ODESSA 1941-44

Defense, Occupation, Resistance & Liberation

Nikolai Ovcharenko

Translated & edited by Stuart Britton

Helion & Company

Helion & Company Limited
26 Willow Road
Solihull
West Midlands
B91 1UE
England
Tel. 01926 499 619
Fax 0121 711 4075
Email: info@helion.co.uk
Website: www.helion.co.uk
Twitter: @helionbooks
Visit our blog http://blog.helion.co.uk/

Published by Helion & Company 2018
Designed and typeset by Mach 3 Solutions Ltd (www.mach3solutions.co.uk)
Cover designed by Paul Hewitt, Battlefield Design (www.battlefield-design.co.uk)
Printed by Gutenberg Press Limited, Tarxien, Malta

Originally published in the Ukraine as *Viis'kove mistetsvo ta traditsii zakhisnikiv Odesi:
Zbirka istorichnikh doslidzhen'* (Odessa: Atlant, 2014)

ISBN 978-1-912390-14-4

British Library Cataloguing-in-Publication Data.
A catalogue record for this book is available from the British Library.

For details of other military history titles published by Helion & Company Limited contact
the above address, or visit our website: http://www.helion.co.uk.

We always welcome receiving book proposals from prospective authors.

Contents

List of Photographs

In plate section

List of Maps

Preface: A People's War

The Second World War left a heavy, bloody imprint on the fate of the Ukrainian people. Ukraine was drawn into a military conflict involving 61 states and four/fifths of the planet's population. Combat operations took place on the territory of forty countries of Europe, Asia, and Africa and on broad expanses of seas and oceans. This war, the bloodiest and most destructive in the entire history of mankind, lasted longer than six years. It resulted in the deaths of more than 50,000,000 people, of which not less than half were the sons and daughters of the peoples of the Soviet Union, including more than 8,000,000 citizens and soldiers of Ukraine.

On 22 June 1941 the Soviet Union was subjected to a perfidious invasion by Nazi Germany. The German fascists and their allies in the aggression struck the USSR with a massive force, including 190 divisions, 3,500 tanks, approximately 5,000 aircraft, and 50,000 guns and mortars.

The Ukrainian people, together with other peoples of the Soviet Union, rose up to repel the German-Romanian aggression. Four and a half million men and women – 10 percent of the republic's residents – fought in the ranks of the Soviet Army; 500,000 partisans fought in the enemy rear; and more than 1.5 million citizens were active participants in acts of sabotage and resistance against the occupiers.[1]

In essence, Odessa was a frontline city from the very first days of the war. Savage fighting on the distant approaches to Odessa unfolded at the beginning of August 1941, and on 5 August the *Stavka* of the Supreme High Command issued an order to defend Odessa "to the very last". Tens of thousands of residents set to work on building defensive lines following an appeal by oblast and city Party organizations. A system of defenses on the approaches to the city was urgently constructed. On 8 August, the city declared it was under a state of siege. On 10 August the enemy began to storm Odessa's fortifications. The Separate Coastal Army, the Black Sea Fleet and the Odessa militia division fought to repel the enemy's savage offensive.

At the end of August, enemy troops broke through to the Dnepr River and seized the expanse between Kremenchug and Kherson. Odessa was now deep in the enemy rear. Despite a five-fold superiority in men and equipment, the enemy's 300,000-strong army was halted outside the walls of the besieged city for 73 days and suffered heavy losses. The Black Sea Fleet was securing the naval lines of communications and reliably covering Odessa from the sea.

The city stood to the death. The population of Odessa courageously bore the burdens and dangers of the siege – systematic raids by enemy aviation, artillery barrages, and food shortages. Under these difficult conditions, the plants and factories never ceased operations for a single day. The soldiers and citizens became a united combat garrison. The enemy never succeeded in taking the city by force. Only in connection with the difficult situation that developed in the Crimea did the Soviet command on 30 September 1941 issue an order to withdraw the Coastal Army from Odessa and send it there.

---

1   *Kniga pamiati Ukrainy: Odesskaia oblast'* [*Ukraine Book of Remembrance, Odessa Oblast*] (Odessa: Maiak, 1994), p. 9.

The superbly organized evacuation of the army proceeded without losses and was completed by the dawn of 16 October 1941. Odessa's lengthy defense tied up significant enemy strength, disrupted his plans to develop naval lines of communication and to execute a rapid advance on the southern sector of the front, and inflicted heavy enemy losses – 100,000 Romanian and German soldiers and officers.

The occupation of Odessa lasted for two and a half years. The Odessa partisans and underground movement struggled with the occupiers under difficult conditions. On 10 April 1944, troops of the 3rd Ukrainian Front liberated Odessa with the active participation of partisans. Seven formations and units, which had most distinguished themselves in the city's liberation, were awarded the honorary title "Odessa". For the heroism and courage displayed in the fighting for the city, 14 men were awarded the title Hero of the Soviet Union, 57 men were awarded the Order of Lenin, and 2,100 men earned other Orders and medals. Approximately 25,000 soldiers and officers were decorated with the medal "For the defense of Odessa".[2]

---

2   *Goroda-geroi Velikoi Otechestvennoi voiny: Atlas* [*Hero-cities of the Great Patriotic War: An atlas*] (Moscow: Glavnoe upravlenie geodezii i kartografii pri Sovete Ministrov SSSR, 1975), pp. 44-47.

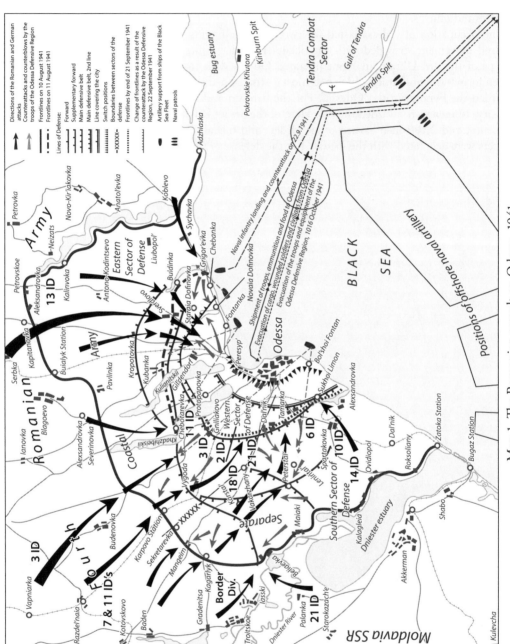

Map 1 The Romanian assault on Odessa, 1941.

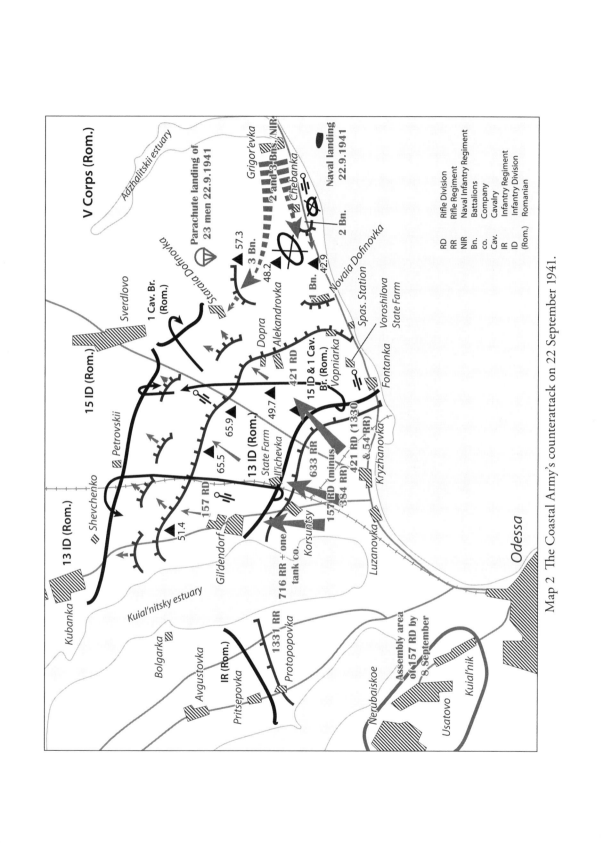

Map 2 The Coastal Army's counterattack on 22 September 1941.

1

The Sources of Odessa's Military Valor

1.1 Odessa's Military History

Odessa is one of Ukraine's four famous Hero-cities. Each city, just like each person, has his or her own genealogy, biography, profession, and unique appearance. The Hero-city with over a million residents is a bearer of age-old military and labor traditions. As Odessans themselves like to say, Odessa was born in a sailor's striped shirt and with a gun in its hands. A lot of brave warriors over the course of centuries have enriched its glory.

The history of the lands of the Black Sea area was difficult and harsh. The first traces of human activity belong to the Upper Paleolithic era (40 to 60 thousand years ago) – a hunting camp of Neanderthals in a cave near the village of Il'inka, 20 kilometers north of Odessa, on the right bank of the Kual'nitskii estuary. Five thousand years ago, on the territory of Usatovo near Odessa, there was a large Bronze Age settlement with enormous burial mounds nearby – these were the first burial structures discovered in the entire Black Sea steppe. In honor of the village where the first archeological diggings were made, the indigenous archeological culture was labeled "Usatov", although it covered much of present-day Romania and Moldavia. The Usatovs drew upon the Tripolitans for their ceramics and manner of residence construction, and adapted the alien steppe-dwellers' practice of raising kurgans above the graves of their ancestors. From these places, the Usatovs migrated to the Balkans, where they played a role in the origin of the local ethnic groups – the ancient Greeks and Phrygians.

The ancient predecessor of Odessa (2,500 years ago) is the ancient Greek city of Gavan Istrian. Its remnants were preserved under the coastal boulevard and the city's central section, while its port was situated where today's Harbor Terminal stands. On the Zhevakhov Hill, which rises between the Kual'nitskii and Khadzhibeiskii estuaries, there was a grandiose Ancient Greek temple in the fifth and sixth centuries dedicated to the goddess of fruitful soil and agriculture – Demeter. The residents of the city were primarily fishermen, and traded actively with the neighboring Scythians for grain and with Ancient Greece for goods and wares. The life of the ancient villages and cities on the northwest coast of the Black Sea came to an end with the invasion of savage nomadic tribes of Huns in 375. For long centuries, the land around the Gulf of Odessa was converted into the unpopulated "Wild Steppes".

During the time of Ancient Rus', eastern Slavs were living on the northern coast of the Black Sea. Then in the XIII Century they were driven out by the Mongol-Tatar hordes. When the Golden Horde fell into decline, in the 1460s the land of the northwestern coast of the Black Sea became part of the fiefdom of the Grand Duchy of Lithuania. The port of Kabichei was built where Odessa now stands; the first mention of it was made in 1415 by the famous Polish chronicler Ia.

Dlugosch.[1] Already at that time, it was a relatively large port, from whence grain was primarily shipped. A castle was also built on the grounds of the settlement.[2]

At the end of the XVth Century, the Black Sea lands were seized by the Ottoman Empire, and from this time the settlement is often mentioned as Khadjibey [Kocibey]. From here the Turks launched raids into Ukraine, plundering and driving thousands of young men and women for eventual sale into slavery, like cattle or objects. In the latter half of the XVIIIth Century, at the behest of the Turkish government, French engineers built a fortress and named it Yeni-Dünya (New Light). This fortress was repeatedly attacked by Ukrainian Cossacks from Zaporozh'e – in 1769, 1770 and in 1774, when it was finally taken. However, according to the terms of the Treaty of Küçük Kaynarca, the fortress was returned to the Turks. The population of Khadjibey was growing; Ukrainians, Greeks, Armenians and others took up residence here. After the defeat of the Zaporizhian Sich [several Cossack keeps on the Dnepr River] at the hands of Catherine the Great's troops in 1775, the former Ukrainian Cossacks were resettled on the territory of Peresyp' and Nerubaiskii, not far from Khadjibey.[3] Grain, delivered from the Dniester lands and Podolia, was shipped out of the harbor.

During the Russian-Turkish War of 1787-1792, on 14 September 1789, a forward detachment of Major General José de Ribas (known as Osip Mikhailovich Deribas in Russia), consisting of Russian troops and detachments of Black Sea Cossack troops, which were formed from the former Zaporozhian Cossacks, fully seized Khadjibey in a daring night assault, which up to this point served as the base of the entire Turkish fleet. In the course of this war, through the joint operations of Russian forces and Ukrainian Black Sea Cossacks, great victories were achieved at Kinburn, Focsani and Rimnik, and important Turkish fortresses were taken: Ochakov, Bender, Akkerman, and Izmail. The newly created Black Sea Fleet under the command of F.F. Ushakov achieved its first victories, primarily thanks to the skillful actions of the Cossack flotilla led by Attamans Sidor Belyi and Fedor Golovatyi, who ensured the destruction of the Turkish fleet and the capture of the Ochakov and Izmail fortresses.

In December 1792, Turkey was compelled to sign the Treaty of Jassy [Iaşi], which returned the Crimea to Russia, as well as the entire northern coast of the Black Sea from the Dniester River to the Kuban. The access to the Black Sea had enormous economic, political and military significance for the Russian Empire.

The Khadjibey's convenient bay permitted the construction of a fortress and port here. The fortress began construction in 1793 under the guidance of A.V. Suvorov, while work on the city began in 1794 according to the plan of Franz Devolan. In the detailed draft of the design he noted that maritime traffic "could move year-round despite any winds", and that it was suitable "to base an acting fleet in wartime and to build a harbor for trade with the wealthy provinces of Podolia, Vohlynia [Volyn] and Galicia bordering the Dniestr."[4] F. Devolan's design was approved by Catherine the Great, and construction of the military harbor "integrated with a quay for merchant shipping" began pursuant to "the highest decree". Major General De Ribas and engineer for port construction Colonel Devolan, under the supervision of A.V. Suvorov, received the assignment to build the harbor and city in five years. At this time, only 8 men and 2 women were counted in the newly conceived city at Khadjibey, for which 30,200 arpents [an old French unit of area

1   *Istoriia gorodov i sel Ukrainskoi SSR: Odesskaya oblast'* [*History of cities and villages of the Ukrainian SSR: Odessa oblast*] (Kiev: Institut istoriia AN USSR, 1978), p. 99.
2   *Zapiski Odesskogo arkheologicheskogo obshchestva, Tom 2* (35) [*Notes of the Odessa Archaeological Society, Volume 2* (35)] (Odessa, 1967), pp. 130-136.
3   A.A. Skal'kovsky, *Istoriia Novoi Sechi ili Poslednogo Kosha Zaporozhskogo* [*The history of the New Sychi or the Last Zaporozhian Kosh*] (Odessa, 1886), p. 190.
4   G.A. Karev, *Odessa – gorod-geroi* [*Odessa – Hero-city*] (Moscow: Voenizdat, 1978), p. 4.

equal to about one acre] were set aside.[5] On 2 September 1794, the first trench was ceremoniously dug, which would mark the layout of the streets of the new city, and stones for the foundation of the first building were set in place. This day in fact became the birthday of the new city. It was bestowed with the name of Odessa, after the name of the Greek colony of Odesos, which was thought to have existed nearby at one time.[6]

The port began to operate almost as soon as the first dock supports were set in place. In 1794, it took in seven merchant ships, in 1795 – 39, and in the following year – 86. Grain and fleece for shipment abroad arrived here along the Dnepr, Bug and Dniester Rivers by horse-drawn transport. In 1805, the port took in 666 foreign and 496 coastal ships, and 120,000,000 kilograms of wheat was shipped away.

Together with the port, the city's population also quickly grew. By 1797, there were now 346 homes, 223 earthen dugouts and various stone buildings here.[7] Soldiers and peasants who had fled to the south to escape the oppression of serfdom were building the city. In 1797, its population, excluding the garrison, amounted to 4,753, including Black Sea Cossacks and their families (187 men and 108 women) who had settled here.[8]

In 1858, the population of Odessa reached 104,000, the third largest city in the Russian Empire by population. Serfdom stimulated the intensive movement of fugitive Ukrainian and Russian serfs, tradesmen and petty merchants from many places of the right-bank Ukraine and Belorussia to the city. After completing their service, Russian and Ukrainian soldiers and officers were granted land and settled here. Greeks and Bulgarians fled to Odessa to escape the Turkish yoke. Italian, Serbian, Slovakian and Polish peasants and tradesmen found shelter here from their persecutors. The Tsarist government, which had become interested in assimilating the vast Black Sea coastal area and the development of foreign trade, was motivated to offer significant financial incentives to working people in order to attract a labor force. Passports weren't demanded of the fugitive peasants; homeless wanderers received accommodations; people of different faith weren't subjected to religious persecution; and after 1834, the so-called "Volunteer Sailors", those who willingly signed up for the organization, were freed from paying special taxes, the obligation to provide accommodations to military personnel when needed, and the obligation to provide recruits from their communities.[9] However, the conditions of work at the port and on construction sites were miserable. The shortage of potable water, the overcrowded living conditions in damp barracks and the very poor diet led to a high mortality rate among the builders of the city.[10]

The hard living conditions, though, didn't break the freedom-loving spirit of its builders and settlers, but rather fortified it, and strengthened their desire for freedom and social justice. Already in the first years of its life, Odessa became a center of the revolutionary and national liberation movement of the Greek and southern Slav peoples. In 1814, a secret Greek national organization called *Filiki Eteria* ["Company of Friends"] was founded here, and its members planned a rebellion

5   E.I. Druzhinina, *Severnoe Prichernomor'e v 1775-1800* [*Northern Black Sea Coast in 1775-1800*] (Moscow, 1959), p. 201.

6   *Istoriia gorodov i sel Ukrainsoi SSR*, p. 100.

7   *Zapiski Odesskogo arkheologicheskogo obshchestva*, p. 363.

8   Druzhinina, *Severnoe Prichernomor'e v 1775-1800*, p. 256.

9   Editor's note: These societies or communities of *Vol'nye matrosy*, which I have chosen to translate as Volunteer Sailors, were established in Novorosiisk in 1834 in order to create a special class of men – national sailors. They consisted of ordinary people from the bourgeoisie, State peasants, libertines and commoners who decided to become sailors in order to alter and improve their lots in life. As an enticement, the volunteer sailors were freed from certain obligations. After completing their mandatory 5 years of service in the Black Sea Fleet, they were given certificates to show that they were experienced sailors and went to work aboard merchant ships. I want to thank author Igor Sdvizhkov for this information.

10   City of Odessa, *Ocherk istoriia goroda-geroia* [*A sketch of the history of the Hero-city*] (Odessa, 1957), p. 19.

of the Greek people against Turkish rule. Later, the "Odessa Bulgarian Rector" was founded here, which became a center of the Bulgarian social and cultural movement. The Italian revolutionary D. Garibaldi repeatedly visited Odessa. The Polish poet A. Mickiewicz lived in exile here. The names of many of the Decembrists were connected with Odessa: P.I. Pestel', M.S. Lunin, M.F. Orlov, V.F. Raevsky, A.V. Podzhno, and A.O. Kornilovich. In 1825, when the secret Decembrist societies were uncovered, Tsar Nikolai I gloomily observed, "from all appearances it is obvious that there must be a nest of conspirators in Odessa ...."[11]

Already in the first decades of its existence, Odessa became a significant cultural center. The first city theater opened in 1809, in which the Italian opera and leading Russian and Ukrainian dramatic troupes performed. The Rishel'evsky Lyceum, which subsequently grew into Novorossisk University, was founded in Odessa in 1817. The second public library in the Russian Empire (after the one in Petersburg) opened here, which with the passage of time became a genuine "free university" for many generations of city residents. Philharmonic and historical societies formed here. Periodic literature began to be published in Odessa in 1820, including the popular Odessa Almanacs, and print shops were opened. A.S. Pushkin resided in Odessa for more than a year, after being exiled to the south by the Tsar for his freedom-loving verses. Here he finished his work on *The Fountain of Bakchisaray*, began work on his narrative poem *Tsygane* [*The Gypsies*], wrote the first chapters of his verse novel *Evgenii Onegin*, and penned many lyrical poems, which widely circulated in the city. In the first half of the XIXth Century, the talented architects and sculptors Francesco Boffo, Thomas de Thomon, Frants Frapoli, H. Toricelli, A. Mel'nikov and I. Martos created marvelous architectural works and monuments in the city.

Odessa first demonstrated its passion for freedom, disdain for danger and the uniform readiness of the multi-national population to defend the city at any cost during the Crimean War (1853-1856). This trading city and port was not at all ready for this war (incidentally, the same could be said for the Russian Empire as a whole). The fortress, which had been built by Suvorov back in 1793, had consisted primarily of earth and timber fortifications, which after two decades had lost their significance and had been adapted as quarantine facilities for arriving crews and passengers of ships. As of 10 April 1854, Odessa's coastal defenses consisted of six batteries:

No. 1 – at Langeron, two 1-pud unicorn cannons [a type of old Russian smoothbore cannon, so called because until 1805 they had a unicorn engraved on the barrel; a pud is an old Russian unit of weight equal to 16.38 kilograms or 36.11 pounds] and six 2-pud mortars.
No. 2 – on the middle face of the Quarantine Mole: six 24pdr howitzers.
No. 3 – on the tip of the Quarantine Mole: ten 24pdr howitzers.
No. 4 – below the boulevard, to the right of the famous Potemkin Stairs: eight 1-pud unicorn cannons.
No. 5 – in the same location, to the left of the Potemkin Stairs: six 24pdr howitzers.
No. 6 – at the tip of the Military Mole: four 24pdr howitzers.

In the majority of cases these cannons were old, cast iron and unsuitable for contemporary warfare. A number of them had been dug into the ground to serve as moorings for arriving ships. The main hope for a successful defense rested upon Nos. 2, 3 and 6 (26 cannons), which protruded into the sea. Unfortunately, the layout of the moles deprived the batteries of the possibility of mutual support, while their low elevation above the sea and their low parapets made them poorly suitable in a military sense. The batteries deployed on the coastal heights were too distant from the hostile

11   Karev, *Odessa – gorod geroi*, p. 7.

ships. The weakest point was the defense's left flank: the four hardly suitable 24pdrs of Battery No. 6 were supposed to defend a wide portion of the Odessa estuary from Peresyp' to the city center.

On 9 April 1854, a powerful Anglo-French flotilla consisting of six battleships, thirteen frigates and nine steamships (more than 350 cannons) entered the Gulf of Odessa and gave an ultimatum to surrender all of the ships that were located in the port. However, the foe received no response.

On the morning of 10 April 1854, the enemy flotilla unleashed all the power of its artillery on Odessa and its few batteries. To the enemy's surprise, the bombardment didn't throw the majority of the Odessan population into panic. At the very height of the bombardment, a holiday church service continued calmly and reverently in a cathedral, even though the salvoes were plainly audible in the tabernacle.

Throughout the entire battle, Battery No. 6 under the command of Chief Warrant Officer A.P. Shchegolov dueled most successfully with the enemy ships, raining red-hot shells down upon them, and thus the nine battleships concentrated their fire exclusively on it. Situated right on the coast, for six hours the battery conducted an unequal artillery duel under the crossfire of several hundred hostile guns and forced the battleships to move back out to sea, having seriously damaged three of them. An attempt to land troops in the vicinity of Peresyp' was thwarted. Having received serious damage to four ships and cannon holes in all the others, and having witnessed the firm resolve of all the defenders to fight for the city, the flotilla sailed away, leaving behind three patrol ships in the estuary.

On the morning of 30 April 1854, in a dense fog, the English 16-gun frigate *Tiger* became grounded beneath the steep bank of the Malyi Fontan, six *versts* [a little more than 6 kilometers] from Odessa. The fire of the garrison's field artillery forced the British frigate to lower its flag. The 225 prisoners, including 24 officers, were removed from the ship and conveyed to the shore, while the frigate itself, which could not be quickly freed, was destroyed on the next day by cannon fire from two other allied ships that had come to rescue the *Tiger* – the *Vesuvious* and the *Niger*.[12] One of the salvaged cannons from this frigate was set up on Primorskii Boulevard in the city and has become an eternal monument to the courage of Odessa's defenders in the Crimean War. In honor of Chief Warrant Officer Shchegolev, one of Odessa's streets and a battery on the Prakticheskii Mole was given his name.

The success of this operation was important not only for Odessa. News about the successful repulse of a strong foe in the first collision with Turkey's allies on native soil quickly spread throughout all of Imperial Russia and had a very encouraging effect. After all, similar facts are very rarely encountered in military history: a peaceful trading city, not at all prepared for war, tenaciously defended itself against two menacing allied fleets – here is something over which one can be proud! The names of General Osten-Saken; Chief Warrant Officer Shchegolev and the ordinary artillerymen of Battery No. 6; Archbishop Innokenty and students Deminitru, Pol' and Bodarevsky have remained in the memory of subsequent generations.

In later years, the significant flow of arriving people contributed to the rapid increase in the city's population (up to 403,800 in 1897) and the development of its industry, transportation and trade. By 1875 there were already 167 enterprises in the city that employed up to 4,000 industrial workers. Eight thousand craftsmen worked in the city's workshops and more than 46,000 manual workers labored in the port, in quarries and at construction sites. In 1888, twice as much grain passed through Odessa's port than through Petersburg, and the city was exporting leather, iron ore, oilcake, timber, hemp, tallow, wax, matting and other items. About a tenth of the government's total imports came in through Odessa. Many Odessan factories and plants worked with imported raw materials.

---

12   V.N. Sanko [chief ed.], *Istoriia Odesi* [*History of Odessa*] (Odessa: Druuk, 2002), p. 118.

The city's infrastructure was developing. Luxurious palaces, beautiful comfortable homes, and bustling shops and cafes were growing in the center of Odessa, while along the coastline entire streets of mansions, villas and splendid dachas were arising. However, the workers occupied cramped quarters of densely-inhabited barracks, damp cellars, wattle and daub huts, "craft apartments" and flophouses, while seasonal workers spent their nights under the open sky, finding shelter in bad weather in the city's catacombs. Hunger, disease and high mortality were their constant companions.

In this period, many of Bulgaria's well-known political and cultural figures maintained ties with Odessa – D. Blagoev, I. Bazov, G. Rakovsky and Kh. Botev. Herzen's *Kolokol* [*The Bell*) and other works circulated widely among Odessa's intellectuals. Unresolved social problems engendered a revolutionary movement. Finding himself in remote exile, the great Ukrainian poet Taras Shevchenko kept connections with Odessa. Leading progressive scholars taught in Odessa University, including D.I. Mendeleev, I.I. Mechnikov, I.M. Sechenov, the founder of surgery treatment in the field N.I. Pirogov, and the zoologist A.O. Kovalesvsky.

During the 1905 Revolution, demonstrations in the city turned into a total political strike by Odessa's workers. Barricades appeared on the city's streets, and armed scuffles began between the workers on one side, and the police and Cossacks on the other. In military units and aboard combat ships moored in the port, Bolshevist groups and organizations began to form. Sailors of merchant ships of foreign and the Caucasus lines flooded the furnaces with water and left their ships.

On 15 June, the rebellious battleship *Potemkin* arrived in Odessa. The workers triumphantly welcomed the revolutionary ship, and when the city's authorities rejected the sailors request for fuel and food, an entire flotilla of fishing boats headed to the battleship with coal and food products. The funeral of the Bolshevik sailor G. Vakulenchuk, who was killed aboard the ship by an officer, turned into a demonstration of the solidarity between the workers and sailors. On the streets and at the port, meetings and rallies took place, at which fiery speeches, which inevitably ended with an appeal for the struggle for self-rule, were given from atop boxes, bales and barrels. A squadron of combat ships was sent from Sevastopol in order to put down the mutiny by the sailors of the *Potemkin*. However, the sailors of the squadron refused to fire upon their mutinous comrades. The battleship cut through the squadron's formation at full speed, and to shouts of "Ura!" drew after it the battleship *Georgii Pobedonosets*, which had decided to join forces with the *Potemkin*. After the departure of the *Potemkin*, the rebellion in the city was brutally suppressed.

The First World War and the revolution that followed it became a genuine tragedy for Odessa. The city became the closest supply center for the 500,000-strong Romanian Front. At the first frontline oblast Council of Soviets' assembly, a Central Executive Committee of Soviets, consisting of soldier, sailor, worker and peasant deputies from the Romanian Front, the Black Sea Fleet and the Odessa Military District (in abbreviation, Rumcherod) was elected. Learning of the revolution in Petrograd, on 14 January 1918 armed detachments of the Red Guard, having seized the train station, the military district's headquarters, the telegraph and telephone stations, the State bank and the arsenal they announced Soviet power in the city. Haidamak paramilitary units[13] and

---

13   Editor's note: The *haidamak* movement consisted of partisan bands of Ukrainian free Cossacks, peasants and rebels who waged guerrilla warfare and staged uprisings against the Polish nobility and collaborationists in the 18th and early 19th Centuries. Ukrainian folklore and literature generally view the actions of the haidamak partisans positively, rather like Ukrainian Robin Hoods, while in the Polish language, the term *Hajdamactwo* became a pejorative label for Ukrainians as a whole. By the late 19th century, the term "Haidamaki" was applied to any strongly nationalist Ukrainian partisans, who were as opposed to Russian hegemony as Polish rule.

officer detachments, equipped with armored cars and artillery, launched combat actions against the Bolsheviks, but they were driven out of the city.

At the end of January 1918, Germany treacherously broke the truce and a 400,000-strong occupational army marched into Ukraine. On 24 February, the city of Odessa went onto a wartime footing. The 3rd Ukrainian Soviet Army, which had been urgently formed, went into battle with the occupiers in the areas of Birzuli and Bălţi. However, under the pressure of the enemy's superior forces, the army was forced to retreat, and on the night of 13-14 March, Austrian-German troops seized Odessa.

The occupation continued until the autumn of 1918, when under the influence of the revolutionary events in Germany and the broad resistance movement in Ukraine, the Austrian-German forces were compelled to pull out of Ukraine. However, on 26 November 1918, other interventionists arrived in Odessa to replace the Austrian-Germans: French, Italian and British ships, and more than 30,000 troops of the Entente. In addition, more than 10,000 White Guards and Deniken units arrived from Ekaterinodar. A new binge of bloody terror began in the city. Soon, under the blows of the Red Army, the interventionists abandoned Odessa in April 1919. However, the departing occupiers plundered city property, port warehouses, bases, industrial enterprises and left with 112 merchant ships – practically the entire merchant fleet.[14] The port ceased to operate. The electricity station wasn't working. Approximately 40,000 laborers were left without work, and hundreds of thousands of citizens were without fuel or food.

At the end of July 1919, approximately 12,000 German colonists from nearby villages marched toward the city with White Guardsmen and troops of Petliura's army. Composite battalions of worker and peasant cadets from infantry and artillery training courses moved out to meet them. The uprising against Bolshevik power was crushed. However, the situation at the front was deteriorating with every passing day. Denikin's army, having received large assistance from the Entente in the form of money, arms and military gear, took the city of Odessa at the end of August 1919 and established a regime of terror and violence, which exceeded the brutalities of all the preceding occupiers. Only on 7 February 1920 was Odessa liberated by a bold raid conducted by G. Kotovsky's mounted troops.

The almost three years of heavy fighting and repeated occupations left the city in economic ruins. The majority of enterprises had ceased to function, the port's docks had been fully destroyed, and the interventionists had either sunk or absconded almost 95% of the merchant fleet.[15]

The entire country began to render assistance to the people of Odessa. Trains carrying equipment to get the industrial factories and port working again came from Moscow and Leningrad. Already by November 1923, Odessa's port was able to receive 32 foreign steamships and 101 coastal boats. By 1928, the resurrected and re-equipped factories and plants exceeded the pre-war production level by 8%. More than 200 large-size factories and plants were working in the city. The shipping fleet, port facilities and foreign shipping lines were gradually rebuilt. Cargo lines began to work regularly – the Odessa – Trieste passenger line. Export cargo, primarily grain, was shipped to Gibraltar, Holland, Norway, Italy, Denmark, France, England, Greece and Latvia.[16]

In the inter-war period, Odessa became one of the country's major industrial, cultural, academic and resort centers, and the most important port on the Black Sea coast. The city's population in

---

14   Karev, *Odessa – Gorod-geroi*, pp. 22-23.

15   *Pravda*, 9 February 1922; *Pod flagom Rodiny: Ocherki istorii Chernomorskogo paraxodstva* [*Under the flag of the Motherland: Sketches of the history of the Black Sea shipping line*] (Odessa: Maiak, 1967), p. 161.

16   *Odesskii morskoi torgovyi port: Otchetnye dannye za 1923* [*Odessa's maritime trading port: Reported data for 1923*] (Odessa, 1924), p. 64; *Odesskie morskoi torgovyi port 1923-1924* [*Odessa's maritime trading port 1923-1924*] (Odessa: Upravlenie morskogo torgovogo porta, 1925), pp. 60-61; *Khoziastvo Ukrainy, 1925* [*Ukraine's economy, 1925*], p. 33.

1939 amounted to 604,000 people. Industry, particularly the metallurgy and machine-building sectors, was growing at a rapid pace. On the eve of the Great Patriotic War, Odessa had 92 industrial enterprises of All-Union significance, and around 350 of All-Republic significance.[17] In connection with the sharply increased international isolation of the Soviet Union under Stalin, almost all of the rebuilt enterprises were re-oriented to domestic raw materials and the manufacture of new products. Instrument-making enterprises, crane machine building plants and chemical industries appeared. By 1941, up to 27,000 students were studying in higher education institutions; 80,000 students were enrolled in 19 technical schools and 132 schools; and 42 scientific research institutes were operating, including the Institute of Ocular Diseases. A large number of health care facilities were open: 16 polyclinics, 7 hospitals, and 4 birthing centers, as well as 80 spas and rest homes. On the eve of the war, Odessa had 56 clubs, a Pioneer Palace, a scientific center, 10 museums, 10 theaters, an open-air stage, a philharmonic orchestra, 93 libraries, including the A.M. Gor'ky Scientific Library with a collection of more than two million volumes.

Three oblast newspapers were published in Odessa – the *Chernomorska kommuna* (until 1929, *Izvestiia*), the *Bol'shevistskoe znamia* (from 1938) and the *Molodaia gvardiia* (from 1923). In addition, the *Moriak* and *Chornomor'skii gudok* gazettes were published here, as well as 28 factory, plant and academic house magazines.[18]

Odessa didn't escape Stalin's repressions of the 1930s. According to official data, more than 30,000 people in the oblast were arrested, of which more than 8,000 were shot; among them were members of various societal levels and professions.[19]

In the years 1936-1939, Odessa rendered assistance to the Spanish people in the struggle against fascist aggression. The struggling Republican side received weapons, medications, clothing and food via Odessa's port. Thousands of children of the Spanish patriots found shelter in Odessa's orphanages.

In the conditions of a rising threat of a new world war, mass civil defense work among the population acquired enormous significance. Marksmanship clubs, aviation and glider clubs and medical troops were being organized in cities and villages. The youth were being trained to drive vehicles and tractors, to handle firearms, and to become pilots and parachutists. The *Osoaviakhim* Organization in Odessa Oblast before the war numbered 164,500 members in its ranks.[20] The successes achieved in the development of the economic, education and cultural spheres contributed to the strengthening of the city's autonomous defensive capabilities.

---

17   *Ukrainskaia SSR v Velikoi Otechestvennoi voine Sovetskogo Soiuza 1941-1945, Tom 1* [The Ukraine SSR in the Great Patriotic war of the Soviet Union, 1941-1945, Volume 1] (Kiev: Politizdat Ukrainy, 1967), p. 204.

18   *Istoriia gorodov i sel Ukrainskoi SSSR*, pp. 127-128.

19   *Odesskii martirolog* [Odessa's Martyrology] Vol. One (Odessa, 1999), pp. 710-711; O.V. Gontar'and Zh.O. Smotrich, "Stalins'ki represii na Odeshchini"//VI Vseukrain'ska naukova konferentsiia z istorichnogo kraeznavstva (Lutsk, 1993), p. 303; D.P. Ursu, "... Osobenno zasoren vrazhdebnym elementom': Odesskii universitet v 20-30-i gody" ["... Especially contaminated with a hostile element: Odessa University in the 1920s and 1930s"] *Demokraticheskoe deistvie* (No. 2, 1955); *Represovane Kraeznavstvo 20-30-i gody* (Kiev, 1991), p. 35.

20   *Kniga Pamiati Ukraina: Odesskaia oblast, 1994*, pp. 9-15. Ed. note: *Osoaviakhim* is a contraction of the words *Soiuz obshchestv sodeistviia oborone i aviatsionno-khimicheskomu stroitel'stvu SSSR*, or Union of Societies of Assistance to Defense and Aviation-Chemical Construction of the USSR. Its purpose was to prepare reserves for the armed forces. It became popular among Soviet youth to earn badges for marksmanship, parachuting and horseback riding at the organization's vast network of its own airfields, firing ranges, parachuting towers and radio clubs. Gradually, training extended to more advanced disciplines like tactics and orienteering. A person could join the Osoaviakhim as early as 14 years of age.

1.2 The Odessa Military District on the eve of the war

Already in the years of the Russian Civil War, Odessa was playing a leading role in the defense of the entire northwestern area of the Black Sea. Soon after taking the city in 1920, the Red Army created a headquarters here for the coastal defense of the Northwestern Fortified District, which was subordinate to the headquarters of the Southwestern Front. Initially it even had the functions of a fleet headquarters. Only after the liquidation of Wrangel's army in the Crimea did the fleet headquarters move to Sevastopol. With the aim of increasing the security of the Soviet Union's southwestern borders, in October 1939 the Odessa Military District was created with its headquarters in Odessa.[21] The defense of the city from the sea was to be secured by the Black Sea Fleet's Odessa Military Naval Base. It had in its possession the cruiser *Komintern*, the minelayer *Shaumian*, a separate battalion of coastal ships, and units of harbor security: two battalions of minesweepers, four battalions of patrol boats, the 2nd Brigade of Torpedo Boats, a naval air squadron, three artillery battalions, an anti-aircraft regiment and other units and elements, including the Ochakovsky sector of defense.

While working out offensive tasks, the command of the Odessa Military District also paid serious attention to the tasks of an active defense, clearly recognizing the ever growing danger of armed aggression. It was far from simple to meet this task. As of 1 June 1941, the Romanian-German forces were far superior to the forces of the Odessa Military District in both numerical and qualitative indicators. Thus in a clarifying note to the operational plan, which was sent to the chief of the Red Army's General Staff General of the Army G.K. Zhukov, the commander of the Odessa Military District Colonel General Ia. T. Cherevichenko emphasized:

> The area of Odessa in all the variants of the operational plan has important significance for the future combat actions of the Romanian front. Meanwhile, with the departure of the 150th Rifle Division the area of Odessa remains weakly provided with both naval strength and ground units. I request that you include the 116th Rifle Division in Border District No. 7, with the restaging of it in the event of military actions from Nikolaev to Odessa, and in addition, to strengthen Border District No. 5 on the Beletsky axis, including the 147th, 196th and 206th Rifle Divisions in the plan of covering the Odessa Military District. I believe it necessary to have two armies within the boundaries of the Odessa Military District in wartime, considering the importance of the Romanian front given by its location and forces in the general strategic plan, as well as by the nature of the actions.[22]

On the basis of the tasks set for it in a directive from the People's Commissar of Defense dated 6 May 1941, the headquarters of the Odessa Military District worked out a "Plan for the defense of the State border".[23] The operational plan of defense, devised by the District's chief of staff Major General M.V. Zakharov, was distinguished by the deep analysis of the strength of the possible adversary, his combat capabilities, the directions of the main attacks, as well as by a principled assessment of the district's own forces. The plan, worked out on a map with a scale of 1:500,000, contains a "Note on the plan of actions of the forces of the Odessa Military District to cover the

---

21   A. Khor'kov, "Krasnoznamennyi Odesskii voenny krug nakanune Velikoi Otechestvennoi voiny" ["Red Banner Odessa Military District on the eve of the Great Patriotic War", *Voenno-istoricheskii zhurnal*, No. 6 (1974), pp. 90-95; Iu.A. Gor'kov and Iu.N. Semin, "Konets global'noi lzhi: ot Chernogo moria do Karpat" [End of a global lie: From the Black Sea to the Carpathians"], *Voenno-istoricheskii zhurnal*, No. 5 (1996), pp. 2-15.

22   TsAMO RF, F.16, op.295, s.253, ark. 1-8.

23   TsAMO RF, F.138, op.7162, s.13, ark. 1-8.

State border according to the Directive No.503874 of the People's Commissar of Defense from 6 May 1941", and is confirmed by the Soviet Union's Commissar of Defense. The document spells out the tasks of the District's forces to cover the national border.[24]

The plan offered an estimate of the enemy's possible strength and groupings opposite the borders of the Odessa Military District on 31 May 1941: 40-45 infantry and motorized divisions, 4 cavalry divisions, 4 mountain rifle brigades, and 2 panzer divisions, of which 17 infantry and motorized divisions and both panzer divisions were German. In response to wartime mobilization, Romania, excluding German forces, might deploy up to 44-45 infantry divisions, 4 cavalry divisions, and 4 mountain rifle brigades. In addition, the plan noted that the deployment of German forces with a total strength of up to 20-25 infantry and motorized divisions on Romanian territory should be expected.

Considering the broadness of the front along the USSR border from Lipcani to the mouth of the Danube River, which extended for up to 500 kilometers (the calculation was made without regard for the Chernovitsy axis) and the possible density of one division per 5 kilometers on main directions of attack, and one division per 12 kilometers on a pinning direction, it would be possible for the adversary to deploy up to 40-45 divisions and two mechanized groups in the first stage of the battle in the area between the Prut and Seret Rivers, as well as in the Northern Dobruja.[25] The enemy grouping on the operational directions (sectors) was foreseen by the plan as follows:

1. In the Lipcani – Iași sector, with a front of up to 150 kilometers and given the presence of 18-20 main communication unpaved roads and two railroads on Romanian territory with a carrying capacity of up to 60 train-pairs and on the territory of the Moldavia SSR of up to 10 train-pairs, the possible enemy deployment of up to 16-18 divisions and one mechanized group in the initial stage was being foreseen.

2. In the Iași – Huși sector with a front of up to 60 kilometers and given the presence of 7-8 main communication unpaved roads and one railroad on Romanian territory with a carrying capacity of up to 26 train-pairs and on the territory of Moldvia SSR of up to 24 train-pairs, the possible enemy deployment of up to 7-8 divisions in the initial stage was anticipated by the end of 1941.

3. In the Huși – Reni sector, with a front of up to 150 kilometers and given the presence of 13-15 main communication unpaved roads and three railroads on Romanian territory with a carrying capacity of up to 55 train-pairs, and two railroads on the territory of Moldavia SSR with a carrying capacity of up to 42 train-pairs, in the initial stage the deployment of 12-13 enemy divisions and one mechanized group was anticipated by the end of 1941.

4. In the Reni – Vilkovo [Vylkove] sector, with a front of 140 kilometers, up to 3-4 divisions should be expected in the first echelon.

The estimate of the composition and grouping of the enemy's air force believed that Romania had a total of 1,100–1,260 aircraft on Romanian territory as of 1 May 1941, of which 540–580 were reconnaissance aircraft; 200–250 were bombers; 300–350 were fighters; and 60–80 were floatplanes. Considering that 20–25% of these aircraft were trainers or unserviceable, it was assumed that 825–900 aircraft could take part in an invasion. In addition, the German *Luftwaffe* had its Luftflotte Four staging from Romanian territory, which consisted of Fliegerkorps IV and Fliegerkorps V with a total of 960 aircraft, including 280 bombers, 300 dive bombers, up to 280

---

24   TsAMO RF, F.16, op.2591, s.253, ark. 9-46.
25   TsAMO RF, F.16, op. 295, s.253, ark. 10.

fighters, and around 100 reconnaissance aircraft.[26] Thus, it was expected that up to 1,800 enemy aircraft of various types could be employed against the Odessa Military District in the opening stage of the battle.

The enemy aircraft were based on 54 airbases and approximately 30 landing fields, of which up to 30 airbases and 27 landing fields were at a depth of 200 to 250 kilometers from the national border. Accordingly, the bulk of the enemy air force was based in the Câmpulung, Braşov, Ploeşti, Bucharest, Constanţa, Prut River sector.

The Romanians had the Danube River Flotilla, which was located in the Galaţi–Brăila area. Its ship and artillery strength consisted of the following (See Table 1.1):

Table 1.1 Ships and artillery strength of the Romanian River Flotilla

Ships		Artillery		Average Armor Thickness	
Type	Number	Caliber, mm	Number of guns	Location of armor	Thickness, mm
Monitors	7	120	23	Flank	40-75
Minesweepers	3	76	4	Deck	25-75
Minelayers	4	47	16	Artillery	50-75
Patrol boats	13	Machine guns	27		
Armed steam ships	3				
Floating batteries	6				
Mortar barges	2				

Thus, it was possible to anticipate an attack by 7 monitors, 3 mine sweepers, 4 mine layers, 13 patrol boats, 3 armed steamships, 6 floating batteries and 2 mortar barges. In total, they were equipped with 23 120-mm guns, 4 76-mm guns and 16 47-mm guns, as well as with 27 machine guns. In addition, a German submarine had been assembled and launched into the water of the Danube River in Galaţi.

Judging from the assessment of the positioning of the forces and means of the German – Romanian forces, the Odessa Military Council assumed that the Romanian Army would operate together with Germany in accordance with a unified operational plan, and that the enemy would launch an attack at the boundary between the Kiev Special and Odessa Military Districts. In the process, the main attacks were expected on the Kamenets-Podol'sk and Jassy – Belets directions.[27] The depth of the operational axis up to the Dniester River was 140-150 kilometers. In order to support the actions of the ground forces, the broad use by the enemy of airborne forces with the task to seize bridges across the Dniester River was expected, in order to block the retreat of our units to the eastern bank. The territory of the Crimea as a base for the actions of the *Luftwaffe* against industrial targets in the USSR was particularly significant for the enemy. Thus, the Odessa Military District command anticipated the combined actions of air and sea landings to seize the territory of the Crimean peninsula.[28]

The command of the Odessa Military District, assessing its own forces, could count upon ground troops, the District's air force, and naval forces. Significant ground strength had been brought up to defend the national border within the boundaries of the Odessa Military District: the headquarters of the 35th, 14th and 48th Rifle Corps; the headquarters of the 2nd Cavalry

---

26   TsAMO RF, F.16, op.295, s.253, ark. 12.
27   TsAMO RF, F.138, op.7162, s.10, ark. 3-6.
28   Gor'kov and Semin, "Konests global'noi lzhi", pp. 5-6.

Corps; the command of the 18th Mechanized Corps; the 176th, 95th, 30th, 25th, 51st, 150th and 74th Rifle Divisions; the 9th and 5th Cavalry Divisions; the 44th and 47th Tank Divisions, and the 218th Motorized Division. In addition, in the Crimea was the 9th Rifle Corps with its subordinate units, the 106th and 156th Rifle Divisions and the 32nd Cavalry Division.

Four rifle divisions and two cavalry divisions, as well as the 18th Mechanized Corps with two tank divisions and one mechanized division, were positioned directly on the border with Romania and in the rear as far as the line of the Dniestr River. The remaining units were positioned east of the Dniestr River. Thus, the average density of the forces of the first echelon to cover the ground border with Romania amounted to one rifle and one cavalry division per 80-85 kilometers. Such an arrangement required the creation of compact groupings with strong reserves only on the separate and most important directions. Upon the declaration of a combat alert, it would require between 4 and 70 hours for the covering units of the first line of defense to move into their defenses. The time necessary for the units to move up from beyond the Dniestr and to arrive in their assembly areas would amount to 30 to 100 hours. The list of the combat composition of the first echelon of covering units was presented in the first appendix to "Memorandum on the plan of actions of the forces of the Odessa Military District".[29]

The quantity of tanks in the district opened broad prospects for their combat use, but this was complicated to a significant extent due to the unsatisfactory mechanical condition of the combat machines. For example, up to 70% of the T-37 tanks as a result of their long-term use were in need of light or major overhaul.[30] Primarily, the older-model tanks had worn-out engines and thus were no longer first-line tanks.[31] The level of motorization introduced in the district required a high amount of equipage with motorized transport and various types of material and technical support.

The actual amount of auxiliary vehicles available to the district's forces on 22 June 1941 is shown in Table 1.2:

Table 1.2 The availability of tractors and trucks as a percentage of authorized table strength, Odessa Military District, 22 June 1941

Type	Percentage of authorized table strength
Heavy tractors	44
Light tractors	46
Trailers	35
Trucks:	
GAZ	82
ZIS	31

In general, the heavy tractors were primarily ChTZ-60 and "Kommunar" tractors that already had 6 to 10 years of use in the district. A number of them were under repair on 22 June 1941.[32] This led to the fact that the tractor pool was insufficient to secure the motorized tow of combat equipment, primarily the artillery. At the start of the war, the district's artillery units were equipped with 1,170 field guns of 76-mm and 152-mm caliber, 470 anti-tank guns, and 536 mortars.[33]

29   TsAMO RF, F.16, op.2951, s.253, ark. 15.
30   TsAMO RF, F.131, op.126009, s.1, ark. 13-27.
31   TsAMO RF, F.138, op.2566, s.29, ark. 1-4.
32   TsAMO RF, F.138, op.2594, s.2, ark. 274.
33   TsAMO RF, F.138, op.2566, s.27, ark. 1

The territory of the Odessa Military District was part of the country's Southern Zone of Air Defenses and was divided into four brigade areas.[34] The anti-aircraft gunners had a large deficit of anti-aircraft guns and machine guns. For example, the units of the 15th Air Defense Brigade on 19 June 1941 had only 50% of their authorized 76-mm and 85-mm anti-aircraft guns, 25% of their large-caliber anti-aircraft machine guns, and 90% of their authorized machine guns.[35]

In order to cover the airspace above national border within the Odessa Military District, it had available the 20th, 21st, 45th and the 65th Composite Aviation Divisions. As of 1 June 1941, the district's air force had 774 operational aircraft, of which 404 were fighters, 116 were ground attack aircraft, and 254 were bombers. Table 1.3 below presents the amount and types of aircraft that were equipping the Odessa Military District's air force on 1 June 1941:

Table 1.3 Composition of the Odessa Military District's Air Force on 1 June 1941

Aircraft	Type	Number	Total number
Fighters	MiG-3	172	404
	I-16	232	
Ground attack	I-153	116	116
	SB	155	
	Pe-2	40	
+Bombers	AP-2	24	254
	Su-2	35	
Grand total:			774

It was planned to significantly increase the size of the district's aircraft pool by the end of August 1941 while simultaneously improving its quality by the introduction of the latest models: 1,155 aircraft, of which 624 would be fighters (MiG-3, Yak-1, LaGG-1), 131 would be ground attack aircraft, and 382 bombers (SB, Pe-2, AR-2, Su-2).

With the inclusion of the 4th Aviation Corps and the aircraft of the Black Sea Fleet, which had up to 700 aircraft of various types, the amount of combat aircraft operating within the boundaries of the Odessa Military District was 1,854.[36] However, the available aircraft were primarily of outdated design and manufacture, while the latest models were only beginning to arrive in the district. Time was also necessary to re-train the pilots in the new aircraft and to reorganize the system of aviation supply, the process of which had only just begun.[37] Up to 12,000 men were mobilized from out of the reserve and 12 construction battalions were formed in order to build airfields, while the Kiev Special Military District supplied another four construction battalions to hasten the work.[38] However, the lack of the needed quantity of mechanized means and special transport for the work on the airbases slowed the process of bringing new airfields into operational use.

As far as the Odessa Military District's naval strength went, it had the Danube River Flotilla located on the Danube River in Izmail, which was part of the covering forces of RP No. 6. It included 5 monitors, 22 river gunboats, 5 mine sweepers and one mine layer. They were equipped

---

34 TsAMO RF, F.138, op.2181, s.2, ark. 395.
35 TsAMO RF, F.138, op.29161, s.27, ark. 394.
36 TsAMO RF, F.16, op.295, s.253, ark. 16.
37 TsAMO RF, F.138, op.7162, s.4, ark. 38-40; TsAMO RF, F.138, op.2181, s.3, ark. 69.
38 TsAMO RF, F.138, op.29161, s.27, ark. 564.

with a total of 2 130-mm guns, 8 102-mm guns and 24 76-mm guns, as well as with 82 machine guns (see Table 1.4)[39]:

Table 1.4 Composition, artillery and armor of Odessa Military District's Danube River Flotilla

Ships	Artillery		Average armor thickness		
Type	Number	Caliber, mm	Number	Location	Armor thickness, mm
Monitors	5	130	2	Flank	7-8
River gunboats	22	102	8	Deck	4
Minesweepers	5	76	24	Artillery	7-30
Minelayers	1	Machine guns	82		

Comparing the combat possibilities of the rival flotillas, it is evident that the Romanian flotilla was superior in number, but also especially with respect to armament (armor and artillery).

The general intent of the operation to cover the national border was as follows: Based on a system of fieldworks, constructed along the line of the national border, and a series of artificial and natural anti-tank obstacles in the depth, the Soviet troops were to cover the most important directions by means of an active defense and to prevent an enemy breakthrough and subsequent penetration into the depth, especially from the Săveni – Iași and the Galați fronts. In the event of an enemy breakthrough of the defensive front, the district command was to eliminate the breakthrough by means of its reserve forces and entire air fleet, relying upon intermediary, rear and cut-off positions.

In accordance with their assigned tasks, the units and formations conducted a reconnaissance of their jumping-off areas, reconnoitered the approach routes, and worked out plans for moving up into the staging areas. In order to bring the troops up to combat readiness in a timely fashion, the commanders of the formations and units repeatedly raised the troops on combat alerts, training them up to a point of an automatic response.[40] In order to reduce the period of time required for the commanders and their headquarters to be ready, the commander of the Odessa Military District compelled the entire command staff to have constantly at hand a full field kit, and for the headquarters to prepare materiel suitable for working in field conditions.

Significant attention was paid in the district to working out the questions of cooperation with the Border Guards. The district headquarters foresaw in advance the assignment of special detachments in the event of "an incursion or the threat of an incursion by armed detachments or groups of troops from the neighboring state."[41] Each detachment consisted of one to three rifle companies (cavalry squadrons or tank platoons), strengthened with light artillery. The chiefs of the border units were given the right to call up support detachments directly through the commanders of the units and formations from which these detachments were organized.

Keeping the district's forces at a constant state of combat readiness was a multi-faceted task. It included an entire complex of various, but interrelated measures, including putting peacetime units onto a wartime footing by bringing them up to table strength in men, weapons and equipment.[42]

---

39   TsAMO RF, F.16, op.295, s.253, ark. 17-18.
40   TsAMO RF, F.138, op.7162, s.10, ark. 19-22; TsAMO RF, F.138, op.2954, s.2, ark. 339.
41   TsAMO RF, F.138, op.7162, s.10, ark. 19-22.
42   K. Peregudov, *Boevaia gotovnost': Kak ee ponimat'* [*Combat readiness: How to conceive it*] (Moscow, 1969); M. Zakharov, "Nachal'nyi period Velikoi Otechestvennoi voiny i ego uroki" ["Initial period of the Great Patriotic War and its lessons"] *Voenno-istoricheskii zhurnal*, No.7 (1961); TsAMO RF, F.138, op.2181, s.2, ark. 43, 472.

Two covering areas (No. 5 and No. 6) were designated to defend the national border. Area No. 7 adjacent to them was protecting the Odessa Naval Base, and Area No. 8, which consisted of the forces of the 9th Separate Rifle Corps, was located in the Crimea. The right-flank Area No. 5, the front of which stretched for 250 kilometers, included the 30th, 95th and 176th Rifle Divisions and the 2nd and 24th Border Guard Detachments.[43] Area No. 6, the front of which extended for up to 280 kilometers, was under the command of the 14th Rifle Corps with its subordinate corps units, the 9th Cavalry Division and the 25th and 51st Rifle Divisions, as well as the Danube Naval Flotilla and the 25th and 79th Border Guard Detachments.

The district's other formations (two mechanized corps, a rifle division and a cavalry division) were designated for launching counterattacks in conjunction with troops of the covering areas. Two fortified districts, which had been created in the 1930s, were defending along the Dniestr River: the Rybnița and Tiraspol Fortified Districts. Work was underway in them to fortify the terrain in a sector of up to 35 kilometers along the river. The 48th Rifle Corps and the 74th Rifle Division remained in the reserve of the Odessa Military District's commander.[44]

On the whole, the totally secret plan for defending the national border contains exceptionally valuable information on the tasks of the District's forces to cover the national border; an assessment of the enemy's strength and groupings opposite the Odessa District; his possible plan of actions; the intent and plan of the District's own operation; the grouping of the covering forces; and their general tasks. Further on, it spells out specific tasks for the combat units in each of the four covering areas; for the District's air force and anti-air defenses; the arrangement of command, control and communications in putting the defending plan into action; and the plan for engineering and logistical support. The appendices to the plan contain a map of the grouping and the rosters of the covering combat units; a directive to raise the District's units on an alert and a timetable for their movement and assembly close to the national border; a plan for staging and using the District's air force; a scheme of the organization, deployment and distribution of the anti-air units; a scheme of the organization and calculation of various types of communications; a scheme of the defensive lines on the territory of Bessarabia and calculations regarding the labor force, materials and transport required to fortify them; and a list of supplies with respect to ammunition, fuel and rations.

Such a serious and not hackneyed or purely formal approach to operational planning and the preparation of the troops to repel an aggression told favorably on the District's fulfillment of the tasks to protect the national border. The lesson of the high-quality work of General Zakharov's staff, received by the commanders of the District's formations and units on the eve of the war, proved to be an excellent experience and a model for the commanders of the Odessa Defensive Area when working out operations in the subsequent organization of Odessa's own defense.

In order to defend the coastline, in February 1940 the Odessa Naval Base was created, which included all of the coastal artillery of the Northwest Area; the Ochakov Fortified District; and the combat ships based in the ports of Odessa and Ochakov, as well as separate army units. The main capital expenditures for constructing the fleet's naval base were planned for 1941-1943. However, just the fact of forming the base and the assignment to it of various types of forces, which from the very first days of the war began to work out the tasks for strengthening the city's defenses, played a major role in the struggle for Odessa.

The Soviet leadership and the Red Army General Staff in the first half of 1941 implemented a number of major measures, which to a significant degree contributed to the enhancement of combat power of the Odessa Military District as well: increasing the number of men in the acting

---

43   TsAMO RF, F.138, op.7162, s.7, ark. 52.
44   Khor'kov, "Krasnoznamennyi Odesskii voennyi okrug", pp. 93-94.

Red Army; accelerating the cadets' course of study in the military schools; moving up armies, corps and divisions from the interior military districts to the border areas; restaging headquarters to field command posts; and so forth.[45] It was intended to create two new fortified districts in the District by the end of 1941, including one for covering Odessa. The District commander, appealing to the General Staff, requested for this purpose the dispatch of "2 million anti-tank mines, 1,000 metric tons of explosives, 1,560 metric tons of obstacles, 11,250 metric tons of barbed wire, 20,000 delayed-action mines, and 200,000 roadside bombs" in 1941.[46]

All these measures could not help but provoke the interest of foreign intelligence agencies. In just the first 25 days of April 1941 alone, 20 German, 7 Hungarian and 3 Romanian agents were exposed in the border sector. They had been assigned to conduct work on Soviet territory both before the start of combat operations and during the war, keeping constant contact over the radio.[47]

The increasing tension in the sector of the Odessa Military District demanded supplementary measures. On 22 May 1941, the District command appealed to the chief of the General Staff to redeploy the 430th Howitzer Artillery Regiment of the Supreme Command Reserve and the 317th Separate Heavy Artillery Battalion closer to the national border.[48] This was followed on 6 June by a request to shift the 48th Rifle Corps to the axis of the enemy's most likely actions. Prior to 15 June, under the guise of a training exercise, the headquarters of the 48th Rifle Corps and the 30th and 74th Rifle Divisions assembled in woods several kilometers to the east of Bel'tsy [Bălţi].[49] Such a regrouping significantly improved the disposition of the District's forces on this axis.

On this same day [6 June] the District headquarters issued an order for the second-echelon artillery regiments and units of anti-aircraft artillery not to assemble for a movement to training grounds, but to remain in their places of constant deployment. The staging of musters of the anti-aircraft units was re-planned to take place in two periods – from 7 May to 5 June at the Akkerman training ground, and from 10 June to 5 September at the Kherson training ground.[50]

Continuous and regular inspections of the combat readiness of the District's forces were conducted. In the course of declared combat-training alarms, the pilots of the aviation divisions and units rehearsed restaging from their permanent bases to operational airfields. In the process, the pilots conduted the sorties of the aircraft with the calculation that having conducted a night flight, they would land at dawn on the operational airfields. Stockpiles of fuel and ammunition had been created in advance at them.

An army field exercise with means of communication, with the inclusion of all the corps and the District's aviation, which had been planned for the end of June 1941, required the assembly of all the headquarters in the Kishinev [Chişinău], Tiraspol area. In the event of combat actions, this might leave the District's forces out of command. Thus, the decision was taken (after obtaining permission from the People's Commissar of Defense) "to raise a detached army command team on combat alert and to send it in vehicles on 19 June 1941 to the reserve command post in Tiraspol", which proved to be very timely.[51] The District headquarters was removed out from under potential enemy air attacks; in addition, this allowed the timely exertion of command and control over the

45 G. Rozanov, *Plan "Barbarossa": Zamysel i final* [*Plan of "Barbarossa": Conception and Conclusion*] (Moscow, 1970); V. Anfilov, *Bessmertnyi podvig* [*Immortal achievement*] (Moscow, 1971).
46 TsAMO RF, F.7162, s.13, ark. 1-8.
47 TsAMO RF, F.25880, op.4, s.5, ark. 106-120.
48 TsAMO RF, F.2181, op.2, s.253, ark. 384.
49 M. Zakharov, M. "Stranitsy istorii Sovetskikh Vooruzhennykh Sil nakanune Velikoi Otechestvennoi voiny, 1939-1941" [Pages from the history of the Soviet Armed Forces on the eve of the Great Patriotic War, 1939-1941] *Voprosy istorii* , No. 5 (1970), p. 45.
50 TsAMO RF, F.138, op.2181, s.24, ark. 11-114.
51 Zakharov, "Strantitsy istorii", p. 45.

forces in order to repel the aggression. A decisive role in timely bringing the District's troops up to combat readiness was played by an order of the District's chief of staff Major General V. Zakharov, which he independently issued to the troops around 2300 hours on 21 June:

1. Raise the headquarters and troops on combat alert and move them out of populated places.
2. The covering units are to take up their areas.
3. Establish communications with the Border Guard detachments.

Simultaneously, the commander of the District's air force was ordered to disperse the aircraft to operational airfields.

Directly in the District's border sector, 7 rifle divisions, 2 cavalry divisions, 2 tank divisions, a motorized division, and two fortified districts were raised on combat alert; by 0400 on 22 June, they were for the most part in their positions.[52] The District's aviation was also timely brought to combat readiness and dispersed among the operational airfields. All this allowed the District's air force to avoid the enemy air strikes, which were launched against the District's air bases between 0330 and 0430 hrs on 22 June 1941; moreover, on the first day of the war, the District's pilots and anti-aircraft gunners downed 20 hostile aircraft in the air.[53] On the whole, the Odessa Military District met the invasion of the German-Romanian forces in an organized manner, firmly and skillfully repulsing the onslaught of the enemy's superior forces and in distinction from the other military districts, suffering fewer losses in the process.

1.3 The first days of the war on the territory of the Odessa Military District

The day of 22 June 1941 will always be marked in history as the beginning of the Soviet Union's Great Patriotic War against Nazi Germany and its satellites. On the enormous expanse of land from the Barents Sea to the Black Sea, bitter fighting developed along the border at dawn on this tragic day. One hundred-ninety select enemy divisions, exploiting the factor of surprise and having concentrated overwhelming forces on decisive directions, swiftly advanced into the country's interior.

From the first days of the war, Odessa was in essence a frontline city. Already on 26 June, it was publicly announced in Odessa that war had reached the city. The Nazi high command gave great significance to the southern axis. It had planned to break through the Southwestern Front with a surprise attack, to envelop the defending Soviet forces from the north, to destroy their main grouping and to seize Kiev, the Donbass and Rostov, thereby depriving our country of vitally important regions in an economic and strategic sense. In addition, the enemy had planned to use aviation to knock-out or destroy the Black Sea Fleet's main forces, and to blockade the remaining ships in their bases until seizing them from the land. The execution of this plan would have allowed the Nazis to use the Black Sea coast for the uninterrupted supply of the German front's southern flank with the aim of the rapid seizure of the entire south of the Soviet Union. These tasks rested upon Army Group South, which included one panzer army and five field armies.

52 P.A. Nekrasov, "Pogranichniki v boiakh za Odessu" ["Border Guardsmen in the fighting for Odessa"], *Nemerknushii podvig: tezisy dokladov konferentsii, posviashchennoi 25-letiiu geroicheskoi oborony g. Odessy v 1941* [Unfading exploit: theses of the reports of the conference, dedicated to the 25th anniversary of the heroic defense of the city of Odessa, 1941] (Odessa, 1966), p. 28.
53 Khor'kov, "Krasnoznammenyi Odesskii voennyi okrug", pp. 93-94.

When preparing for the invasion of the Soviet Union, Germany took measures to take the bases and aerodromes in the western part of the Black Sea region. With Romania and Bulgaria having signed up to join its aggressive pact, Germany introduced its troops onto their territory and in essence established occupation regimes in these countries. This allowed German to make full use of their territory, military bases and forces in the interests of the war that was being readied against the Soviet Union. By the start of the war, the Germans were expanding the network of airfields on the territory of Bulgaria and Romania, enlarging and improving bases and organizing the defense of them. All of this to a significant degree changed the initial face of the future theater of combat operations. The enemy's aviation in the theater amounted to 650 Romanian aircraft of various types and 450 German aircraft.[54]

The Nazis didn't have a fleet in the Black Sea at the start of the war, but the Romanian fleet had four destroyers, three torpedo boats, one submarine, three PT boats, three patrol craft, two minelayers, ten minesweeping boats and small auxiliary ships, which were based in Constanța and Sulina. It was supplemented by another 7 monitors, 3 floating batteries, 15 river gunboats and 20 patrol craft of the Danube River Flotilla. The German command had a low opinion of the Bulgarian and Romanian fleets in a possible war against the Soviet Union; therefore, it took full leadership over the available forces in the Black Sea into its own hands. Back at the beginning of 1941, the Commander-in-Chief of the German *Kriegsmarine* Admiral Raeder reported to Hitler: "… It is necessary to organize the active cooperation of the available Bulgarian and Romanian navies; for this purpose, in addition to the operational leadership implemented by an admiral – the commander of the Southeast *Kriegsmarine* and his communications staff, it is proposed to attach German naval officers and German technical personnel to the crews of the ships."[55] Germany also strengthened the defense of the Romanian and Bulgarian coastlines through the construction of coastal batteries and the deployment of mine barriers.

By the number of combat ships, the Soviet Black Sea Fleet was significantly superior to the fleets of the other states bordering the Black Sea. It had ships of all classes under its control, including the battleship *Parizhskaia Kommuna* [*Paris Commune*], contemporary cruisers, destroyers, submarines, ten torpedo boats, gunboats and needed auxiliary ships of various types. The Black Sea Fleet had a developed system of naval bases with its main base in Sevastopol.

Thus, at the start of the defense of Odessa, the correlation of forces on the sea with respect to the main classes of warships was in our favor. However, with respect to air strength, the enemy had in the theater an indisputable quantitative superiority. In addition, the enemy air forces had more than 500 aircraft of the latest types, whereas the aviation of the Black Sea Fleet had only just begun to receive modern aircraft. Thus, it was the correlation of naval and air forces that would have a decisive influence on the conditions of conducting combat operations in the Black Sea region.

Combat operations started in the Black Sea at 0315 hrs on 22 June. The *Luftwaffe* conducted a raid against Sevastopol. However, the Black Sea Fleet had been put on the alert at midnight on 21 June, blackout measures had been initiated, and the enemy bombers came under sailors' anti-aircraft fire. The Germans managed to drop only several magnetic mines in the main entry channel and in the Northern Bay; the majority of the mines fell on land, and some of the German aircraft had turned back before reaching their target.

54   I. Popescu-Tuturi, I., G. Zahariia, et. al. *Rumyniia vo vtoroi mirovoi voine* [*Romania in the Second World War*] (Bucharest, 1964), p. 17; N.P. V'iunenko, *Chernomorskii flot v Velikoi Otechestvennoi voine* [*Black Sea Fleet in the Great Patriotic War*] (Moscow: Voenizdat, 1957), pp. 19-20.

55   K.V. Penzin, *Chernomorskii flot v oborone Odessy (1941)* [*Black Sea Fleet in the defense of Odessa (1941)*] (Moscow: Voenizdat, 1956), pp. 8-9.

In the course of the first day of the war, reconnaissance patrols by surface craft were initiated from all the bases of the Black Sea Fleet, including from Odessa, and the deployment of mine fields began. Submarines were sent out to the area between Constanţa and Sulina and between Constanţa and Burgas (Bulgaria) to operate against the enemy's communication lines. The Black Sea Fleet was given its main assignments: to cover and support the naval flank of the ground forces with the fire from ships, aerial attacks, and the launching of attacks from the sea against the enemy's rear and flank areas; to disrupt the enemy's naval communications and to protect their own shipments; and to defend its naval bases stoutly.

Romania was a main source of oil for Germany – a most important strategic raw material, necessary for supporting the combat operations of the *Wehrmacht*'s motorized and mechanized units, the *Luftwaffe* and the *Kriegsmarine*. The primary port for the shipment of oil to Germany was Constanţa – the enemy's main naval base on the Black Sea. The Black Sea Fleet received the mission to block the shipment of Romanian oil to countries of the fascist bloc.

Already on the night of 22/23 June, the first raid was launched against Constanţa's military targets. Aircraft of the Fleet's 63rd Aviation Brigade dropped bombs on oil and fuel tanks in the vicinity of the port, sparking secondary explosions and flames. In the course of the day (23 June), three more air raids were conducted against Constanţa and two against Sulina. On 24 and 25 June, aircraft of the 2nd and 40th Aviation Regiments escorted by fighters of the 62nd Fighter Aviation Brigade again made bombing runs over targets in Constanţa.[56] On 7 July six Pe-2 aircraft under the command of Captain A. Tsurtsumiia bombed Ploesti and shot down two enemy Me-109 fighters. Starting on 10 July, the Southern Front's air force took part in attacks against Ploesti. In the course of a week, 20,000 metric tons of oil products were set ablaze in this area. On 13 July, SB and TB-3 bombers under the command of Hero of the Soviet Union Major P.L. Tokarev bombed Tulcea. On 10 August, six TB-3 bombers suspending I-16 fighters beneath them instead of bombs and six Pe-2s bombed the Cernavodă Bridge. The I-16 fighters separated from their carriers and bombed the bridge from low altitude. As a result, the railroad bridge and the oil line that crossed it were knocked out. In these combat operations, the pilots under Captain A.V. Shubikov and A.P. Tsurtsumiia particularly distinguished themselves.[57]

The enemy's main base, Constanţa, was subjected not only to bombings from the air, but also an artillery bombardment from the sea by ships of a Black Sea Fleet squadron. The approaches to Constanţa were blocked by a minefield with a narrow passage through it. The mine barrier itself was being protected by the fire of coastal artillery, including the three heavy-caliber 280-mm cannons of the twin-turreted German Tirpitz Battery. Numerous German and Romanian bombers and fighters were based in Constanţa and on nearby airfields. Combat surveillance ships were screening the approaches to the minefield: 30 miles to the northeast, a gunboat was on patrol; beyond the margin of the minefield were two destroyers serving in the role of pickets; 30 miles to the southeast, a torpedo boat was on patrol, supported by two more destroyers. A minelayer and a gunboat were based in Constanţa, but at the moment of our ships' hit-and-run foray, they were out on a raid; at a distance of approximately 60 miles in the direction of Sevastopol, a Romanian submarine was on patrol. Aerial reconnaissance was being conducted from Constanţa in the direction of the Crimea.

For the attack against Constanţa, a strike group consisting of the Leningrad-class destroyers *Khar'kov* and *Moskva* under the command of Captain 2nd Rank M.F. Romanov was created. The

---

56 N. Grechanok, "Udary Chernomorskogo flota po ob'ektam protivnika v 1941 godu" ["Attacks of the Black Sea Fleet against enemy targets in 1941"] *Voenno-istoricheskii zhurnal*, No. 12 (1975), pp. 26-34.

57 P. Bolgari, N. Zotkin, D. Kornienko, M. Liubimov, and A. Liakhovich, *Chernomorskii flot: Istoricheskii ocherk* [*Black Sea Fleet: A historical study*] (Moscow: Voenizdat, 1967), p. 144.

support group consisted of the cruiser *Voroshilov* and the destroyers *Soobrazitel'nyi* [*Agile*] and *Smyshlennyi* [*Sagacious*]. The strike group departed from Sevastopol on the evening of 25 June; the support group under the command of Vice Admiral T.A. Novikov followed in its wake. The ships' passage to the area of combat operations went smoothly. At 0500 on 26 June, the destroyers opened fire at the oil tanks in the port of Constanța from a range of 130 cables [a nautical unit of measure equal to 1/10 of a nautical mile]. The bombardment continued for 10 minutes, and over this time the destroyers fired 350 130-mm shells. A strong fire was observed in the vicinity of the oil tanks. In response, the ships came under fire from the 280-mm German battery, which managed to bracket the destroyer *Moskva*, which was in the lead. The commander of the strike group gave the signal to cease fire and to withdraw from the firing position under the cover of a smokescreen. Evading the fire of the enemy's coastal artillery, the destroyers retreated with a zig-zag course at a speed of 30 knots. At 0520, as the ships were already about to exit beyond the margins of the minefield, the destroyer *Moskva* struck a mine. Ruptured in the vicinity of the first boiler room, it began to sink quickly. At this time, enemy aircraft appeared overhead, which began to machine-gun the sailors in the water. The attempt by the destroyer *Khar'kov* to render assistance to the perishing sailors was not crowned with success, since it was simultaneously being attacked by enemy aircraft and coming under fire from large-caliber artillery. *Khar'kov's* boilers were damaged by shell explosions – the destroyer's speed dropped to 6 knots, which in the circumstances of the unceasing barrage threatened it with destruction. Boiler room machinists P. Grebennikov and P. Kairov repaired the damaged boilers despite the very high temperatures, and this allowed the *Khar'kov* to gain speed and to return to base safely. For the courage and fearlessness they displayed, sailors P. Grebennikov and P. Kairov were awarded with the Order of the Red Banner.

The boldness and effectiveness of the raid by the detachment of ships was recognized even by the German command. For example, in the diary kept by the leader of the German fleet's training center in Romania, which was located at this time in Constanța, it was noted on 26 June 1941: "It must be acknowledged that the bombardment of the coastline by the Russian destroyers was very audacious. The fact that as a result of this bombardment an oil tank was set ablaze and the flames subsequently spread to an ammunition stockpile, is inarguable proof of the bombardment's success. Moreover, as a result of damage to the railroad, the Bucharest – Constanța line was cut; in connection with the great damage to the train station, inflicted by the bombardment, difficulty with fuel deliveries has arisen."[58]

As a result of the active operations of Soviet submarines and aircraft, the enemy was compelled to implement supply shipments across the Black Sea with only small, solitary ships, which hugged the coastline in transit. In clashes on the Black Sea the crews of the submarines "Shch-211", which sank a transport ship and an oil tanker; "Shch-214", which sank a tanker and a schooner with its cannon's fire; and "Shch-215", which sank a transport; particularly distinguished themselves.[59]

The German Eleventh Army, plus the Romanian Third and Fourth Armies and the Hungarian VIII Corps conducted the offensive on the Eastern Front's southern flank – a total of 24 divisions and 15 brigades.[60] The Soviet 51st "Perekop" Rifle Division was defending the sector along the Danube stretching from the Black Sea to Lake Yalpug. The 79th "Izmail" Border Guards Detachment was directly covering the left bank of the Danube. It included an NKVD battalion

58 *Boevoi put' Sovetskogo Voenno-Morskogo Flota* [*Combat path of the Soviet Navy*] (Moscow: Voenizdat, 1964), pp. 427-428.

59 V. Vorob'ev, "Boevye deistviia podvodnykh lodok Chernomorskogo flota 1941-1942 gg." ["Combat operations of the submarines of the Black Sea Fleet 1941-1942", *Voenno-istoricheskii zhurnal*, No. 6 (1976), pp. 46-53.

60 *Velikaia Otechestvennaia Voina Sovetskogo Soiuza 1941-1945: Kratkaia istoriia* [*Great Patriotic War of the Soviet Union 1941-1945: A brief history*] (Moscow: *Voenizdat*, 1965), p. 88.

of naval border security – 4 submarine chasers and 25 small river cutters. The Danube River Flotilla (commanded by Vice Admiral N.A. Abramov) was patrolling the waters of the Danube. It had bases in Izmail, Reni, Kilia and Vilkovo [Vilkovo]. The flotilla consisted of monitors, patrol boats, armed airboats, minesweepers and other ships, as well as a separate rifle company, the 17th Machine-gun Company, the 46th Separate Anti-aircraft Battalion and the Danube Sector of Coastal Security: six artillery batteries of various calibers and the 96th Fighter Aviation Squadron.[61] The area of naval bases was being covered by the system coastal defenses and anti-aircraft batteries. The main mission of the Danube River Flotilla was to prevent an enemy invasion across the Danube River into Southern Bessarabia.

Thanks to the anticipatory actions of the District's chief of staff M.V. Zakharov, by 0400 on 22 June the majority of the units of the 25th and 51st Rifle Divisions had deployed into the fortified positions along the bank of the Danube River. Intervals between the divisions were being covered by elements of the 79th Border Guards Detachment. At 0415 Romanian artillery batteries opened fire at the Soviet side, targeting Reni, Kartaly, Izmail, Kilia, Vilkovo and the ships of the flotilla. Izmail was also being bombarded by two Romanian monitors, which had departed from Sulina and had entered the Kilia branch of the Danube River. Having grasped the critical nature of the situation, Vice Admiral Abramov at 0420 independently gave the order to open fire. The barrage from the Romanian bank of the river lessened somewhat. However, the enemy heavy artillery, which was firing from defilade positions, didn't cease its fire. In the afternoon, the hostile artillery switched to constant harassing fire, systematically suppressing targets that had already fallen silent, because the Soviet batteries relied upon ammunition that arrived from the Black Sea, and the path to the sea from the beginning of the war was under the targeted fire of Romanian batteries that had been deployed on the right bank of the Danube River. During the artillery barrage, the flotilla and the coastal batteries didn't suffer serious losses, but the Izmail port was completely knocked out.

Below Izmail, in the Kilia sector, which was being defended by the 23rd Rifle Regiment of the 51st Rifle Division, the Romanians at 0900 made their largest attempt to force a crossing of the Danube River. On 22 June, all the enemy's attempts to cross the Danube River were repulsed by the combined efforts of Red Army units, Border Guardsmen and the flotilla: one in the vicinity of Beshiktash and Lake Razdel'nyi; three in the area of Kilia-Nova; two – at Vilkovo; and four attempts to ford the Prut River near Reni.

Only approximately a half-kilometer separated the town and port of Izmail (including the main base of the Danube River Flotilla) from the Romanian Cape of Satul-Nou on the opposite bank of the Danube River. Thus from the very first minutes of the war, the enemy held the entire port under targeted fire, including machine-gun and mortar fire as well. But the main threat presented by the bluff of the Cape of Satul-Nou was that it served as an ideal position for correcting the fire of the heavy artillery batteries positioned in the Tolcea area. Through the precise information of the artillery spotters atop the bluff, an enemy battery from the range of approximately 20 kilometers placed effective fire on units of the 51st Rifle Division, the navigable channel, the port and even on the area of the positions of the Danube Flotilla's main forces in the Kislitsia delta arm of the Danube.

The ranks of the town's defenders included thousands of volunteers, who had deep knowledge of the local terrain. The seizure of the enemy batteries and the maintenance of a bridgehead on the

---

61   A. Vakhmut, "Pervye dni voiny na Dunae" ["First days of the war on the Danube"] *Voenno-istoricheskii zhurnal*, No. 9 (1970).

right bank of the Danube River would make it possible to support the successful combat operations of the flotilla on the river, as well as to maintain a firm defense on the line of the border.[62]

On the evening of 22 June, Vice Admiral Abramov decided to seize the Cape of Satul-Nou standing opposite the town of Izmail, and to suppress the hostile artillery batteries. Quickly, in the course of a day, a landing force was prepared to storm the opposite bank. The landing force included a composite company of Border Guardsmen, and the Danube Flotilla's machine-gun and rifle company. Five gunboats would ferry the men across the river. Artillery support for the landing was provided by three batteries on the eastern bank and the monitors *Udarnyi* [*Striking*] and *Martynov*. The landing force assembled in the Kislitsia branch of the Danube.

On the morning of 24 June, after an artillery preparation, the gunboats quickly deposited the men on the western bank of the river. In a swift action, the Soviets destroyed two Romanian companies and took 70 officers and soldiers as prisoner. A battalion of the 51st Rifle Division crossed the river to exploit the success, and expanded the bridgehead's front up to 40 kilometers.[63] The attackers suffered no fatalities; 10 men were wounded.

The Soviet command decided to take advantage of the achieved success quickly, and set about preparing a larger river crossing in the vicinity of Kilia-Veche, where the enemy's main forces were located. The second attack included three battalions of the 23rd Rifle Regiment (commanded by Major P.N. Sirota). Four gunboats and 10 coast guard motor boats would transport the battalions across the river. Considering the small quantity of boats, the landing would take place in three echelons, one rifle battalion in each.

The first echelon began crossing on the night of 25 June directly at Kilia-Veche. The night attack came as a surprise and the Romanians spotted the approach of the Soviet boats too late. Despite the artillery fire that was opened up, which damaged two of the motor boats, the Soviet infantry were deposited on the Romanian bank. The Romanian garrison in Kilia-Veche was unable to offer resistance; a panic erupted in the town, and it was taken in the night fighting. By 1000 hrs on 26 June, the Soviets had fully seized a fortified region and were occupying a bridgehead up to 4 kilometers wide and 3 kilometers deep. A Romanian infantry battalion was crushed, along with its attached artillery and border guard complement. The enemy lost more than 200 soldiers and officers killed, and approximately 500 (according to other data, 720) were taken prisoner. In addition, 8 cannons, 30 machine guns and more than 1,000 rifles were captured.[64]

In the course of 26 June, the flotilla's gunboats transferred elements of the 51st Rifle Division to the Romanian bank, which drove the Romanians away from the entire coastal area and took militarily-important villages and islands. The two bridgeheads became merged into one. As a result, both banks of the Kilia mouth of the Danube, from the Rapidy River to Peripravy (which extended for 75 kilometers), came under the control of Soviet forces. The Danube River Flotilla obtained freedom of action and could now render effective support to the ground units.

As a result of the numerically-small Soviet forces on this sector of the front and the difficult overall situation on the Soviet-German front, it was impossible to count upon the arrival of reinforcements in order to develop the offensive further into Romanian territory. The division commander gave the order to hold the occupied bridgehead firmly and to dig in on the lines attained. The initial attempts by Romanian naval infantry to eliminate the bridgehead were repulsed on 27 and 29 June. Starting on 1 July, the enemy launched daily attacks; particularly

---

62   Ibid., p. 5.
63   *Kniga pamiati Ukrainy: Odesskaia oblast', Tom 1*, p. 12.
64   I.I. Loktionov, *Dunaiskaia flotiliia v Velikoi Otechestvennoi Voine* [*Danube Flotilla in the Great Patriotic War*] (Moscow: *Voenizdat*, 1962), p. 26.

savage and bloody fighting unfolded on 3, 4 and 6 July. Altogether, 18 major attacks by Romanian forces were driven back with a heavy toll exacted on the attackers.

By the end of July the German-Romanian forces, using the successes they achieved on other sectors of the front, broke through to the east and began to threaten the northern flank and rear of the Southern Front with encirclement. Therefore the *Stavka* of the Supreme High Command ordered the removal of the Soviet forces from the border along the Danube and to take up a defense along the Dniester River. Only then, on 19 July, was the bridgehead beyond the Danube abandoned at the order of higher command. The Danube River Flotilla removed the Soviet troops from the bridgehead on hostile territory in an organized manner and without losses, left the Danube River, and reached Odessa across the open and stormy sea. Having completed the passage across the sea, which was uncommon for riverine ships, the flotilla assembled in Kherson and Nikolaev. There, in the course of two weeks they repaired their combat ships and subsequently fought with the aggressors on the Lower Bug and the lower Dnepr Rivers.[65]

The seizure and holding of the bridgehead across the Danube in the war's early days had not only an operational-tactical, but also a powerful psychological and morale significance. Literally within several days from the start of the invasion, the entire Soviet Union, but most importantly, the Red Army learned that the enemy could be defeated even on his territory. For their exploits performed during the river crossings, many soldiers and officers, including the commander of the 23rd Rifle Regiment Major P.N. Sirota, the first assistant of the regiment's chief of staff Lieutenant A.M. Ovcharov, the secretary of the regiment's Komsomol committee Burov, and many others were decorated with high government honors.[66]

The overall situation on the Danube – Prut sector of the front was especially tense. Forces of the Southern Front consisting of the Soviet 9th and 18th armies (the latter commanded by General of the Army I.V. Tiulenev) were opposing three armies of the aggressor – the German Eleventh and the Romanian Third and Fourth – from Lipcani to the mouth of the Danube River. On this slice of the Soviet-German front that extended for 480 kilometers, the enemy had a numerical superiority, which was particularly large in the Danube sector that extended for 170 kilometers and was defended by units of Major General D.G. Egorov's 14th Rifle Corps. Here, on average there were only five defenders for each kilometer of the border, against which up to an enemy company was operating. Only the courage and heroism of the soldiers and commanders of the left flank of the Southern Front made it possible not only to hold the foe at the border, but also to seize a significant bridgehead on enemy territory, as well as a lot of prisoners and booty. About these events, Colonel M.I. Krylov (who at the time served as the chief of staff of the Danube Fortified District) later wrote: "Without the resolute defense of the Danube and the Prut, and later along the Dniester, it would have been hardly possible to stop the foe in front of Odessa."[67] In reality, in such daring operations, the soldiers and commanders of the Red Army were quickly learning to fight "in a new way" – with close cooperation between all types of forces and the maximal freedom of action by the responsible commanders, in accordance with the combat situation as it was developing.

65   *Boevoi put' Sovetskogo-Morskogo Flota*, pp. 429-430.
66   Vakhmut, "Pervye dni voiny na Dunae".
67   As cited by Tsymbal, E., *Trassy zhizni* [*Traces of life*] (Odessa: Maiak, 1975), pp. 104-105.

Part I
The Defense of Odessa 1941

2

The situation on the Southern Front in the summer of 1941

In July 1941, the German forces of Army Group South, while fighting to take possession of Ukraine's capital, the city of Kiev, also conducted an offensive to the southeast and south, striving to seize the Donbass and the naval bases of the Black Sea Fleet. In the middle of July, they launched major offensives in the sector stretching from Berdichev to the mouth of the Dniester River. The German Eleventh Army, the Third and Fourth Romanian Armies and the VIII Hungarian Corps were attacking Southern Front's 9th and 18th Armies and its Coastal Group of Forces. A total of 24 Soviet divisions, which had been greatly weakened in the preceding fighting, were facing 24 divisions and 15 brigades of the enemy.[1]

The German Seventeenth Army after three days of bloody fighting managed to breach the Soviet defensive front at the boundary between the Southwestern and Southern Fronts. It began to exploit in the direction of Zhmerinka. The German Eleventh Army at this time was striving to force a crossing of the Dniester River in the vicinity of Mogilev-Podol'skii. Soviet troops were offering stubborn resistance. The heavily-battered units of the 130th Rifle Division and the garrison of the Mogilev-Podol'skii Fortified District held their positions on the left bank of the Dniester River for 10 days. In this sector, the Germans lost more than 5,000 of their soldiers and officers. However, owning a superiority in strength, the enemy managed to create a bridgehead across the Dniester and in the course of 16-18 July crossed five divisions to the left bank. A threat arose to the entire left flank of our 18th Army.

At this same time, the Romanian Fourth Army with the support of a large quantity of aviation launched an offensive toward Kishinev [Chișinău] in the south. At the cost of heavy losses, the Romanians succeeded in taking the city.[2] The serious danger arose of the possible isolation of Southern Front's Coastal Group of Forces and the enemy's seizure of Odessa. In this situation, the Soviet command decided to withdraw the 9th Army and the Coastal Group of Forces to the left bank of the Dniester River, and to restage the Danube Flotilla to Odessa and Nikolaev.

On 18 July 1941, the Coastal Group of Forces was given an assignment by a directive of the Southern Front headquarters: "In cooperation with the Black Sea Fleet, prevent an enemy breakthrough in the direction of Odessa, holding it under any circumstances."[3] On 19 July, the *Stavka* converted the Coastal Group of Forces into the Separate Coastal Army, and appointed an

---

1   *Ukrainskaia RSR u Velikii Vitchiznianyi viini Rad'ianskogo Soiuza 1941-1945 rr., u 3 tom* [*Ukrainian RSR in the Great Patriotic War of the Soviet Union 1941-1945, in 3 volumes*] Volume 1 (Kiev: Politizdav Ukraini, 1967), p. 211.

2   V.G. Berezhin'skii, "Odes'ka oboronna operatsiia: 60 rokov tomu" ["Odessa Defensive Operation: 60th anniversary"], *Narodna armiia*, (No. 2) 2001.

3   TsAMO RF, F.288, op.9960, s.2, ark. 25.

experienced commander who had experience in the fighting for Odessa in the years of the Russian Civil War, General G.I. Safonov to command the new army. Between 19 and 25 July 1941, the adversary made a swift advance to the bridges across the Dniester, but the Separate Coastal Army's forces held them in heavy fighting while organizing a defense on the distant approaches to Odessa.

At this time, the overall situation on the Soviet-German front was deteriorating with catastrophic speed. By the end of July the enemy, continuing its swift advance, created the threat of a breakthrough to Leningrad, and was striving at any cost to overcome the resistance of Soviet forces at Smolensk and Kiev. In connection with the enemy's appearance in the Kiev area and the breakthrough of the Southern Front near Mogilev-Podol'skii, a real threat was created of the encirclement of Southwestern Front's 6th and 12th Armies, as well as of Southern Front's 9th and 18th Armies. In order to prevent the encirclement, on 17 July 1941 the *Stavka* ordered these armies to withdraw to the Belaia Tserkov' – Gaisin – Kamenka – Dniester River line. On 21 July, the enemy's XXXXVIII Motorized Corps managed to create a breach in the Uman' area, but it was counterattacked by forces of the 2nd Mechanized Corps from the Southern Front reserve and hurled back 40 kilometers to the north. This somewhat improved the situation, but not for long. The Soviet armies continued to be threatened with encirclement.

In connection with this, the Soviet high command issued an order for the forces of the Southern Front to withdraw to the Talnoe – Christinovka – Bălţi line. Meanwhile the enemy, developing its strategic offensive with superior forces on 26 July launched attacks against weak sectors of the Southwestern and Southern Fronts. The German 72nd Division, making use of its experience when it had forced a crossing of the Prut River, forced the Dniester River and created a bridgehead north of Grigoriopol' at the boundary between the 9th Army and the Separate Coastal Army. From the march, the enemy was trying to split the Soviet armies apart and to seize Odessa and Nikolaev.

The situation was made worse by a German breakthrough out of the Berdichev area in the general area of Uman', Pervomaisk and Voznesensk by von Kleist's Panzer Group 1. On 2 August, motorized corps of this panzer group broke through to Pervomaisk and emerged in the rear of the Soviet 6th and 12th Armies. From the northwest, units of the German Seventeenth Army reached the same place. Divisions of the 6th and 12th Armies in the Uman' area fought their way out of the closing pocket to the area south of Pervomaisk, but approximately 65,000 men fell into encirclement. Squeezed by the enemy's compact ring, the trapped soldiers and officers of the 6th and 12th Armies defended courageously and tenaciously. They made every effort to break out of the cauldron. Counterattacks came one after the other, but were unsuccessful. The Soviet troops fought in encirclement until 13 August. Only isolated groups of soldiers and officers were able to make their way out of the pocket; the rest became prisoners.

At this time, 46 enemy divisions, including 6 panzer and 4 motorized divisions, were attacking opposite the Southern Front. The German high command had given them the order to encircle and destroy the main forces of Southern Front. The Front commander General I.V. Tiulenev subsequently wrote about these terrible days: "Our troops were conducting heavy fighting with a pivoted front, repelling enemy attacks not only from the west, but also from the northeast."[4]

On 4 August 1941, the Southern Front's Military Council reported to the *Stavka*:

> Possession of Odessa has large political and operational significance. The enemy will be constantly connected on the flank. The defense of Odessa must be conducted under the conditions of the Fleet's superiority in the Black Sea. The defense on land is eased by the presence of major water barriers on the flanks – the Dniester estuary to the west, and the Kual'nitskii

---

4   Tiulenev, I.V., *Cherez tri voiny* [*Through three wars*] (Moscow, 1960), p. 160.

and Khadzhibeiskii estuaries to the east. Only the 30-40 kilometer neck of land along the Paliovo – Vygoda Station – Beliaevka line remains to be defended. For this, the Coastal Army can at first assign three rifle divisions (the 25th, 95th and 30th) and people's militia. Leave all means of air defense, which is presently there, in order to provide air cover. Add a regiment of fighter aviation; the latter not at the expense of the Front.[5]

The *Stavka* accepted the proposal and on 5 August 1941 issued a directive to the commander of the Southwestern Direction Marshal of the Soviet Union S.M. Budennyi: "Do not surrender Odessa and defend it to the last possibility, employing the Black Sea Fleet for this." I.V. Stalin personally dictated the directive.[6]

On 5 August the forces of the Southern Front was falling back with fighting on the line from Pervomaisk to Tiraspol. The Coastal Army was in retreat to the Odessa area, while the 9th and 18th Armies were defending the bridges across the Southern Bug in the Nikolaev area. The Danube River Flotilla, covering the bridges from Voznesensk to Nikolaev, was offering great assistance to the Soviet ground troops.[7]

After the Romanians forced a crossing of the Dniester River, Hitler sent a letter to I. Antonescu, in which he congratulated him with the "return of the provinces" and expressed gratitude for Antonescu's intention to "fight to the last on Germany's side". Thus Antonescu, with all the forces of his reinforced Fourth Army and with the support of units of the German 72nd Infantry Division strove to capture the virtually defenseless Odessa.

The commander of the Coastal Army, in view of the threat and the proximate danger, as well as in the conditions of organizational chaos and the absence of communications between formations, sought to organize a front to defend Odessa as quickly as possible with his meager forces. The left flank was continuing to hold a defensive line from Karolino to Bugaz along the coast of the Dniester estuary, and further to the north along the Dniester. But on the right, eastern flank, a gap arose that was approximately 50 kilometers wide, in connection with the fact that the 30th Rifle Division, which was supposed to be holding the line of defense here, had been cut-off by the enemy and was retreating toward the Southern Bug together with units of the 9th Army. Units of the German 72nd Infantry Division and a Romanian cavalry brigade were pushing through this gap with the aim of taking Odessa from the march.

General Sofronov was compelled to send the regiments of a cavalry division that was in the process of forming up in Odessa to the army's right flank, in the attempt to seal the breach with slashing attacks and, if possible, to make contact with the cut-off 30th Rifle Division. The cavalrymen, led by their General Petrov, galloped across the enormous expanse of the steppes in search of the 30th Rifle Division, while launching unexpected flank attacks against the enemy's marching columns, drawing the enemy troops into fleeting clashes, disrupting their columns and slowing their pace of advance. Continuing to follow their orders, the cavalrymen made a deep penetration and emerged in the enemy's rear. Fighting their way back to Odessa through the German and Romanian units, the cavalrymen constantly harassed the enemy's rear echelons, spending days and nights in the saddle. In the course of this cavalry raid, the cavalry regiments adopted the following combat formation: Sabre squadrons advanced in front; headquarters and the regiment's specialized elements marched in the middle; and machine-gun carriers covered the rear. The enemy deployed a tank screen in the effort to intercept and destroy the Soviet riders. However, the cavalrymen,

---

5   TsAMO RF, F.251, op.646, s.4, ark. 121.
6   *Istoriia Velikoi Otechestvennoi Voiny Sovetskogo Soiuza 1941-1945, v 6 t.* [*History of the Great Patriotic War of the Soviet Union 1941-1945, in 6 volumes*], Volume 2 (Moscow: Voenizdat, 1971), p. 113; N.G. Kuznetsov, *Na flotakh boevaia trevoga* [*Combat alert in the fleets*] (Moscow: Voenizdat, 1971), p.119.
7   Bolgari, et. al., *Chernomorskoi flot*, p. 149.

putting an artillery battery into action, knocked out several of the tanks and broke through the screen, having taken prisoners from among the crews of the knocked-out tanks. In order to inspire his troopers, exhausted by the constant fighting, the commander of the 7th Cavalry Regiment Captain Blinov placed the captured tankers in front of the regiment's formation and directed, "Take a look, boys, at these fascist shrimps, take a good look. Really, can't we whip 'em? Each of you, who meet the fascists in combat, will be facing just such despicable cowards."[8]

The daring raid by General Petrov's riders into the rears of the attacking enemy divisions slowed the pace of their offensive and prevented them from breaking through to Odessa from the northeast from the march. The time that was won allowed the Coastal Army headquarters to shift the 54th "Razinskii" Regiment of the 25th "Chapaev" Division, the 26th Composite Border Guard Regiment, the just-formed 1st Regiment of Naval Infantry, a battalion of the reserve 136th Regiment and two destroyer battalions from among the number of Odessa volunteers to the undefended eastern sector. The motley elements and units were commanded by Brigade Commander S.F. Monakhov, who from them organized a firm defense of Odessa from the east in the Buldynka – Grigor'evka area.[9] Having suffered substantial losses in the course of the multi-day raid into the enemy rear, the regiments of Petrov's cavalry division were withdrawn into the Coastal Army's mobile reserve beyond the Adzhalykskii estuary.

The forces of Odessa's naval base consisted of a detachment of combat ships, three battalions of fixed and mobile long-range coastal artillery, the 73rd Anti-aircraft Regiment, three squadrons of naval aviation and specialized elements of coastal security. According to its complement of ships, the base was one of the best in the Black Sea Fleet.[10] Odessa's base was hosting the auxiliary cruiser *Komintern*, the destroyer *Shauman*, a separate battalion of gun boats (*Krasnyi Adzharistan, Krasnaia Gruziia, Krasnaia Abkhaziia* and *Krasnaia Armeniia*), and a brigade of 23 torpedo boats. To secure the base's waters, there were 17 MO-4 cutters, 2 mine sweepers, 4 patrol boats and the minelayer *Lukomskii*.[11] By the start of Odessa's defense, preparation of the naval sector had been completed: all of the coastal artillery batteries were combat-ready; the defensive mine barrier had been laid; and the base had deployed a picket ship. All of the attention of Odessa's base command in this period was focused on working out the tasks of joint operations with the army and completing the formation of new units, necessary for the direct struggle for the Fleet's base. All of the following steps were taken: arrangements were made for artillery support for the flanks of their forces; pilots of MBR-2 aircraft were trained to correct the fire of ships at ground targets; batteries were reinforced with a second line of barbed wire obstacles, explosive mines and delayed-action mines; detachments were created to defend important base facilities; aerial observation, illumination and signal posts were set up; and the coastal artillery positions were camouflaged. In order to protect Odessa against aerial attacks from the sea, schooners with barrage balloons and floating anti-aircraft batteries had been prepared.[12]

The capture of Odessa was given a large place in the plans of Germany and its allies. Aware of the evident superiority of the Black Sea Fleet in submarines and surface ships, the aggressors could not count upon victory in naval actions. They were hoping to destroy the Black Sea Fleet by seizing its bases from the land, and first of all, Odessa. In addition, the fascist command believed that the rapid capture of the city would help it crush the Soviet forces of the Southern Front and to take possession of the Donbass and Crimea, followed by the Northern Caucasus and the

---

8   TsAMO RF, F.288, op.9960, s.2, ark. 39.
9   Kuznetsov, *Na flotakh*, p. 117.
10   TsVMA MO RF, F.204, s.29364, ark. 81.
11   TsVMA MO RF, F.204, s.23690, ark. 70-80.
12   K.V. Penzin, *Chernomorskoi flot v oborone Odessy (1941 god)* [*The Black Sea Fleet in the defense of Odessa (1941)*] (Moscow: Voenizdat, 1956), pp. 14-16.

Trans-Caucasus. The supremacy of the Soviet fleet in the Black Sea was very unsettling to the Nazi generals. They understood that until the Black Sea Fleet had been deprived of its bases, any territorial successes of the German forces in the Soviet Union's south would be insecure.

Odessa's military command and civilian authorities began to prepare for a defense even before the Soviet forces fell back to the line of the Dniester River. Two regiments of naval infantry had been formed up before 5 August; the coastal artillery had been re-arranged in order to fire at ground targets; and test firing to adjust the fire of the combat ships in accordance with the tasks of the land defense had been conducted. The command of the Odessa Naval Base undertook measures to strengthen the base's protection from the sea and was assigning base personnel to construct ground lines.

Since Odessa Oblast' from the very first day of the war was in the frontal zone, this required particular efficiency and speed in reorganizing the entire life of the city on a wartime basis. From the start of the war, more than 155,000 residents of all nationalities from Odessa or from the surrounding oblast' were mobilized or volunteered for the Red Army or Black Sea Fleet – Ukrainians, Russians, Jews, Moldavians, Armenians, Georgians and others. More than 18,000 Communists and 73,000 Komsomol members flowed into the combat ranks of the army, including 3,200 females who were sent to the front as medics, nurses and signal personnel. Various opinions can be held of Communist ideology, but it is impossible to underestimate its organizational and mobilizing role in those days. In addition, 3,755 various automobiles, 340 tractors and 186 motorcycles were mobilized from the economy in order to serve the Red Army's needs.

People's militia played a particularly important role in the fighting for Odessa. Out of the 55,000 militia volunteers, an entire division was formed, and replacements were obtained for other combat units of the defensive area.[13] Over a short period of time, 45 militarized formations were created in Odessa, including 6 destroyer battalions, which had a total strength of 11,420 men. They patrolled the city's streets, guarded important military sites, and conducted the struggle against hostile infiltrators and diversionists. The local anti-air defense was strengthened with 3,500 men.

In these difficult conditions, ignoring the proximity of the front, a harvest of crops began. Students went out to the farms to aid the village workers. From Odessa State University alone, more than 8,000 students and professors traveled out to the oblast's collective farms and State farms.[14]

On 8 July 1941, the evacuation of cultural treasures and machinery and equipment from the city's industrial plants began. An enormous burden and responsibility fell to the lot of railroad workers and longshoremen. The property of the V.I. Lenin machine-building factory, of the January Uprising factory, of a fuel refining plant, of the Red Profintern factory and of other plants and enterprises were evacuated by rail. A stream of particularly heavy loads, the handling of which required enormous care and experience, was sent to the port. The work of the longshoremen came under the control of the naval command.[15] The situation became complicated when the German cut the railroad connection with Odessa at the end of June (before this happened, 51,000 metric tons of equipment and materials had been evacuated). The port became the sole transport link that connected the city with the rest of the country. The longshoremen reduced the amount of time needed for loading and unloading ships to a minimum. In July 1941 alone, 67 ships carried out shipment operations in the port of Odessa. Over one month, 46,000 military personnel and

---

13   Kniga pamiati Ukrainy: Odesskaia oblast', pp. 17-18.
14   *Istoriia Odes'kogo universitety, 1865-2000* [*History of Odessa University, 1865-2000*] (Odesa, 2000), p. 108.
15   *Ocherki istorii Odesskoi oblastnoi partiinoi organizatsii* [*Essays on the history of the Odessa Oblast' Party organization*] (Odessa: Maiak, 1981), pp. 339-340.

civilians and 58,000 metric tons of loads were shipped out of Odessa, and the port received 5,300 metric tons of ammunition. Altogether, almost 10% of Ukraine's population and 150 plants and institutes were evacuated through Odessa's port.[16] Already by the month of October, the Odessa enterprises that had been evacuated to the East began to produce items for the needs of the country's defense.

After the factory machinery and equipment was loaded on board each ship, as a rule, civilians that were due to be evacuated were then taken on board. Frequently, the embarkation exceeded all norms and rules of sea shipments – people had to be saved. En route to their destinations, the ships were subjected to bombing attacks; several also struck mines. One of the greatest tragedies involved the loss of the steamship *Lenin*, which on 27 July 1941 hit a mine – of the 2,500 passengers, primarily women and children, only around 500 were rescued.[17]

In order to hold the defense, it was necessary to create a system of fieldworks quickly. At first, during our forces' withdrawal from Bessarabia, it was intended to construct four lines of defense on the land surrounding Odessa. However, in connection with the rapidly changing situation, it was decided to focus primarily on the construction of three: the first line, 60 kilometers outside of Odessa; the second line, 40 kilometers outside of the city, and the third, just 20-25 kilometers from the city. As a result of the enemy's rapid advance, the first and second lines of fortifications were incomplete and left almost undefended by troops.[18] The main efforts were concentrated on setting up the third line of defense, nearest to the city.

The engineer units of the Coastal Army and of the Odessa Naval Base, which numbered no more than 12,000 men, were not capable of carrying out the task of fortification construction over a short period of time through their own efforts. Civilians of the city and its suburban areas came to their assistance. From them, 12 fortification labor battalions of 500 men and women each were created. Every day, 10,000 to 12,000 residents of Odessa left the city to work on the fortifications. In the days of August 1941, of the 360,000 inhabitants that remained in the besieged city, more than 100,000 took part in the construction of defensive fortifications. For the most part, these were women – this was a major accomplishment of Odessa's females. The fortifications created by the hands of the soldiers of the engineering forces and the residents of the city enabled the conversion of the city into a powerful fortress.

The Southern Front's chief of engineers Hero of the Soviet Union General A.F. Khrenov directed the defensive construction work The fascists subjected the work sites to a systematic artillery barrage and bombings from the air. There were casualties among the people who were building the fortifications. The difficulty of the construction work was increased even more by the fact that the majority of the work was being done by hand. The summer heat and the lack of water also made it hard to work. However, this didn't break the iron will of the Odessans. In a matter of days, they performed an amount of work that would have required months in peace time, and surpassed even the boldest expectations.

By the end of August 1941, three main and several intermediary lines of defense had been built. Each line was divided into sectors, and each sector into battalion areas of defense with a unified system of fire. The scale of the defensive construction work can be judged by the following facts: 138 kilometers of anti-tank ditches, 22 kilometers of escarpments, 45 kilometers of trenches and communication trenches were dug; several hundred machine-gun nests and emplacements for guns were set up, including approximately 2,000 firing positions for mortars, anti-tank rifles and

16   Grigor, M., *More – moia sud'ba: Vospominaniia kapitana* [*The sea was my fate: Recollections of a ship captain*] (Odessa, 1987), p. 105.
17   Shternshtein, Ia., *Morskie vorota Ukrainy* [*Ukraine's sea gates*] (Odessa, 1985), pp. 86, 92.
18   A.D. Borisov, "Oborona Odessy (avgust – oktiabr' 1941)" ["The defense of Odessa (August – October 1941)], *Voennaia Mysl', 1942*, No. 8, pp. 56-57.

machine guns; 45 kilometers of dragon's teeth, sheathed with barbed wire, were deployed; and more than 40,000 anti-tank mines and anti-personnel mines were emplaced.[19]

The forward line, which was 20 to 25 kilometers outside the city, prevented the enemy from shelling the city with field artillery. It ran along the line Adzhalykskii estuary, Blagodatnoe, Kubanka, Chebotarevka, Paliovo, Vygoda, Karstal', Beliaevka, eastern bank of the Dniester estuary as far as Karolino-Bugaz inclusively. It ran for 140 kilometers, with a depth of 1.5 to 2.5 kilometers.

The main line of defenses consisted of two belts of fortifications at a distance of 6-14 kilometers outside the city (the first belt: Grand Adzhalyskii estuary – Il'ichevka – Kholodnaia Balka – Dal'nik – Sukhoi Liman; the second belt: Kryzhanovka – Usatovo – Zalog – Liusdorf [present-day Chernomorka]). It extended for 80 kilometers and had a depth of 3.5 kilometers. The line was strengthened with several switch positions.

The rear line (the line covering the city's evacuation) lay 8-9 kilometers from the city center on the outskirts of Odessa: Kuial'nik – Krivaia Balka – Bol'shoi Fontan. This line extended for 40 kilometers and had a depth of 1.5 to 2.5 kilometers.[20]

The forward system of defensive fieldworks was supplemented within the city by barricades, anti-tank obstacles and firing points. Even the elderly and schoolchildren were building them. From the morning until late in the evening they were throwing up barricades made from rubble taken from the broken-up streets and bags filled with sand and clay, converting large buildings into strongpoints, reinforcing firing positions, setting up anti-tank "hedgehogs", and adapting the water sewers for secret links between areas. Over a short period of time, 243 street barricades were thrown up in the city. Each was capable of withstanding a hit from a 155-mm shell. Three lines of barricades and firing positions were covering the port and the city center. In order to defend them, detachments totaling a number of 11,000 men were formed.[21]

Before the start of the war, a unified plan for Odessa's defense from the ground, sea and air did not exist. According to the views that were in circulation at that time, Odessa was located in the rear, and its defense was being guaranteed by its location relative to the front line. The plan for Odessa's defense, with regard for the experience of the First World War, was oriented toward protecting it from an approach by sea. Thus a general plan for Odessa's defense from all directions was being created and implemented on the fly already during the war.

It should be noted that in the first stage of the war, in the conditions of the forced retreat, all the shortcomings concerning the cooperation of the two military People's Commissariats during peacetime were being particularly acutely felt. Thus, the army and navy chiefs interpreted the irregular expression "call upon the Black Sea Fleet" differently, and at times disagreements arose even over this matter. The high command of the Southwestern Direction strove to use the Fleet's ships as much as possible for the defense of Odessa, paying little regard for the other tasks for which the Fleet was responsible.

In the first days of the defense, there were two commands in Odessa: the command of the Separate Coastal Army headed by Lieutenant General G.P. Sofronov, which was subordinate to the Southern Front, and the command of Odessa's naval base headed by Vice Admiral G.V. Zhukov, which was subordinate to the commander of the Black Sea Fleet. Thus, until that time that the *Stavka* decided to create the Odessa Defensive Region, there was a lack of agreement in the actions of the Black Sea Fleet's and Separate Coastal Army's commands.[22]

19   V.G. Berezhinsky, *Odesskaia oboronitel'naia operatsiya (5 Avgust – 16 Oktiabr' 1941)* [*Odessa's defensive operation (5 August – 16 October 1941)*] (Kiev: NITSGP VSU, 2001), pp. 5-6.

20   A.D. Borisov, *Odessa – gorod geroi* [*Odessa – hero city*] (Moscow, 1954).

21   *Kniga Pamiati Ukrainy: Odesskaia oblast'*, pp. 15-16.

22   Kuznetsov, *Na flotakh boevaia trevoga*, p. 118.

The fate of Odessa in the initial phase of the defense would be decided by whether or not the Coastal Army, relying on still weak defensive lines, would be able to stop the offensive by superior enemy forces. In the subsequent fighting for Odessa, the defense's success depended on the stubbornness and endurance of all our forces and the Black Sea Fleet's capability to keep the army resupplied, using the only route available to it – the sea. This success depended as well on the effectiveness of the support that the Fleet could render to the ground forces with ship-to-shore fire from its ships and with its air force.

By the nature of the combat operations, Odessa's defense can be divided into four main stages: from 5 to 18 August – the preparation of the defense and the fighting on the distant approaches to the city; from 19 August to 21 September – the combat on the near approaches to the city; from 22 to 30 September – the counterattack by the forces of the Odessa Defensive Region and the stabilization of the front; and from 1 to 16 October – active combat operations with the simultaneous concealed evacuation of the forces and equipment of the Odessa Defensive Region.

3

Defensive fighting on the distant approaches to the city

The task to cover the Odessa axis and the city of Odessa itself was given to the Separate Coastal Army. Simultaneously, the Soviet command took a number of steps to make maximal use of the ships of the Black Sea Fleet and in particular the coastal artillery to assist the ground troops. The fleet, in addition, was given the mission in the event of Odessa's encirclement to keep the ground forces supplied from the sea.

The theater of combat operations represented a gently rolling plain (with hills up to 50 meters in elevation). The Black Sea coastline was high and poor for making amphibious landings, with tall bluffs and narrow sandy and stony beaches. In separate locations, deep ravines and estuaries run perpendicular to the coast. The estuaries are separated from the sea by sand spits (as in the case of the Kual'nitskii and Khadzhibeiskii estuaries) or else freely connect with the sea. The coast offers a splendid view in the direction of the sea, while from the sea only ravines, bottom lands and estuaries are visible among the tall coastal bluffs. This circumstance complicated the use of the Black Sea Fleet's naval artillery.

The estuaries, which separate the coastline into a number of isolated sectors, present significant obstacles to the direct movement of troops in a coastal zone that extends from 10 to 40 kilometers from the sea. The width of the estuaries varies between 1.2 and 5 or more kilometers; their depths vary between 3 and 8 meters. The coastal spits are 250 meters to 4,000 meters wide. The upper reaches of all the estuaries dry out in the summer, but their bottoms remain covered with a 2-6 meter layer of sticky mud. In the course of the defense, the estuaries were used to anchor the flanks of the Red Army units. The latter rested at first on the Tylihul and Dniester River estuaries, and then the right flank was anchored on the Adzhalykskii and Bol'shoi Adzhalykskii estuaries, while the left flank rested on the Sukhoi estuary. During the fighting for Odessa the terrain was covered with head-high cornfields. These eased the approach of offensive forces when on the attack and complicated the defense.

Assessing the ground surrounding Odessa, it must be said that it wasn't very suitable for setting up a defense. However, the use of the estuaries to anchor the flanks eased the creation of a stiff defense.[1]

By 10 August, the German Eleventh Army (the 50th, 72nd and 73rd Infantry Divisions) and the Romanian Fourth Army (the 3rd, 7th, 11th, 14th and 15th Infantry Divisions), as well as the Romanian 1st Guards, 1st Border and 1st Cavalry Divisions, were operating on the Odessa axis. In addition, the enemy had more than 100 tanks and 100 aircraft. Thus, the enemy at the start of

---

1   A.D. Borisov, "Oborona Odessy, Avgust – Oktiabr' 1941" ["The defense of Odessa, August – October 1941"], *Voennaia mysl'* – 1942, No. 8, pp. 52-54.

the operation had 11 divisions together with means of reinforcement. By the end of the operation, the German command had assembled up to 18 Romanian and German divisions at Odessa.[2]

The Separate Coastal Army consisting of the 25th "Chapaev" Rifle Division and the 95th Moldavian Rifle Division were opposing the enemy's forces. A light cavalry division was in the process of forming up. In addition, the city's defenders included the 136th Reserve Rifle Regiment, the 26th NKVD Composite Border Guard Regiment, the 15th Anti-aircraft Brigade, the 47th Pontoon Battalion, machine-gun battalions of the 82nd Fortified District and other elements. Militiamen and destroyer battalions comprised the primary reserve for replacing losses. The Odessa Naval Base formed the 1st and 2nd Naval Infantry Regiments. A fire-support ship detachment (approximately 30 gun barrels) provided active support to the field artillery, which at the start of the city's defense numbered 303 cannons (including the 45-mm guns). The divisions of the Separate Coastal Army had been significantly weakened in the preceding fighting. In separate regiments there were no more than 280-300 men. The army had no tanks suitable for combat, while its attached 69th Fighter Aviation Regiment had no more than 25-33 operational aircraft. Five battalions of personnel, 500 heavy machine guns and 321 light machine guns, which had been transferred to it from the Tiraspol Fortified District upon the latter's retreat, somewhat strengthened the positions of the Separate Coastal Army. This asset provided the opportunity to create a significantly dense pattern of machine-gun fire.

Thus, the attacking enemy had a general superiority of 3.5 times the defender in personnel and aircraft and an overwhelming superiority in tanks. However, Odessa's defenders were immeasurably superior to the enemy in an ideological and psychological sense. The deep understanding of the war's aims, the love for the Motherland and their city, the understanding of personal responsibility for the fate of families and friends, gave rise to mass heroism, resolve and tenacity in the struggle among the soldiers, commanders and citizens of the city, which was vividly demonstrated during the city's defense.

The German and Romanian troops at first attempted to take Odessa from the march. Their hard-headed self-confidence was so high that they set 10 August as the day for a parade of their troops in Odessa, long before entering the city. The plan of the German command had been worked out with full regard for the terrain and the existing combat conditions. However, the German and Romanian generals underestimated the morale of the soldiers of the Red Army and the combat resolve of Odessa's population, as well as the possibilities of the Black Sea Fleet in support of the ground forces. Their calculations that Odessa's garrison, being isolated from the main forces of the field army, would quickly collapse under the blows of bombers, tanks and infantry and surrender their positions didn't come to fruition. Therefore the offensive operation of the German and Romanian troops became prolonged and didn't foretell a rapid success.

The Soviet command had the primary tasks of tying down as many enemy forces as possible for as long as it was able, to wear down the enemy troops and bleed them white with a stubborn defense, and to hold a staging area for the possible development of a counteroffensive and attacks against Romania's oil-producing areas. The Coastal Army, conducting a retreat to the Berezovka – Razdel'noe – Kuchurganskii estuary line, was putting up stubborn resistance to the enemy. The fascists put constant pressure on the retreating units, hoping on their heels to break into Odessa. The danger was increased by the exposed eastern flank of the city's defense, which had been created after the 30th Rifle Division had been cut-off by the enemy. It was into this gap that the forces of the German 72nd Infantry Division and the Romanian cavalry brigade were thrown, which had the task to break into the rear of our forces and block their path of retreat to Odessa. Only thanks

2   *Istoriia Velikoi Otechestvennoi Voiny Sovetskogo Soiuza 1941-1945* [*History of the Great Patriotic War of the Soviet Union 1941-1945*] in 6 volumes (Moscow: Voenizdat, 1963); Vol. 2, p. 113.

to energetic measures taken by the Coastal Army command was the dangerous breach in the front plugged. The German 72nd Infantry Division, having failed to reach its objective, fell back to the east, and the Romanian 15th Infantry Division took up its positions.

On 8 August through an order of the chief of the city's garrison Vice Admiral G.V. Zhukov, a state of siege was announced in Odessa. On other sectors of the front surrounding Odessa, soldiers and commanders of the 25th and 95th Rifle Divisions were repulsing furious attacks by superior enemy forces in the area between the Kual'nitskii and Khadzhibeiskii estuaries, the railroad hub of Razdel'noe, and in the direction of the district center of Beliaevka. Despite their limited strength, extreme exhaustion and shortage of weapons, with the skillful shifting of forces and bold counterattacks, the men of the Coastal Army were increasing their resistance to the enemy with each passing hour.

However, the Coastal Army was unable to hold its positions as directed by the Southern Front command and at the end of day on 10 August fell back to a line of incomplete defensive fortifications. The line of defense rested in the northeast on the Adzhalykskii estuary, before continuing on through Buldynka, Sverdlovo, Il'inka and Chebotarevka (sector held by S.F. Monakhov's group). In the center, the line moved away from the city, running through Aleksandrovka, Brinovka, Sekretarevka (sector held by units of the 95th Rifle Division); on the left the line continued on through Mangeim (present-day Kamenka) and Beliaevka to the Dniesterovskii estuary (held by units of the 25th Rifle Division).

From the beginning, Odessa's defense was characterized by the activity of the Soviet troops' operations. In the course of 11 and 12 August alone, the defenders repulsed 9 major enemy attacks, having killed more than 4,000 enemy soldiers and officers. In addition, with anti-tank artillery and Molotov cocktails they knocked-out 14 enemy tanks, while 7 enemy aircraft were shot down in aerial combat. The initial days of fighting played an important role in the subsequent defense of the city – the foe was stopped. Our troops gained valuable time to strengthen their occupied positions. Units of the Coastal Army by 12 August had fallen back to the line of Grigor'evka, Sverdlovo, Il'inka, Beliaevka, Ovidiopol' and Karolino-Bugaz, which is to say, directly to the previously-designated third line of defense. There was not enough time to complete all the fortification work on this line by the moment the retreating units took it up. In particular, the construction of anti-tank ditches, escarpments and counterscarps hadn't been completed. Thus the troops that took up the line had to complete the constructions in the course of fighting. With the withdrawal of Soviet forces to this line of defense, work to create the following defensive lines became more active:

1. Forward lines:
   a) Adzhalykskii estuary – Petrovskii – southern outskirts of Kubanka – Il'inka – Chebotarevka – Palievo – Vygoda – Karstal' – southern outskirts of Beliaevka;
   b) Palievo – Dubinovo – Vakarzhany – Krasnyi Pereselenets – Perestal' – Frantsfeld.
2. Auxiliary forward line: Dalnikh – Lenintal' – Aleksandrovka.
3. Main line of resistance: Voroshilov State Farm – southern outskirts of Gil'dendorf – Protopopovka – Gniliakovo – Dal'nik – Tatarka – Sukhoi Liman.
4. Secondary line of main resistance: Kryzhanovka – Mezhdulimannye – Usatova – Zastava Station – Sukhoi Liman – Liustdorf.
5. Switch position: Nerubaiskoe – Dal'nik.
6. Inner line covering the city: Zhevakhov Hill – Krivaia Balka – Chubaevka – Bol'shoi Fontan.

Within the city limits, barricades, firing positions, anti-tank obstacles and other fortifications were being created.

The forward lines, which were separated by 20-23 kilometers from Odessa's outskirts, secured the city and port from artillery fire. Both flanks of the forward lines were anchored on difficult obstacles to overcome – the Alzhalykskii and Dniesterovskii estuaries. This line stretched up to 80 kilometers. The main lines of resistance lay 8-14 kilometers outside the city and stretched up to 60-62 kilometers; its flanks rested on the sea. The secondary line of main resistance lay 6-10 kilometers outside the city.[3]

Both lines of main defense lay too close to the city. The interior screening lines were, in essence, designed to protect the city against enemy rifle and machine-gun fire and might have significance only for conducting a rear-guard action during the evacuation of units from Odessa. However, considering the conditions in which the Odessa defenses had to be constructed, it must be recognized that the decision taken to organize and lay out the defensive lines corresponded to the existing situation and was correct.

On 12 August Romanian units undertook an unsuccessful attempt with small forces (groups of 1-2 battalions each with tanks) to penetrate our defense in the directions toward Buldynka, Bol'shoe Festerovo and Beliaevka. In the course of the next two days, the fascists again tried to go on the offensive in those same sectors following an artillery and mortar preparation, but these attacks were also driven back by the defenders. Particularly stubborn fighting unfolded in the eastern sector of defense in the Buldynka area where the enemy managed to push back some of our defending units. However, our soldiers, demonstrating exceptional heroism and launching repeated counterattacks, restored the position.

On 13 August at the cost of heavy losses the enemy troops reached the Black Sea coastline near Adzhiaski (present-day Rybakovka) and fully isolated the defenders of Odessa. The only line of communication remained naval communications with the deep Soviet interior. It was because of this that the naval and transport fleet would play a special role in the defense of the city. Soviet forces could not hold out for a long time in a besieged city without food and ammunition, replacements and weapons, which could only be delivered to Odessa by sea. The fleet also evacuated cargo that was important to the military economy to the deep interior, launched attacks against enemy ships and ports, and disrupted enemy attempts to blockade Odessa and make naval landings. The fleet command also was to form and send units of naval infantry to the ground front; support the Coastal Army with fire from ships, coastal artillery and means of naval aviation; launch counterattacks against the enemy together with the ground units; and in case it became necessary, secure the evacuation of ground troops and combat gear.

The ground, upon which the fighting unfolded, presented a treeless, gently rolling plain that gradually descended to the sea. This made camouflaging the Soviet units and the organization of an anti-tank and anti-air defense more difficult. The estuaries restricted the ability to maneuver, and complicated concerted action and command and control over the Soviet forces. Thus the Coastal Army command found a correct way out of the situation, deciding to regroup its forces and to reorganize the entire system of defense in accordance with the concrete conditions. On 13 August 1941, the army commander General G.P. Sofronov ordered for the entire front of defense to be split into three relatively independent sectors: an Eastern, Western and Southern Sector.

The Eastern Sector on the right flank was covering the approaches to Odessa from the east and north on a front of 40 kilometers. Its boundary line on the left ran along the Khadzhibaevskii estuary to Peresyp'. Its defenders consisted of the 54th Rifle Regiment of the 25th Rifle Division, the 1st Regiment of Naval Infantry, the 26th NKVD Composite Border Guards Regiment, and a rifle battalion of the 136th Reserve Regiment. Brigade commander S.F. Monakhov was appointed commandant of the Eastern Sector.

---

3   Borisov, "Oborona Odessy (avgust – oktiabr' 1941)", pp. 56-57.

The Western Sector extended for 25 kilometers and covered the city from the north. The sector commandant was the commander of the 95th Rifle Division Major General V.F. Vorob'ev. On the right was the boundary with the Eastern Sector, and on the left – from Sekretarevka through Vakarzhany it continued on to the coastline in the Chubaevka area. The sector's defenders were the 90th, 161st and 241st Rifle Regiments of the 95th Rifle Division and the 1st Machine-Gun Battalion of the Tiraspol Fortified District.

The Southern Sector secured the defense from the west and the south on a 70-kilometer long front, more than half of which consisted of the Dniesterovskii estuary, where the positions were at first being held by small elements of regular units and soldiers of the Ovidiopol'skii Destroyer Battalion. This sector's forces included the 25th Rifle Division (minus its 54th Rifle Regiment) and the 2nd Composite Machine-Gun Battalion of the Tiraspol Fortified District. On the right was the boundary with the Western Sector, and on the left – the Dniesterovskii estuary. Command of this sector went to the commander of the 25th Rifle Division Colonel A.S. Zakharov, who replaced General I.E. Petrov on 20 August.

The forces that occupied these sectors of defense received the mission to hold stubbornly the line running from Grigorovka through Buldynka, Il'inka, Chebotarevka, Brinovka, Sekretarevka, Mangeim, Beliaevka and Ovidiopol' to Karolino-Bugaz. The Coastal Army had in reserve the 1st Cavalry Division, the 47th Separate Pontoon Battalion, and the city's destroyer battalions. The commander of the Odessa Naval Base had the 2nd Regiment of Naval Infantry in reserve. Because of the length of the front and the small number of available troops, the army command had to arrange the combat formations in a single echelon, but with the constant support of the army's reserve.

The Coastal Army's artillery regiments and artillery battalions, as well as the artillery of the Odessa Naval Base, were also allocated to the sectors. In addition, it was planned to employ the cannons of the ships of the Northwest Sector. All types of artillery were directed by the Coastal Army's artillery chief Colonel M.K. Ryzhi. A routine for calling upon the naval artillery, a probable plan of their fire and a system for correcting the fire were all worked out by the army's artillery headquarters together with the Odessa Naval Base's chief weapons officer. In order to support the infantry with heavy firepower, mobile artillery groups were created out of the corps, division and coastal artillery.

The creation of specific sectors of defense allowed the fluid use of reserves, improved command and control, and facilitated better cooperation with the forces of the Odessa Naval Base. The defense of the coastal areas of Odessa in the Dniesterovskii estuary – Tendrovskaia Spit (a hook-shaped barrier beach sheltering Tendrovskii Bay) sector and the support of the infantry with naval artillery fire were implemented by the forces of the naval base under the command of Rear Admiral G.V. Zhukov.

In the initial stage of Odessa's defense, the Coastal Army's 69th Fighter Aviation Regiment (commanded by Major L.L. Shestakov) was based upon the city's airfields, as well as three separate aviation squadrons of the Black Sea Fleet: the 7th and 82nd Flying Boat Squadrons and the 70th Bomber Aviation Squadron. With the enemy's approach to Odessa, the defenders were almost left without any airfields, which didn't allow the possibility to reinforce the aviation units. Black Sea pilots of the 9th Fighter Aviation Regiment (commanded by Lieutenant Colonel K.P. Malinov and military commissar Battalion Commissar N.A. Kuz'min), which was based in the Nikolaeva area, provided help to the defenders of Odessa in the first days of the fighting. The Black Sea pilots courageously engaged the fascist bombers in battle, blocking their path to Odessa and Nikolaeva. On 8 August 1941, a flight commander of the 3rd Fighter Aviation Squadron Lieutenant V.L. Red'ko took on a group of fascist bombers. With accurate fire he shot down one bomber; the rest aborted their mission, turned around and flew away.

On the following day, pilots of this same regiment Senior Lieutenant V. Kulikov and Junior Lieutenants B. Cherevko and V. Grek were on duty at the airfield. A group of fascist bombers was approaching the city. The flight took off. Cherevko was the first to spot nine Junker bombers and over the village of Nechaiannoe he disrupted the bombers' formation, having shot down the lead bomber. Flight commander V. Kulikov attacked another bomber of the group and shot it down. Having lost two bombers, the fascists turned back, having jettisoned their bombloads. Cherevko went into another attacking run and set ablaze another Junkers. At this time another pair of our fighters hurried to join the action. The element's leader Lieutenant G. Lazarev took on four Messerschmitts that were covering the bombers' retreat, and one of them riddled his cockpit and set his plane on fire. B. Cherevko rushed to aid the wounded Lazarev, but it was too late. Lazarev's damaged fighter plummeted to the ground.

Six more of our fighters approached and a new dogfight flared up. Captain A.P. Kolobkov and Lieutenant L. Danchenko were the first to lead their machines at the foe. In the ensuing action Captain Kolobkov's fighter was shot down, but Lieutenant Danchenko managed to damage one Messerschmitt. However, a pair of German fighters immediately pounced on Danchenko's fighter. After a short clash the motor in Danchenko's fighter went dead and the lieutenant had to make a forced landing. The enemy dove after the stricken machine, but B. Cherevko, V. Grek and V. Kulikov attacked them, and the latter shot down another enemy fighter. Having lost three Junkers and three Messerschmitts, the fascists exited the battle. Lazarev, Kolobkov and Danchenko didn't return to their airfields.

On 10 August the *Luftwaffe* made an attempt to break through to Odessa from the direction of the sea. Black Sea Fleet pilots of the 9th Fighter Aviation Regiment intercepted them. In the following aerial combat Lieutenant V.E. Karpechkov shot down the first enemy aircraft. The enemy's heavy machine plunged into the sea. Another enemy aircraft shared the same fate, having been shot down by the pair of Junior Lieutenants V.F. Grek and P.A. Kachalk.

On 12 August another dogfight erupted above the Odessa area. This time the army pilots and Black Sea pilots jointly repulsed enemy attempts to break through to the city. Deputy commander of the Black Sea Fleet's 9th Fighter Regiment's 2nd Aviation Squadron Senior Lieutenant I.K. Kalinin shot down one enemy aircraft in the first attacking pass. In this same clash a pilot of this same squadron Senior Lieutenant A.F. Berestovsky also shot down a German aircraft. The rest of the enemy's pilots lost their nerve, and they high-tailed it away.

The pilots of the Fleet's 32nd Fighter Aviation Regiment had several combats on the distant approaches to Odessa. Captains K.P. Bukhtiiarov and A.V. Shubikov, Senior Lieutenants A.A. Shchukin and I.I. Skachkov, Lieutenants I.I. Shevchenko and K.A. Rusakov, and Junior Lieutenant A.M. Artiukhin each shot down one enemy aircraft.[4]

The importance of the Party and political work, which had an enormous significance for strengthening the combat spirit of Odessa's defenders, must also not be forgotten. The Coastal Army's Political Department in the first stage of the defensive fighting reinforced the elements of the Party and Komsomol organizations that had been weakened as a result of the heavy losses among the Communist Party members in the preceding fighting. Many Communists and Komsomol members in the rear were transferred to the front to rebuild the Party cadres. In addition, 146 of the best-trained Communists among the rank and file and junior command staff were promoted to political work. The Odessa District Party Committee sent 300 Communists from the staff of the city's Party organization to army units; among them were two City Committee Secretaries and the entire instructor's staff that were capable of bearing arms. Almost all of Odessa's Communists were

4   G.I. Vagneev, Chernomortsy v Velikoi Otechestvennoi voiny [Black Sea Fleet men in the Great Patriotic War] (Moscow: Voenizdat, 1978), pp. 33-34.

appointed as political workers in the units. Using various means of ideological rallies, brief meetings and discussions; Party and frontline press; and radio and visual propaganda, they fostered a high conscientiousness and sense of patriotic duty among the city's defenders, and a readiness to perform acts of bravery for the sake of the Motherland.

To a decisive degree, the defense of Odessa depended upon the complete and proper use of the city's economic and human resources. Odessa's city administration did large work to mobilize all of the forces and means to repulse the foe. On 10 August 1941 there took place a meeting of the city's core group, which laid out concrete measures to improve the readiness of the combat replacements for the Coastal Army and the construction of defensive fortifications; to organize the smooth operation of the local anti-air defenses; and to provide for the repair of combat equipment. City and district operational groups ("troikas") were created to provide clear and concrete direction of the mobilization of internal reserves; these operational groups included the secretaries of Party committees, the heads of executive committees, and the chiefs of NKVD or police departments. The Party City Committee's First Secretary N.P. Gurevich headed the city's operational group, while the operational groups of the city's districts were led by the Party secretaries of the district committees. The troikas oversaw the construction of defensive fortifications; the combat and political training of the people's militia; the work of the local anti-air defenses; the maintenance of social order in the city; and the security of enterprises, water supply sources, etc.

Many of the militiamen had no combat training, and thus the training of the new recruits was organized both on the basis of a reserve regiment, and on local police schools and their inter-regional training course. Once the initial training was completed, a specially-appointed detachment of up to 1,200 men was created, which at first took part in guarding the rear lines of defense, before being fully shifted to the front. This detachment under the command of Major G. Baryshnikov fearlessly fought the enemy in the vicinity of Dal'nik.

Collectives of industrial plants rendered enormous assistance to the city's defenders. At the beginning of August, the January Uprising factory produced the first armored train. The employees of this and other Odessan factories put damaged tanks back into service and repaired artillery pieces, armored cars and motorized transport; produced anti-tank obstacles and anti-tank and anti-personnel mines; manufactured barbed wire and entrenching tools; and fabricated Molotov cocktails and the wicks for them. Enterprises of the textile and food industries worked around the clock to furnish the army with uniforms and food. Like elsewhere in plants and factories across the country, youth and women replaced the men who had gone into the army. This process particularly increased after the city wound up encircled and new detachments of Odessan workers left the factories for the front. More than 17,000 housewives and female students of higher classes took up position in front of machine tools and lathes, where weapons were forged for the defense of Odessa. Elderly pensioners, former employees of these factories, also returned to the assembly lines.

The city that had been encircled by the enemy was subjected to systematic bombings from the air. The first massed air raid took place on 22 July. Often large groups of enemy aircraft struck the city 12-15 times a day, leaving behind ruins and conflagrations. All of the services of the city's local anti-air defense, the chief of which was the chairman of the city council B.P. Davidenko, fearlessly fought the consequences of the enemy air raids. City firefighters entered devastated buildings and brought out dust-covered people, rendered first aid to victims, restored to service the transportation and communication system left damaged by the bombers, and contained and extinguished fires. Members of the Self-Defense League, primarily women and youth, exhibiting tremendous stamina and composure, maintained around-the-clock watch on the roofs of buildings and during air raids neutralized hundreds of incendiary bombs, thereby preventing the outbreak of many fires.

A large amount of work was done in the city to provide the people with good air raid shelters. The cellars of many buildings were adapted for this, and more than 4,924 trenches were dug into courtyards, public squares and wide streets. However, in areas of the city near the port, where the enemy air raids were particularly intensive, these shelters couldn't be adequate. From the latter half of August, many residents at their own initiative began to resettle in the catacombs beneath the city. Approximately 38,000 people eventually took secure shelter in the catacombs at a depth of 18-30 meters beneath the city. In the daytime, when all the able-bodied population went to work, only seniors, children and the sick were left in the catacombs. However, the conditions in the catacombs were hard, so on 22 September 1941 the decision was reached to improve them, which foresaw the strengthening of passages, the arrangement of ventilation, the installation of electric lights, and the delivery of water and bread to the people. The authorities were able to implement these measures only partially.

Hundreds of wounded men were brought into the city each day from the front. Over these days, 18,000 of the city's residents became blood donors and gave their blood to save the lives of wounded warriors. After a hard day, hundreds of women and female adolescents kept watch over the patients in the hospitals, easing their suffering with their attentive care.

The strength of the Soviet troops' and population's resistance grew with each passing day. The bodies of thousands of fascist soldiers and officers covered the ground on the approaches to the city. On 15 August 1941, the Southern Front's Military Council announced its gratitude to all the personnel of the Coastal Army for the valor and courage they'd demonstrated in the defense of Odessa.

In the course of the operation, the Romanian command had to change the axis of the attacks they launched several times. At first they focused the main efforts against the eastern sector of our defense, developing the main attack from Adzhiaski toward Sychavka. Next they strove to take Odessa with an attack out of the northwest direction, from the direction of Razdel'naia toward Vygoda, and from the direction of Iasski toward Beliaevka. The enemy command also called for an attack along the entire front, in order to squeeze the ring of encirclement, especially from the flanks. Exploiting the offensive against the eastern sector of our defense, the enemy intended, having seized the Dofinovka – Chebanka area, to obtain the possibility of bombarding the Odessa port with artillery fire and thereby deprive the besieged city of its lone remaining line of communication by sea. An offensive in the center from the direction of Razdel'naia, along the rail-road toward Vygoda Station and from the Iasski direction toward Beliaevka allowed the broader employment of tanks, although this would require a frontal attack. Thus, this axis of advance was an auxiliary one.

In the middle of August, having lost the opportunity to take the city from the march, the enemy changed tactics: from 15 August the main attacks were launched against the flanks of the lines of defense. For this purpose the Romanian command brought up its reserves. Opposite the front of Odessa's defenders there were already seven enemy infantry divisions, and one tank and two cavalry brigades. Two more infantry divisions and another cavalry brigade were brought up to Odessa.

On 15 August the Romanian troops went on the offensive in the area of the eastern sector of the defense. Here, units of the Romanian 15th Infantry Division and 1st Cavalry Brigade, supported by a large quantity of tanks and with air support, were attacking Brigade Commander Monakhov's composite detachment, the strength of which didn't exceed one division. The main attack struck the line of the 1st Regiment of Naval Infantry, which was commanded by a veteran of the Russian Civil War Colonel Ia.I. Osipov. The enemy attacks came one after the other, both in daylight hours and at night. Up to two battalions of infantry, supported by tanks, broke through our defenses and seized Buldynka. The naval infantry under Colonel Ia.I. Osipov's command launched a counterattack against the enemy penetration. Supported by the fire of the destroyer *Nezamozhnik* [*Ukrainian peasant*] and the gunboat *Krasnyi Adzharistan* [*Red Adzharistan*], the Black Sea infantrymen recaptured Buldynka, in the process having driven back approximately one enemy battalion into an estuary. Regiment Commander Ia.I. Osipov was wounded in the arm, but refused to leave the front and continued to direct the fighting. Red Seaman S. Klimenko particularly distinguished himself in the battle with the foe. Having made his way into the enemy rear unnoticed with a light machine gun, he suddenly opened fire on the enemy from behind and killed many enemy soldiers, but the main thing was that he prompted a panic.

On 16 August the enemy continued an offensive in the direction of the Bol'shaia Adzhalykskii estuary. An infantry battalion with a company of tanks broke through to the area of Shitsli, but could advance no further. The commander of the 1st Regiment of Naval Infantry decided to encircle the enemy that had broken through. The naval infantrymen, vigorously supported by the Border Guardsmen of Major A.A. Malovsky's regiment, launched a counterattack, encircled the enemy group that had penetrated in the Shitsli area, and destroyed it. Up to 200 prisoners were taken, and 18 guns, 3 tanks, 1 armored car and other battle spoils fell into Soviet hands. In this battle the military commissar of the 1st Regiment of Naval Infantry Senior Political Instructor V.A. Mitrakov demonstrated heroism by his personal example. He personally led the attacking troops from a position out in front of them, rallying others to follow him.

On this same day, the naval artillerymen of Captain I.V. Zinov'ev's 412th Coastal Battery scored a major success. Intelligence reported that the enemy had brought up a battery of heavy artillery to the Beliary area. Zinov'ev's battery was given the task to destroy it. A forward artillery spotter soon provided the coordinates of the enemy battery. Just 18 rounds were necessary, and the enemy battery, which hadn't managed to fire a single salvo at our positions, was destroyed.

The villages of Buldynka and Shitsli, which were important in an operational sense, changed hands several times on 16 and 17 August. In the course of the fighting for them, the enemy lost more than two regiments of infantry and a lot of military gear. There were also heavy losses among the Soviet troops.

Despite heavy casualties, the Romanian units that were attacking in the South Sector in the direction of Kagarlyk and Karstal' managed nevertheless to penetrate our defenses south of Kagarlyk. With the aim of eliminating the penetration that had been created in the sector at Kagarlyk, the Coastal Army command assigned the task to the army's reserve with attached assets to assemble with a night march by the morning of 17 August in the Petrovskii (east) – Rus. Mendrovo – Korsunitsy area, and subsequently to encircle and destroy the enemy's Kagarlyk grouping with an attack in the general direction of Kagarlyk and Gradenitsa. Simultaneously, Zakharchenko's units were ordered to prevent the enemy's further advance to the east, and to counterattack the fascists in the direction of the southwestern outskirts of Kagarlyk with part of their forces. All day long on the day of 17 August, intense fighting went on in the Kagarlyk area and the task was carried out.

After this, the fighting in the East Sector noticeably subsided. The separate attempts to breach our defenses undertaken by the enemy had all been repulsed. The sector's troops had been supported by naval fire and the guns of the coastal artillery. The gunship *Krasnyi Adzharistan* had repeated placed fire on aggregations of enemy troops despite the enemy's air attacks. It received an underwater breach due to the nearby explosion of one bomb. The ship's boatswain Warrant Officer R.S. Segal together with a group of sailors managed to plug the breach quickly, and the gunboat returned to base under its own power.

Simultaneously with the offensive in the East Sector, as already mentioned enemy troops launched strong attacks as well in the area of the South Sector of defense. Having assembled up to two of their divisions and 70 tanks at the boundary between the 31st and 287th Regiments of the 25th Rifle Division, the fascists at the end of the day 15 August broke through the forward edge of defense in the Kagarlyk area near Beliaevka. The thinned elements of the 25th Rifle Division (minus its 54th Rifle Regiment) offered stubborn resistance, repeatedly launching counterattacks.

A platoon of the 31st Rifle Regiment's mortar company, which was commanded by Junior Lieutenant V.P. Simonok, offered support to the 4th Rifle Company's counterattack. At a critical moment, when the company became pinned down under intense rifle and machine-gun fire, V.P. Simonov himself took control of a mortar and destroyed the enemy firing points. Afterward, with a pistol in his hand, he rose on the attack, leading all the other men with his élan. As a result the enemy was driven out of Kagarlyk. For this and other exploits in the fighting at Odessa, V.P. Simonov was deemed worthy of the highest title in the land, Hero of the Soviet Union.

Approximately one battalion of Romanians attacked the 25th Rifle Division's motorized rifle company, headed by Junior Lieutenant P.M. Monail. The Soviet troops accepted unequal battle, in the course of which they killed more than 350 enemy soldiers and officers. Junior Lieutenant K.T. Lysyi's artillery battery played no small role in this. When the Romanians breached the line of defense, the artillerymen rolled out the battery into an exposed position and began to fire at the enemy with canister rounds, and fired at the tanks with armor-piercing shells. Two enemy tanks were destroyed.

In a different sector the artillerymen of Lieutenant D.P. Boiko's battery over the course of 19 hours repulsed the Romanian attacks with fire over open sights. They knocked out 12 heavy enemy guns. D.P. Boiko was one of the first defenders of the city to be awarded with the Order of Lenin.

On 16 August enemy troops made a 1-3 kilometer advance southeast of Kagarlyk. Even such an insignificant change in the front lines created a threat of the enemy's emergence in the rear of the 25th and 95th Rifle Divisions. The 25th Rifle Division fell back somewhat. In order to eliminate the breakthrough, the Coastal Army command organized a shock group consisting of the reserve 1st Cavalry Division, the 136th Reserve Regiment and two battalions of the 95th Rifle Division. The troops fought valiantly without regard for their lives, but their forces and means were small; the shortage of shells was particularly acute. In the course of the counterattacks the ranks of the shock group quickly melted away – the companies were left with just 25-30 men each. This combat operation of the shock group had no success.

Simultaneous with the launching of attacks against the defense's flanks (in the eastern and southern sectors), on 17 August the enemy began an offensive in the center, along the Razdel'naia – Odessa railroad. Tanks advanced in front of the infantry, some of which were armed with flame-throwers. However, here too the enemy was stopped. The troops of the 95th Rifle Division were tenaciously holding their lines.

On 18 August the enemy, having assembled up to 8 infantry and cavalry divisions, went on the offensive along the entire front, launching the main attacks in the sector between the Adzhalykskii and Bol'shaia Adzhalykskii estuaries, and in the Western Sector – along the railroad, where enemy infantry with the support of 60 tanks went on the attack in the direction of Vygoda. The fascist tanks used flamethrowers. At the same time, the attacks didn't cease on the Kagarlyk axis. Savage fighting flared up on the open ground, cut by shallow depressions. Soviet artillerymen fired at enemy tanks over open sights, and when the tanks approached to within close range, the soldiers began tossing Molotov cocktails at them. The anti-tank artillery battalion under the command of Captain V.I. Barkovsky demonstrated courage, resourcefulness and composure by destroying 25 enemy tanks. This was a great victory. It was the first time during the defense of Odessa that so many enemy tanks had been knocked out or left burning in one action. The gun layer of one anti-tank gun, M.D. Magarichov particularly distinguished himself in the fighting, having personally destroyed 4 tanks.

The infantry elements, inspired by the success, launched a counterattack. The entire staff of the 161st Rifle Regiment under the command of Colonel S.I. Serebrov fought courageously against the enemy. Its 3rd Rifle Battalion encircled and destroyed more than 1,200 enemy soldiers and officers north of Vygoda Station. The commander of this battalion, the 22-year-old Senior Lieutenant Ia.G. Breus was awarded the title Hero of the Soviet Union.

The appearance of Armored Train No. 21, which was built and equipped by the workers of the January Uprising factory, at the height of the fighting at Vygoda was a great surprise to the foe. The armored train broke into the enemy's position and with fire from both sides was wiping out enemy men and equipment. The foe couldn't withstand this onslaught, and his attack, which lasted for 15 hours, faltered.

On the afternoon of 18 August, our aerial reconnaissance neutralized an attempt by the enemy to make a naval landing in the Odessa area. They spotted 8 large and 4 small naval transports and 10 patrol boats approaching from Sulina. Dispatched bombers attacked and sank two naval transports and damaged another, while the rest scattered and retreated.

Despite the numerous attacks, reinforced with the massed support of aircraft, artillery and mortars, the enemy failed to break through the defenses, and along the entire front he was hurled back to the line of departure. Only in isolated sectors was the enemy able to make a 1-2 kilometer advance.

In these first battles, the German and Romanian troops suffered enormous losses. Thousands of corpses were blanketing the approaches to Odessa. Under the heat of the sun, they quickly rotted, creating unbearable conditions for our soldiers who were manning the front lines. Along with the dead were a lot of wounded men who hadn't been recovered, the groans of which in the periods of calm were audible along the entire front. The Soviet command proposed a ceasefire so as to gather the wounded and the dead, and ceased fire at the set time. The Romanians didn't respond to this suggestion, and then it was decided to spread chloride of lime over the rotting corpses under cover of darkness.[5]

On 18 and 19 August, the enemy attacks against the positions of the naval infantry resumed with new strength. The last reserve held by the Coastal Army command – the 151st Signal Battalion, numbering 500 men, and the 100 men of the Lenin District's destroyer battalion – was sent to aid the naval infantry. The soldiers of the army and fleet held the lines with unparalleled bravery; even the wounded warriors refused to leave the battlefield, remaining in formation. An enemy battalion with the support of three tanks encircled Captain A.S. Lamzin's company. The men fought in encirclement for eight hours, killing approximately 200 fascists and knocking out 2 tanks, before breaking out of encirclement and linking back up with their own unit. The names of Red Navy sailors D.M. Voronko, S.G. Klimenko, A.M. Khmelevsky and many others have been immortalized by their feats of arms in the struggle with the foe. The 412th Coastal Battery and the guns of the Northwest Sector's detachment of combat ships rendered substantial assistance to the troops of the Eastern Sector and particularly the regiment of naval infantry. In addition, the ships of the main naval base supported the defense in the Eastern Sector: the frigate *Tashkent*, the destroyers *Frunze, Dzerzhinsky, Besposchadnyi* [*Merciless*], *Smyshlennyi* [*Sagacious*], and the cruiser *Krasnyi Krym* [*Red Crimea*]. In the Western Sector, the cruiser *Krasnyi Kavkaz* [*Red Caucasus*] and the destroyer *Sposobnyi* [*Capable*] provided fire support to the ground troops.

On the morning of 19 August the Romanian troops continued to attack, with particular persistence in the Shitsli and Kagarlyk areas. By evening the situation was deteriorating in the Southern Sector; on the next day enemy broke through the defenses in the Kagarlyk, Beliaevka sector and continued to exploit in the direction of Karstal' (present-day Shirokaia Balka). The 25th Rifle Division was unable to withstand the onslaught. The enemy broke into Beliaevka. A counterattack didn't yield positive results. The enemy's capture of Beliaevka seriously worsened the condition of the troops and the city, because the water pump station *Dniester*, which was located there, kept the city supplied with fresh water from the Dniester River.

---

5   A.D. Borisov, "Oborona Odessy (avgust – oktiabr' 1941)", p. 58.

At the same time, part of the 95th Rifle Division's force of the Western Sector was fighting in the Kagarlyk area and the enemy command conducted an offensive against this division. Even though it was of an auxiliary nature, in the event of success the enemy might break through to the city along the shortest path – along the Razdel'naia – Odessa railroad.

Altogether, the Romanian offensive forced the Coastal Army command to withdraw the sector's left flank in order to avoid encirclement. The retreating troops were only able to stop and consolidate on the Varazhany – Perestal' – Frantsfeld line. The withdrawal of the troops in the Southern Sector demanded the withdrawal of the troops of the Western Sector as well – otherwise the enemy might appear in their rear. At an order, the troops of the Western Sector took up a new defense on the Paliovo, Vygoda, Petrovskii, Vakarzhany line.

On 19-20 August the enemy managed to penetrate the defense of the city's defenders in the Eastern Sector in the sector of the 1st Regiment of Naval Infantry. The 2nd Regiment of Naval Infantry was sent to its relief. The enemy, having a three-fold superiority in force, was counting upon a victory. In the course of eight hours the Romanians conducted countless attacks. The Black Sea soldiers fought tenaciously and drove back all the attacks, having killed up to 200 enemy soldiers and officers and destroyed 2 tanks in the process.

The troops of the 26th Border Guards Regiment and 54th Regiment of the 25th Rifle Division, which were defending the northeastern approaches to Odessa, were defending just as tenaciously as the sailors. Here, in the 54th Regiment, the young women N.A. Onilova and L.M. Pavlichenko gained their fame. A young worker of an Odessan fabric factory, Nina Onilova voluntarily headed to the front. Having received a machine gun, she declared, "With it I will cut down the fascists, and there will not be and cannot be any mercy to the hated foe."[6] She carried out her vow. Already in her first battle with accurate machine-gun fire she killed approximately 40 aggressors, and over the entire time of Odessa's defense and later in the fighting near Sevastopol, she killed more than 350. The graduating college coed L. Pavlichenko also voluntarily joined the army. Having become a sniper at the front, she killed more than 100 fascists at Odessa.

By 19 August 1941 as a result of almost two weeks of fighting, the enemy had lost more than 50% of his men and combat equipment of the first-echelon divisions, but had been unable to seize Odessa from the march according to the initial plan. Each regiment of the Coastal Army was opposing approximately two enemy divisions. However, the men of the Coastal Army in the course of the bitter fighting had also suffered large losses – up to 40% of its soldiers and officers were now dead or wounded. The losses were especially significant among the command cadres.

The enemy, though, having introduced fresh reserves, was intensifying the attacks. The defensive front given the available quantity of troops had become quite extended, and thus the threat of a breakthrough was growing. So on the night of 19-20 August, the Soviet command decided to withdraw its troops to the main line of resistance: Il'inka – Paliovo – Vygoda – Karstal' (present-day Shirokaia Balka) – Ovidiopol' – Karolino-Bugaz. The combat operations shifted to the nearest approaches to Odessa.

Despite the enemy's more than five-fold advantage in strength, in the first defensive stage (between 5 and 19 August 1941) Odessa's defenders in heavy fighting drove back every enemy attempt to seize the city from the march. In the bitter fighting they became combat-hardened and their military skill grew. So even though the enemy managed to shove back the Soviet units, just as before he was unable to break through the front of defense of the Eastern Sector. Meanwhile, the enemy's losses in personnel and equipment were enormous.

The complexity of the situation required an improvement in the leadership of the defense. The command and main forces of the Southern Front, which had retreated to the east of the Dnepr

---

6   TsAMO RF, F. 288, Op. 9905 – Spr. 10, Ark. 185.

River, were located far from besieged Odessa. Difficulties arose in the operational communications between the Coastal Army and Southern Front's Military Council. Smoother coordination in the actions of the besieged army with the Black Sea Fleet was also necessary. Thus the Commander-in-Chief of the Southwestern Direction Marshal of the Soviet Union S.M. Budennyi on 16 August appealed to the *Stavka* of the Supreme High Command with a request to subordinate the Coastal Army to the Military Council of the Black Sea Fleet and to appoint an operational ground commander to assist the naval command.

On 19 August the *Stavka* issued a directive about creating the Odessa Defense District, which included the forces of the Separate Coastal Army, the Odessa Naval Base and some of the ships of the main nucleus of the Black Sea Fleet. All of the forces and means of the Odessa Defense District became subordinate to the Military Council of the Black Sea Fleet.

When creating the Odessa Defense District, the *Stavka* preserved the already existing structure of command which had already showed its competence in the fighting: the highest organ of command in the Odessa bridgehead area now became the Military Council of the Odessa Defense District. The commander of the Odessa Naval Base Rear Admiral G.V. Zhukov was appointed commander of the troops of the Defense District.[7] His deputies became the commander of the Coastal Army Lieutenant General G.P. Sofronov (for the ground defense), the new commander of the Odessa Naval Base Rear Admiral I.D. Kuleshov (for defense of Odessa from the sea), and Brigade Commander V.P. Katrov (for the District's air force). The assistant commander of the Odessa Defense District for defensive construction was Major General of Engineering Troops A.F. Khrenov. Major General Ia.D. Shishenin directed the headquarters of the Odessa Defense District, while Colonel M.I. Krylov assumed direction over the headquarters of the Coastal Army.[8]

The *Stavka* of the Supreme High Command gave the assignment to the Odessa Defense District to hold Odessa to the last possibility; to increase the construction of fortifications, having mobilized for this the able-bodied civilian population; and to make effect use of all available equipment and other military property. As a result of the creation of the defense district and the reorganization of the command, a single, orderly system of the defense's leadership took shape, which gave the possibility to arrange efficiently the cooperation of all types of troops and to make better use of local resources for the front's needs. The creation of the Odessa Defense District secured flexible command of all different types of troops that were taking part in the defense of the naval base, while the subordination of the Odessa Defense District's Military Council to the Military Council of the Black Sea Fleet had enormous significance in the conditions of the ground blockade of Odessa. On 20 August, a public appeal was made on the ships of the Fleet and in the units of the Crimea Fortified District about recruiting volunteers for the naval infantry for the defense of Odessa.

The last 10 days of August and the beginning of September 1941 became one of the most intense and critical stages of the entire period of Odessa's defense. In the *Sovinformburo*'s bulletins in these days, the Odessa direction was called one of those sectors of the Soviet-German front where the fighting was of the bitterest nature. It was to the heroes of these battles that the well-known poet K. Simonov dedicated the following poetic lines, having written them in besieged Odessa:

In daylight hours, having strained a drop of water into each flask
Going into close combat a hundred times
Having taken off the bloody striped shirt
The sailors are silently dying …

7   N.G. Kuznetsov, *Na flotakh boevaya trevoga* [*Combat alert in the fleets*] (Moscow: Voenizdat, 1971), pp. 120-121.
8   S.A. Vol'sky, *Velichnyi podvig* [*Greatest achievement*] (Kiev: 1967), p. 51; I.I. Azarov, *Osazhdennaia Odessa* [*Besieged Odessa*] (Odessa, 1975), p. 72.

4

The fighting on the nearest approaches to the city

The Romanians prepared for a new round of fighting and were receiving reinforcements. By 20 August the adversary had assembled 17 divisions and 7 brigades in front of Odessa. The forces defending the city were significantly smaller – they barely numbered 34,500 men equipped with 660 submachine guns, 418 heavy and 703 light machine guns, 303 artillery pieces, just 2 operational tanks and 19 aircraft to cover a line with a frontage of more than 80 kilometers![1]

The Nazi leadership was plainly dissatisfied with the delay in Odessa's capture. On 20 August the Chief of the OKH [*Oberkommando des Heeres* – Supreme High Command of the German Army] General Staff F. Halder made the following entry in his diary: "Odessa remains a sore spot." After a phone conversation with the Chief of the OKW [*Oberkommando der Wehrmacht* – Supreme High Command of the Armed Forces] Wilhelm Keitel, Halder jotted down: "Without Odessa, no Crimea. Logistical reasons."[2] Hitler on 22 August wrote: "For Germany the liquidation of the Russian airbases on the Black Sea coastline, first of all in the Odessa area and in the Crimea, has decisive significance." This matter agitated the *Führer*, especially from the point of view of keeping the Romanian oil fields undamaged, which were extremely important for supplying Germany's Army and Navy with fuel.[3]

Back in 1940 Hitler and the fascist ruler of Romania Ion Antonescu had come to an agreement, according to which Romania in exchange for its participation in the war would receive, in addition to Moldavia, all of the territory between the Southern Bug and Dniester Rivers and Odessa's industrial zone. The intention was to convert this area into a Transnistria governorship, with its center in Odessa.[4] Thus for the Romanian command the question of seizing Odessa became a matter of national prestige.

Ion Antonescu issued an order, in which he was forced to recognize his troops' weak morale and low combat-effectiveness: "It is a disgrace to such an army, which has a four-fold or even five-fold

---

1 *73 geroïchnikh dnia: Xronika oboroni Odesi v 1941 r.* [*73 heroic days: Chronicle of Odessa's defense in 1941*] (Odessa: Maiak, 1988), p. 91.

2 *Ukraïns'ka RSR u Velikii Vitchizniachii viini Radian'skogo Soiiuza 1941-1945 rr: u 3 t.* [*The Ukrainian RSR in the Great Patriotic war of the Soviet Union 1941-1945: in 3 volumes*] (Kiev: Politvidav Ukraïni, 1967), Vol. 1, p. 229; F. Halder, *Voennyi dnevnik v 3 t.* [*War diary in 3 volumes*] (Moscow: Voenizdat, 1989), Vol. 1, p. 291. English text taken from Charles Burdick and Hans Adolf Jacobson (ed.), The Halder War Diary 1939-1942 (Novato, CA: Presidio Press, 1988).

3 *Odesskaia oblast' v Velikoi Otechestvennoi voine 1941-1945: Dokumenty i materialy* [*Odessa Oblast in the Great Patriotic War 1941-1945: Documents and materials*](Odessa: Maiak, 1970), p. 52

4 *Kniga Pamiati Ukrainy: Odesskaia oblast'* [*Ukraine Book of Memory*] (Odessa: Maiak, 1994), Vol. 1, p. 21.

numerical superiority over the enemy and is superior in armaments, especially when it is being held in place by small Soviet units."[5]

In a different order to the Romanian troops, Ion Antonescu declared:

> Dismiss those formation commanders, as well as those commanders of regiments, battalions and companies, the units of which are not attacking with complete resolve, turn them over for trial, and deprive them of the right to a pension. Deprive those soldiers, who fail to go on the attack with the proper élan or who abandon a defensive line, of their property and government assistance for the rest of the war. Execute on the spot those soldiers who lose their weapon. If a formation retreats without justification, the chief is obliged to deploy machine guns in their rear and to shoot the fleers pitilessly.[6]

In confirmation of his order, Antonescu relieved a number of generals and officers of their commands, while many soldiers and junior officers who were suspected of cowardice were shot.

The Romanians created groupings of several divisions each on separate directions and launched furious attempts to break through the Odessa Defense District's line of defense. On 20 August they went on the offensive across the entire front. By the start of the fighting on the outskirts of Odessa, the enemy had concentrated five army corps consisting of 12 infantry, one tank and two cavalry divisions opposite the Eastern Sector's three rifle divisions and composite detachment. The 13th and 15th Infantry Divisions were attacking the Eastern Sector, while seven divisions (the 3rd, 7th, 11th, 14th, 21st Infantry Divisions, the 1st Guards Division and the 1st Border Guards Division) attacked the Western Sector. The enemy probed for the boundaries of our units, and then, after conducting a powerful artillery and mortar preparation, hurled the infantry into the attack. Covered by the cornfields, the Romanians infiltrated the boundaries and widened the gaps with fighting, forcing our units to pull back their flanks. This forced our units in isolated sectors to fall back to new lines.

Day and night, the enemy's artillery and air force were shelling or dropping bombs on the combat positions of the Coastal Army, the ships of the Black Sea Fleet, and the city itself. The attacks struck the troops of the Eastern, Western and Southern Sector simultaneously. Odessa's situation became ever more threatening with each passing day. However, even at this time, the city refused to submit to the foe, although the situation became still more complicated. From 25 August, targeted artillery fire on the city and port began. The city's defenders were showing maximal tenacity, refusing to yield a single meter of native soil without combat. Ukrainians and Russians; Belorussians and Moldavians; Georgians and Armenians; Azerbaijanis and Kazakhs; Uzbeks and Turkmen; Tadzhiks and Kirghiz; Latvians, Estonians and Lithuanians, as well as representatives of 27 other nationalities were heroically fighting for Odessa.

The troops of the Odessa Defense District as a result of strong counterattacks in the Eastern Sector inflicted heavy losses to the enemy, especially to the 15th and 13th Infantry Divisions. In the Western Sector of the defense, the enemy's 3rd Infantry Division was decimated. The Romanian 5th and 7th Infantry Divisions also took heavy losses. The defenders of the Southern Sector bled the 1st Guards and 21st Infantry Divisions white. However, despite the enormous casualties, the Romanian command kept feeding fresh divisions into the battle.

In the course of bitter, bloody fighting the enemy succeeded in pushing back the units of the Odessa Defense District. Suffering serious losses, they fell back 4 to 15 kilometers from the line of defense that they had been occupying up until 20 August. In the Southern Sector the enemy broke

---

5   *Krasnaia Zvezda*, 15 October 1941; *Znamia kommunizma*, 5 October 1971.
6   I.I. Azorov, *Osazhdennaia Odessa*, p. 84.

through the defenses in the Kagarlyk – Beliaevka sector and exploited the success in the direction of Karstal', Vakarzhany, Dal'nik and Odessa. Retreating, the Southern Sector's troops were only able to halt the retreat and dig in along the Vakarzhany, Perestal', Frantsfeld line. Perestal' (present-day Petrolinevka) was seized.

In the Western Sector the enemy launched an attack in the Maki, Odessa direction. At the order of the commander of the Odessa Defense District, the Sector's troops fell back with fighting to the Paliovo, Vygoda, Petrovskii, Vakarzhany line. The Romanian troops managed to shove back the 95th Rifle Division's 161st Rifle Regiment and to take Vygoda Station. The Coastal Army's headquarters sent a machine-gun company of the former Tiraspol Fortified District and Armored Train No. 22, which had been built in Odessa to aid the division. The sector commander Major General V.F. Vorob'ev committed his final reserve, 100 men under the command of the 95th Rifle Division's chief of operations Captain V.P. Sakharov, into the fighting. Almost the entire headquarters staff and the members of the division's Political Department were fighting at the front, and put a stop to the further development of the breakthrough.

On 21 August the troops of the Southern and Western Sectors launched a counteroffensive with the aim of taking back Vygoda Station and other lost positions, but without success. The enemy managed to stop our units' offensive and then drive them back.

On 22 August Ion Antonescu arrived at Vygoda Station near Odessa with the intention to take leadership of the troops, which were to seize all of Odessa on 23 August – his birthday. In addition, a parade of Romanian troops on Odessa's main square (Cathedral Square) was set to take place on the same day. Antonescu made an appeal to his army: "Soldiers! Make the final effort to end the struggle. Attack! Over the next two days you will take possession of the most important port on the Black Sea. The entire world is watching you, in order to see you in Odessa."[7]

However, instead of a parade on Odessa's main square, the enemy once again had to rotate shattered units out of the line for refitting. The heavy losses in front of Odessa were forcing the Romanian command to send all of its rear area, construction and specialized units to the front, as well as soldiers of older ages, who had been left behind in the field works in Bessarabia. Despite all this, the Romanian Fourth Army had been unable to breach Odessa's defenses.

On 22 August the commander of the Western Sector received a detachment of volunteer sailors, numbering around 600 men, under the command of Major A.S. Potapov, which had arrived from Sevastopol the evening before. On the night of 22/23 August, the detachment assembled on the forward edge and took up a jumping-off position in the sector of Colonel S.I. Serebrov's 161st Rifle Regiment. Early on the morning of 23 August, the sailors and the regiment's troops went on the attack and began to push back the enemy. A powerful "Ura!" rang out amidst the clouds of dust and smoke. The sailors broke into the enemy's trenches and became tied up in brief hand-to-hand combat; the enemy quickly broke and fled. The Black Sea Fleet's volunteer sailors continued the onslaught and made a deep penetration into the enemy's disposition, re-taking the village of Kalinin. Only that evening did Major A.S. Potapov issue the order to the detachment to halt and make no further advance. He called for a conference of his subordinate commanders, during which they reached the decision not to abandon their present positions, but to operate in the enemy's rear. So the sailors moved out and raised havoc in the enemy rear, destroying garrisons and military stockpiles and disrupting communications. Only on the third night did the sailors attack the hostile troops that were opposite the 161st Rifle Regiment from the rear, overrun the enemy and link back up with friendly forces. Many of the Red sailors, who distinguished themselves in this bold raid, were awarded government decorations, while their commander Major A.S. Potapov was deemed worthy of the Order of Lenin.

---

7   *Znamia kommunizma* [Communism's banner], 22 August, 1971.

The naval artillerymen of the 40th Mobile Artillery Battalion of a coastal defensive base (led by Captain I.B. Iablonsky) demonstrated self-sacrifice and courage. They had to fight off furious enemy attacks from positions among the rifle regiments and divisions, to which they'd been made operationally subordinate. Brave scouts to a large extent contributed to the artillerymen's success in destroying enemy personnel, equipment and military targets. They were not only scouting out targets, but often acted as spotters and adjusted the artillery fire themselves. The sailor-scouts I. Gogolenko, G. Ubransky, V. Polomarchuk, A. Makusheva, M. Kolodin, A. Podkovka, A. Nechipurenko and others particularly distinguished themselves by their ability to penetrate into the enemy rear and to scout his forces.

By the end of 22 August units of the 95th Rifle Division fell back with fighting to the Hill 94.5, Novaia Beliaevka, Dubinovo, Vakarzhany line. The 25th Rifle Division had dug in on the Vakarzhany – Peterstal' – northern outskirts of Frantsfeld line. In the Eastern Sector, the enemy remained inactive on 20 August, but on 21 August the Romanian 15th Infantry Division went on the attack together with two German companies, striving to break through the defenses in the sectors held by the 1st Regiment of Naval Infantry and the 54th Rifle Regiment. Particularly heavy fighting went on in the area of Buldynka and Shitsli. Elements of the 2nd Regiment of Naval Infantry were sent to assist the Eastern Sector's troops.

Over the course of eight hours the enemy undertook attacks against the positions of the Eastern Sector's troops, but without result, and in the Buldynka, Hill 41.7 sector the Romanians were forced to go over to the defense. Supporting fire from the destroyers *Frunze* (commanded by Lieutenant Commander P.A. Bobrovnikov) and *Dzerzhinsky* (commanded by Lieutenant Commander P.I. Shevchenko), the gunboat *Krasnaia Armeniia* (commanded by Commander, Captain 3rd Rank A.I. Koliada) and the 412th Coastal Battery made a large contribution to this. On the following day they were joined by the cruiser *Krasnyi Krym* (commanded by Commander, Captain 2nd Rank A.I. Zubkov) and the destroyers *Shaumian* (commanded by Commander, Captain 3rd Rank K.P. Valiukh) and *Nezamozhnik*. Placing fire on the areas of Buldynka, Sverdlovo and I'lnika, the ships inflicted heavy damage to the enemy's troops and equipment. Particularly effective was the fire from the *Krasnyi Krym*'s large-caliber guns, for which the cruiser's entire crew received an expression of gratitude from the commander of the Coastal Army.

On 23 August the enemy attempted to seize Shitsli, but failed to do so. The sector's troops received support from the cruiser *Krasnyi Krym*, the destroyer *Frunze*, and the field artillery of the 412th Coastal Battery. Over 21 minutes the 412th Coastal Battery fired 130 180-mm shells and 2,000 45-mm shells at the enemy, as well as approximately 2,000 mortar shells. From the battery's fire, the enemy lost more than 500 soldiers and officers.[8]

Besieged Odessa was in acute need of air support. With the creation of the Odessa Defense District, the number of aircraft didn't increase, but quickly began to diminish, since the flying boats of the 7th and 82nd Aviation Squadrons soon re-staged to Gelendzhik, and the 70th Bomber Aviation Squadron restaged to the Crimean peninsula. The situation on the Coastal direction became more complicated with each passing day and the Fleet's command began to switch a significant amount of its air power over to operations over the ground front.

On 22 August the 8th Fighter Aviation Regiment's 1st Fighter Aviation Squadron (equipped with I-16 fighters) under the command of Captain F.I. Demchenko and the 46th Separate Aviation Squadron of rocket-equipped Il-2 ground attack aircraft under the command of Lieutenant N.P. Kuteinikov restaged to Odessa. Later, some of the Yak-1 and I-15 fighters from the 94th Separate Fighter Aviation Squadron transferred to Odessa. In addition, the Black Sea Fleet command decided to use its bombers and torpedo aircraft flying from Crimean airfields, as well as aircraft

---

8   TsMVA VO RF, F. 204, Spr. 9333, Arzh. 10.

based at the Krasnaia Znamenka airbase in the Bekhter area, for operations against the enemy troops in the Odessa area and against rear area targets.

The city's defenders were standing to their deaths, even though they were suffering significant losses. The replacements that began to arrive in Odessa from the sea were unable to bring the numbers of defenders back up to where they were on 20 August. By 30 August, not more than 25,000 men were still reporting for duty. The situation stood even worse with weapons. On 23 August in the Coastal Army's journal of combat operations, it was noted: "In the army's units there is a large deficit of rifles, machine guns, mortar rounds, 76-mm shells for the regimental and divisional guns, and 122-mm shells ... the trained reserved are now completely depleted, while we have 400 untrained men."[9]

Bitter fighting resumed in the Eastern Sector on 24 August. Under enemy pressure, units on the sector's left flank retreated. There was the threat of a flank attack against the sector's right-flank units. In view of this the Odessa Defense District's command issued an order for a withdrawal to a line behind the Bol'shoi Adzhalyskii estuary. The front lines now ran at a distance of just 8-12 kilometers from the city.

On the morning of 25 August, the 412th Coastal Battery had to blow up its guns. Its personnel merged with the 1st Regiment of Naval Infantry. Over its time of combat at Odessa, the battery had destroyed approximately 20 tanks and 40 vehicles, killed a lot of enemy troops, and had suppressed 12 hostile batteries.

The enemy command immediately took advantage of the withdrawal, having positioned long-range batteries in the area of Novaia Dofinovka. On 25 August they began to place targeted artillery fire on the city and port. Not only the moorings, the port's facilities and the access routes to them came under the artillery fire, but also the maritime entrance to the port. This significantly complicated the entry of ships to the port and their exit from it, but also all of the loading and unloading work. The Odessa Defense District command and the local authorities took urgent measures to build temporary moorings in the areas of the Arcade and the 16th Station of the Bol'shoi Fontan (the Gold Beach), which light and medium transports could use without being subjected to enemy fire from the east. The temporary moorings were built by the city's workers under the guidance of engineers of the Odessa Naval Base within 10 days.

Between 21 and 24 August the enemy abruptly changed tactics. Previously it had gone on the attack in dense combat formations and as a result had suffered large losses. Now the Romanians switched to cautious advances in separate sectors, using tanks to break through the defenses.

On 25 August the enemy hurled nine divisions into combat, striving to obtain success in all three sectors. Over two days the enemy forces had been reinforced with two more infantry divisions. Heavy fighting went on until the end of August. With the aim of conserving food reserves in the city after 25 August, ration cards were introduced for separate types of food products – bread, sugar and fats (there was no shortage of fruits and vegetables).

On 26 August, not only the two regiments of naval infantry that had been formed in Odessa were fighting in the defensive lines protecting the city, but also four volunteer detachments that had arrived from Sevastopol totaling 1,620 men. On 28 August, two more detachments of volunteer sailors numbering more than 1,000 men were shifted to Odessa.[10]

Just as before, coastal artillery and combat ships were providing fire support to ground troops defending Odessa. Daily, the 21st Battery (commanded by Captain A.I. Kuznetsov) of the 44th Separate Anti-aircraft Artillery Battalion, which was positioned on the cape near Fontanka, fired

9   *Chernomors'ka komuna*, 24 August 1941.
10   G.I. Vagneev, *Chernomortsy v Velikoi Otechestvennoi voine* [*Black Sea Fleet sailors in the Great Patriotic War*] (Moscow: Voenizdat, 1978), pp. 47-48.

at the attacking enemy. The days after 25 August, when the 412th Coastal Battery was no longer in Chebanka, were especially tense, and the 21st Battery wound up immediately in the path of the advancing enemy troops. By the morning of 26 August, shells in the battery were running low, but the enemy was still pressing. The naval infantry rose on the counterattack and needed fire support. When the ammunition ran out, the battery commander Captain A.I. Kuznetsov made contact over the telephone with the commander of the artillery battalion and personally adjusted the fire of the artillery battalion's other batteries. In the course of the battle he was mortally wounded and died in the arms of his subordinates. The commander's death enraged the artillerymen. Having received a resupply of shells, for five more days successively they fired at the enemy. Over the entire period between 15 and 30 August the battery conducted 82 firing missions, expending 900 shells in the process. A lot of combat equipment and up to 2,000 enemy soldiers and officers were destroyed by its fire.

The artillery crews of the 411th Battery (commanded by Captain I.N. Nikitenko) and the 39th Battery (commanded by Captain E.N. Shkirman) in the tense days between 25 and 30 August fired missions to suppress enemy batteries, as well as to place fire on enemy troop aggregations and his attacking columns in the Perestal' area, so intensively that their gun tubes often glowed red.

Every day, six to eight combat ships took part in the artillery support for the troops of the Odessa Defense District. On 27 August, the destroyers *Bodryi* [*Sprightly*], *Smyshlennyi*, *Shauman* and *Nezamozhnik* and the gunboats *Krasnaia Armeniia*, *Krasnaia Gruziia* and *Krasnyi Adzharistan* fired at enemy positions in the Sverdlovo, Kubanka area.

The *Stavka* of the Supreme High Command, aware of the Odessa Defense District's plight, at the end of August sent 10 march battalions numbering more than 9,000 men to the Odessa front. Meanwhile, the Black Sea Fleet command formed new detachments of naval infantry with a total number of 1,620 men and sent them to Odessa. The replacements immediately replenished the forward units.

At Odessa, the line between the front and rear had become blurred not only in a psychological and political sense, but also with respect to territory. The troops and civilian population comprised a single battle camp of the city's defenders. On 21 August 1941 at the height of the fighting that began on the close approaches to Odessa, the city's administration published an appeal "To the citizens of the city of Odessa":

> Comrades! The foe is standing at the gates of Odessa – one of the most vital centers of our Motherland. Our native, sunny city is in danger. Everything created in it by the hands of the workers is in danger. The lives of our children, wives and mothers are in danger. The fascist cutthroats want to turn us, the freedom-loving citizens, into slaves. The time has come when each of us must rise to the defense of our native city. It is the duty of each citizen to forget everything personal and to give all of your efforts to defend the city. It isn't the first time that Odessa's workers are standing up for the honor and independence of our Motherland and of our native city. The moment has arrived when the glorious combat traditions of the Odessan proletariat must be embodied in new combat achievements of male and female workers, workers of science, technology and the arts, and housewives in the defense of our native city against the fascist barbarians.
>
> The defense of our city is the cherished cause of our population. To defend our native land, our native city, together with the Red Army's units – that is what our Motherland expects and demands from us.
>
> Each building, each factory must become a fortress, upon which the fascist bandits will break their teeth. Arm yourselves with everything possible. A Molotov cocktail tossed at a tank; a stone hurled from a window; boiling water dumped onto the head of the cannibals can forge our victory over the foe.

More organization, no panic, no loss of composure! Now enormous orderliness, unity, self-sacrifice and a readiness to make any sacrifice are necessary. Struggle decisively and pitilessly against panic-mongers and those who sow discord. The holy duty of each is to give every effort, and when necessary, their life as well for the Motherland, for our native city, and for the lives of our children.[11]

One of the important factors of success, which played a decisive role in these critical days, was the contribution of Odessans in the defense of their native city. With the creation of the Operational-Productive Group (or the Defense Commission), the Odessa Defense District's Military Council was now able to to bring together all of the combat actions under its leadership, which unquestionably increased the defense's effectiveness. The Defense Commission was an important link that tied the military command and the city's leadership into a single organizational structure. It encompassed all of the issues that were one way or another connected with mobilizing the city's human resources for the needs of the front and its intellectual and economic potential.[12]

A decree from the bureau of the Ukrainian Communist Party's oblast committee on 22 August, entitled "On measures to support the city of Odessa's defense" played an important role in these days. This was in essence a Party order, which demanded of the city's Operational Group to strengthen the anti-air defenses, to establish around-the-clock watch of the apartment blocks and especially the sources of water, and to take food supplies under control and distribute them according to a plan. The decree compelled the Party district committees to send all of the Communists and Komsomol members still capable of carrying a weapon to military units in order to defend the city and to render necessary assistance to military registration and enlistment offices in conducting supplementary mobilization. The Chief of the Red Army's General Staff Marshal B.M. Shaposhnikov on 26 August demanded in a telegram sent to the Commander-in-Chief of the Black Sea Fleet "... to exploit fully the efforts of the local population and the means and possibilities of Odessa."[13]

Odessa's population became an important source of human replenishments for the Coastal Army. In the course of the Party's mobilization in the latter half of August, approximately 2,000 Communist Party members additionally departed for the front. By the end of the month there were only 1,908 Party members and candidate members remaining in the city's Party organization, which was less than 10% of its pre-war number, and only 2,963 (or 6% of the pre-war figure) Komsomol members. A special detachment numbering 1,200 men under the command of Major P.I. Demchenko was formed from Odessa's police force with the task to struggle against enemy diversionary groups. By this time virtually all of Odessa's people's militia detachments had already joined the acting army and on 21 August they comprised 12% of its total manpower.

The mobilization of draft-eligible men of older ages (up to 55 years of age) began in Odessa. Nearly 10,000 replacements were generated, and 1,000 to 1,200 men each were distributed among the 25th and 95th Rifle Divisions and the 1st Cavalry Division. The bulk of those called up for military service, numbering approximately 5,000 men, was used to form a new rifle division. This division, which was staffed up to 50% with people's militia, was organized around a nucleus of an experienced, composite detachment of troops of the Eastern Sector of defense. At first this division was called the Odessa Division, but later it received the numeric designation of the 421st Rifle Division. Colonel G.M. Kochenov was placed in command of the division. The soldiers and

11   *Odessa v Velikoi Otechestvennoi voine Sovetskogo Soiuza. Sbornik dokumentov i materialov* [*Odessa in the Great Patriotic War of the Soviet Union. Compilation of documents and materials*] (Odessa, 1947), pp. 67-68.
12   N. Stanko [chief editor] et. al., *Istoria Odesi* [*History of Odessa*] (Odessa: Druk, 2002), p. 377.
13   Ibid.

commanders of the 421st Rifle Division stood to their deaths for one and a half months on the lines of the defense's Eastern Sector. The presence of Odessans at the front from the very beginning was an effective, acting factor.

On 24 August 1941, self-defense detachments of workers began forming up in Odessa, consisting primarily of people's militiamen. Over a short period of time six such detachments were formed (one from each city district) with a total of 3,600 members, including 250 women. A self-defense reserve numbering 7,600 members was created in Odessa's factories and businesses for cooperating with the Odessa Defense District's forces in the event of an enemy breakthrough into the city.

Many of the workers, including women as well, without taking a break from work learned military specialties and went to the front as volunteers. The oblast newspaper *Chernomorska kommuna* talked in its pages about women who went to the front as nurses or even pilots.[14] The previously mentioned sniper L. Pavlichenko and machine-gunner N. Onilov acquired their military specialties in this way, and for the courage and heroism that they demonstrated from this time they were deemed worthy of the title Hero of the Soviet Union.

The front demanded not only human resources; no less needed were weapons and ammunition. Immediately after the war's breakout, 24 of Odessa's industrial factories were converted to produce military items at an order from a People's Commissariat. These factories were responsible for the production and repair of various types of weapons and equipment for the Southern Front. However, soon the largest factories and plants were evacuated to the east together with a large portion of their qualified employees at an order from the government. Thus from the first days of Odessa's defense, the remaining resources of the city's enterprises were used to repair and produce military items for the nearby front, which at this time already ran near the city itself, in essence along its outskirts. Odessa had become a frontline city in the full sense of these words. Yet in spite of this Odessa's workers not only continued to go to work, but also as far as possible increased the output of military goods. The troops needed a significant number of anti-tank and anti-personnel mines, explosives, wicks for Molotov cocktails, iron anti-tank obstacles, barbed wire, booby traps and other types of military gear. It was also necessary to get the production of armored trains, armored cars, mortars, flamethrowers and hand grenades up and running. One can imagine how difficult this was to do. After all nearly all of the factories' modern equipment had been evacuated to the deep rear, and a majority of the highly-trained workers and technical staff had either gone to the front or had been evacuated to the country's east together with the heavy machinery. The reserves of raw materials and fuel were also quite limited, and prior to the war Odessa hadn't produced weapons to defend the city and hadn't acquired or mastered the means for their production.

In order to ensure the urgent fulfillment of the front's demands, the institution of commissars was introduced in the factories and plants; the commissars came from among the number of leading Party and workers. An initiative from the city's residents arrived to help. A manufacturing commission in the course of three days compiled an account of all the available factory equipment, semi-finished goods, raw materials and fuel. Machinery that had been in small manufacturing facilities, factory training workshops, secondary technical schools and universities replenished the assembly lines and shops of the January Uprising and October Revolution factories, the Petrovsky shipyard, and others, which were required to shoulder the main burden of military production. Raw materials and fuel could be expended only with the authorization of the manufacturing commission. The leading factories went to a 24-hour work schedule. Broad cooperation among the factories helped overcome the enormous difficulties. They all carried out the tasks of the front according to a single plan, supplying each other with the necessary semi-processed materials or

---

14 *Chernomors'ka Komuna*, 24 August 1941.

prepared parts needed for the manufacture of weapons. A widespread competition developed among the workers to see who could carry out the front's requests most quickly. A movement of multi-tasking, the simultaneous operation of several machine tools, as well as a movement of those who over-fulfilled their shift targets by 200 percent or 300 percent became particularly widespread. At the January Uprising factory, the arc welder A.I. Kal'ianov and pattern maker S.Kh. Zhabrotsky replaced two of their comrades that had departed for the front and daily over-fulfilled their production targets by 200-250%. G.M. Kruglyi's labor brigade over the course of several days never left the works of the shipyard, arming and repairing naval transports. The foreman of the October Revolution factory's assembly works I.P. Osipenko made more than 20 labor-saving suggestions, which contributed to production improvements, and working on the welding and assembly of armored tractors, doubled his target norm of output.

The examples of labor heroism had an effect on the youth as well. At the port, in the shipyard, at the January Uprising and October Revolution factories, at the bread factory and at many other enterprises, Komsomol members without exception over-fulfilled their production targets by 200-250%.

Workers of the January Uprising factory V.M. Karpov, G.S. Bondarenko, K.A. Buria under the leadership of machine shop manager G.G. Koliagin spent more than 70 hours without interruption positioned at their work places. They took a break only after all the preparatory work to manufacture armored trains had been completed. Thanks to their efforts, the "January" factory got the production of armored trains underway. Plates of ship armor were applied to an ordinary steam engine and flat cars. Guns and machine guns were mounted on the flat cars. Troops of the Odessa Defense District and workers of the city manned the armored train. Already on 11 August the labor collective of the January Uprising factory handed the first armored train over to the city's defenders, which became a mobile reserve of the Coastal Army's headquarters. Tanks also underwent repairs at this factory. A second armored train (No. 21 or "The Black Sea Sailor") was built at the Odessa Ship Repair Factory No. 1.

The production of military goods and weapons reached a genuinely sweeping scale in the last 10 days of August 1941, when the Odessa Defense District's Military Council decided to get the output of weapons that were acutely needed by the city's defenders up and running within a week. Quickly the production of makeshift tanks began at the January Uprising factory (headed by A.N. Likutin). For this purpose, tracked ChTZ-5 tractors were overlaid with armor, before being equipped with machine guns and cannons. The result was a menacing looking machine, which the Odessans, who are inclined toward humor at any time, jokingly called "NI" tanks (*Na ispug* – a play on the expression *brat' na ispug*, to frighten or scare, but also calling to mind the Russian negative, "not tanks". The first combat trials of these tanks took place in fighting at the Dal'nik, where these makeshift tanks fully justified themselves. The factory's chief engineer P.K. Romanov and an engineer of the Odessa Naval Base Captain U. Kogan proposed the idea of converting tractors into tanks. Quickly the production of NI tanks was up and running at the October Revolution factory as well. Already on 4 September the first series model of NI tanks left the factory's workshop.

Women of Odessa were working side by side with the men. A female welder of the October Revolution factory S.K. Tkachuk systematically over-fulfilled her production targets to repair cannons by 300%. A.S. Bankovaia, a worker of a knitting factory, serviced 17 machine tools during these days of Odessa's defense. The top producer at the Bread Factory No. 3 M.P. Kokun was working in place of her son and daughter, who were both fighting on the approaches to Odessa. She daily fulfilled the norms for 2-3 people. K.D. Darmostuchenko manufactured mortars, having replaced two specialists who had gone to the front. A highly-qualified machinist of the Red Profintern factory A.Iu. Shevtsova over-fulfilled the output norms by 180-200% and simultaneously taught her specialty to 8 young women.

The activity of innovators and creators reached a never-before-seen scale. Every day, dozens, and sometimes hundreds of the most various proposals and suggestions came in from engineers and workers that would allow the factories and workshops to come to grip with the production of a needed weapon. Suggestions included a technique to replace the special steel for armoring trains and tractors with three layers of armor made from boiler plates and rubber; a method to use alloyed pipes to manufacture mortar tubes; and a way to get the local manufacture of flamethrowers and fuses for grenades up and running.

At this time the city's factories were being subjected to aerial bombings and artillery barrages. Dozens of bombs and shells fell on the grounds of the factories and workshops. People were killed by these strikes, buildings were destroyed, but the work of Odessa's industry never ceased even for an hour. The January Uprising and October Revolution factories and the shipyard produced armored trains, tanks, mortars and anti-tank "hedgehogs", and repaired tanks, cannons, and both combat and transport ships. The Dzerzhinsky factory produced flamethrowers. The Petrovsky, Kinap, Red Profintern and Khvoristin factories manufactured grenades, as well as anti-tank and anti-personnel mines. Explosives were produced in the Bol'shevik factory. The factories Red Guards, 10th Anniversary of the Red Army, Starostin, Transporter, Red Proletariat, Remmashtrest and many others produced mortars, shells, anti-tank hedgehogs, caterpillar tracks for vehicles, barbed wire, cables for naval ships and for suspending underwater mines, and entrenching tools, but also worked to repair combat equipment and vehicles.

The most difficult conditions for production activity were at the October Revolution factory – here, after the evacuation of machinery and specialists to the country's interior, less than a tenth of the employees and only aged, worn-out equipment remained. Moreover, the factory's workshops were just 6 kilometers from the frontlines, well within the reach of enemy artillery, and thus on some days up to 60 artillery shells and bombs fell on its grounds. Despite this, its workers kept laboring and supplying the front with such vitally necessary items: over the entire period of defense, they produced 105,000 shovels, 14,000 pickaxes, 12,000 axes, and 3,000 anti-tank hedgehogs made from rail.

Medium-sized and small enterprises and workshops made their own contribution to the defense. Bottle-based improvised incendiary weapons , the so-called Molotov cocktails, from the very first days of the defense were an important weapon in the struggle against enemy tanks, but the lack of wicks for them was a great inconvenience (both time and a sufficient amount of skill were necessary to make something to ignite the bottle's contents). Professors at the Odessa University came up with an original means for making ampules containing a self-igniting liquid. The question arose about their serial production. The city's production group directed the Komsomolka chemistry workshop, which before the war had manufactured shoe polish, to produce these vital wicks. The workshop's collective dealt with their assignment with honor and quickly raised the output of wicks up to 8-10,000 pieces a day. This not only fully met the needs of the Odessa Defense District, but also allowed the "export" of Molotov cocktails to the Crimea. It is possible to cite a lot of such examples: the Bol'shevik toy coop manufactured 100,000 shells; the Tel'man coop (which before the war had manufacture housewares) produced 750,000 parts for grenades; and the Lastochkin and Fifth-Year Plan No. 3 sewing companies manufactured 15,000 life jackets, up to 16,000 quilted jackets and cotton trousers, and 35,000 knapsacks.

Enterprises of the food and manufacturing industries got the uninterrupted supply to the defenders of their own output up and running, even though many of them were located in the zone of continuous artillery fire (like the meat-processing plant) or became the victims of air raids (like Bread Factory No. 2). At a decision of the Odessa Defense District's Military Council, workers who were fulfilling military orders were to receive the same food rations as the frontline Red Army troops.

Under the siege conditions, Odessa's factories and businesses manufactured and repaired 134 types of armaments. They sent to the front 5 armored trains, 55 tanks, 1,262 mortars, 965 flame-throwers, more than 310,000 hand and anti-tank grenades, approximately 250,000 anti-personnel mines, more than 57,000 demolition charges, 90,000 Molotov cocktails, hundreds of kilometers of telephone cable, 4,500 anti-tank hedgehogs, more than 2,000 metric tons of cement, and 300 metric tons of barbed wire. They also repaired and put back into service 42 tanks, more than 300 artillery pieces, 962 machine guns, 6,502 rifles, 69 tow tractors and approximately 600 trucks and cars. A manufactured or repaired weapon immediately left the factories and went to the front. There is the following authoritative evidence about the production rates of "Odessan" weaponry from the Coastal Army's Chief of Staff N.I. Krylov: " … the production of 50-mm mortars reached such a scale, that we had the possibility to send a batch of them to the naval infantry brigades that were forming up in the Crimea."

This was a massive labor achievement by Odessa's residents, which was accomplished in conditions when there was not only a lack of equipment and raw materials, but even when water was being distributed in the besieged city according to ration cards. For this self-sacrificial work in the days of Odessa's defense, the employees of a number of enterprises – the January Uprising and October Revolution factories; the Ukraine, Red Guards, Bol'shevik, Kinap, Petrovsky, and the steel wire cable factories; as well as of the shipyard, Odessa's shipping line, Odessa's port and the Odessa – Kishinev railroad – were honored with the medal "For the defense of Odessa".[15]

The defenders of besieged Odessa were also being supported by the rest of the country, which the Odessans called "the big land". In August, 9,800 metric tons of military cargo arrived in Odessa, and in September – 23,500 metric tons. To assist the besieged troops, various ships from other parts of the country delivered 10,000 metric tons of ammunition. Replacements arrived to replenish the combat ranks: 9,000 in August, and more than 37,000 in September, including 8,000 naval infantrymen. The crews of the transport ships of the Black Sea Fleet completed 911 voyages to the fighting Odessa under the conditions of relentless air strikes and despite the danger of mines.[16]

Odessa was connected with the rest of the country only by sea. Thus the port was being protected like the apple of one's eye. Anti-aircraft gunners of Odessa Naval Base's 37th Anti-aircraft Regiment and the 15th Anti-Air Defense Brigade were defending the area of the port. The enemy command tried at any cost to knock out the port and thereby cut the unvanquished Odessa off from the rest of the country. There were days when up to 250 heavy-caliber shells and hundreds of high-explosive and incendiary bombs fell on the grounds and docks of the port. However, the port's service personnel and workers demonstrated exceptional fortitude and aplomb. The loading and unloading of cargo went on around the clock and didn't cease even during enemy air raids and artillery barrages.

It was in such difficult conditions that the dockworkers daily received and dispatched up to 5,000 metric tons of cargo. The longshoremen of N.T. Nikitiuk's, Kh.R. Pokrass', F.P. Tsapok's, M.I. Maklakov's and other teams showed themselves to be fearless patriots. They were unloading naval transports twice as fast as they did prior to the war. From the ports, military cargo was quickly delivered to the front. The successful unloading of the transport ships in the port was just as important for Odessa's defenders as successful combats at the front. Over the time of the city's defense, the port served the stopovers of 303 transport ships. Odessa's longshoremen together with sailors unloaded 41,800 metric tons of weapons, ammunition and food, delivered to Odessa's

---

15   *Kniga Pamiati Ukrainy: Odesskaia oblast [Ukraine's Book of Memory: Odessa Oblast]* Vol. 1 (Odessa: Maiak, 1994), p. 23.
16   Ibid., p. 25.

defenders from the country's deep interior, and in addition loaded and sent off more than 188,000 metric tons of valuable factory equipment to Caucasian ports. The dockworkers assured the evacuation by sea of more than 31,000 wounded Soviet soldiers and approximately 300,000 civilians.

In order to ensure that military loads were delivered as intended without delay required the particular dedication of the sailors of civilian steamships. The crews of the ships of the transport fleet *Armeniia, Fabritsius, Pestel', Krym, Tashkent, Valerii Chkalov, Kuban', Berezina, Kalinin, Uralles* and others worked heroically under the leadership of experienced captains V.Ia. Plaushevsky, M.I. Grigor, S.M. Vislobokov, A.K. Kravchenko, I.F. Ivanov, I.F. Korotky and others. Despite the danger of mines and continuous bombings, they each made 10-12 trips to Odessa from the Crimea and the Caucuses, and together with the combat ships that were escorting them, fought off more than 200 attacks by fascist aircraft. Alongside the large transport ships, motor-sailing ships were widely used. Altogether these smaller ships completed 215 missions without any protection, and 696 voyages in convoys.[17]

Enemy aviation was the main obstacle to the uninterrupted assurance of communications with Odessa. At first during the war, the enemy strove to disrupt naval communications with Odessa by dropping magnetic mines, aerial attacks, and artillery salvos on the ships that were entering or leaving the port, as well as while they were docked at the port. The enemy also attempted to torpedo the ships from the air and with attacks by torpedo boats, which were based in Sulina and Burgas. Romanian torpedo boats made several forays, but they were all successfully repulsed. During the period of Odessa's defense, the only submarine available in the Romanian fleet, the *Delfinul* [*Dolphin*], made two forays to our shores, but failed to conduct a single attack.[18]

In order to protect the ships standing in the dock against enemy air attacks while they were being loaded or unloaded, it was necessary to enhance the anti-air defenses. Defense against attacks from the air was being secured by our aircraft on-duty at their airbases and by fighter patrols in the air, as well as by anti-aircraft artillery. The gun crews of the 161st Anti-aircraft Battery (commanded by Lieutenant A.P. Kushnir) of the Odessa Naval Base's 7th Anti-Aircraft Artillery Regiment stood out for their accurate and smooth performance while repelling enemy air raids by shooting down several enemy aircraft.

Enemy aircraft, which were initially based on airfields at Varna, Constanța, Braila and Focșani, and subsequently on airfields seized in the Ukraine, kept changing their combat tactics during the struggle to disrupt our naval communications. This forced corresponding alterations in our means of countering the attacks when defending the lines of communication. In the initial stage of the war, when the enemy was placing his main hopes in bottling up our fleet in their ports with minefields, enemy aircraft operated against Soviet lines of communication chiefly with solitary aircraft, and only during daylight hours. They were using horizontal bombing runs from high or medium altitude. The accuracy of such attacks was very low, and our transports that were making independent movements without escorts or air cover as a rule arrived at their bases undamaged.

When the foe failed to blockade the bases of the Black Sea Fleet by deploying magnetic mines (and failed to seize them on the ground), the German command restaged dive bombers and torpedo-carrying aircraft with experienced crews from the Mediterranean to captured Ukrainian airbases. Solitary torpedo-laden aircraft, flying along scouted routes, conducted searches for Soviet transport ships and conducted an attack upon the most valuable target that it came across. For example, on 21 August 1941, an enemy aircraft torpedoed the naval transport *Briansk* in the vicinity of Sychavka, which was in route to Odessa from Sevastopol. The ship sank. The appearance of torpedo-carrying aircraft became a serious danger. Measures were adopted to increase the

---

17 *Morskoi sbornik* [*Naval digest*] No. 12 (1969), p. 23.
18 G.I. Vagneev, *Chernomortsy v Velikoi Otechestvennoi voine*, pp. 56-57.

protection of transports and convoys by employing not only combat ships for this, but also aircraft. The Commander-in-Chief of the Black Sea Fleet ordered the commander of the Odessa Defense District to dispatch transports from Odessa only with the onset of twilight, no later than 2000, so by sunrise they would be in the Tarkhankut – Evpatoriia sector, where they could be covered by fighter aircraft of the Black Sea Fleet.

In September 1941 the enemy began to employ attacks by groups of dive bombers, including against combat ships. Also, in the latter half of September, using the close proximity of their airfields, the Germans began to make broad use of Me-109 fighters as fighter-bombers against the naval transports, especially in the area of the Tendrovskii combat sector.

The enemy also made use of coastal artillery, positioned on the coastline in the Sychavka – Koblevo area, to the north of the village of Fontanka, and also in the area of the Sukhoi estuary, to disrupt Soviet communications by sea. By placing artillery fire on the port and the approaches to it, the adversary was making not only anchorage in the port, but also the entry to it and exit from it, hazardous.

The Soviet fleet used inshore routes that ran along the Ak-Mechet' – Tarkhankut – Sevastopol line most intensively. Initially the convoys were not in columns. The transports covered a portion of the route between Odessa and Sevastopol in daylight hours with protection, but sailed the rest of the route after sunset independently. Then the method of escorting the convoys with screening ships as far as the intermediary base of Ak-Mechet', where a new shift of escorts would take over for the rest of the route, began to be used. However, enemy aircraft discovered this and began to launch attacks against our transports in Ak-Mechet'. Thus it became necessary to avoid stopping at the intermediary base.

The screening ships carried the responsibility not only of providing anti-air defense for the transports, but also anti-submarine defense and anti-ship defense. In order to provide anti-air defense of individual transport ships and convoys, wide use was made of the Black Sea Fleet's fighters. On-duty fighter pilots at the airbases in response to an alarm would sortie to cover the transports and convoys and boldly take on the German raiders. For example, on 10 August 1941, Junior Lieutenants B. Cherevko and V. Grek of the 9th Fighter Aviation Regiment, who were on-duty at their airbase, received an order to cover a passage of the *Kursk* transport ship (commanded by V.Ia. Trush), which had citizens that were being evacuated from Odessa on board. The two fighters immediately took to the sky. On the approach to the transport our pilots spotted three enemy Dornier-215 bombers. B. Cherevko made an attacking pass against the lead bomber. Having closed to within 50 meters, he opened fire and the enemy aircraft burst into flames. Dropping out of formation, the stricken bomber turned around and began to flee to the west. V. Grek attacked it, but at this moment the two other bombers were homing in on the transport. Seeing this, Cherevko attacked one of them and forced it to jettison its bombs far from the target. However, the third Dornier continued onward. Cherevko made a chandelle and bore down on it with an attacking run. Having pressed the trigger, the ammunition almost immediately ran out. The pilot maneuvered to ram the bomber, and he succeeded in striking the enemy aircraft's tail assembly, and the Dornier immediately plummeted into the sea. However, Cherevko's aircraft also became uncontrollable and went into a vertical dive. After failing to regain control of his fighter, Junior Lieutenant Cherevko bailed out of his aircraft at an altitude of 1,000 meters and splashed down into the sea. A patrol boat under the command of Lieutenant F.V. Malakhov that was escorting a different convoy headed toward the place of Cherevko's splashdown and plucked him from the water. Thanks to the combined actions of the fighter aviation and the anti-aircraft gunners, the enemy's aircraft were unable to paralyze the sea lines of communication with Odessa.

After the city became besieged on land, the evacuation of the industrial enterprises from August 1941 was conducted only by sea. Up to 5,000 freight cars loaded with cargo, grain and factory equipment had accumulated at the port. Everything possible was done to send them out by sea.

The unfinished diesel-electric ships *Prut* and *Proletariat* with a capacity of 10,000 metric tons each, which were standing in the shipyard, were brought to the Platonovsky jetty. There they were loaded to capacity and then towed away to Mariupol'. A floating dock was employed to evacuate the steam engines. On 10 August Icebreaker No. 5, the tugboat *Typhoon* and the tow ship *Simeiz* began to tow the floating dock that was loaded with the steam engines. The port of Nikolaev was the floating dock's destination. The gunboat *Krasnaia Armeniia* and two patrol boats of a Border Guards battalion were escorting the floating dock. Fighter aircraft were covering the ships and floating dock from the air.

The captain of the tugboat *Typhoon* I.K. Omel'ianov made the following entry in the logbook: "… in the morning enemy aircraft appeared and began to drop high-explosive bombs athwart Sychavka to Ochavka itself. There were 11 air raids before 1900 and 78 bombs were dropped."[19] Six enemy bombers alone took part in the first attack, but not a single one of them managed to break through to the convoy. One of the enemy bombers was shot down by the concerted fire of the ships and plummeted into the sea. Our fighters intercepted a second attempt by enemy bombers to attack the ships. Junior Lieutenant V. Grek courageously dove upon one of the hostile aircraft. The Junkers began smoking from his accurate fire and jettisoned its bombs into the sea far from the targets. While Grek was engaged with the dive bomber, a different Stuka winged over and began to dive on the floating dock. Any delay was out of the question, and Grek quickly maneuvered to ram it. At the cost of his own life, V.F. Grek prevented the fascist pilot from dropping his deadly load.

The city's residents had to suffer significant deprivations because of the enemy siege. Local authorities sought to ease their situation. A meticulous account of all food supplies was made, and a careful storage and economical expenditure of them was arranged. A great aid to the city's defenders was the delivery of 5,000 metric tons of flour, 2,000 metric tons of groats, 1,200 metric tons of meat and 800 metric tons of tinned foods from the rear. Simultaneously, agricultural produce that was arriving from suburban collective farms and State farms was added to the food reserves. The farmworkers gathered the harvest under enemy shells and bullets, and at night trucks hauled bread, vegetables and fruit into the city. The implemented system of food rationing and the search for various ways to replenish the food reserves made it possible to deliver bread, fats, sugar and other food items to the population without interruption throughout the entire period of defense, albeit in limited amounts.

Especially important was keeping the city supplied with water. After the enemy seized the water pump station in Beliaevka, Odessa lost its main source of water. The small reserves of water that were left in the city couldn't meet the needs of the population and industry for very long. In addition, a lot of the water went to put out the fires that arose as a result of the enemy artillery barrages and bombardments. Having failed to break Odessa's defenders by force of arms, the aggressors began to threaten them with death resulting from dehydration and epidemics. They were dropping provocative leaflets over the city, proposing the cessation of resistance, in return for which the people would supposedly be given water. However, here the enemy too miscalculated. At the behest of the city council, a group of hydrologists determined places where it was possible to dig new wells. More than 1,200 of the city's residents went to work to dig them. Simultaneously, old, abandoned wells were repaired. Over several days through the efforts of the population and army engineers, 6 boreholes were drilled in the city and 58 common and artesian wells were dug or repaired, which met the minimal needs of the population for fresh water.

In order to put out fires in the city, 15 water storage basins were built with a capacity of 200 cubic meters of water each; factories constructed 40 cistern tanks in places of production; and

---

19   Ibid., p. 60.

1,600 wooden barrels with a capacity of 40 draw buckets and 82 metal receptacles were established in apartment complexes. All the containers were filled with water, the use of which was permitted only for putting out fires. The authorities delivered sea water to fill these containers, which could only be used to put out fires.

In order to provide a regular supply of potable water to the people and to prevent any abuses, on 10 September 1941 the city council decided to introduce a ration system for water. The daily ration was set within the limits of 4 to 5 liters per person. This amount of water was inadequate, but the population steadfastly endured the difficulties of the city's state of siege.[20] Agitation and explanatory work among the city's residents to strengthen their morale played a large role in the conditions of the siege and the enemy's propaganda. Its main message was the just, liberating nature of the war with the aggressor, and the nurturing of a feeling of hatred toward the invaders. More than 1,800 agitators worked to sustain morale and martial spirits in the city. The militant call of the agitators and propagandists resounded in factories and institutions, in defensive works and militia units, residential buildings and shelters: "Everything for the front, everything for victory over the foe, everything for the defense of our native city." The oblast newspapers *Bol'shevistskoe znamia*, *Chernomorska kommuna* and *Molodaia gvardiia* played an important role in this work. The newspapers told about the heroism of the troops that were defending Odessa, filled the workers' hearts with confidence in victory over the fascist aggressors, and called upon the people to strengthen the city's defenses, increase vigilance and expose enemy agents. Visual propaganda was broadly utilized: Posters showing the appeals of the country's leadership and local authorities were pasted up on public squares and gathering places, at the entrances of buildings, and in factories and workshops, as were slogans and bulletins. They called upon the people to give a stern rebuff to the fascist invaders. During the time of the siege, 68 titled addresses to the people, and leaflets, placards and posters with a total printing of 34 million copies were published and circulated among the civilian population and combat units. It was particularly interesting for the defenders of Odessa to read the satirical post cards and letters to Hitler and Antonescu, composed in the style of the Ukrainian Zaporozhian Cossacks' famous reply to the Turkish Sultan. The letter to Hitler stressed the self-identification of Odessa's defenders as followers of the glorious Ukrainian tradition of defenders of their native soil:

> We, the grandchildren and great-grandchildren of the glorious and militant Zaporozhian Cossacks of Ukrainian land, which is now part of the Soviet Union, decided to write you this letter, damned Catheaux, just as our ancestors and grandfathers wrote to all who were causing Ukraine big harm. You, you perfidious Judah and snake, attacked our country and want to plunder our factories and plants; land, forests and water, and introduce here barons and capitalists like you, you greatest of all barons and capitalists. This will never happen. We know how to stand up for ourselves. The sword of Daniel Galitsky and the sabre of the Cossack Bogdan Khmel'nitsky struck you down, you nasty piece of work; in 1918 we drove the Kaiser's soldiers out of Ukraine like dogs. We've always beat the Knight-dogs, so let us now smash the Hitlerites and followers of Goebbels.
>
> To assure you that this letter was written by Ukrainian Zaporozhian Cossacks, brave and courageous warriors, we've attached a copy of I. Repin's painting [Repin's famous painting entitled "Reply of the Zaporozhian Cossacks to the Turkish Sultan"].[21]

20   V.N. Stanko et al., *Istoriia Odesi*, p. 383.
21   *Ukrainska RSR u Velikii Vitchiznianii viini Rad'ianskogo Soiuzu 1941-1945 u 3 t.* [*Ukrainain RSR in the Great Patriotic War of the Soviet Union 1941-1945 in 3 volumes*] (Kiev: Politvidav Ukraini, 1967), Vol. 1, p. 237.

The letter to Antonescu ended with the eloquent conclusion, below which thousands of Odessa citizens and defenders of the city signed their names: "Our Odessa will never see you, dog." This letter was read with delight, passed from hand to hand, and was cited in transit and at the front. They understood the inner spirit of the people, who decided to resist and to prevent the foe from entering their native city.

The fact that despite the enemy's siege, the incessant bombing raids and artillery barrages, the city's communal economy continued to work practically without interruption is worthy of astonishment. The city's electrical station was continuing to supply the military facilities, industrial enterprises and the population's daily needs. The city's trolley system didn't stop operating for a single day: Odessa's streetcars continued to roll to the front as well, bringing military cargo, mail and other items, and returning with the wounded. The workers of the power plant's workshops and of the streetcar depot also made parts for mortars, anti-tank obstacles, maintained watch of the skies in the city's anti-air defense teams, and taught their young replacements their craft. Odessa's telephone operators were working with striking accuracy and harmony. Maintaining communications with telephone stations that were proximate to the front, they kept the population timely informed about the approach of enemy aircraft, provided for uninterrupted telephone connections in the city and among the troops, and facilitated the correspondence of the city's residents with the front and the rest of Russia. Throughout the course of almost the entire siege, Odessa's telegraph was exchanging telegrams with all of the country's cities. The sole distinction from peace time was the inscription above the small window of the receiving telegraph operator: "A delivery time is not guaranteed." Daily, the doors of shops, dining halls and cafes were open to serve the people until 2000. Laundries, bath houses and hair salons continued to operate without interruption just as they did before the war. Performing troupes, comprised of actors, actresses and musicians of Odessa's theaters, actively operated at the front and in the city.[22] The city's movie theatres were restored to operation and showed such films as *Chapaev, Frontovye podrugi* [translated into English as *Girl from Leningrad*], *Fed'ka, Traktoristy* [*Tractor drivers*], *Novyi gorizont* [*New horizon*], *Chetvertyi periskop* [*Fourth periscope*], *Moriaki* [*Sailors*] and others.[23]

The courage and tenacity of the city's defenders prompted the feeling of deep respect and admiration of the entire country and all the people of free will around the world. Odessa was continuously connected with Moscow by radio. Radio exchanges regularly took place with Kiev, Khar'kov, Sevastopol and Leningrad. Promptly at 1700, the broadcaster of Moscow Radio would announce: "Attention! Odessa is speaking!" and the entire world would hear the voices of Odessa citizens and the city's defenders, who were now located in the deep rear, but who hadn't laid down their weapon and hadn't submitted to the foe. At 1730 the studio of a frontline wireless radio station would begin transmissions from the basement accommodations at the address 49 Manezhnaia Street.[24]

The city's radio broadcast would enter the country's radio waves every three days. In one of the transmissions, it stated, "Odessa's defenders swear to you, *Bat'kivshina* [Ukraine Fatherland], to destroy the pernicious fascist thieves; to deal with the bloody enemy by fire and sword; and to avenge the blood spilled and the tears of the widows, old men and children." More than once, the troops of the defensive area and the workers of Odessa sent congratulations and words of brotherly solidarity to the defenders of Leningrad and Ukraine's capital, Kiev.[25] In return, the defenders of Odessa themselves heard congratulations and words of praise for their tenacity from the workers of Moscow, Kiev,

22 *Bol'shevistkskoe znamia*, 3 September 1941; *Odesskaia oblast' v Velikoi Otechestvennoi voine 1941-1945*, pp. 80-83; A. Nedzvedskii, *Odesskaia tetrad'* [*Odessa notebook*] (Odessa: Druk, 2001), p. 36.

23 *Znamia kommunizma*, 25 August 1971.

24 "V boiiakh za rodnuiu Odessu" ["In the fighting for native Odessa"], Issue 4 (Odessa, 1941), pp. 34-35.

25 *Bol'shevistkoe znam'ia*, 14 September 1941.

Leningrad and other cities and towns of the Soviet Union.[26] Over the period of Odessa's defense, there were 27 cross-talks between Odessa and other cities of the country. Accordingly, its defenders and civilian population were constantly sensing the entire country's support.

The role of the press was also significant. During that time, regional publications played the main role, since the central newspapers reached the city by sea via Sevastopol only with great delay. Oblast newspapers *Bol'shevistkoe znam'ia* and *Chernomorska kommuna* were published daily in 70,000 copies and inspired the people with confidence in eventual victory over the foe, called upon them to be vigilant, and informed them about the life of the city. The oblast newspapers also reprinted articles of the central newspapers with the aim of keeping Odessans more informed about them. From them, the city's citizens learned that Odessa's stubborn defense was resonating around the world. On 6 September 1941, for example, a communication from workers of the Don region to the defenders of Odessa was published. The people of Rostov wrote, "We have a request to convey our admiration of their struggle to the soldiers of the Red Army and the People's Militia, the glorious Black Sea sailors, and the heroic land and sea falcons [pilots], and our confidence in victory over the foe." On 11 September, the *Pravda* newspaper published the following warm, touching words in a lead article:

> Millions of people daily wake up with thoughts of Leningrad, Kiev and Odessa. We are anxious about them; we live with them and with their feelings, thoughts and insurmountable confidence in victory. They know that the entire country stands behind them. They are strong with the entire nation's support.

In this same edition, words of congratulations to the citizens of Odessa from the residents of Bristol, England were published. On 16 September 1941, Odessa's oblast newspapers published congratulations to Odessans from England, which contained the prophetic words: "A glorious and important page is being written and will be written into the book of Odessa's victory."[27]

This work bore its fruit. Despite the fact that the enemy had massed large forces against the defenders of Odessa, the Commander-in-Chief of the Odessa Defense District Vice Admiral G.V. Zhukov recalled, "It would be incorrect to say that the adversary was superior to us. Yes, he had a lot more manpower and equipment. However, the spirit of Odessa's defenders was incomparably higher. We had received an order – to defend our native city. Everyone was full of firm resolve to carry out their duty to the end."[28]

The printed word also gave a lot of attention to morale building in the army as well. The army newspaper *Za rodinu*, the navy's newspaper *Krasnyi chernomorets*, divisional newspapers and the collections of essays *V boiakh za rodnuyu Odessu* [*In combat for native Odessa*], *Vrag u sebya* [*Foe at the doorstep*] and *Litso dvunogikh zverei* [*Face of two-legged beasts*] through numerous examples of combat life taught the soldiers to hate the foe and to fearlessly crush him at every turn.

Of particular significance in the Odessa Defense District was the strengthening of close, friendly ties between the civilian population and the soldiers and commanders of the Red Army. More than 2,000,000 rubles worth of items for the troops were collected and sent to the front. Each gift package contained warm letters and words of congratulations as well. Delegations from among the number of the top workers and community representatives would drive out to the forward positions in order to distribute the packages to the soldiers and commanders. In the trenches, they

---

26 *Geroicheskaia Odessa: Sbornik statei i materialov* [*Heroic Odessa: Collection of articles and materials*] (Odessa, 1945), p. 38.

27 *Pravda*, 11 September 1941; *Chernozemnaia kommuna*, 24 September 1941.

28 A. Shternshtein, *Morskie vorota Ukrainy* [*Sea gates of Ukraine*] (Odessa: Odesskoe oblastnoe izdatel'stvo, 1958), pp. 100-101.

would talk about how the people of Odessa were supporting the front with intense work, sparing no strength. This inspired the city's defenders to new feats of arms. When a particularly difficult situation arose at the front in the latter half of August and the beginning of September 1941, Odessa's workers three times made patriotic appeals to the troops. One of their messages stated:

> We are proud of your valor and heroism. We bow our heads before your fearlessness. Your boundless bravery and selfless dedication to the Motherland inspires our confidence that the foe will not pass, that the enemy will be defeated. … Comrade soldiers, commanders and political workers! Your fathers, mothers, wives, sisters and children appeal to you. Continue to beat the fascist robbers just like you are doing now. Throw back the bloody foe with fire and sword. Take vengeance against him for the spilled blood and for the tears of the widows and children. Blood for blood and death for death! Beat the fascists pitilessly, like stray dogs.
> Let the hordes of the Romanian-German fascists find an inglorious death on the broad steppes of the Black Sea coast. A dog's death for dogs! So let all of our forces become united and with a powerful blow we'll crush the villainous foes. We are with you, comrades, and whatever the trials that befall our city, we will struggle to the end, until complete victory over fascism.[29]

Such appeals were fervently discussed in all the units of the defensive area for the next several days. Everywhere a common answer was given to the city's residents: "We promise you, dear comrades, to fight to the last drop of blood, and to smite the foe unerringly."[30] Practical combat actions went on underneath these words.

The sailors of the Black Sea Fleet fought at Odessa in close combat comradeship and cooperation with the ground troops; already in those days, their exploits were already becoming a legend. Colonel Ia.I. Osipov's naval infantrymen launched counterattacks 5-6 times a day. Over three days of fighting in the beginning of September, the soldiers of this regiment destroyed up to two regiments of enemy troops, captured a mounted squadron together with its commander, and seized 6 operational tanks, 18 field guns, 17 machine guns, and several thousand shells and grenades. In a different sector, in the area of Vygoda Station, 300 sailors led by Major A.S. Potapov broke into the enemy's positions and spent the next several days rampaging through the enemy's rear areas, before returning to friendly lines. Other detachments of volunteer sailors fought just as valiantly. Up to 8,000 of the naval infantrymen served at the front at Odessa. The heroism of the naval infantry was reflected in a poem by the writer K.M. Simonov, who visited besieged Odessa as a war correspondent of the *Krasnaia Zvezda* newspaper:

> We marched from the Black Sea in sailors' jackets,
> Like a black wall.
> After the battle the fascists called us "the Black Cloud" …
> We go into bloody battle upright, exposing our breasts,
> Lighting the way forward with our Black Sea glory.[31]

Alongside the others, militia men fought courageously. A squad of People's Militia comprised of former workers of the city's factories and Odessa's port fought in the area of the village of Dal'nik. The tiny handful of brave men repelled 16 enemy attacks and held their occupied line for 5 days.

---

29 *Odessa v Velikoi Otechestvennoi voine Sovetskogo Soiuza: Sbornik dokumentov i materialov* (Odessa, 1947), Vol. 1, pp. 124-125.
30 *Bol'shevistskoe znamia*, 7 September 1941.
31 *Chernomorska kommuna*, 25 September 1941.

Toward the end of the fifth day, of the 10 men in the squad, only two remained alive: L. Rudnev and the female volunteer N. Voskoboinik. A tank and a group of enemy soldiers were advancing toward them. Rudnev ordered the young woman: "Crawl back to our own guys; tell them there, in Odessa, that we fought honorably to the last breath.[32] He then went to meet the tank with a bundle of anti-tank grenades.

Junior Sergeant A.A. Nechipurenko, a deputy of the Odessa Oblast Soviet, demonstrated ingenuity and bravery in the struggle with the foe. Together with other brave men, more than once he made his way behind enemy lines with a radio, and from there he would adjust the fire of Soviet artillery batteries. Once, on a solitary patrol, A.A. Nechipurenko came upon an enemy anti-tank battery. Accurately tossing grenades, he killed several enemy soldiers and caused the rest to flee. The battery was left unmanned. The brave warrior harnessed horses to one of the anti-tank guns and several caissons, and raced back to his unit. The gun was fully operational, and the caissons contained 70 shells and 200 armor-piercing and rifle cartridges. For this exploit, A. Nechipurenko was deemed worthy of a high honor – the Order of Lenin.

Artillerymen played a large role in Odessa's defense. The city's defenders didn't have a lot of guns and mortars – from 476 to 589 tubes at various times. However, with their accurate, concentrated fire the artillerymen and mortar crews inflicted enormous losses on the enemy, more than once disrupting his offensive operations. The 265th Regiment of corps artillery under the leadership of Major M.V. Bogdanov, a deputy of the Ukraine Soviet Socialist Republic's Supreme Soviet, enjoyed deserved fame. The mobile batteries of this regiment kept showing up wherever the defenders were having more difficulty repelling the foe's attacks. Just the mention of Bogdanov's name alone evoked horror among the fascists. To his combat score, Bogdanov had several regiments of enemy infantry that were scattered by accurate artillery fire; 10 destroyed batteries; more than 40 destroyed tanks; and a lot of other combat equipment.[33]

A.I. Kuznetsov's 21st Coastal Artillery Battery was engaged in the area of the most stubborn fighting, on the defense's right flank; according to plan, it was covering the entrance to Odessa from the sea. However, at the end of August, when the enemy was threatening to breakthrough to the port, the 21st Coastal Artillery Battery found itself on the forward edge of defense. Here is how the chief of staff of Odessa's Naval Base Captain 1st Rank K.I. Derevianko describes those days

> It was in the last days of August. Having started to repel an enemy onslaught at long range, the battery was driving back attacks, shooting up the foe at point-blank range whenever the enemy closed on the positions. Several times matters reached the point of hand-to-hand combat. L.I. Kuznetsov was always located at the front. The situation was such that the battery telephone operator more than once interrupted calls in order to engage in hand-to-hand combat with the enemy.[34]

The artillery of 27 ships of the Black Sea Fleet, which had 130 guns between 76-mm and 180-mm caliber, were widely supporting the combat actions on the ground. The naval ships were conducting combat operations in difficult conditions. The *Luftwaffe* reigned supreme in the skies and was systematically launching attacks on the ships. They were also dropping mines of enormous explosive power on the naval lines of communication. Enemy artillery was firing at the ships from the coastline. Nevertheless, with accurate fire the ships' guns were suppressing the fire of enemy artillery and mortar batteries and smashing aggregations of enemy troops and equipment.

---

32   Borisov, *Odessa: Gorod-geroi*, p. 35.
33   "V boiiakh za rodnuiu Odessu", Issue 4, pp. 34-35.
34   Kuznetsov, *Na flotakh boevaia trevoga*, p. 124.

The ships' crews were demonstrating exceptional courage and resourcefulness, carrying out their assigned tasks at any cost. Over the period of Odessa's defense, the Black Sea Fleet's ships poured approximately 15,000 shells onto enemy positions. The cruisers *Krasnyi Kavkaz* (commander – Captain, 2nd Rank A.M. Gushchin), *Krasnaia Ukraina* (commander – Captain M.E. Basistyi) and *Krasnyi Krym* (commander – Captain A.I. Zubkov); frigate *Tashkent* (commander – Captain, 3rd Rank V.M. Eroshenko; destroyers *Besposchadnyi* [*Merciless*] (commander – Lieutenant Captain G.P. Negoda, *Boikii* [*Sprightly*] (commander – Lieutenant Captain G.F. Godlevsky), *Bezuprechnyi* [*Irreproachable*] (commander – Lieutenant Captain P.M. Buriak), *Frunze* (commander – Lieutenant Captain P.A. Bobrovnikov) and others especially distinguished themselves in inflicting attacks against the enemy. Their commanders were often receiving messages from the shore: "You're firing on-target, sailors, give them some more" or "The target has been blanketed, the enemy is retreating … Give all the men our frontline thanks."[35]

The few aircraft of the defensive area were not only providing cover to the city from the air, but were also launching strikes against the enemy's frontline forces. In addition to the small quantity of Il-2 ground attack aircraft, in the course of the fighting for Odessa fighters, equipped with rockets and bombs, were widely used in a ground attack role. On 26 August pilots of the 8th Fighter Aviation Regiment V. Mironchuk, A. Zhalkovsky, G. Levchenko and I. Berishlivi, led by deputy squadron commander Captain V.N. Val'tsefer, successfully conducted an attack against enemy forces in the Vakarzhany area.

On the next day early in the morning, enemy aircraft suddenly appeared above Odessa from behind some clouds. Junior Lieutenants I. Bereshlivi and V. Mironchuk instantly took off to intercept them. They sliced through the formation of enemy aircraft, and with accurate fire Bereshlivi shot down an aircraft bearing a swastika. The flight of Senior Lieutenant I. Skachkov that was hurrying to their assistance destroyed two more fascist aircraft. The remaining enemy aircraft aborted their mission and refused combat.

Several pilots of the Coastal Army and the Black Sea Fleet proved themselves to be genuine aces during the fighting for Odessa. The small collective of fighter pilots of the Coastal Army's 69th Fighter Aviation Regiment engaged in combat 7-10 times a day with large groups of enemy aircraft, which were conducting raids against the city and ground positions. Aerial reconnaissance provided Odessa Defense District's Military Council with information on the location and concentration of enemy forces and the directions of their advance. At a command order, fighter pilots would take off to launch ground attacks against enemy positions, thereby easing the situation of our ground units. Many of them failed to return from combat missions. More than once it happened when after a dogfight only 5-6 aircraft fit for flying remained in the aviation regiment; the rest had serious damage. But by the morning of the following day, thanks to the selfless work of the repair teams up to 20 aircraft would be in service, and the commander would report on the regiment's readiness to carry out new missions. In addition to the paucity of aircraft, their obsolescence, and the wear and tear on the machines, there were other particular difficulties in the combat activity of the 69th Fighter Aviation Regiment. At the end of August, enemy artillery began to shell the airfield from which the aviation regiment was staging. It was now no longer possible to base aircraft on it. The workers of Odessa arrived to help the pilots. Under the direction of military engineers, they worked at nights to build a new airfield within the city's limits, between the 6th and 7th Stations of the Bol'shoi Fontan line. In the course of a week, a runway was laid down in brick, revetments with rail track overheads were built, and the new airbase became serviceable. The Odessa Defense District's air force was based on it until the end of Odessa's defense. It required extreme skill on the part of the pilots to take off and make landings without brushing the roofs of buildings with their undercarriage or wings.

---

35 Penzin, *Chernomorskoi flot*, p. 76-77.

It was under just these conditions that the pilots of the fighter regiment flew 3,781 individual combat sorties and engaged in 576 aerial combats. In these dogfights many fighter pilots shot down 6-8 enemy aircraft. But the most important thing that the pilots of the 69th Fighter Aviation Regiment accomplished was to prevent accurate bombing on the port and city. Even the fascist pilots after the war acknowledged that not even once were they able to perform targeted bombing.

To achieve this, the regiment commander L.L. Shestakov, lacking sufficient force to neutralize the enemy aircraft, imposed his own rules of combat on them above Odessa. In order to prevent the fascist bombers from descending to lower attitudes to permit targeted bombing, he arranged his fighters in small groups at various altitudes, thereby making a so-called "stack". As a result, not a single ship – target No. 1 for the enemy aircraft – was ever sunk in Odessa's port because of any direct hits, although many of them had tens or even hundreds of holes caused by nearby exploding bombs. In addition, the city's buildings primarily remained intact and functioning, together with thousands of lives of Odessans. Convincing evidence of this still exists today; when passing through the city's Old Quarter, you can see preserved tablets on buildings testifying to their 100 to 150 years of age.

The Motherland highly evaluated the pilots' achievement. For the defense of Odessa, regiment commander L.L. Shestakov and squadron commanders and pilots M.E. Astashkin, A.A. Elokhin, I.G. Korolev, S.A. Kunitse, A.A. Malanov, Iu.B. Rykachev, V.T. Topol'sky, V.A. Serogod'sky, M.I. Shilov and A.T. Cherevatenko were all awarded the title Hero of the Soviet Union.

The aircraft of the Black Sea Fleet also supported the troops of the defensive area despite its distance from their bases on Crimean airfields. They were covering the naval lines of communication and the anchorages of the ships from the air; launching bombing attacks against the lines of communication and oil fields in Romania; and striking aggregations of enemy troops and equipment. Naval pilots A.K. Kondrashin, N.A. Tokarev and A.P. Tsurtsumiia gained fame in the aerial combats over Odessa and became Heroes of the Soviet Union. The Black Sea Fleet's air force flew 1,647 individual aircraft sorties to the Odessa area.

On 28 August striving to reach the northern shore of the Gulf of Odessa, in order to cut off the single sea route connecting the city with the rest of the world, the enemy broke through to the Luzanovki area. Coastal artillery, the guns of almost of the available ships in the Odessa area, as well as ground attack and fighter aircraft were employed to eliminate the breakthrough.

Between 29 and 31 August 1941, the frigate *Tashkent*, the cruiser *Chervona Ukraina*, five destroyers and two gunboats took part in providing artillery support to the ground troops.[36] On 31 August 12 combat aircraft of the 8th Fighter Aviation Regiment led by Captain F.I. Demchenko struck a lengthy enemy motorized column on the Ivanovka – Aleksandrovka road and destroyed it. In the dogfight that ensued, Captain Demchenko and his deputy Captain V.N. Val'tsefer each shot down an enemy aircraft, while Junior Lieutenant I.S. Bereshvili at a critical moment employed the weapon of the brave – a ramming attack. He destroyed an enemy aircraft, but was himself killed in the combat.[37]

By the end of 31 August, the troops of the East Sector managed to liquidate the breakthrough and to hurl the enemy back from the Luzanovki area. They dug in on the Fontanka – Il'ichevka State Farm – southern outskirts of Gil'dendorf (present-day Krasnoselka) line.

At the beginning of September organizational changes were implemented by the Odessa Defense District's Military Council. On the basis of the troops of the East Sector, a rifle division (the 421st Rifle Division) was formed, having initially received the designation "Odessa". The 1st Naval Infantry Regiment and the 26th Border Regiment were included on its unit roster as the 1st

36   N.E. Basistyi, *More i bereg* [*Sea and coast*] (Moscow, 1970), p. 54.
37   TsVMA MO RF, F. 1080, Op. 3, D. 6, l. 6.

and 2nd Rifle Regiments, and temporarily the 421st Rifle Division also controlled the 54th Rifle Regiment from the 25th Rifle Division. Of the artillery units, the 134th Howitzer Regiment was added to the division. Colonel G.M. Kochenov was appointed as the division commander.[38] This change permitted more streamlined control over the sector's troops.

In the bitter fighting, the combat skills of the defenders of Odessa were growing. The enemy suffered heavy losses in personnel and combat equipment. In the first half of September, only 25-30% of the men were left in many of the Romanian regiments, battalions and companies of the first echelon. The Romanian command was hastily replenishing the enormous losses. By the beginning of September, it had concentrated almost half of the entire Romanian Army at Odessa – 18 divisions, of which 15 were in the first echelon. On the front of the South Sector opposite the played-out 25th Rifle and 1st (later the 2nd) Cavalry Divisions, seven Romanian divisions and five battalions of German troops were attacking.

By the beginning of September, the men of the Coastal Army were defending on the following line: Point 47.4 (1 km west of Fontanka – Point 53.6 – Agrokombinat – Il'ichevka – Point 66.5 – Point 66.3 – Protopopovka – Point 85.6 – Vakarzhany – Point 76.3 – Point 67.5 – Point 79.4 – Krasnaia Iukhimova – Kalagleia – Karolino-Bugaz.[39] As a result of savage fighting, the fascists had been able once again to shove back the forces of the East, West and especially the South Sector. In the South Sector, on 31 August the enemy had seized Liliental' and had begun to attack the boundary between the South and West Sectors in the direction of Dal'nitskii and Dal'nik.

By this time the commander of the 25th "Chapaev" Rifle Division Major General I.E. Petrov had set up his observation post on a nameless rise northeast of Dal'nik. The observation post of the 411th Battery was located in the same place. On the morning of 2 September columns of attacking enemy troops appeared from multiple directions. At General Petrov's order, the 411th Battery with fire from three 180-mm howitzers smashed the columns of attacking troops.

On the night of 2-3 September, for the first time the enemy launched a massive night attack, delivering the main attack in the center, along the railroad and south of it. The 95th Rifle Division put up stubborn resistance. Allowing the Romanians to close within a range of 100 meters, the Red Army troops shot them up at pointblank range and repeatedly went over to counterattacks with fixed bayonets. With repeated attacks and by committing reserves, the enemy managed to push back our units in certain places by up to 1 to 1.5 kilometers, but was unable to breach the front. On the following days the enemy, having assembled superior forces in the Krasnyi Pereselenets, Liliental' area attempted to break through the defense in the direction of the Bulgarian hamlets, thereby creating a direct threat of breaking into the city. The Odessa Defense District ordered a counterattack from both flanks in order to eliminate the enemy penetration. However, this counterattack had no success.[40]

Between 5 and 9 September 1941, mass meetings and assemblies of workers with representatives of the army and fleet took place in Odessa, which were dedicated to the first month of the city's defense. It was by 5 September that the construction of its main line of resistance was fully completed. It extended along a front of more than 60 kilometers and ran at a distance of 14-15 kilometers from the city. The following data speak to the scale of the conducted work on the nearest approaches to Odessa: over just one week of intensive work, 1,500 trenches of various profiles were dug; more than 20 kilometers of posts and barbed wire were installed; more than 40,000 anti-tank and anti-personnel mines were laid; and 32 battalion areas of defenses were created. The construction of blocking obstacles on rear lines was completed along 35 kilometers of the front and at a

---

38   TsVMA MO RF, F. 204, Spr. 9105, l. 9.
39   Borisov, "Oborona Odessy (avgust – oktiabr' 1941), p. 58.
40   Ibid., p. 59.

distance of 8-10 kilometers from the city following the line: Kryzhanovka – hamlets between the Kulianitsky and Khadzhibeevsky estuaries – Usatovo – Sukhoi Liman – Liustdorf. In the event of the city's evacuation, a covering line was created on the line: Kryzhanovka – Krivaia Balka – Chubaevka – Bol'shoi Fontan. On this line, 550 emplaced flamethrowers were set up, which enabled the creation of a ring of fire around Odessa that extended for almost 55 kilometers. More than 100,000 Odessans in a maximally short time completed field works, which involved the movement of approximately 300,000 cubic meters of earth, while the overall length of the main and intermediary lines of defense equaled 250 kilometers.

Meanwhile, in the event of an enemy breakthrough, the construction of street barricades went on in the city. A total of 243 barricades were built, which in three concentric belts butted up against the sea. Basements of buildings at city crossroads were equipped as firing points. The first belt of barricades ran through the city's outskirts; the second – the city's center, and the third protected only the port. Each barricade was calculated as strong enough to take a direct hit from a 150-mm shell: they were built out of bags of sand and dirt (the burlap factory produced 300,000 such bags), and they were girded by the wreckage of trolley and railroad cars. All of this was covered by cobble and stones. Each barricade had artillery, machine-gun and rifle embrasures. Only narrow passages were left un-barricaded for the movement of transport and pedestrians, but on the city's outskirts even they were blocked by anti-tank obstacles.

Having failed to break the resistance of the troops defending the city, the aggressor in impotent fury unleashed a storm of air raids and artillery barrages on the city. Over the two days of 6 and 7 September alone, 59 buildings were destroyed, 92 people were killed and 130 wounded; the public water supply and drainage systems were damaged; in five places the tram tracks were blown up; and fires broke out – material valuables and priceless cultural monuments perished in the flames. However, the city courageously fought with the consequences of the barbarous attacks. All of the links of the local anti-air defense service were working harmoniously and promptly; up to 3,500 men and women were enrolled in the service. Self-defense groups that had been created in practically every enterprise and house management office contributed to their activity.

The activity of the city's fire-fighting service, which enlisted approximately 800 men, was particularly smooth and responsive. They were organized into 14 teams. Odessa's fire chief F.V. Vinogradov headed the service. However, without the active assistance of Odessans, the work of the service wouldn't have been as effective; after all, often the fires enveloped several city blocks simultaneously, and at night the glow from them was visible from many kilometers outside the city. Fire-fighting teams were also present in every major factory. The following figures testify to the scale of their activity and significance. Over the entire period of the city's defense, Odessa experienced more than 350 air raids, from which more than 3,000 civilians became casualties. Four hundred and forty buildings were either partially or completely destroyed. Among them were businesses, schools and medical facilities, unique monuments of culture and architecture, multi-family dwellings and so forth. Without the selfless participation of 11,000 members of the groups of self-defense (the overwhelming majority of which were women), the consequences of the air raids and artillery barrages would have been significantly more tragic.

The experience of the initial air raids demonstrated that the ordinary cellars of many buildings were unsuitable for protecting the population: people were dying under the ruins of collapsed buildings. The narrow anti-air slit trenches proved to be a more reliable shelter. They were dug throughout the entire city: in squares, in parks, at trolley stops, in courtyards and on factory grounds. Altogether, there 4,294 such trenches with an overall length of 90,000 meters. They saved the lives of hundreds and thousands of people.[41]

---

41   *73 geroicheskikh dnei: khronika oboroni Odessy v 1941*, p. 39.

Medical workers made an enormous contribution to the cause of Odessa's defense. All of them, from professors down to nurses were living a barrack-like existence and working under hard conditions. Doctors and sanitary activists worked in the medical-sanitation service of the city's anti-air defense system. They staffed approximately 1,500 medical posts. Risking their own lives during air raids and artillery barrages, they gave first aid to the wounded and rescued people from burning buildings and collapsed cellars.

The most highly-qualified portion of the city's medical personnel worked in the hospitals, into which 800 to 1,200 wounded soldiers were admitted each and every day. For 20 hours without relief and with only short breaks, professors and docents of Odessa's Medical Institute and the Institute for the Advancement of Doctors labored over the operating tables. A portion of the hospitals also served the urban population. All of the city's polyclinics received the sick and ill. Thanks to the selfless work of Odessa's doctors, over the entire time of the city's siege and the strictly rationed water, there was not a single epidemic outbreak.

The families of the dead and sufferers from the bombings sensed the concern on the part of the city's leaders. They were given monetary assistance in the amount of up to 100 rubles and free general merchandise worth between 200 and 500 rubles. The families of frontline soldiers were surrounded with constant attention – twice a month they regularly received monetary assistance. In August they each received a supplemental 70 rubles of a lump-sum allowance. The executive committees of all levels created departments of government support for families of military servicemen. Trade union organizations of the January Uprising and October Revolution factories and of other enterprises distributed aid out of their own funds to the families of frontline soldiers. Female sanitary volunteers combined work in the factories, where they replaced mobilized male workers, with care for the badly-wounded soldiers. School-age children also visited the wounded; they read them letters from their families and performed amateur concerts.

The foe tried at any price to break the resistance of the Odessans, including by means of demoralizing them. In order to sow panic in the city, provocative rumors circulated and saboteurs infiltrated the city. However, the population remained vigilant and rendered support to the destroyer battalions, and thus the fascist agents were unable to create major disturbances in Odessa.

The encirclement of Odessa became increasingly tighter, but the defenders were standing to their deaths, suffering significant losses. In separate regiments the number of combat-capable Red Army men didn't exceed 170-300 men. Local human reserves had essentially become exhausted. Between 5 and 12 September the *Stavka* of the Supreme High Command sent 15 march battalions with a total strength of 15,198 men to Odessa. This was sufficient only to replace the recent losses, but not to restore the regiments to their original strength.

5

Tanks in the battle for Odessa

During the Second World War, tanks became the main shock force in ground battles. In the defense of Odessa, the employment of tanks had its own unique features, worthy of a closer examination in this section of the book.

The use of tank units and formations for inflicting an effective strike against the enemy from the very beginning required from commanders significant operational and tactical skill, a high degree of organization of the cooperation among the different types of armed forces in their application, as well as qualified, experienced personnel who supported their combat deployment and provided service and repair. The expertise and high morale of the tank crews, the combat cohesion of the elements and units, as well as the commander's flexibility of thought and experience in assessing a rapidly-changing situation made this intimidating type of weapon even more effective. The process of the development of production of tanks and their combat employment had specific characteristics in the armies of different countries.

During the First World War, in 1915 on the Western Front the opposing armies ultimately dug into the ground. The multitude of trenches, communication trenches and the labyrinth of barbed wire obstacles strengthened the positions to the extent that despite powerful artillery, the Allies were unable to create a decisive, strategic breakthrough of the front. Active search for new means of breaking through a fortified defensive front began. Most suitable for this purpose were armored machines with caterpillar tracks, capable of pushing the artillery and machine-gun fire into the depth of the enemy's defense – into the area of the dispositions of the enemy's artillery batteries. Initially Great Britain began work on this project under the conditions of strict secrecy. With the aim of misleading the enemy, the British circulated a rumor that the production of mobile cisterns, which in English are called "tanks", was underway at an order from the government of Imperial Russia. In February 1916, the first tank model in the general shape of a rhombus demonstrated good results in tests, and their serial production began. On 15 September 1916, 49 British tanks took part in the Battle of the Somme. Although this came as a complete surprise to the Germans, the British were unable to achieve a complete victory. The loss of tanks in this battle was significant – 31 of the machines were knocked out: 17 of them were damaged by enemy fire, and 14 as a result of mechanical breakdowns. Post-action analysis of the use of the tanks indicated that the main mistake was their deployment in small numbers. In addition, a number of technical shortcomings were revealed – the fragility of the tracks, the tanks' underpowered engines, etc. The Germans on the other hand, having received notice, began working out the capabilities and means for an anti-tank defense.

At the same time France was conducting independent projects to design and build armored fighting vehicles. On 14 April 1916, 132 machines of the Schneider type were assembled at Craon for an offensive. During the attack, the tanks reached the Germans' first line of trenches, which had been especially expanded; the trenches had a width of 4-5 meters. There, the Schneider tanks were stopped by heavy fire. The loss of tanks in this action was also significant – up to 58% of the machines. This allowed the following conclusions to be drawn: 1) the advance detection of the tanks had to be avoided; and 2) in order to seize and hold an area, the tanks had to operate together with infantry. In subsequent fighting more attention was given to escorting the tanks with infantry; their use at night; camouflaged paint schemes; the use of previously-prepared fascines in order to overcome anti-tank ditches; and the narrowing of tasks, boiling down primarily to clearing paths through barbed wire obstacles and destroying enemy firing positions. The development of light tanks also got underway.

The most successful use of tanks in the course of the First World War was the joint attack by the British and the French at the Battle of Amiens on 8 August 1918. Here, the infantry, supported by 600 tanks, attacked in a dense fog. Seven defending German divisions were caught by surprise. As a result, 25,000 prisoners and 400 guns were captured, and the date became a day of mourning for Germany. The unexpected appearance of massed light tanks played a major role in the final defeat of the Germans. On 2 October 1918, a member of the German High Command in the Reichstag testified: "… the hope to defeat the enemy disappeared. The first factor that had a decisive influence on the outcome of the battle was the tanks. The enemy is using them in enormous masses."

Germany, the artillery of which relatively easily inflicted heavy losses to the Allied tanks in the initial battles, during the war didn't pay significant attention to the development of its own tank production. However, after the war, the Germans paid particular attention to the production of tanks, their employment, and especially to the preparation of experienced crews and commanders to conduct impetuous combat actions with an emphasis on making independent decisions in the course of the battle. Speed and the independence of actions became the main task of the German panzer troops. The tactics of their use foresaw the massing of a large number of tanks on the main directions and rapid maneuvers to bypass major knots of resistance with the active support of self-propelled artillery and ground support aircraft.

In prior research devoted to the lengthy and successful defense of Odessa, on the whole little attention has been given to tanks. However, a lot of disagreement exists in the analyses of various times and authors. We'll examine the quantitative and qualitative characteristics of the armored forces and tanks of the opposing sides, as well as the order and effectiveness of their use.

Odessa, according to the plans of the German command, was supposed to become an important supply base for the *Wehrmacht* forces attacking toward Crimea and the Caucasus. Therefore the fascists committed the entire Fourth Romanian Army to the capture of Odessa, as well as units of the German 72nd Infantry Division. Altogether up to 18 divisions took part in the assault on Odessa; of this total, one was a tank division with approximately 100 tanks. The separate Coastal Army, which consisted of two rifle divisions and one cavalry division, was defending the city. At the beginning of August 1941, these divisions practically had no operational tanks. Having created a six-fold superiority in strength and means, the enemy was counting upon taking Odessa from the march, and had already scheduled a parade of its forces on Cathedral Square on 10 August 1941. However, the Soviet troops repulsed all of the attacks by the superior forces of the Romanian army and inflicted heavy losses on the attacking troops.

The problem in researching the history of the use of tanks in the Odessa defensive area consists of the narrowness of the base of sources on the actions of the ground troops of the Coastal Army. The archives of the Coastal Army were destroyed in the Crimea in 1942, while Romania's own archival materials are extremely sparse. Thus many historical articles on the use of tanks at Odessa are only a repeat of the G. Penezhko's memoirs *Na Odesskom platsdarme* [*At the Odessa bridgehead*] written back at the end of the 1940s, which unfortunately contains quite a few mistakes and ideological blemishes.[1] For example, obviously from the pre-conceptions of the political censors of that

---

1   G. Penezhko, *Na Odesskom platsdarme* [*At the Odessa bridgehead*] (Odessa: Oblizdat, 1950).

time (Romania was part of the camp of socialist countries), G. Penezhko speaks about knocked out German tanks (or in the best case, fascist tanks) at Odessa. In his memoirs there is no real assessment of the quantity, quality and losses of tanks or the tactical combat practices with the use of tanks of the opposing sides. In general in the indicated work, more attention is given to the history of re-equipping tractors into the armored NI tractors, leaving without attention the fact repaired combat tanks had greater combat significance.

At the start of Odessa's defense, the Coastal Army had only few tanks in good working order. As a matter of fact, the Red Army on the eve of the war had a significant number of combat machines, but the bulk of them were lost in the very first weeks of the war. There were several reasons for such truly shocking losses. The service life of the engines equipping the tanks of the Red Army was very short and amounted on average to just 50 operating hours, sufficient for only a few days of combat use, and thus 40% of the Soviet tanks were knocked out in the first days of the war due to mechanical problems, breakdowns, wear and tear on parts, etc. In addition, serious breakdowns quickly increased because of the large losses among experienced tankers and mechanics. A large quantity of combat machines was abandoned or destroyed due to the lack of fuel and ammunition – the ammunition and fuel stockpiles had been subjected to enemy air strikes and artillery attacks as one of the primary objectives in the border zone. In the chaos of the initial stage of the war, there was only rare success in bringing up fuel and ammunition to resupply the tanks. Moreover, Soviet commanders in the very beginning of the war often abandoned tanks in combat without the support of infantry, aircraft and artillery, and even when lacking radio contact, which led to additional losses. At the same time Red Army commanders sought to build their defenses according to a linear principle on a broad front, without adequate depth, and without regard for enemy tactics, details of terrain or the importance of defending key directions. Boundaries and flanks were poorly secured. To all of the above one must add the lack of normal intelligence or radio communications, continuous strikes from the air, and the inexperience of the crews (just 5 hours of practical training was given to the driver-mechanic of a tank, while many had only 1.5 to 2 hours of driving time in training; in the Werhmacht, tank drivers were given not less than 50 hours of driving time in training), and also the absence of an organized and well-supplied repair service in the Red Army. As a result we obtain an exhaustive description of that woeful fact why the entire tank force of the Coastal Army in the first days of the defense of Odessa consisted of six light tanks and approximately 30 armored cars and lightly armored tractors, equipped with machine guns.

Romania, which had fought on the side of the Entente during the First World War, received its first tanks from France in the 1920s. These were 76 light Renault FT-17 tanks (48 equipped with cannons and 28 with machine guns), and until the end of the 1930s these made up the basis of Romanian armored units. In 1939 the Romanian Army began to re-equip with new tanks that had been purchased abroad. These included 126 R-2 tanks that had been purchased from Czechoslovakia which went to equip the 1st Tank Regiment. In 1940, the 1st Armored Division was formed, which included the 1st Tank Regiment, four battalions of the 3rd and 4th Infantry Regiments, as well as the 1st Motorized Artillery Regiment. At the beginning of 1939, the 2nd Tank Regiment began forming, equipped with 41 Renault R-35 tanks that had been purchased in France. In September 1939, another 34 R-35 tanks were added from the number interned after Poland's defeat.

The numerous Romanian cavalry, like the French Army, was armed with light tankettes equipped with machine guns in a pivoting turret. For this, at the beginning of 1939 35 AH-IVR (Romanian) had been purchased in Czechoslovakia; once in Romania, these tanks received the designation R-1 (*Carul de Recunoastere* R-1). Organizationally, each of the six Romanian cavalry brigades had a motorized cavalry regiment and a reconnaissance squadron that included four R-1 tankettes. The rest of these machines were either located in the cavalry training center (in Sibiu) or had been attached to formation headquarters for reconnaissance and communication.

At the end of the 1930s the Romanian industry made an attempt to initiate the independent production of armored vehicles. An agreement was signed with France about licensing the production of 300 Renault UE armored transports, which in Romania received the name *Malaxa*. The assembly of these tankettes took place in a factory of the same name in Bucharest, primarily with domestically-manufactured parts. Only the engine and transmission system were delivered from France. With the capitulation of that country, the delivery of engines ceased and in March 1941, after the output of 126 machines, their production ceased. The armored transports, 12 machines each in an anti-tank company, were used to tow the 47-mm anti-tank guns. Altogether by the moment of the invasion of the Soviet Union, the Romanian Army had 178 tankettes, both of their own production and those given to Romania by Germany after the victory over France, as well as several interned Polish TK and TKS.

On the eve of the war, the Romanian Army's tank pool included 35 R-1 tankettes and 126 R-2 light tanks, bought in Czechoslovakia; 75 French R-35 (41 purchased in France and 31 interned in 1939 in Poland); and 60-75 outdated Renault FT-17. Altogether the Romanian Army had 480 armored transport vehicles.[2] This number included the Malaxa tankettes, both purchased in France and assembled by license in local factories. Only the R-2 tanks met the requirements for combat of that time.

German military specialists took an active part in the organization and combat training of the Romanian 1st Armored Division. However, a problem could not be avoided: the French and Czech tanks differed so much in their combat capability and roles that the 2nd Tank Regiment had to be withdrawn from the 1st Armored Division and given to the Fourth Army. The 1st Tank Regiment was equipped with R-2 (Skoda LT-35), while the 2nd Tank Regiment had the R-35 (the Renault light escort tank; slow-moving, but with excellent armor). Both tanks were armed with 37-mm cannon. As it stood, the 1st Armored Division was left with only the 1st Tank Regiment. Likely, that is why in Soviet literature the Romanian division is called a motorized brigade. By the start of the fighting for Odessa, all of the Renault FT-17 tanks were combined into a separate training battalion and used exclusively for training tankers and guarding the oil fields near the town of Ploești. The technical characteristics of the Romanian tanks are shown in Table 5.1 (see next page).

In 1941 the Romanian Army had no combat experience with the use of tank units. Nevertheless, the 1st Armored Division in July 1941 made a successful debut in the course of Operation München in Moldavia. On 8 August units of the 1st Armored Division together with the Romanian 1st Cavalry Division took Katarzhino (present-day Krasnoznamenka in the Ivanovskii District).

In the fighting at Odessa, the Romanian Fourth Army opposed the Coastal Army with approximately 100 light tanks of Czech and French manufacture, not including the armored cars and armored tractors, equipped with machine guns. It should be noted that the Romanian military often used the armored tractors as combat machines. The Romanian command primarily used tanks in small groups. The proper level of cooperation between the tanks and the infantry hadn't been laid down, which led to the fact that the tanks were frequently left without infantry escort.

The initial experience with the mass employment of tanks on a narrow sector of the front, in the battle for Karpovo, led to a catastrophe, after which the remnants of the 1st Armored Division were withdrawn into the Fourth Army's reserve. On 21 August 46 damaged tanks (knocked out or broken down) were sent back to Kishinev. The remaining 20 tanks, as part of the Romanian I

---

2   R. Forstmeier, *Odessa 1941. Der Kampf um Stadt und Hafen und die Raumung der Seefstung 15 August bis 16 Oktober* [Frieburg, 1967].

Table 5.1 The characteristics of the Romanian tanks

Type and source country	R-1 tankette; Czechoslovakia's AN-IV	R-2 light tank; Czechoslovakia's LT-35	Renault R-35 light tank; France	Renault F-17 light tank; France
Number in the army as of 22 June 1941	35	126	35	48 armed with cannons and 28 armed with machine guns
Year of production	1936-1938	1936	1935	1917
Combat weight (metric tons)	3.9	10.5	10.6	6.5/6.7
Maximum speed (km/hr)	45	34	20	7.8
Operational range (km)	170	160	140	35
Engine horsepower	55	120	82	39
Height (meters)	1.67	2.37	2.37	2.14
Width (meters)	1.73	2.06	1.85	1.74
Armor thickness, front (mm)	12	25	40	16
Armor thickness, side (mm)	6	16	40	16
Gun caliber (mm)	–	37	37	37
Armor penetration	–	40mm of armor plating at a range of 500 meters	30mm of armor plating at a range of 1,000 meters	12mm of armor plating at a range of 500 meters
Muzzle velocity (meters/sec)	–	675	Up to 701	400
Ammunition load	Up to 3700 cartridges	78	116	237
Number of machine guns and their caliber (mm)	1 7.92 1 ZB vz. 26	2 x 7.92	1 x 7.5	1 x 8.0
Crew size	2	3-4	2	2

Corps, took part in the capture of Freidental', before being formed into a composite group (subsequently retitled the 1st Assault Group) under the command of Lieutenant Colonel Ion Eftimiu. The 2nd Tank Regiment, which was equipped with R-35 tanks, continued to fight at Odessa. It was directly subordinate to the headquarters of the Fourth Romanian Army.

The Coastal Army didn't have its own separate tank elements in July 1941. By the table of organization, only the reconnaissance battalions of the 25th and 95th Rifle Divisions should each have had one tank and one armored car company. I've had no success in finding out how many of these tankettes and armored cars were left in these divisions after the 16 days of the border battles. Light, semi-armored tractors of the type T-20 Komsomolets were used to tow the 45-mm anti-tank cannons in the rifle battalions, regiments and separate artillery battalion. It had a speed of 47.5 km/hour and a ball-mounted DT machine gun, which allowed the defenders of Odessa to use them everywhere as machine-gun tankettes.

At the beginning of August, the first BT-7 tanks, which had been repaired in the January Uprising factory in Odessa, arrived in the Coastal Army. The repair work had been done by the 15th Repair Brigade on a tank-repair basis, although the factory itself had been evacuated to the Urals. Here, capital repair work was done on light tanks, and they were given supplemental armor in the form of protective 30-mm plates of ship steel. Auxiliary protective armor plating was mounted on the hull and turret of the BT-7 and BT-5 tanks at the initiative of a member of the Coastal Army's Department of Mechanized Forces Senior Lieutenant G. Penezhko. The plates provided decent defense against the fire of the Romanian battalion cannons. The tanks with the strengthened turrets (the plates were a half-meter wide and were mounted on both sides of the cannon) had an oddly menacing appearance. BT-7 motors, after small adjustments, were mounted in the BT-5 tanks. In the course of the fighting for Odessa, the BT-7 and BT-5 fought successfully against the light tanks that equipped the Fourth Romanian Army. The most frequently-used tactical method was tank and tank-cavalry ambushes, and in favorable circumstances, counterattacks. The tankers strove to attack the enemy at top speeds while firing intensively on the move and with short halts, destroying infantry and gun and machine-gun crews. They sought to maneuver on the battlefield, using folds in the ground to emerge on the flank and rear of the enemy's positions.[3]

The combat workdays of the tankers of Senior Lieutenant G. Penezhko's incomplete tank company (6 BT-7 tanks) began on 6 August, when the company became subordinate to the commander of the 95th Rifle Division, the headquarters of which was located in Razdel'niaia Station. The division commander sent the tankers to the area of Migaevo Station on the division's extreme right flank, with the assignment to cover the boundary with the neighboring 9th Army. Here on 7 August the tank company, covering a railroad bed, spent the entire day skirmishing with the forward units of the German 72nd Infantry Division. After attacks by German aircraft, the tankers often had to change positions. In this action the tankers didn't lose a single machine, though several tankers received light wounds. However, the Germans outflanked the station and continued to advance to the east, creating the threat of encirclement for the right-flank elements of the Coastal Army. It was necessary to forestall the enemy. Thus on the night of 7-8 August the tank company with sailors of the 1st Naval Infantry Regiment mounted on board, bypassing Danilovka which had been occupied by the Germans, broke into the village of Zhelepovo from the direction of the hamlet of Lozovyi. Here, on the main street, the composite detachment unexpectedly attacked a column of enemy vehicles. The tank riders and tankers forced the Romanians to flee in panic. The naval infantry regiment took up a defense in the Zhelepovo – Baranovo sector, while the tankers were ordered to tie in with the neighboring division. In order to do this, they had to move out in the direction of Oktiabr'skoe. On the night of 8-9 August the tankers rolled through Gudevichevo and Volkovo, and then, diverging slightly from their route, they came upon the village of Liubotaevka, where in the darkness they collided with a German forward tank detachment. G. Penezhko's tankers opened fire first and forced the Germans to withdraw. Early on the morning of 9 August the tankers, exiting Liubotaevka and advancing to the north along a balka, encountered scouts of the 1st Cavalry Division, which had been urgently sent from Odessa and were fighting on the boundary with the 9th Army. In the area of the Marinovo railroad junction, the tank company commander received an order over the telephone from the army commander to become subordinate to the naval infantry regiment. The tankers helped the sailors drive back the initial and subsequent enemy attacks against the position at Marinovo, and then on the line: Serbka – Svoboda – Chernogorka. With the aim of intercepting the enemy, which was striving to get on the rear of the sailors, the tank company was sent with a company of naval infantry on board as a forward detachment to threatened sectors. This mobile detachment in the course of three days repelled enemy attacks until the arrival of the main forces of the naval infantry regiment, initially in the area of Chernogorka, then Serbka, and later on the lines Buialyk Station – Kairy and Blagodatnoe – Spiridonovka (present-day Pervomaiskii) – commune *Zaria Truda*. Up until 12 August the tankers helped the naval infantrymen repulse enemy attacks in the Budlinka – Sverdlovo area.

After carrying out the assignment to stabilize the front in the East Sector of defense, the tanks passed to the subordination of the commander of the 95th Rifle Division, where they helped restore a position. At Karpovo Station, in cooperation with an armored train, the tankers captured a Romanian train that was carrying knocked-out Soviet tanks. The armored train *Chernomorets*

---

3   *Tank v boiu* [*Tanks in battle*] (Moscow: Voenizdat, 1946), pp. 156-163.

hitched up the railcars that were transporting the knocked-out tanks and pulled them back to Odessa for repair.

Next the Coastal Army's tank reserve passed to the operational control of the 25th "Chapaev" Rifle Division. The tankers helped the men of the division to regain possession of the village of Mangeim (present-day Kamenka). On 17 August the tankers took part in the fighting at Beliaevka, and on the night of 17-18 August, together with the "Pugachev" Regiment, the tankers fully demonstrated their capabilities in a night attack. In this action a lot of prisoners were taken, but three tanks were lost. Later, in a battle at Mangeim, the other three tanks were lost, but the losses were quickly replenished by tanks that had been repaired at a factory in Odessa.

As we see, the small detachment of Soviet tanks performed a role as a mobile fire brigade, which was directed to threatened sectors of the front and helped hold back the enemy attacks. The maneuvering of the tank reserve to various sectors of defense created the illusion in the Romanian command that the Coastal Army had a large tank force. There, wherever the Soviet forces used 4-6 tanks, according to Romanian intelligence the Soviets had 8-10 tanks. Despite their limited number, the tankers often achieved success; the fact that the Romanian infantry was poorly equipped with anti-tank guns contributed to this. A psychological factor also played a role. The bulk of the Romanian Fourth Army consisted of poorly trained reservists. The simple Romanian peasant, dressed in a military uniform, not only poorly understood what he was doing on foreign soil, but was also poorly prepared to meet armored machines. As a result, the appearance of just a few tanks gave rise to panic among the Romanian soldiers. Of course, several machines couldn't compensate for the overall lack of tanks, and for a long time the Romanian side had a serious advantage in tank numbers. Thus already in the first days of the defense, as a substitute for tanks, the command of the Coastal Army was forced to employ the semi-armored Komsomolets-10 artillery tractors, which were armed with machine guns.

From the middle of August, the repair base in Odessa managed to put two tanks back into operation each day, and by the time Odessa was evacuated, 44 combat tanks had been repaired: 10 BT-7, 2 BT-7M, 4 BT-5, 1 BT-2, 2 T-26, 8 T-20, 5 BA-20, and 12 T-37 and T-38. Some of them went through repairs several times. The repair base also managed to assemble one tank from a tank boneyard that remained at Odessa-Tovarnaia Station and damaged tanks that came back from the front. G.P. Penezhko, the future Hero of the Soviet Union and the permanent representative of the Coastal Army's Department of Mechanized Forces at the factory, provided technical direction. The tank crews were formed from volunteers – factory workers, drivers and artillerymen.[4] The military correspondent and writer K. Simonov, who was in Odessa during the siege, observed: "Tanks were being repaired by everyone together – both workers and tank crews, who had come out of battle two or three days ago. The tanks were primarily BT-5 and BT-7. As it turned out in this war, they had armor that could be penetrated too easily, so in the workshops they were attaching supplementary plates of armor to the tanks' turrets."[5] In the beginning of September, the number of repaired tanks allowed the command of the Coastal Army to form a tank battalion, which was commanded by Senior Lieutenant Nikolai Iudin. The battalion's 1st Company was equipped with BT-7 tanks, the 2nd – with BT-5 tanks, and the 3rd – with armored tractors.

As previously mentioned, the deficit of combat tanks was compensated by armoring tractors, which were in mass production in Odessa and were actively used in the course of the city's tenacious defense. Work to build the armored tractors began in the middle of August 1941. The chief engineers of the January Uprising factory P.K. Romanov and combat engineers A.I. Obednikov and

4   Odessa Regional History Museum – Inv. No. D-3578, p. 1.
5   K.M. Simonov, *Raznye dni voiny. Dnevnik pisatelia* [*Various days of the war. Diary of a writer*] (Moscow: Khudozhnaia literature, 1982), p. 118.

V.G. Kogan devised the project to add armor to the tractors and arm them. Plates of ship armor steel were used to armor the tractors, as well as two-ply boiler plate given special thermal treatment and joined by welding. In order to strengthen the crew's protection, a layer of wood or rubber was inserted between the armor and the inner plating. The box-like armored body was mounted on the chassis of the STZ-NATI tractor while retaining its overall configuration: a kerosene engine with a capacity of 52 liters was mounted on the forward part of the frame; behind it was a place for the driver-mechanic; and beside it was the fighting compartment with a cupola. In front, along both sides of the engine, were two armored superstructures: the right-hand one for the observer, the left-hand one for the machine gunner. Observation of the enemy was handled through open vision slits. The crew consisted of 3-4 men. The transmission had four forward gears and one rear gear. The tractor running gear was fixed and had on each side four bogies, two idlers and a rear drive sprocket. The machine turned out to be overloaded, prone to capsize, and could accelerate to no faster than 7 km/hour (though a few could reach 20 km/hour). The engine quickly overheated, and the field of vision from within the machine was extremely limited.[6] The machine was armed with light 37-mm or 45-mm cannons, or else DShK machine guns, in a revolving turret, as well as with two 7.62-mm DT (DP) machine guns. A few of the armored tractors were equipped with long-range flamethrowers.[7] The turrets came from damaged T-26 M1931 tanks or were of self-fabricated construction. The turret base rings for the fabricated turrets were made in the streetcar workshops, where the necessary equipment could be found.[8]

A proving ground was created at the factory for tests, and there the first tanks successfully passed the factory trials – the armor offered protection against small-caliber shells, shell fragments and bullets. The unique tanks immediately went into serial production.[9] The first two machines, which were built on the basis of the STZ-5 artillery tractors, were ready on 20 August. The October Revolution factory applied the armor to the tractors. The former secretary of the Party's Lenin District Committee N.G. Lutsenko, who supervised this work, recalled: "Between 20 August and 15 October, 55 tanks were built out of STZ-5 tractors." Other sources give a different number – 69. The most reliable is the "Otchet ob oborone Odessy" [Account of the defense of Odessa], written in 1943 shortly after the events. It stated:

> In the middle of August, the process of converting tractors and trucks into tanks and armored cars was organized at the January Uprising and October Revolution factories. A 45-mm cannon and two Maksim machine guns were mounted on each of them. The tanks were covered with armor from ship-building steel with a thickness of 14-20-mm; on the armored cars, the thickness of the armor increased up to 25-mm. The fabricators laid down wooden joist and planks between the armor and the interior plating. In combat the armored cars were vulnerable from the front, since from that direction the tires lacked any protection. It was necessary to give the rear of the vehicles reliable protection and drive the armored cars into battle in reverse gear, which yielded a positive result. Subsequently the wheels of the armored cars were equipped with tracks, which gave them a high degree of mobility. By 14 September 31 machines were produced, which allowed a tank battalion to be formed. On 14 September the armoring of another 15 tractors began.[10]

---

6   *73 geroicheskikh dnei: Khronika oborony Odessy v 1941 godu*, p. 276.

7   *Voennye znaniia*, No. 8 (1993); A. Karev, *Odessa – gorod geroi* [*Odessa – hero-city*] (Moscow: Voenizdat, 1977), p. 65.

8   Ibid.

9   M.V. Kolomiets, *Bronia na kolesakh. Istoriia sovetskovo broneavtomobilia 1925-1945* [*Armor on wheels: History of the Soviet armored car 1925-1945*] (Moscow: Iauza, Strategiia KM, Eksmo, 2007).

10 Ibid., pp. 332-334.

This document brings a bit more clarity – the number of armored tractors included armored cars fabricated from trucks as well. The Chief of the defensive area's Mechnanized Forces Maksimov, in the document "Otchet o rabote otdela avtobronetankovykh voisk v period oborony Odessy s 1 avgusta po 15 oktiabria 1941" ["Account of the work of the Department of Mechanized Forces"], which was produced on 11 March 1942 notes: "The extremely inadequate quantity of tanks in the Coastal Army compelled the Department of Mechanized Forces to take the path of creating the so-called "Odessa tanks". In the course of a short period of time, through the efforts and means of the separate repair battalion and local enterprises, 49 STZ-5 tractors were fully armored and armed, and commanders and driver-mechanics were trained."

Weakly armed and with poor mobility, they nevertheless performed successfully in combat. Already in the first action on 1 September at Dal'nik, three "NI" tanks together with one BT helped the 25th Rifle Division repulse Romanian units, the men of which were frightened by the appearance of the "strange tanks". After the attack, the tankers towed back 4 captured cannons.[11] The inspection of the tanks at the factory after the first battle showed that on the whole, the machines successfully passed their first combat tests: fragments and bullets left only impressions in the armor, and one 45-mm shell penetrated the armor through and through, without hitting the crew or engine.[12] After the battle, soldiers of the 161st Rifle Regiment asked the commander of the armored tractor that took the penetrating hit from the 45-mm shell why he decided to go on the attack in such an unreliable machine. He, with the traditional Odessan wit replied: "The enemy can kill me only with a direct hit. But according to theory, in order to achieve this he must expend the greater portion of his ammunition, and for two tanks he doesn't have enough shells."[13]

The characteristics of the tanks that equipped the Coastal Army are given in Table 2.2:

Table 5.2 Characteristics of the Coastal Army's tanks

Type:	T-26	BT-7	NI-1
Year of production	1937	1939	1941
Combat weight (in metric tons)	10.5	14.6	Around 7.0
Maximum speed (km/hr)	30	62	20
Operational range (km)	200	600	140
Engine horsepower	97	400	52 to 56
Height (meters)	2.33	2.70	2.4
Width (meters)	2.46	2.23	1.9
Armor thickness: front (mm)	15	20	10-20
side	15	13	10-20
Gun caliber (mm)	45	45	37-45
Range of fire (km)	4.8	4.8	
Muzzle velocity (meters/second)	760	760	
Ammo load	165	188	
Number of machine guns	3	3	1 or 2 7.62mm DT machine guns

---

11   A.K. Filipenko, "K voprosu ob uchastii tankov v boiakh pod Odessoi" [On the question of the participation of tanks in the fighting at Odessa"], *Odessika: Istoriko-kraevedcheskii al'manakh* [*Odessika: Regional history almanacs*] Issue 12 (Odessa: Pechatyi dom, 2011).

12   Odessa v Velikoi Otechestvennoi voine Sovetskogo Soiuza, Volume 1 (Odessa, 1947), p. 109.

13   Kolomiets, *Bronia na kolesakh*, p. 66.

The tankers took part in repulsing two Romanian general offensives on 28 August and 12 September, supporting counterattacks by the infantry units. The armored tractors were used in mass for the first time in a night attack on 20 September 1941 at the village of Velikii Dal'nik in the South Sector of Defense. Calculations were based more on the psychological effect than on their firepower. For this purpose, the armored tractors were equipped with sirens and floodlights, while the wild rumble and the chattering of the machine guns taken together with the surprise caused the Romanians not just to withdraw long-held positions, but to flee openly. On the next day they tried to justify this behavior by saying that the Coastal Army men had hurled some terrifying secret weapon against them. The armored tractors' shortcomings – the noisy engines, the squeaking tracks and the loudly rattling armor – were converted into a positive. The night attack of the armored tractors was a resounding success. It was after this legendary attack made by the NI-1 armored tractors (the factory name was "Na istreblenie" [exterminate]) received the new name "Na ispug" [frighten or scare]. Such a nickname is also explained by the fact that because of the lack of large-caliber guns, the barrels of the light cannons were given larger jackets in order to give the tanks a more "serious" appearance, and sometimes simply dummy guns were mounted on the tanks. In addition, as veterans remember, when in motion the tank made an appalling din.

The tankers also played an important role in supporting two of the most important counteroffensive operations at the concluding stage of Odessa's defense; in particular, in the famous Grigor'eva operation on 22 September. On the eve of the operation, the Coastal Army's tank park was replenished with a tank company of the 141st Reconnaissance Battalion of the 157th "Kuban" Rifle Division that had arrived with 15 BT-7 tanks. The Coastal Army's Chief of Staff Nikolai Krylov recalled the first hours of the counter-offensive: "The first reports from the observation posts were brief and openly exuberant: 'There they go! … They're making headway! … The tanks are surging ahead!'" Only the 157th Rifle Division was attacking with tanks. The 421st Rifle Division couldn't even be supported by the Odessan armored tractors – at this time they were helping repel attacks on different directions.[14] The tank company was directly operating together with the 716th Rifle Regiment, which was attacking in the sector between the Kuial'nitskii estuary and the railroad leading to Gil'dendorf (Novoselovka), while one tank platoon was operating with the 633rd Rifle Regiment toward the Il'ichevka State Farm. The tank attack to a great extent contributed to the success of the Soviet counter-offensive, which managed to throw back the Romanian forces to a point 5-8 kilometers from Odessa.

The tanks of the Coastal Army also played a key role in the subsequent counter-offensive on 2 October at Dal'nik. The main attack was launched in the direction of Lenintal'. Under the cover of an artillery barrage, the tanks were brought up to the enemy's very trenches, which ensured the shock of their attack. The army's tank battalion consisting of 35 (according to other data, 39) combat machines under the command of Senior Lieutenant Nikolai Iudin overran the Romanian line and broke through to Lenintal', where it overran Romanian artillery positions, before returning to the Soviet lines with 24 captured guns and a lot of machine guns and mortars. According to information from Romanian sources, their artillerymen, left without covering infantry, on their own engaged in combat with the Soviet tanks and infantry. Using grenades and Molotov cocktails, and also fire over open sights from their guns, they claim to have destroyed 12 Soviet tanks. This happened after Romanian fighter aircraft separated the Soviet infantry from the tanks and left the tanks without infantry escort. Incidentally, Soviet sources speak about the loss of just two tanks, which became separated from the battalion's combat formation during a pursuit of the enemy.[15]

---

14   N.I. Krylov, *Ne pomerknet nikogda* [*It will never grow dim*], 2nd ed. (Moscow: Voenizdat, 1984).

15   73 geroicheskikh dnei. Khronkika oborony Odessy v 1941 godu.

In the fighting at Odessa the tankers, considering the small quantity of tanks and their weak armor, really looked after their machines. They reverently took care of their "offspring", made by their own hands – the tank crews were often formed from the workers of the factories that produced them.[16] A lot of cases have been identified, when the tankers, leaping out of their tanks, killed enemy infantry with fire from a rifle or grenades, in order to avoid damage to their machines, each of which was worth its weight in gold and which by their participation in battle saved many lives of our soldiers. That is how gunner Voloshin and battalion commander Senior Lieutenant Iudin acted in one battle. In the tank attack at Lenintal', the heroism of the tankers was on a mass scale, as recorded in the reports of the commanders of the attacking units and in the Coastal Army's journal of combat operations. Of the 10 BT-7 tanks that took the most active part in fighting, 5 were destroyed in battle. Flamethrowers were mounted on the T-26 tanks, and frames for firing aircraft rocket projectiles were installed on 13 Komsomolets tractors.[17]

At the beginning of Odessa's defense, the Coastal Army had just several BT tanks, but by the time the troops were evacuated to Sevastopol, it now had an entire tank battalion of three-company composition. It should be considered that in a short period of time, through the improbable efforts of Odessa's factory workers, more than 100 armored fighting vehicles were delivered to the front – approximately 50 damaged tanks were restored to combat serviceability, and about 60 armored tractors were produced. During the evacuation of the Coastal Army, the "NI" tank company was positioned on the western outskirts of Odessa with the assignment to support the rear guard elements. However the enemy didn't detect the stealthy nighttime departure of our troops, and thus made no attempt to pursue. The "NI" tank crews were the last to leave their combat positions, having disabled or blown up their machines. Some of them were repaired and used for training purposes by the Romanians. During the Coastal Army's evacuation from Odessa, it was able to bring out 14 tanks and 16 armored cars together with it.

As we've seen, the information from both sides on the use of tanks and on their losses is very contradictory. If to believe Soviet sources, then just the pilots of the Black Sea Fleet's air force alone destroyed 168 enemy tanks at Odessa. If you add the number 55 of the tanks knocked out by ground units, then on the whole it turns out that the Soviet troops destroyed each and every Romanian combat machine at Odessa. The Romanians place their own losses at 19 tanks (this figure appears in contemporary Romanian books about the Battle of Odessa), which also raises questions.[18] True, there exists a well-known difference between the concept "knocked-out tank" and "destroyed tank" – the latter means it must be written-off. However, primarily, as often happens in reports from the front, we are dealing with an exaggeration of the enemy's losses and an understatement of our own. Obviously, Soviet sources include the Romanian Malaxa armored transports in the total of knocked-out or destroyed Romanian machines. The latter were used by the Romanians for towing anti-tank guns, and in each infantry division there were 12 of them, while an additional 40 Malaxa were part of the 1st Armored Division. The Romanians didn't assign them to the category of "combat machines".[19] In the summary note, prepared by the Fourth Army's Intelligence Department soon after the occupation of Odessa, there is the statement:

Just as during the combat operations in Bessarabia and the combat operations in the Transnistria, Soviet forces used combat machines primarily in small elements (up to a

---

16   Odesskii istoriko-kraevedcheskii muzei, Inv. No. D-3578.

17   A.A. Cherkasov, *Oborony Odessy. Stranitsy pravdy* [Defense of Odessa: Pages of truth] 1st ed. (Odessa: Optimum, 2006).

18   *România în anii celui de al doilea război mondial.* 3 vol. (Bucharest, 1989).

19   Stroitel'stvo i boevoe primenenie sovetskikh tankovykh voisk v gody Velikoi Otechestvennoi voiny [Building and combat use of the Soviet tank forces in the years of the Great Patriotic War] (Moscow: Voenizdat, 1979).

battalion, with a maximum of 20-30 machines). The single instance of the massed employment of combat machines was during the counterattack by the 157th and 25th Rifle Division against Romanian units in the area of Dal'nik on 2 and 3 October, when 42 combat machines were activated on a front of up to 4 kilometers. During other counterattacks the enemy used small groups of combat machines numbering 3-5 or 8-16. The armor counterattacks, as a rule, were repelled by our infantry with the help of anti-tank weapons. In the majority of cases, the counterattacking groups of combat machines were scattered by the fire of our artillery. When conducting fire over open sights, a large number of enemy combat machines were knocked out. Primarily, the Soviet forces were using combat machines not as a means for breaking through our front, but as a means for supporting the operations of the rifle units. Incidentally the weight of the armored machines didn't exceed 20 metric tons. On the Odessa Front, cases were noted where the Soviet troops employed armored tractors, equipped with machine guns or flamethrowers. The armoring of the tractors was done in Odessan factories.[20]

Such evidence from the Romanian archives requires a weighty comparative-analysis approach. Speaking on the losses of Soviet tanks, it is necessary to take into consideration both Romanian sources and G. Penezhko's memoirs. On the whole, Soviet irrecoverable tank losses can be put at 10-15.

The Romanian command in the assault upon Odessa was in fact unable to realize the significant potential of its sole tank division in order to break through the defenses. At first the Romanians used tanks in small groups and often without infantry support, yet their first massed tank attack ended in a catastrophe for them.

The tankers of the Coastal Army, despite their small numbers, in the extreme conditions of the struggle for their survival of their native city quickly gained combat experience and made a significant contribution to the defense of Odessa. A difficult task was their lot – given the enemy's large superiority in force, they had to plug breaches in the line and strengthen weak sectors, and support the infantry during counterattacks and offensives. At Odessa, they did this with several dozen tanks, which in the initial phase of the war were not under the control of large Soviet tank formations. The tanks were used both on the offensive and the defensive. In the defensive fighting the tanks, reinforcing the infantry, didn't receive their own sectors of defense, but were used together with the infantry or used as the armored reserve of the Coastal Army's commander-in-chief in order to counterattack enemy breakthroughs. The main task during counterattacks was the destruction of the enemy's infantry units and their firing means. The tanks based their combat operations on surprise and their maximally concentrated use in favorable terrain. Surprise was extremely important for the utmost success of an attack.[21] After all, if the direction of attack intended for the armor became known to the enemy beforehand, he could assemble a large number of anti-tank means in this sector, and the tank attack would be made more difficult. In order to achieve the element of surprise, the Soviets exploited the shielding properties of natural concealment – woodlots, populated places, the reverse slope of hills, etc., as well as every possible military subterfuge and deceptive measure. The surprise use of tanks, especially with elementary psychological pressure (at night, floodlights, sirens, the rattle of tracks and fire) strongly enhanced their effect on enemy troops. This allowed the tankers to carry out their tasks successfully with the fewest possible losses.

---

20   Filipenko, "K voprosu ob uchastii tankov".
21   *Boevoi ustav bronetankovykh i mekhanizirovannykh voisk Krasnoi Armii* [*Combat manual of the armored and mechanized forces of the Red Army*] Part 1 (Moscow: Voenizdat, 1944), p. 4.

When using the tanks, consideration was given to their technical possibilities, details of terrain, and measures to overcome natural and artificial obstacles. Reconnoitering and the study of the ground of forthcoming operations and the enemy, the disposition of his anti-tank firing means and anti-tank obstacles, and the correct choice of the areas and directions of the tanks' actions had decisive significance for their success. The proper and clear organization of the cooperation with the infantry and artillery; the high degree of preparation of the crews and tanks for battle; their timely maintenance and repair in field conditions (the repairs were organized close to the frontlines through the efforts of the factory mobile workshops) were also substantive factors in the successful employment of tanks in battle.

6

The joint counterattack by the defenders of Odessa and the stabilization of the front

At the beginning of September, the territorial gain by the enemy in the area of Fontanka allowed the enemy to deploy artillery batteries within range of Odessa's port, and their fire was preventing the port's operation, which seriously and adversely affected the defender's combat capabilities. There was an analogous situation in the South Sector of Defense, so the city faced the threat of overlapping enemy artillery fire. In order to search for a way out of this critical situation, on 6 September the Commander-in-Chief of the Black Sea Fleet Vice Admiral F.S. Oktiabr'sky and the Soviet Navy's deputy chief of staff Vice Admiral G.I. Levchenko arrived in Odessa. Having assessed the situation on the ground, the Black Sea Fleet's commander-in-chief fully agreed with the opinion of the Odessa Defense District's Military Council that it was possible to protect the city and port from enemy artillery fire only by driving the enemy from his occupied positions in the East Sector. However, there wasn't enough strength in Odessa to conduct such an offensive. It was decided to ask the *Stavka* to send a rifle division to Odessa for the offensive and to prepare a landing by sea in the area of Novaia Dofinovka in order to launch a preemptive attack into the rear of the enemy grouping in the East Sector. In principle, the question was decided about preparing a combined attack against the enemy with the joint forces of the Odessa Defense District and the Black Sea Fleet.

The situation at Odessa was becoming increasingly tense. The German command, having brought up fresh forces and having implemened a corresponding regrouping (having assembled up to 11 infantry divisions with tanks opposite the West and South Sectors), initiated a new, decisive offensive. The attacking units were supported by a significant amount of artillery (up to 80 tubes per kilometer of front). The units defending Odessa, as a result of many days of combat spent resisting the enemy's incessant attacks, had already suffered significant losses. A lack of weapons was perceptible.[1]

By 12 September, reserves were melting away, while the enemy was continuing to press. Considering the emergency situation that Odessa now faced, on 14 September the Military Council of the Odessa Defense District sent an alarming telegram to the *Stavka*:

> The enemy is receiving replenishments. Fresh divisions are being brought up. Under the pressure of his superior forces, the danger has arisen of a retreat by our units to the Gniliakovo – Dal'nik – Sukhoi estuary line. The population, the airfield, the city, the port and ships will

---

1   TsAMO RF, F. 288, Op. 3365, D. 1, ll. 71-72.

suffer enormous losses from enemy artillery fire. Our air force will be forced to restage to the Crimea. The 421st Rifle Division, which was created out of local reserves, has an insufficient quantity of machine guns and artillery. The other divisions also need replacement machine guns and artillery. The rifle divisions have an overall 42% deficit of command staff. The march battalions have all joined the units. Over the last month of the defense, losses in wounded alone reach 25,000. Over the day of 12 September alone, there were 1,900 wounded (taken from hospital admittance records). In order to prevent a breakthrough and artillery fire on the airfield, city and port, one rifle division is necessary, as well as further replenishments with march battalions.[2]

On the following day, 15 September an answer was received. At the most difficult time for Odessa's defenders, the *Stavka* responded to them not with a categorical order that was typical for the Stalinist regime, but with a request: "Give the Supreme Commander-in-Chief of the *Stavka's* request to the soldiers and commanders that are defending Odessa to hold out for 6-7 days, in the course of which they will receive assistance in the form of aircraft and armed replenishments … I. Stalin."[3] This text had been personally dictated by the Supreme Commander-in-Chief. Already within two hours, the following directive, which promised help despite the difficult situation on other fronts, was set down on paper and ready to be sent to Odessa – the Odessa Defense District would receive the well-prepared 157th "Kuban" Rifle Division from Novorossiisk.

It isn't surprising that such a personal appeal from the Supreme Commander-in-Chief quickly inspired the ordinary soldiers. Without hiding the problematic situation with reserves, the *Stavka* with one simple word "request" raised their combat spirits. The *Stavka* directive was announced in every unit of the Odessa Defense District without exception, and its contents were made known to each soldier. In the units and elements and aboard the ships, meetings were held under enemy fire, at which the soldiers and sailors swore not to retreat a single step. This work strengthened the resolve of Odessa's defenders in the struggle. As Rear Admiral G.K. Zhukov wrote in his memoirs, "Each soldier, commander and militia man was ready to take on any difficulties and trials, just to carry out the mission."

On 15 September, the enemy forces went over to a general offensive. In order to prevent a disaster, there remained only one way out: to withdraw the left flank of the South Sector of Defense to the western bank of the Sukhoi estuary, where a defensive line had already been prepared. On 16 September, the command of the defensive area executed this forced withdrawal. This allowed a major reduction in the front line, which in turn increased the density of fire and allowed the 31st Rifle Regiment to be removed from the front and become the Coastal Army's sole reserve, which was urgently necessary for the defense.

In connection with the withdrawal of the troops of the South Sector, the coastal belt, upon which the Odessa defenders relied to secure the flank, was reduced to 30 kilometers. The adversary was now in direct proximity to the city not only from the east, but also on its southwestern side. Having deployed long-range artillery, from the west they began to shell the rebuilt temporary quays of the Arcadia and the 16th Station of the Bol'shoi Fontan. A regular barrage on the city began, and also on the ships approaching it. The fascists were keeping the airfields, moorings and approach routes under artillery fire. The loading and unloading of ships, which were delivering ammunition and equipment, as well as the evacuation of the wounded, became possible only in the hours of darkness. In addition, the enemy began dropping magnetic mines by parachute in the area of the port, in order to blockade the maritime zone. All this made it more difficult for the

2   N.G. Kuznetsov, *Na flotakh boevaia trevoga*, p. 118.
3   TsVMA MO RF, F. Sht., Spr. 783, Ark. 115; N.G. Kuznetsov, *Na flotakh boevaia trevoga*, pp. 122-123.

Black Sea Fleet to maneuver in the bay of Odessa and to support the troops of the defensive area. The delivery of replacements and ammunition to the besieged Odessa became extremely complicated. Its connection with the rest of the country was under threat.

In order to deprive the foe of a prominent landmark and save the port from targeted fire, on 15 September the Vorontsov Lighthouse was blown up. The chief of staff of the Coastal Army Colonel M.I. Krylov in his memoir emphasized that the days of mid-September were tragic for Odessa's defense. In the course of 15-18 September the enemy, introducing his reserves into the battle, resumed the offensive, launching the main attack (with the forces of up to three infantry divisions with tank support) in the general direction of Vakarzhany and Dal'nik. The attacks continued day and night. On separate sectors the enemy managed to penetrate the defenses, but counterattacks restored the situation.

A complication of the forthcoming Soviet counter-offensive consisted in the fact that ordinarily an offensive requires at least a 3-1 advantage in numbers over the enemy, but at Odessa, even including the arriving reinforcements, the enemy had a four-fold superiority in strength. The density of the Odessa Defense District's artillery also amounted to just 5-6 artillery tubes per kilometer of front, which was 3-4 times less than the norms accepted in pre-war times. Thus the command of the Odessa Defense District was persistently seeking every possibility to accumulate strength for a decisive counterblow. This included the formation of the Odessa Defense District's first tank battalion by 10 September. Of the 44 machines that emerged on this day through the gates of the January Uprising factory, there were 39 tanks (primarily BT-7 and T-26) and "NI" armored cars. Senior Lieutenant N.I. Iudin was placed in command of the tank battalion.[4] Over two weeks since the end of August, 25 march battalions (25,300 men) had arrived in Odessa. However, just as before, an acute deficit of command staff, particularly junior commanders, was perceptible: in all the divisions of the Odessa Defense District by the middle of September 1941, there was a deficit of up to 50% of the authorized number. Over one month of fighting alone, the 95th Rifle Division alone lost three platoon and company commanders. All of the headquarters without exception had a shortage of command staff.

The command of the Odessa Defense District was addressing this problem as well through internal resources. For this purpose, the Coastal Army's Department of Combat Training opened courses for junior lieutenants. This yielded for the units more than 300 new platoon commanders, previously sergeants and privates, who had practical combat experience and who stood out for their organizational skills. Even though these men didn't have the necessary theoretical training, given those circumstances this was the only real way out of the situation. Over the entire period of defense, approximately 700 sergeants, soldiers and Black Sea Fleet sailors, who replaced their fallen commanders directly on the battlefield, received the rank of junior lieutenant.

Meanwhile, the Bucharest radio had announced a new date for the capture of Odessa. This time it was set for 10 September 1941. The Odessa Defense District command, preempting the foe's offensive, on the evening of 9 September issued an order to the commander of the 25th Rifle Division Major General I.Iu. Petrov to launch an attack in the most threatened sector of the defense's left flank – in the area of the Lenintal' salient. Simultaneously, the forces on other directions as well went over to offensive operations.

Despite all the dangers, in the city, confidence in the possibility to save Odessa continued to grow. One of the clearest examples of this conviction was the decision to begin a new calendar year in the city's schools. On 15 September, children sat down for parties in 35 schools to celebrate the new school year. The children of the families that had resettled in the catacombs were also

---

4   L. Vladimirisky, "Eskadra Chernomorkogo flota v oborone Odessy" ["Squadron of the Black Sea Fleet in the defense of Odessa"] *Znamia kommunizma*, 3 September 1971 and 11 September 1971.

not forgotten. Many of the teachers had gone to the front, so lecturers of Odessa's special middle schools and of higher education institutes made up for the shortage of pedagogical personnel. The students were supplied with textbooks (including some already published in 1941), notebooks and school materials. The schools provided free breakfasts to the children; cafeterias were working in the schools. Classes continued until the last day of the city's defense.

On 15 September, the Black Sea Fleet's Military Council called for the commander-in-chief of the Odessa Defense District to launch an offensive on the night of 16-17 September in the Sverdlovo, Kubanka direction, and to make demonstration attacks in the West and South Sectors, while the Fleet on that same night would initiate a tactical amphibious landing at Grigor'evka at 0100.[5] However, the Odessa Defense District command couldn't agree with the proposal of the Fleet's Military Council. There wasn't enough strength for a defense, let alone for an offensive. By this time, the 157th Rifle Division that had been promised by the *Stavka* still hadn't arrived from Novorossiisk, while in the South Sector the enemy had again launched an attack and had forced our troops to fall back to the line of the Sukhoi estuary. The Military Council of the Odessa Defense District unanimously insisted on the start of the operation only after the arrival of the 157th Rifle Division, which is to say, on 21 September.

The decision of the Defense District's Military Council came down to launching an attack with the forces of the 421st and 157th Rifle Divisions in the general direction of Sverdlovo; the ships of the Black Sea Fleet would lead off with a landing of the 3rd Naval Infantry Regiment at Grigor'evka, while aircraft would drop paratroopers in the Shitsli – Buldynka area with the aim of disrupting command and communications, as well as sowing panic in the enemy rear.[6] The plan allocated 5 hours to complete the landing of the 3rd Naval Infantry Regiment at Grigor'evka, while the offensive of the units of the East Sector would begin at 0800. In addition, the Odessa Defense District's Military Council proposed not to conduct any preliminary artillery preparation, but to open fire from the ships against revealed firing points and approaching enemy reserves as the regiment advanced.[7]

The Fleet's Military Council agreed with the Odessa Defense District Military Council's proposal, and the operation was shifted to 21 September 1941. The merchant vessels *Dnepr*, *Abkhazia*, *Armeniia*, *Ukraina*, *Vostok* [*East*], *Belostok* [*Bialystock*] and *Kursk* were activated to ship the 157th Rifle Division. Units of the division began to arrive in Odessa on 18 September. The division numbered 12,618 soldiers and officers, 70 guns, 15 tanks and other equipment. Several days later, a battalion of "Katiusha" rocket-launchers was delivered to Odessa. The arrival of such a significant attachment supported the confidence of Odessa's defenders. In a most difficult situation for the government, when the foe was already at the gates of Leningrad, lunging toward Moscow, and conducting active operations on the left bank of the Dnepr River in Ukraine, the *Stavka* of the Supreme High Command was still able to find a way to help the defenders of Odessa. The Chief of the General Staff Marshal of the Soviet Union B.M. Shaposhnikov in a special telegram directed the command of Odessa's defensive area to use the 157th Rifle Division on the axis of the main attack, and not to dissipate its strength in order to pursue secondary objectives.[8]

Eighteen companies of march replacements were still on their way to Odessa. With their arrival, the correlation of force at Odessa settled at a 1 to 4 ratio. The commander of the 157th Rifle Division requested the Military Council of the Odessa Defense District to petition the *Stavka* of the Supreme High Command about also sending the 422nd Heavy Howitzer Regiment, which

---

5   TsVMA MO RF, F. 204, Spr. 9571, ll. 32-33.

6   N. Bellous, "Pervyi desant morskikh pekhotintsev" ["First landing of naval infantrymen"] *Voenno-istoricheskii zhurnal*, No. 4 (1972), pp. 46-47.

7   TsVMA MO RF, F. 204, Spr. 9571, ll. 33-36.

8   I.I. Azarov, *Osazhdennaia Odessa* [*Besieged Odessa*] (Odessa, 1975), p. 141.

was attached to his division, to Odessa. His request was satisfied. Meanwhile, the adversary was striving to demoralize the Odessans – on the night of 18-19 September, for eight hours in a row air raids struck the city, but news about the arrival of a significant combat reinforcement was already on the lips of everyone. This was further encouraging the confidence and optimism of the city's residents. Women, children and old men were greeting the troops that were arriving in Odessa. Despite the fact that enemy attacks were coming one after the other, both day and night, especially in the Vakarzhany – Dal'nik sector right up to 21 September, the troops of the defensive area continued to withstand this furious onslaught.

Preparations for the counter-offensive were in full swing. All of the documents were drawn up with the participation of the headquarters of the units that were readying for the offensive. The plan precisely set the sequence of attacks and the cooperation among the units. In order to organize the cooperation between the naval landing and the counterattack by the forces of the Odessa Defense District, officers from the Black Sea Fleet's Operations Department were sent to Odessa. They let it be known that the proposals from the Odessa Defense District's Military Council had been taken into consideration only because the Military Council's members had been so insistently, obstinately and unanimously advocating for them.

The 3rd Naval Infantry Regiment (commanded by Captain K.M. Koren') had been created in Sevastopol literally over a matter of several days. Small groups of volunteer sailors from surface ships and submarines, and from units and offices of the Black Sea Fleet had joined it. The troops, which had gathered at Cossack Bay, were training to embark upon ships, and then from the ships onto cutters and barges, and also to disembark on an unimproved coastline, both in the dark and in daylight hours. Simultaneously, the regiment's procurement of weapons and equipment was underway (it lacked a sufficient number of machine guns), while staff officers in headquarters worked to complete the paperwork for the operation.

A large amount of Party-ideological work also went on as the troops trained for the landing. Party and Komsomol organizations were created in all the units, and agitators were assigned. They were primarily responsible for forging cohesion within the units; analyzing the practical and political qualities of the troops; and educating the sailors in the spirit of allegiance to combat traditions: the feelings of an unbreakable fleet friendship and combat comradeship, esprit de corps in combat, and the highest discipline. Matters of preparation to resolve combat tasks were discussed at meetings. Combat veterans spoke to the green sailors and petty officers. Primarily, these veterans were sailors that had been discharged from hospitals, who had previously taken part in fighting on the Danube and at Odessa and Nikolaev. Those who stood out in training exercises received attention in combat leaflets, while the agitators talked up their experience. The sailors conscientiously sought to grasp the tactics of ground combat, and readied themselves seriously for the hard trials that awaited them.

Simultaneously, combat ships and landing craft assigned to transport the men by sea and disembark them were preparing. Solitary patrols by picket ships and torpedo boats were deployed on the outer edge of the minefields in the Odessa area, as well as in the area of Tendry, and reconnaissance photographs were taken of the designated landing places. The headquarters of the Odessa Defense District supplied the landing force with intelligence from ground reconnaissance.

On 20 September the Military Council of the Odessa Defense District heard the report from the commander of the Coastal Army Lieutenant General G.P. Sofronov, who had overall responsibility over the troops that were to launch the counterattack in the East Sector. The Military Council approved the preparatory measures and confirmed the plan of action, which was reported to the Fleet's Military Council.

The participants in the joint offensive were given their objective:

- The 421st Rifle Division (commanded by Colonel Kochenov) with its attached artillery and fire support from the 37th and 38th Batteries of the Odessa Naval Base and the Fleet's ships was to attack toward Kryzhanovka, with the immediate task to seize the lines: Voroshilov State Farm, DOPRa dairy farm, and Hill 65.9.

- The 157th Rifle Division (commanded by Colonel Tomilov) with its attached artillery and a tank detachment was to launch attacks in the direction of Luzanovka, Korsunitsy and Hills 52.3 and 69.7, having the immediate task to seize Hills 65.9, 65.5 and 51.4.

- The 3rd Naval Infantry Regiment (commanded by Captain Koren') under the cover of artillery fire from ships of the landing force after disembarking was to seize the villages of Grigor'evka, Chebanka, and Staraia and Novaia Dofinovka, thereby to assist the offensive by the 421st and 157th Rifle Divisions and prevent the enemy's retreat from the area of the Voroshilov State Farm in the direction of Novaia Dofinovka.

- A group of consisting of 23 men dropped by parachute were to disrupt communications in the enemy's rear, sow panic among his troops, and disorganize command and control.

- The landing force of ships included the cruisers *Krasnyi Kavkaz* and *Krasnyi Krym* and the destroyers *Boikii* [*Sprightly*] and *Bezuprochnyi* [*Irreproachable*].

- The detachment of landing craft included the tug boat *Alupka,* 19 cutters of various types, and 10 barges.

- The artillery support group included the gunboat *Krasnaia Gruziia* and 5 patrol boats, which had been assigned to transport the landing parties from the cutters to the shore.

- Air support for the landing rested upon the Fleet's aviation brigade, staging from Crimean airfields, and the Odessa Defense District's aviation regiment.[9]

The commander of the naval operation, Rear Admiral L.A. Vladimirsky and the deputy chief of staff of the Odessa Defense District Captain, 1st Rank S.N. Ivanov, who had departed from Sevastopol en route to Odessa aboard the destroyer *Frunze* at 0600 on 21 September, were supposed to report on any last-minute changes to the operation to the Military Council of the Odessa Defense District.

At 1330 on 21 September 1941, the cruisers *Krasnyi Krym* and *Krasnyi Kavkaz*, the destroyers *Boikii* and *Bezuprochnyi* with 1,900 landing troops aboard left Cossack Bay (Sevastopol) and set a course for Odessa at a fleet speed of 18 knots. The commander in charge of the landing operation was the commander of the brigade of cruisers, Rear Admiral S.G. Gorshkov. During the passage to the invasion site, the ship captains and the commanders of the 3rd Naval Infantry Regiment appealed to the troops with a call to act boldly and decisively when landing on shore. The commander of the 3rd Company of the 3rd Battalion Junior Lieutenant I.D. Charupa petitioned the command for permission for his company to be the first to land on the shore. His request was approved, because his company was one of the best prepared, and his men had a reputation for combat audacity. The combat mission was held in strict secrecy, and the sailors learned about it only after the ships left Sevastopol. En route, the political workers and experienced sailors held discussions with all of the regiment's men, igniting enthusiasm and a desire in the sailors to meet the hated foe in battle, in order to relieve the besieged city.

According to plan, the ships moving from Sevastopol with the landing troops were supposed to link up at 2400 with a detachment of landing craft from Odessa (the gunboat *Krasnaia Gruziia*, the tugboat, 22 cutters and 10 barges). However, the detachment failed to show up at the designated time. The delay was caused by the fact that the commander of the landing operation Rear Admiral L.A. Vladimirsky had arrived in Odessa much later than had been anticipated. Enemy aircraft had attacked and sunk the destroyer *Frunze*, which had been carrying the admiral. Vladimirsky

9   Azarov, "Nash pervyi morskoi desant" ["Our first naval landing"] *Morskoi sbornik*, No. 9 (1961), p. 45.

received a light wound, but the deputy chief of staff of the Odessa Defense District Captain, 1st Rank S.N. Ivanov, who was carrying the papers for the operation, was killed.

All this happened in the following fashion: On the morning of 21 September, en route to Odessa, on the approach to Tendry the *Frunze* spotted the gunboat *Krasnaia Armeniia*, which had been attacked and damaged by enemy aircraft. The destroyer approached the gunboat in order to render assistance, but was attacked by enemy dive bombers. The first attack against the ship was successfully repulsed by friendly anti-aircraft fire. During the second attack, the destroyer received a hit in the aft deck, where the main anti-aircraft cannons were mounted. Control over the rudder was knocked out, and the ship began taking on water. L.A. Vladimirsky ordered to head toward a spit of land. Before reaching it, the *Frunze* became grounded. The tugboat *OP-8* that was accompanying the destroyer and which had earlier helped put out the fire on the gunboat, took men off the *Frunze* and continued to head toward the spit of land. Almost immediately it was attacked by enemy aircraft, and from the damage it took it settled onto its side. The personnel of the destroyer and the crew of the tugboat swam their way to shore. Several of the sailors, petty officers and officers of the destroyer *Frunze* were killed. Both Lieutenant Captain V.N. Eroshenko, who commanded the destroyer and Rear Admiral L.A. Vladimirsky received light wounds. Enemy aircraft sank the *Krasnaia Armeniia* and some of its crew perished. After the admiral was administered first aid, he departed for Odessa aboard a torpedo boat.

Vice Admiral F.S. Oktiabr'sky, having received a telegram about the loss of the *Frunze* and having no information about the fate of Rear Admiral L.A. Vladimirsky, in order to avoid the failure of the landing ordered the Defense Military District's Military Council and Vice Admiral S.G. Gorshkov, who was in charge of the landing: "Conduct the operation, land at 0300. The cruisers are to sail away from Tendry by dawn. The fleet destroyers are to remain to provide fire support."[10]

At 1945, the ships re-deployed into a column and at 2110 closed upon the approach point to the Odessa Naval Base's navigation channel. Vice Admiral I.I. Azov later recalled, "There was no sleep on the night of 21-22 September. During Rear Admiral L.A. Vladimirsky's snap visit to the headquarters, everything had been finalized. However, Vladimirsky wasn't able to return to the cruiser *Krasnyi Kavkaz* by the start of the landing operation." At 2150 the cruiser *Krasnyi Kavkaz* received a message from the chief of staff of the Odessa Naval Base. He was reporting that the gunboat *Krasnaia Gruziia* and cutters would arrive at the rendezvous point by 0100 on 22 September. The task force from Sevastopol decreased its speed in order not to arrive there before the indicated time.

At 0114 the task force arrived in the area of the landing site and the ships began to take up their positions, but the landing craft were late, so Rear Admiral S.G. Gorshkov decided to begin the landing with the means at hand, without waiting for the arrival of the gunboat and cutters. The embarkation of the first wave aboard the ships' lifeboats went smoothly. However, time was running short to land all of the invasion troops. In connection with the enemy air force's high activity, the process had to be completed before dawn so as not to subject the cruisers to risk of attack; they'd been ordered to get underway immediately to Sevastopol before sunup. At 0123 the cruisers and destroyers, positioned about 2,778 meters from shore opened a powerful fire on previously designated targets – enemy artillery and mortar batteries and other firing points. The barrage generated intense fires on the shore, which subsequently became guide marks for our landing craft.

At 0130 the order rang out: "Initiate the landing!", and five minutes later the first lifeboats left the ships and headed for the shore. Lieutenant Charupa's 3rd Company of the 3rd Battalion comprised the first wave. The landing troops were in a hurry, in order to get ashore before the enemy came back to his senses after the preliminary artillery barrage. There still remained 100-150

---

10   Ibid.

meters to the shore when the boats ran aground, and the enemy opened up scattered rifle and machine-gun fire at them. At the command "Into the water!" the sailors and commanders, having raised their rifles and grenades above their heads, leaped overboard. In places, the water was up to their chests, but everyone had only one thought: to reach the shore as quickly as possible.

Lieutenant I.D. Charupa was one of the first to emerge from the sea. More of the landing troops linked up with him. Charupa led the soldiers toward the enemy, which was firing at the incoming boats, and forced the firing points to fall silent. By 0200, all the units of the first wave had landed ashore without having met strong resistance. Signal fires were set on the shore to guide the following waves in. Right after the 3rd Company, two other companies of the 3rd Battalion landed, having the task in the first phase to take Grigor'evka and to prevent the enemy from placing fire on the landing party's main force. Together with them, a mortar battery landed with correcting stakes. In the wake of the 3rd Battalion, Senior Lieutenant B.P. Mikhailov's 1st Battalion came ashore with the task to seize Chebanka and Novaia Dofinovka, where it would link up with units of the 421st Rifle Division.

Only at 0240 did the gunboat *Krasnaia Gruziia* pull up beside the cruiser *Krasnyi Krym*, and having immediately taken aboard some of the remaining landing troops, it headed toward shore. However, it was unable to approach any closer than 555 meters. In the meantime, barges that were supposed to take aboard the landing troops arrived. Patrol boats which had also arrived by that time took the rest of the invasion troops from the cruiser *Krasnyi Krym* and the destroyers and delivered them to shore in order to accelerate the landing operation. By 0510, the process of landing was completed. *Krasnyi Krym* and *Krasnyi Kavkaz*, liberated from their landing duties, in accordance with the radio message from the Fleet commander-in-chief began to depart at 0400 and returned to Sevastopol at 1630. The destroyers remained behind in order to provide fire support for the landing.

Once all of its troops were ashore, the 3rd Naval Infantry Regiment went on the attack. Senior Lieutenant I.D. Cherupa's 3rd Company of the 3rd Battalion, moving in the vanguard, ran into intense machine-gun and mortar fire. It turned out that it was impossible to approach Grigor'evka following the planned route of advance: it had a concentration of enemy firing points. So the commander resorted to cleverness. Leaving behind a small detachment of soldiers with the order to keep up a rapid fire, he moved out with the company's main force to outflank the enemy positions and with a bayonet attack overran them. The destruction of the enemy garrison was completed with the arrival of two other companies led by battalion commander Senior Lieutenant I.F. Matvienko. The enemy soldiers, having tossed aside their weapons and gear, fled. In the battle to take Grigor'evka, Senior Lieutenant Matvienko was wounded three times by shell fragments, but having bandaged the wounds, he continued to lead the battalion forward. At a critical moment of the battle, an exploding shell cut down a machine gun team. The badly-wounded Sergeant Major Boiko crawled over to the machine gun to keep up the fire with the thought to prevent the enemy from counterattacking. The soldier continued to fire the machine gun until his strength left him.[11]

In the course of the offensive, the landing troops came upon a well-camouflaged battery of four cannons, which the hastily-retreating enemy had left behind without disabling them. The fact that the enemy minelayers hadn't had time to remove the signs that marked the boundaries of the minefields also testified to the surprise effect of the invasion. This significantly eased the naval infantrymen's task. Subsequently the captured cannons, which had been pitilessly shelling the city and port, were paraded through the streets of the city by the sailors. On the gun shield and barrel was an inscription in chalk: "It was firing at Odessa. It will do so no longer." With applause,

---

11   Azaraov, *Osazhdennaia Odessa*, pp. 154-155.

Odessans accompanied the soldiers that were escorting the cannons through the streets. Later, these cannons were put on public display at the History Museum in Sevastopol.

In separate sectors the enemy was putting up fierce resistance to the landing troops. The 1st Battalion under the command of Senior Lieutenant B.P. Mikhailov, attacking toward Chebanka and Novaia Dofinovka in order to link up there with units of the 421st Rifle Division, encountered heavy opposition in the vicinity of Chebanka, where a Romanian headquarters was located. The resistance was broken only thanks to the artillery support from the destroyers *Boikii*, *Bezuprechnyi* and *Besposchadnyi*. The commander of a reconnaissance group, Red Seaman Bukarev, having discovered an enemy battery in the Chebanka area, stealthily crept up to it and seized it. Red Seaman Petrenko, conducting reconnaissance near Staraia Dofinovka, bumped into a group of enemy soldiers and boldly wielded his weapon against them. When more Red sailors came upon him Petrenko was lying dead, surrounded by 10 dead enemy soldiers.

The naval landing, having broken enemy resistance with the support of fire from the offshore ships and ground attack aircraft, by 1800 on 22 September reached its objectives and emerged on the line: Chebanka – Hill 57.3 – Novaia Dofinovka. On the morning of 23 September units of the 3rd Naval Infantry Regiment linked up with units of the 421st Rifle Division in the vicinity of the Voroshilov State Farm.

Simultaneously with the naval landing, at 0130 23 men led by Sergeant Major Kuznetsov dropped by parachute from a TB-3 airplane in the area of Hill 37.5 next to the village of Shitsli. Although the wind scattered the landing team, the men acted decisively even when alone. For example, M. Negreba destroyed the headquarters of a Romanian unit, having audaciously snuck up and tossed grenades into it.[12] After the operation, I.I. Azarov recalled the stories of the parachutists:

> Leningrad resident G. Eliseev after landing acted alone: He cut a communications wire that he came across, silenced guards, and killed enemy soldiers and officers. In this way he wiped out a machine-gun crew and captured a heavy machine gun with several boxes of ammunition belts, and then turned it against enemy soldiers. The group of parachutists A. Kotikov (the group commander), P. Litovchenko and A. Leont'ev, as well as Luk'ianenko, Perepelitsy, Reznikov and Khrulenko, with whom they subsequently linked up, acted exceptionally boldly and successfully. It conducted active combat operations and took a lot of prisoners. During one of the sharp clashes, a tragic episode nearly took place. Some of the prisoners, who were prostrate on the ground, seeing that no one was paying attention to them, pounced on the wounded Litovchenko. Kotikov saved him. They showed no mercy to anyone who attacked when a man's back was turned.[13]

According to the testimony of prisoners, throughout the entire night the command of the Romanian 15th Infantry Division was unable to figure out what was happening. No one knew from where the Soviet units were attacking: from the sea, from the air or from the direction of Odessa. More importantly, they couldn't figure out the strength of the attackers. The small airborne landing played its role. The choice of the landing spot for the parachutists had been chosen successfully – exactly in the center where communication lines intersected and the paths lay for shifting enemy reserves. It caught the enemy's attention, and the dark night and daring actions of the parachutists in several places simultaneously created an exaggerated image of the strength of the airborne landing in the enemy and prompted panic. After carrying out their tasks, the parachutists linked up with landing troops of the 3rd Naval Infantry Regiment.

---

12   V.N. Stanko, chief ed., *Istoriia Odesi* [*History of Odessa*] (Odesa: Druk, 2002), p. 390.
13   Azarov, "Nash pervyi morskoi desant", pp. 50-51.

The exploit of the 23 parachutists "hot on the heels" of the events was described in a well-known frontline essay by L. Sobolev, "Batal'ion chetverykh" ["Battalion of four"]. The essay introduced all of the heroes and gave their real names. In this essay, Red Seaman Roman Perepelitsa assesses the strength and combat capabilities of his comrades in the following manner: "One sailor is a sailor; two sailors – a platoon; three sailors – a company. How many were we? Four? A battalion, I say."[14]

The landing by sea and air in the rear of the enemy's divisions proved to be a complete surprise, and the Romanian reaction were weak. The surprise actions of the landing troops from sea, the supporting fire from the offshore ships, the successful operations of the team of parachutists in the enemy rear, the strikes by our air force on enemy air bases in the area of Baden and Zel'tsy, followed by a second wave of airstrikes against the enemy's second echelon in the areas of Aleksandrovka, Il'ichevka, Sverdlovo and Gil'dendorf threw the enemy forces into confusion.

While the 3rd Naval Infantry Regiment was fighting successfully for Grigor'evka and other points, diverting the enemy's attention, regiments of the 421st and 157th Rifle Divisions went on the attack out of the East Sector at 0800. Overcoming enemy resistance in the vicinity of Fontanka and Hill 58.0, units of the 421st Rifle Division persistently pushed ahead. The enemy offered tough resistance. By 1100 the 421st Rifle Division had advanced to the Agrokombinat, Il'ichevka, Fontanka line, and with the introduction of the 54th Rifle Regiment into the battle, by 1600 the division finally captured Hill 58.0. The Romanian resistance crumbled, and tossing aside weapons, their men began to retreat. By the end of the day, the regiments of the 421st Rifle Division was occupying the Voroshilov State Farm, Vapniarka, Aleksandrovka, the DOPRa dairy farm and Hill 65.9, and had linked up with units of the 157th Rifle Division.

The 157th Rifle Division, with the forces of the 716th Rifle Regiment and the support of the Odessa Defense District's tank battalion launched its main attack in the direction of Gil'dendorf. The 633rd Rifle Regiment was operating in the direction of Il'ichevka State Farm. With its first attack it breached the enemy's fortifications and in the wake of the tanks broke through into the depth of the enemy's defenses. The impetuosity of the attack by the units of the 157th Rifle Division threw the enemy ranks into a panic, and the Romanians hastily fled, leaving behind their wounded. By 1330 the 716th Rifle Regiment reached the eastern outskirts of Gil'dendorf, while the 633rd Rifle Regiment – the Il'ichevka State Farm. A fresh attack by the regiments of the 157th Rifle Division that started at 1600 threw the enemy into a disorderly flight. The decisive actions of the 157th Rifle Division brought about the rapid defeat of the enemy's forces. At the end of 22 September, units of the 421st and 157th Rifle Divisions had arrived at their designated lines, having fulfilled their combat orders with honor.

On that same day [of 21 September], in order to disorient the foe regarding the direction of the main attack and to deprive him of the possibility of shifting reserves to meet the attack at Grigor'evka, a diversionary attack against the enemy was launched in the South Sector of Defense at 0300, several hours prior to the main attack. The air forces of the Coastal Army and the Black Sea Fleet were actively supporting the offensive on the ground and from the sea. It inflicted powerful bombing strikes against enemy airfields and troop groupings in the areas of Sverdlovo, Kubanka, Aleksandrovka, Gil'dendorf and the Il'ichevka State Farm. At dawn 19 airplanes of the 69th Fighter Aviation Regiment with several strafing runs destroyed 8 tents, a lot of fuel cisterns and killed 3 pilots, while knocking out 21 enemy aircraft on the airfields close to Baden (present-day Ocheretovka) and Zel'tsi (present-day Limanskoe).

However, our air force wasn't alone in the air. At 1300 on 22 September, enemy dive bombers targeted the destroyer *Bezuprechnyi* with 36 bombs. Our fighters with their attacks hindered

---

14   L.S. Sobolev, *Izbrannye proizvedeniia* [*Selected works*], Vol. 2 (Moscow, 1962), p. 420.

accurate bombing, but bombs fell close to the ship. Its commander Lieutenant Captain P.M. Buriak with artful maneuvering avoided any direct hits. However, the destroyer received heavy damage from a blast wave and bomb fragments (more than 300 holes). The 1st and 2nd boiler rooms were flooded as well as the port engine. The destroyer lost power and was left with killed and wounded aboard. Only thanks to the skillful actions of the crew in the struggle for survival, the ship remained afloat and was towed back to Odessa.

Meanwhile at 1730, 19 enemy bombers attacked the destroyer *Besposchadnyi* and released 84 bombs. The result was no direct hits, but a blast wave crumpled the prow up to the 44th cross rib and flooded the control center and the 1st, 2nd and 3rd bunkrooms. The ship was taking on a lot of water. However, the competent actions of the ship's commander Lieutenant Captain G.P. Negoda and the selfless work of the crew not only kept the ship afloat, but allowed it to reach Odessa by running in reverse. The destroyer *Boikii* also received a lot of minor damage from enemy aircraft. Even so, despite the enemy's air force's strong reaction, the destroyers carried out their missions.[15]

On the whole, the counteroffensive concluded successfully. The agreed-upon coordinated actions of the ground forces with the naval and parachute landings totally disrupted the enemy's prepared new offensive, which significantly eased the situation for the Odessa Defense District's defending units. As a result of the landing operation, the Romanian forces were thrown back by 5-8 kilometers away from Odessa in the East Sector and the Romanian 13th and 15th Infantry Divisions were shattered; the Romanians lost up to 6,000 soldiers and officers killed or captured, including around 2,000 dead. Our forces captured 83 guns and mortars, 6 tanks, 127 machine guns, 1,100 rifles and machine pistols, 13,500 mines and hand grenades, 3,000 shells, more than 100 kilometers of telephone cable and a lot of other military gear.[16] The Soviet pilots destroyed 40 enemy aircraft either in the air or on the ground.

However, the most important achievement of the operation was the fact that the shelling of the city, port and approaches to it from the northeastern direction ceased completely. The port was left in a zone that was out of range for the enemy artillery. Over the single day of the counterattack, the Coastal Army expanded the area of the Odessa bridgehead by 120 square kilometers.[17] In order to take this ground, the enemy had conducted bitter fighting accompanied by heavy losses for one and a half months, while in contrast, for example, the 157th Rifle Division on 22 September lost only 19 killed and 237 wounded to win it back.[18]

The success of the joint counterattack substantially affected the future course of the combat operations at Odessa. In connection with his heavy losses, the enemy lessened its pressure on the city. The enemy command now anticipated a counteroffensive by Soviet forces along the entire front. It brought up two fresh divisions and issued instructions to its troops that no longer placed emphasis on how to attack, but on how to defend better. The contents of Operational Order No. 73 to the Romanian troops dated 5 October 1941 confirm this: "The recent offensive by the enemy, as well as the intelligence that is available today, allows the conclusion to be drawn that the enemy is preparing the deployment of his main forces. The divisions must be ready to repel an enemy offensive."[19]

It was also important that demoralization among the Romanian soldiers and officers, who were losing hope to capture Odessa further increased: the number of desertions increased, and incidents

---

15 Azarov, "Nash pervyi moskoi desant", pp. 49-50.
16 TsVMA MO RF, F. 204, Spr. 6772, Ark. 420.
17 K.V. Penzin, *Chernomorskii flot v oborone Odessy* [*Black Sea Fleet in the defense of Odessa*] (Moscow, 1956), p. 104.
18 *Znamia kommunizma*, 3, 21, 22 September 1971; N. I. Krylov, *Ne pomerknet nikogda*, pp. 203, 206.
19 *Ukrains'ka RSR u Velikii Vitchiznanii viini Radians'kogo Soiuzu 1941-1945*, Vol. 1 (Kiev: Politvydav Ukrainy, 1967), p. 247.

of self-inflicted wounds became much more frequent. Realizing that the war was being fought in the interests of German fascism and that they faced certain death, many Romanian soldiers and officers voluntarily surrendered to Soviet troops and appealed to their compatriots to follow their example. One such appeal, signed by 200 Romanian soldiers and officers, stated: "Not wishing to spill blood on behalf of Hitler and his sycophants, we, soldiers and officers of the Romanian Army, today voluntarily surrendered to the Red Army ... Brothers, end the war! Turn your weapon against your own enslavers and kill them! Hail the free Romanian people!"[20] News of the debacle suffered by Romanian divisions at Odessa filtered into Romania and made a dismal impression on the country's inhabitants, increasing their dissatisfaction with I. Antonescu's fascist regime.

Even the foe was noting the success of the counteroffensive. In his war diary, the chief of the OKH General Halder wrote: "... the defense of Odessa had a nature of resistance with no thought about retreat; the defense was distinguished by offensive actions, and was active"[21] and also: "The Romanians are receiving unexpected attacks from the rear."[22] If in the first two days following the Soviet counteroffensive the Romanian command still attempted to launch attacks in the South Sector of Defense, then after "Katiusha" rocket launchers were employed on 25 September in the area of Dal'nik, for the first time since 5 August calm settled over the front.

This operation demonstrated the growing military skill and mass heroism of the defenders. The commander of the 157th Rifle Division D.G. Tomilov wrote in his report: "It is very difficult to single out soldiers and commanders for their feats, since all of the men rushed forward, and the individuals who showed courage and heroism obviously remained unobserved.[23] On 23 September, a decree of the Presidium of the Supreme Soviet was published about awarding 43 participants in the offensive operation with Orders and medals.[24]

The situation of Odessa's defenders eased, and the conditions for delivering everything necessary from the sea improved. In addition, in order to plug the breach torn into his front, the Romanian command was forced to transfer fresh forces to the eastern sector at the expense of reserves, and weaken the attacks against other sectors of the Odessa front. Full of resolve to defend the city even longer, the Soviet troops began to prepare for combat operations in winter conditions. An order was issued about arranging heat in the bunkers and about preparing fuel and items for winter; warm clothing and footgear for the troops of the defensive area was being produced at an increased tempo. Even though the front's breath was perceptible at every step, the city continued to function almost normally. Communal facilities were operating, electrical power stations were producing electricity; the trolley cars continued to run, and stores, polyclinics, hospitals, movie theaters and performance art theaters remained open. Classes were even underway in schools – and this was something very symbolic. The city was beginning to prepare for a winter under siege conditions. In order to resolve the fuel problems, the Soviet Council of People's Commissars allocated 125,000 metric tons of coal, 22,000 metric tons of heating oil and petroleum, 118,000 metric tons of coke and 178,000 metric tons of firewood to Odessa.[25]

Furthermore, the Odessa Defense District command began to plan another counterattack in the southwestern direction. Up until the end of September, the Coastal Army received another 36

---

20   *Krasnaia Zvezda*, 1 October 1941.
21   F. Halder, *Voennyi dnevnik: v 3 t.* [*War diary in three volumes*] Vol. 1 (Moscow: Voenizdat, 1971), p. 367, 370. [Ed. note: These quotes cannot be found in the highly edited single volume English translation of Halder's war diary, so the translation of them in this book is from the Russian.]
22   Ibid., p. 376.
23   TsAMO RF, F. 288, Op. 9900, D. 18, l. 42.
24   *Odesskaia oblast v Velikoi Otechestvennoi voine 1941-1945: Dokumenty i materialy* [*Odessa Oblast in the Great Patriotic War 1941-1945*] (Odessa: Maiak, 1970), pp. 104-105; *Znamia kommunizma*, 14 September 1971.
25   Stanko [chief ed.], *Istoriia Odesi*, p. 392.

companies of replacements, more than 8,000 men. On 29 September, two transport ships arrived in Odessa with 35 train cars of ammunition. After the successful counterattack, on the night of 22-23 September the forces of the Odessa Defense District underwent a regrouping. The most combat-capable 157th Rifle Division was transferred to the West and South Sectors, while the troops of the 421st Rifle Division and the attached 3rd Naval Infantry Regiment continued to hold the defense in the East Sector. In the remaining days of September, our troops dug in on their achieved lines and repulsed all of the enemy's attacks. The situation at Odessa stabilized.

The headquarters of the Coastal Army completed the preparations of a combat order and the compilation of a plan for an offensive on the left in the South Sector, with the launching of the main attack in the direction of Lenintal'. The plan designated the operation to begin on 2 October 1941.[26] However, an offensive by the German armies of Army Group South, which began at this time at Khar'kov and in the Donbas, as well as the genuine threat of an enemy breakthrough into the Crimea, sharply changed the plans of the higher Soviet command with respect to the Odessa bridgehead. The concluding stage of Odessa's defense, no less difficult than the preceding one, lay ahead.[27]

---

26   Krylov, *Ne pomerknet nikogda*, pp. 206, 213.
27   *Operatsiia Sovetskikh Vooruzhennykh Sil v Velikoi Otechestvennoi voine 1941-1945* [*Operation of the Soviet Armed Forces in the Great Patriotic War 1941-1945*] Vol. 1 (Moscow: Voenizdat, 1985], p. 171 and insert 21.

7

The evacuation of the Odessa defensive area

In September 1941, besieged Odessa was continue to hold out against the massed attacks of a 300,000-man grouping of German and Romanian forces, while periodically conducting well-prepared counterattacks. The city had learned to live under the hard conditions of a siege, and was keeping the forces of the Odessa Defense District supplied with replacements, weapons, ammunition and other necessary means, as well as supporting the living conditions of its citizens as much as possible. In Odessa, transportation, electrical supply and the rest of the city's infrastructure continued to operate, as well as everyday services, cafes, theaters and movie houses. The people of Odessa were so confident in the solidity of the city's defense that on 15 September, a new calendar schoolyear began in Odessa's schools. Here is how the commander of the 25th Rifle Division V.F. Vorob'ev saw Odessa on 5 October 1941: "Upon entering the city, the barricades that obstructed the city's streets leaped to the eye. In many places, the paved roads were strewn with the rubble from demolished buildings. However, the trolleys were going around, shops were open, school kids were hurrying to classes, and fresh billboards were advertising new films."[1]

However, the overall situation that had taken shape on the Soviet-German front by the end of September was much more tragic. The fascist troops were lunging toward Moscow and Leningrad. They had taken Kiev, broken into the Donbas, and were surging into the Crimean peninsula. A direct threat to the capture of the Black Sea Fleet's main naval base – Sevastopol – was forming. In this situation the Military Council of the Black Sea Fleet appealed to the *Stavka* of the Supreme High Command with a proposal to re-position the combat-capable and experienced troops of the Odessa Defense District in order to strengthen the defense of the Crimea. Despite the alarming situation in the Crimea, at first the *Stavka* didn't want to issue an order to abandon Odessa, where bitter yet successful combats were unfolding. Later the People's Commissar of the Navy Admiral N.G. Kuznetsov wrote:

> The thoughts of I.V. Stalin in connection with Odessa's evacuation were known to me. He asked me to question the Military Council of the Black Sea Fleet about the expedience of leaving some of the forces, up to two divisions, in Odessa in order to hold the city and to tie up enemy forces there. I sent such a telegram on 4 October. The chief military headquarters and the Military Council of the Black Sea Fleet reported to me that such half-measures were not useful. Subsequent events confirmed that a delay with the evacuation of Odessa or leaving some of forces there might have had a fatal effect on the defense of Sevastopol, and by itself, on the fate of Odessa's defenders.[2]

---

1   As cited by N.G. Kuznetsov, *Na flotakh boevaia trevoga*, p. 126.
2   Ibid., p. 126.

Only after receiving the Military Council of the Black Sea Fleet's confirmation of the need to evacuate all of the troops from Odessa, on 30 September 1941 the *Stavka* issued a directive: "The soldiers and commanders of Odessa's defensive area, who have bravely and honorably carried out their orders, are to evacuate in the shortest time possible to the Crimean peninsula." The troops of the 51st Separate Army were ordered to cover and hold the northern approaches to the Crimea until the arrival of the Coastal Army's forces.[3]

The *Stavka*'s directive to evacuate the forces brought the Deputy People's Commissar for the Navy Vice Admiral I. Levchenko from Sevastopol to Odessa. On this same day the Military Council of the Odessa Defense District met, at which Rear Admiral G.V. Zhukov announced the directive. For the Military Council and the soldiers of the Odessa Defense District, not to mention the city's people, such a decision was completely unexpected – the defense of Odessa by this time had stiffened and seemed to be of an enduring nature. However, the Fleet command insisted on conducting the evacuation of troops from Odessa.

During the Great Patriotic War, the Soviet command had to evacuate forces and the population on a major scale three times: from Tallinn, Odessa and Khanko. In each case the circumstances were different, but in each instance posed a challenge. The evacuation had to be implemented literally within the sights of the enemy guns. Moreover, the more stubbornly, to "the last possibility", the fighting that was going on, the more difficult it was to evacuate.

In Tallinn the command had just several days to prepare for the evacuation and to conduct it. The Germans were pressing and moreover had a large superiority in forces. Upon the enemy's discovery of the evacuation, he inflicted significant losses to the Soviet fleet and the evacuating troops.

Thus the evacuation of the Odessa Defense District's forces received much more careful preparation. The evacuation of the Odessa defensive area's forces and means was an extremely precarious and complex combat operation, the successful implementation of which demanded the harmonious, stealthy work of all the forces of the Coastal Army, Black Sea Fleet and steamships. It was necessary to extract by sea 5 divisions together with their rear units and weapons, the most valuable remaining factory equipment, their most highly qualified workers and the families of the servicemen in the shortest possible time, between 1 and 16 October 1941. The evacuation by sea of a major force grouping is especially dangerous by the fact that the enemy obtains the possibility to place damaging fire on the evacuating troops for an extended period of time: when being removed from the front, when marching to the port, when embarking onto the ships, when leaving the harbor and when sailing to the new destination. Evacuation on a large scale requires a sufficient amount of time for preparations, camouflaging, and organizing the thorough cover and maximal concealment of the operation.

Immediately after the receipt of the *Stavka*'s directive, on 1-2 October 1941 the 157th Rifle Division, which had only recently arrived at Odessa from Novorossiisk, left for Sevastopol. On the evening of 1 October, the *Ukraina*, the first transport ship carrying elements of the 157th Rifle Division departed from Odessa and set a course for Sevastopol; on the following day, the transport ships *Zhan Zhores* and *Bol'shevik* left Odessa with the rest of the 157th Rifle Division.

In order to conceal the start of the evacuation from the enemy, as well as to throw him into confusion and disrupt his plans for an offensive toward Odessa, on 2 October 1941 a major counterattack with forces of the 25th Rifle Division and the 2nd Cavalry Division was launched in the South Sector of Defense. After an intense, 20-minute artillery and mortar preparation, in the course of which a battalion of "Katiusha" rocket launchers fired 5 salvoes, the Soviet forces went on the attack in the Dal'nitskii – Lenintal' sector. By the evening, they had penetrated 4 kilometers

---

3   TsAMO RF, F. 407, Op. 7852, D. 1, ll. 111-112.

into the depth of the enemy's defenses and had fully destroyed four battalions of Romanian infantry. The Odessa Defense District's tank battalion (39 tanks and armored tractors) under the command of Senior Lieutenant I. Iudin, with the support of infantry from the 25th Rifle Division, breached the enemy's defenses. The tanks surged forward and conducted a daring foray into the enemy's rear areas, destroying enemy personnel and equipment, but the infantry lagged behind. Thus on their return back the tankers had to fight their way through an anti-tank screen that had been deployed by the Romanians and took losses. However, despite the enemy's intensive fire, the tankers overran the Romanian artillery and towed back 30 artillery pieces they had captured in the battle. As a result of this counterattack, the adversary lost approximately 1,000 soldiers and officers. Among the captured loot were 44 guns of various calibers and 48 heavy machine guns.

The initial evacuation plan foresaw a gradual contraction in the front lines with a subsequent withdrawal of troops from the main line of defense to rear defensive lines, and then to the barricades in the city. Such a scenario for the evacuation process gave rise to the threat of having to conduct it under intense enemy fire, and consequently, with heavy losses, especially among the army's rear guard units.

On 5 October 1941, General I.E. Petrov was appointed commander of the Coastal Army in the place of General G.P. Sofronov, who had departed due to illness. Having assessed the situation that was fraught with heavy losses in the Coastal Army's personnel, General I.E. Petrov devised and insisted upon a new plan for the evacuation, which envisioned the simultaneous, stealthy removal of all of the Odessa Defense District's main forces directly from the main line of defense and their subsequent evacuation in a single echelon, as well as a reduction in the time given to the evacuation to five days and its completion by the night of 15-16 October. According to Petrov's new plan, our main forces were to hold their positions on the main line of defense until the evening of 15 October, while exhibiting combat activity and feigning preparations for new attacks. Then only with the onset of darkness, covered by rear-guard battalions detached from each division and with offshore fire support from the Black Sea Fleet's ships, the main forces would disengage from the enemy and conduct a concealed march on foot to the port, embark upon the ships, and head out to sea. Leadership over the preparation and conducting of the evacuation was implemented by an operational command group headed by the commander of the Coastal Army General I.Iu. Petrov. Everything was calculated and weighed down to the last details. This was a bold plan, although one not without risk, based upon the acquired combat experience with a numerically superior foe and on a deep faith in one's own troops and their capabilities.

A most important condition for the success of the evacuation was the secrecy of its preparation and the concealment of its implementation, as well as keeping the enemy confused and clinging to disinformation. In addition to the measures to increase the activity of the Soviet forces at the front, this was achieved by spreading word about an operational rotation of the forces and relieving pressure on the city's services and infrastructure for the winter by evacuating some of the population. Soviet scouts dropped off fictitious materials for the enemy about the transfer of additional army and navy units to Odessa. Along the roads leading to the front under enemy observation, columns of trucks with canvas-covered beds kept moving, feigning the arrival of major reinforcements. Transport ships, sailing into the port in daylight hours, had bags of flour and other products on their decks. With the demonstrative transfer of an outwardly appearing significant volume of cargo into covered vehicles, this suggested to enemy spies that food was being accumulated in Odessa for wintertime delivery to the troops and population. The construction of heated dugouts was also organized, while iron stoves in large numbers arrived by sea, delivered to the dugouts and lit inside them, giving the appearance that the troops on the defensive line were preparing for winter.

Meanwhile, each night 3 to 6 large transports would stealthily leave the port with men, weapons and property of the army's rear. Under the cover of ships and aircraft of the Black Sea Fleet, without losses they would arrive at their destinations. Over 10 days, between 1 and 11 October, 51,690 men, 208 artillery pieces of various calibers, 16 aircraft, 868 vehicles, 162 tractors, 18,000 metric tons of equipment of the factories and port, and a lot of other military property was brought out of Odessa. The restaging of such a large quantity of men and military loads couldn't escape the attention of enemy reconnaissance. Signs of the evacuation were noted by the enemy and he again increased the pressure on Odessa.

On 9 October the enemy forces launched an offensive along the entire front of the Odessa defensive area, but met with a decisive repulse and were forced to fall back to their jumping-off positions. On the next day the fascists undertook an attempt to achieve their objectives by a human wave attack in the South Sector. After a strong artillery preparation, they went on the offensive in compact columns of battalions. The artillery of the South Sector opened fire at them. Shells were exploding in the midst of the attacking columns, but they kept coming on, continuing to advance. The enemy troops managed to break through the first line of trenches and penetrate into the depth of the Soviet defenses. Soldiers of the 25th Rifle Division and 2nd Cavalry Division responded with a bayonet charge. As a result, the Romanian 10th Infantry Division was smashed. Its 38th Infantry Regiment was hit particularly hard, suffering the loss of 1,200 men killed and wounded and up to 500 men taken prisoner, including the regiment commander and his staff officers. The penetration was eliminated and the front restored to its previous lines.

The success achieved in this counterattack by troops of the Odessa Defense District again misled the enemy command. It could not imagine how an army that was implementing an evacuation could launch such a powerful response. Thus, as became known already after the war, on 12 October Bucharest radio announced that the final assault on Odessa would be postponed until the spring of 1942. In order to keep the enemy in a state of confusion, all of the Coastal Army's artillery still within the bridgehead was ordered on 13 October to begin around-the-clock, systematic shelling of the enemy's combat positions, particularly intensively from the morning of 15 October. At nights, signs of future changes were clear: enlivened traffic toward the port, a large number of arriving transport ships, etc. However, in the daytimes Odessa was continuing to live under the routines that had become established during the siege – communal enterprises, the power station, and the city transportation system were still working; oblast newspapers were coming out; and classes were continuing in the schools. Indirect confirmation of the enemy's lack of information about the Odessa Defense District's plans for evacuation might be the text of a Hitler's letter to I. Antonescu on 5 October 1941, in which he proposed "easing the offensive against Odessa for the Romanian troops without excessive blood."[4]

In the course of 14-15 October, 17 ships of large tonnage, 2 cruisers, 4 destroyers, 4 minesweepers and a large quantity of cutters, tugboats, barges, schooners and so forth arrived in Odessa's port for the simultaneous evacuation of the Odessa Defense District's main forces. This was the last voyage by transport ships to the besieged city. The crews of the following ships, which became military transports and made a weighty contribution to the overall cause of Odessa's defense, were ready for their final voyage from Odessa's shores: *Ukraina* (Captain P.A. Polovko), *Abkhaziia* (Captain D.D. Dzhurashevich), *Armeniia* (Captain V.Ia. Plaushevs'ky), *Gruziia* (Captain M.I. Fokin), *Kuban'* (Captain G.M. Vislobokov), *Krym* [*Crimea*] (Captain R.Iu. Slipko), *Pestel'* [*Pestel*] (Captain S.M. Kushnarenko), *Anatolii Serov* (Captain K.K. Tret'iakov), *Kalinin* (Captain I.F. Ivanov), *Chapaev* (Captain A.I. Chirkov), *Kursk* (Captain V.Ia. Trush), *Voroshilov* (Captain A.F. Shantsberg), *Zhan Zhores* (Captain G.M. Lebedev), *Fabritsius* (Captain M.I. Grigor'ev) and other ships took part. In

---

4   *Niurnbergskii protsess: Sbornik materialov v 8 t.* [The Nuremburg trials: Collection of materials in 8 volumes], Vol. 3 (Moscow, 1989), p. 576.

addition, the transport ship *Bol'shevik* (Captain E.I. Freiman) was delayed in setting out toward Odessa due to mechanical problems. Combat ships of the Black Sea Fleet were committed to escort the transport ships: the cruisers *Krasnyi Kavkaz* and *Krasnaia Ukraina*, the destroyers *Smyshlennyi*, *Bodryi*, *Nezamozhnik*, and *Shaumian*, the frigates *Petrash* and *Kuban*, 4 minesweepers, 20 patrol boats and an assortment of tugboats, barges and schooners. Even though the ships sought to disperse across all the moorings and to camouflage themselves, such a significant and unusual aggregation of ships in Odessa's port was spotted by enemy aerial reconnaissance.

At daybreak and in the evening of 15 October, massed air attacks, in which more than 40 enemy aircraft took part, launched raids on the port. They were repulsed by the ships' and coastal anti-aircraft artillery together with the Odessa Defense District's fighters. In the course of one of the enemy's attacks, a bomb struck the aft deck of the steamship *Gruziia*. It triggered a fire which was extinguished by the crew only later that evening; 120 wounded men were taken off the burning ship. The *Gruziia* was towed out of the port by the destroyer *Shaumian*, and then under its own power made its way to Novorossiisk, carrying on board approximately 2,000 evacuees and wounded.

On 15 October leadership over the evacuation, according to plan, was executed from the flag-ship cruiser *Chervona Ukraina*. It was from its bridge that the final order to the troops of the Odessa Defense District went out, signed by Rear Admiral G.V. Zhukov. In particular, it ordered:

1. Begin the withdrawal of the Odessa Defense District's troops at 1900 on 15 October 1941, complete the embarkation on the night of 15-16 October, according to the plan of 13 October that I've confirmed.
2. I am placing responsibility for the execution of the withdrawal and embarkation on the commander of the Coastal Army Major General Petrov.
3. I am subordinating the commander of the Odessa Naval Base Rear Admiral Kuleshov to the commander of the Coastal Army.
4. I demand from the commanders and commissars of the formations and units under their personal responsibility that all property, materiel and supplies, which are impossible to evacuate, to be destroyed. Take along with yourselves side arms and crewed weapons. Destroy facilities of government and strategic significance according to the plan I've confirmed.

On the day before the evacuation of the Odessa Defense District's troops, 20 bombers of the 40th Aviation Regiment left Crimean airfields and struck enemy airfields and positions in the area of Sukhoi Liman, Bolgarskie Khutory and other populated places.

On 15 October at 1900 the main forces of the defensive area began to withdraw from the forward line of defense under the cover of rear-guard units and fire from the Black Sea Fleet's ships. Units of the 25th, 95th and 421st Rifle Divisions and the 2nd Cavalry Division together with their weapons, having completed a hard night march reached the city and moved further along its streets, which had previously been especially covered with lime and ground chalk so that no one would lose their way in the darkness, to the port. At 2300 the troops from the march began to embark upon the transport ships at every point of embarkation.

In the memoirs of I.I. Azarov, who was a member of the Odessa Defense District's Military Council it is possible to find a description of the grueling march and embarkation of the soldiers:

> I still clearly see silent men trudging along and climbing aboard the ships, so burdened with ammunition that it is surprising that a man could move with such a load. They were marching for kilometer after kilometer, and also at night ... Some of the soldiers couldn't even climb the gangway and collapsed under their burdens. Red Navy sailors and petty officers, without

waiting for an order, helped them get up, having donned the soldiers' weapons and packs onto their own shoulders.[5]

As soon as they were loaded, the transport ships cast off and moved out into the open harbor before setting on their course. The overall direction over the embarkation of the troops onto the ships was handled by the commander of the Odessa Naval Base Rear Admiral I.D. Kushelov and his headquarters' staff. At 2100, the rear guard battalions of the divisions began to withdraw from the forward edge of defense. Taking advantage of the nighttime darkness, under the cover of fire from the coastal artillery and offshore ships, they abandoned their forward position without hindrance and up until 0300 were arriving at the port in vehicles. After their withdrawal, combat engineers began mining all the roads, in order to hamper a possible pursuit by the enemy. From the coast, the rear-guard battalions were delivered by longboats to the cruisers *Krasnyi Kavkaz* and *Krasnaia Ukraina*.

That same night in the city, specially assigned teams under the command of the Coastal Army's chief of engineers Colonel G.P. Kerdinsky destroyed key facilities that were important in a military respect. Even before this, according to the adopted plan, more than 100 delayed-action mines were emplaced around the city at the airfield, the port, the electrical power station and in other important buildings; the building on Marazlievsky Street that housed the headquarters of the NKVD was also prepared for demolition.

On the whole in the course of several nighttime hours, the main forces of the defensive area numbering 35,000 men with their combat gear and personal weapons were completely removed from their combat positions, marched to the port and loaded upon ships. At 0510 on the morning of 16 October, the last transport ship carrying troops of the Odessa Defense District left the Odessa harbor. Only after this did the coastal artillery cease their fire, which had continued without interruption throughout the night on enemy positions, and then the guns were blown up. The artillerymen of the coastal batteries and the demolition teams that had destroyed strategic facilities in the city were the last to board ships. Faithful to the traditions of the Navy, the last to leave the burning port was its chief P.M. Makarenko. Then the base's minelayer *BTShch-15* dropped mines into the Odessa harbor and around its outer perimeter.

At 0530 a duty officer reported to the command: "The evacuation of Odessa has been fully completed. No losses in men and equipment." The entire array of measures to evacuate the Odessa defensive area passed without detection by the enemy. Up until nearly noon on 16 October, the Romanians conducted an artillery barrage and bombed the forward edge of defense and the city, which had been abandoned by the Soviet troops. Toward noon enemy aerial reconnaissance spotted a large convoy of Soviet ships in the Tendry area. However, the enemy initially didn't pay any significant attention to this finding. Indeed, it was only after reconnaissance probes of the positions of our troops along the entire front did the enemy become convinced that the entire Coastal Army had been evacuated from Odessa.

Enemy aircraft began a pell-mell pursuit of the convoy of Soviet ships; 56 enemy bombers, torpedo planes and fighters more than once tried to conduct a massed attack against the convoy and destroy it. However, the command of the Black Sea Fleet had anticipated such a threat. In addition to the anti-aircraft guns of the combat ships that were accompanying the transports, more than 50 fighters of the Black Sea Fleet and the Coastal Army's 69th Fighter Aviation Regiment provided air cover. At least 12 Soviet fighters were constantly patrolling the skies above the convoy. Intercepting the enemy attacks, the Soviet pilots became engaged in 23 aerial combats and shot down 17 enemy aircraft. The anti-aircraft gunners aboard the ships claimed another three fascist aircraft downed. Our pilots in this aerial battle lost 6 fighters. The transports and ships remained

---

5   Azarov, *Osazhdennaia Odessa*, p. 194.

undamaged and continued on their voyage. Only the transport ship *Bol'shevik*, which was moving empty at the tail of the convoy as a reserve, was sunk by an enemy torpedo attack. Before the ship sank, its crew was rescued by patrol boats of the 2nd Brigade of Patrol Boats.

At 2200, the main forces of the Odessa Defense District arrived at Sevastopol. Altogether between 1 and 16 October, approximately 111,000 soldiers and commanders of the Coastal Army and the Odessa Naval Base (including 31,000 wounded), 15,000 civilians, 462 guns, 19,103 metric tons of ammunition, 24 tanks and tankettes, 16 armored cars, 3,625 horses, 1,158 vehicles, 500 automobile engines, and more than 9,725 metric tons of various equipment from Odessa's factories and port were evacuated from Odessa and delivered to the Crimea and Caucasus. For the evacuation, 24 transport ships that displaced more than 159,000 metric tons of water were used, and they made 51 voyages to the besieged city. In escort, 23 combat ships completed 33 voyages. The Black Sea Fleet and the naval steamships successfully met a difficult challenge.[6]

Compelled by order, the city's officials that were abandoning the city put up posters around the city addressed to all the citizens of Odessa and Odessa Oblast, which explained the reasons for the evacuation of the Coastal Army's forces, emphasized the significance of the city's heroic defense for the future inevitable defeat of the foe, and set tasks for the further struggle against the occupiers:

> The heroic defenders of Odessa, the Red Army and the Black Sea Fleet, supported by all the workers, defended the Soviet Black Sea coast with unprecedented heroism and courage. They carried out their duty to the Motherland with honor. Dozens of Romanian-German divisions and hundreds of thousands of fascist bandits perished ignobly on the approaches to Odessa.
>
> Now, however, in connection with the fact that Odessa has wound up remote from supply bases and has lost its previous strategic importance, the Soviet government and the *Stavka* have decided to abandon Odessa, shifting its forces to other sectors of the front ...
>
> Dear friends! ... We will not yield to the German brigands the goods we have earned with our blood and sweat; we will not yield ourselves to the German bandits in bondage and slavery. We are our own masters, we love our regime, we love our sunny Soviet Ukraine, we love our great Soviet Union, and for them we will fight to the last drop of blood. We will beat the foe cruelly, incessantly, until his complete destruction!
>
> Deal pitilessly with the German-Romanian aggressors, beat them at each step, pursue and destroy them like scurvy dogs. Let death lie in wait for the foe in each building, yard and street and on roads large and small. Instead of bread, give him a bullet, instead of refuge – fire. Create sabotage groups for struggle against units of the hostile army, in order to blow up bridges and roads; damage telephone and telegraph cables; set fire to woods, stockpiles and wagon trains; create intolerable conditions for the foe and all of his henchmen; follow and destroy them at each step; sabotage and disrupt all of the aggressors' measures.[7]

The evacuation of the Coastal Army from Odessa to the Crimea became a major accomplishment of military skill. Never before previously in the history of wars were there cases when an enormous army imperceptibly to the enemy abandoned their positions and at night, over the course of several hours, embarked upon ships together with all of their gear, made a lengthy maritime trip and without losses re-stage to a different front. The combat operation to evacuate the forces and means of the Odessa defensive area, by its results and the skill shown when conducting it remained unsurpassed right up until the end of the Second World War.

---

6   Odessa v Velikoi Otechestvennoi voine Sovetskogo Soiuza. Sbornik dokumentov [Odessa in the Great Patriotic War of the Soviet Union. Collection of documents] Vol. 1 (Odessa, 1947), p. 267.
7   Ibid.

Speaking about the strategic significance of Odessa's defense, it is necessary first of all to note that in the most difficult and tragic initial phase of the Great Patriotic War, the city's defenders tied up 300,000 Romanian troops in front of its walls – nearly half of the armed forces of one of Nazi Germany's main strategic allies. In the heavy fighting they were worn down, bled white, destroyed by one-third and left significantly demoralized. While Odessa maintained the defense, the enemy had no possibility to supply Army Group South by sea from the ports of Bulgaria and Romania or to use the single coastal railroad line, which also ran through Odessa. All this strongly and adversely affected the pace of the German offensive on the coastal axis and delayed their shift to decisive operations to seize the Crimea and Caucasus.

Factually speaking, the tenacity of the lengthy defense by the defenders of Odessa made a weighty contribution to the disruption of Hitler's plan of a blitzkrieg war. Even members of the German command recognized this. For example, the head of the German military mission in Romania Major General Arthur Hauffe reported to Hitler's headquarters:

> The Russian units in Odessa carried out their task to gain time. They prevented for another two months the time planned by us to convert Odessa into our own supply base. They were tying down the overwhelming portion of the Romanian ground forces and moreover inflicted heavy losses to the Romanian Fourth Army; it was left with only 60% of its personnel, and those troops were worn out by the fighting.[8]

In the course of the fighting for Odessa, a new operational form for defending a naval base was created – a defensive area, with a medley of forces and combat means from diverse types of troops and local resources under unitary command. Following this example, subsequently the Sevastopol, Kerch, Novorossiisk and Tuapse defensive areas were created. Indeed here, as Admiral N.G. Kuznetsov accurately noted, very important was the comradeship-in-arms of the Army and Navy.[9] Pilots of the 69th Fighter Aviation Regiment also made a major contribution to the overall cause. Equipped with just 36 I-16 fighters, they flew combat missions under the conditions of a 3-1 advantage in favor of the enemy, but they were able to devise aerial combat tactics that virtually prevented targeted bombings of the city and port. Even fascist aces later recognized this in their memoirs. Altogether, the Soviet pilots flew 3,500 individual combat sorties, engaged in 576 aerial combats, and shot down or destroyed on the ground 94 aircraft and 4 gliders. Twelve of the regiment's pilots were deemed worthy of the high title Hero of the Soviet Union, and the regiment was awarded the Order of the Red Banner and given the honorific title "Odessa".[10]

The successful amphibious landing at Grigor'evka and the subsequent actions of the naval infantry on land have entered forever the annals of military history. Here one must again emphasize that even this success was ensured by the proper choice of the axis of attack and the accurate, continuous support of the ground forces by the Black Sea Fleet and aircraft.[11] The acquired experience and tactical skill of the commanders were later used in many of the Fleet's future landing operations.

In the fighting for Odessa, on a local front separated from the main Red Army, the command cadres gained combat experience and became tempered by combat more quickly. This experience allowed them to conduct combat operations successfully on other fronts: during the defense of

---

8   P. Voinovsky, *Moe naivishche schastia: Spomin* [*My highest happiness: Memoirs*] (Kiev, 1999), pp. 245-247.

9   Kuznetsov, *Na flotakh boevaia trevoga*, p. 118.

10   L.L. Shestakov, "V nebe Odessay istrebiteli 69-go aviapolka" ["Fighters of the 69th Aviation Regiment in the skies of Odessa"] *Oni srazhalis' za Odessu: Sbornik vospominanii* [*They fought for Odessa: Collection of recollections*] (Odessa, 1998), pp. 54, 62.

11   Istoriia voenno-morskogo iskusstva [History of naval arts] (Moscow: Voenizdat, 1969), p. 264.

Sevastopol, the Caucasus and Stalingrad, and subsequently in offensive operations to smash the German forces. The USSR People's Commissar of Defense Iosif Stalin remarked:

> The soldiers and commanders of the Red Army, not having even adequate combat experience, learned to beat the adversary surely, to destroy his personnel and equipment, to disrupt the enemy's plans, and to defend our cities and villages tenaciously against the foreign aggressors. The heroic defenders ... of Odessa demonstrated models of selfless bravery, iron discipline, tenacity, and the ability to win. Our entire Red Army is equal to these heroes.[12]

Odessa was also a unique example of the mobilization of the material and human resources of a city for the struggle against a foe. The ranks of the Odessa Defense District's troops were replenished by more than 30,000 Odessan militiamen, and tens of thousands more fought in the city against saboteurs and the consequences of air raids. The residents of Odessa together with the engineering troops created solid, fortified lines for the stubborn defense of their native city. Under artillery fire and the explosions of dropped bombs, more than 100,000 workers and employees, housewives and pensioners, students and teachers, and workers of culture and the arts toiled to build the system of anti-tank and anti-infantry obstacles. The workers of Odessa's factories produced or repaired 134 types of weapons and ammunition, and for the most part kept the Odessa front supplied.

The achievement of the troops of the Coastal Army, the Black Sea Fleet sailors and the citizens of Odessa is one of the bright pages in the history of the Second World War. The collective exploit of Odessa's defenders have been worthily evaluated. Odessa was one of the first to be considered worthy of the title "Hero City". Fourteen Soviet soldiers who defended Odessa were bestowed the title Hero of the Soviet Union, 57 men were decorated with the Order of Lenin, 379 with Order of the Red Banner, 659 with the Order of the Red Star, 21 with the Order of the Badge of Honor, 500 with the medal "For bravery", and 551 with the medal "For combat merits". All of Odessa's defenders were awarded the medal "For the defense of Odessa", which the USSR Supreme Soviet especially authorized on 22 December 1942 as evidence of the nationwide recognition of their contribution on the altar of victory.

The Ukrainian people hallow the memory of those who gave their lives in the fighting for Odessa. Many streets of the city bear the names of heroes of the defense. Songs have been written about them, movie films made, and books written. In the T.G. Shevchenko City Park there is a Monument to the Unknown Sailor, at the feet of which burns an eternal flame of honor – a symbol of the memory of those who were killed while defending their native city and the Motherland.

---

12   I. Stalin o Velikoi Otechestvennoi voine Sovetskogo Soiuza [I. Stalin on the Great Patriotic War of the Soviet Union] (Moscow: Voenizdat, 1984), p. 80.

Part II

The Occupation and Liberation of Odessa 1941-44

8

Odessa under occupation

Ah, Odessa,
You've known much grief…

The occupiers didn't immediately decide to enter Odessa, which had already been abandoned by its defenders. Only on the evening of 16 October 1941 did groups of enemy scouts appear on the empty streets of the city. However, this didn't prevent Romanian propaganda from boastfully declaring that Odessa had been "taken with fighting". The first infiltrating groups of enemy soldiers quickly headed toward the port, hoping to capture Red Army units that hadn't had time to evacuate. However, at the port they found only the ruins of burning buildings and a desolate, ominous wasteland. One of the darkets periods in the life of Odessa began – the 907 days of occupation by German and Romanian conquerors.

Life in the city came to a stop in its tracks and its businesses and plants were not open. In a lead article of the *Pravda* newspaper, there was the comment: "The Nazis have given Antonescu's clique the richest city and the collective farms and State Farms of the oblast for emptying and plundering as an award for the service of the Romanian government to Hitler's Germany. The Germans are paying off the Romanians with the life, property and freedom of the Soviet citizens."[1]

Odessa and the territory between the Southern Bug and Dniester Rivers were given by Hitler to the Romanians for plunder. On this territory, the occupiers created the Transnistria [Trans-Dniester] governorship centered first on Tiraspol, and then on Odessa. The captured southwestern Ukrainian lands were included in the new governorship: all of the Odessa Oblast and parts of the Nikolaev and Vinnitsa Oblasts (west of the Southern Bug River), as well as the left bank areas of Moldavia. The provisional western border of the Transnistria was the Mogilev-Podol'sky – Bar – Zhmerinka line.[2]

The border of the Romanian zone of occupation east of the Dniester River was finally determined by an agreement, signed on 30 August 1941 in Bendery by representatives of the German and Romanian military commands. The agreement defined the special status of the Transnistria as a zone of interest for both Romania and Germany simultaneously. This found a reflection in the existence of a dual demarcation line: the first along the Dniester River (the boundary with Romania proper), the second along the Southern Bug (the boundary with the Bug – Dnieper zone). Such an approach eloquently spoke to the presence of strategic divergences in the views of the partners regarding the plundering at the expense of post-war Europe as a whole, and south

---

1   As cited by Ia. Shternshtein, *Morskie vorota Ukrainy – Odessa* [*The naval gateway of Ukraine – Odessa*] (Odessa: Odesskoe oblastnoe izdatel'stvo, 1958), p. 146.
2   E. Volkl, *Transnistrien und Odessa (1941-1945)* [*Transnistria and Odessa, 1941-1945*] (Regensburg, 1996), p. 27.

Ukraine in particular. You see, back on 16 July 1941 at a conference in Hitler's headquarters, Hitler, commenting upon Romanian claims for Ukrainian land between the Dniester and the Southern Bug, emphasized: "It is now important that we don't disclose our ambitions to the entire world … However we ourselves at the same time must recognize now that we will never leave these oblasts."[3]

From the beginning, the geographical and strategic significance of the region compelled the German command to ensure that Romania would receive a mandate only for a temporary administration over the Transnistria and the economic exploitation of it. The boundaries of the 64 districts that made up the Transnistria almost fully coincided with the pre-war borders. Counties were created to oversee the administration of several districts; there were 13 of these.[4] A prefect, the authorized representative of the governorship, headed each county and controlled the police, the gendarme in the countryside and the socio-economic services. The prefect was the highest authority in the county and in his activity relied upon two assistants – sub-prefects, one of which was to be a local citizen.

Professor Gheorghe Alexianu, a former lawyer from Chernovtsy, was appointed as the governor of Transnistria.[5] When working out his program of activity, G. Alexianu upon his arrival in Odessa declared, "We will be operating with particular cruelty."[6]

The occupational regime from the start didn't trust the local population. That was why G. Alexianu appointed representatives from Romania, typically veterans of the Bessarabian counter-revolutionary *SfatulȚării* [Country Council][7] or officers that held the highest government decorations to the top administrative posts.[8] In order to control the cities and villages, functional structures were created headed by a *primarius* (in the city – the chief, in the village – the *starosta*) in order to help him implement his legal authority. The chief or *starosta* and his assistants simultaneously served as the prefect of a district, or, in certain cases, of a county. Two cities, Odessa and Tiraspol, had municipal governments.[9]

Gherman Pântea, a veteran of the *SfatulȚării* movement was appointed as mayor of the Odessan municipality. In order to execute the main duties in the city administration, other veterans of this movement arrived in Odessa together with him. The most important questions of city life were regulated by "committees" created within the municipality.[10]

Directorates comprised the executive apparatus of the governorship of Transnistria. They were in charge of questions of administration, justice, finance, commerce, labor, industry, agriculture, the food industry, monopolies, economics, culture, health care, communications and others. G. Pântea quickly gathered a large amount of authority in his hands – even a number of the directorates were either directly subordinate to him or to G. Alexianu. Gradually, some of the departments of the directorates, the number of which constantly multiplied, passed to the full control of

3   *Niurnbergskii protsess: Sbornik materialov v 8 t.* [*Nuremburg trials: Collection of materials in 8 volumes*], Vol. 2 (Moscow, 1989), pp.581-582, 689.

4   DAOO, F.R. 2242, Op. 4, Spr. 23, Ark. 11.

5   V. Gridin, "Eshche raz ob Odesse I Transnistrii v 1941-1944" ["Once again about Odessa and the Transnistria in 1941-1944"], *Iug*, 30 June 1995.

6   DAOO, F. R. S/393, Op. 1, Spr. 677, Ark 125.

7   Ed. note: the *SfatulȚării* was a council that was organized to unite political, public, cultural and professional organizations in the territory of the Governorship of Bessarabia when the Russian Empire was collapsing. It proclaimed the independent Moldavian Democratic Republic in December 1917 and then unification with Romania in April 1918.

8   *Molva*, 11 April 1943.

9   DAOO, F. R. 2243, Op. 2, Spr. 53, Ark. 23.

10 Shternshtein, *Morskie vorota Ukrainy – Odessa*, p. 146.

the municipality.[11] A "Government Zone" was created in Odessa in order to provide accommodations for this army of bureaucrats. It was bounded by the streets Marazlievsky, Duce Mussolini (Evreiskaia) and as far as Korol' Mikhail (Preobrazhenskaia) Street, then from Koblevskaia Street to the intersection of Torgovaia Street with Kherson – Sofievskaia Street, including all the alleys and lanes leading to the sea. Taken altogether, this land comprises the city center.[12]

Punitive functions on the territory of the Transnistria were carried out by the gendarme, who also carried out police duties in Odessa; their headquarters was located in the city. The precincts of the Odessa police force were directly subordinate to the *primarius* of the Odessa municipality and its head G. Pântea.

The headquarters of the constabulary oversaw 6 battalions, 4 of which operated according to the principle of "clustering", with reliance on the gendarme legions of neighboring districts. The legions were divided into platoons, and those, in turn, into groups. The numerically strongest was the 4th (Odessa) Gendarme Battalion (approximately 1,500 men). It included the gendarme legions of Odessa, Ovidiopol', Ochakov and Berezovka. In addition, within the prefecture of the Odessa police were the 1st and 7th Gendarme Battalions. The legions were primarily staffed by local residents; there were a total of 150 professional policemen from Romania.

The prefecture of the Odessa police (the city was divided into 9 sectors) had departments of control over the administrative police (traffic control, order in the streets, personnel, etc.). In September 1943 it was reorganized into two offices: the Administrative Police and the *Siguranța* – the police's secret security service, which primarily struggled against the resistance movement. Departments of the *Siguranța* existed within each battalion and legion of the gendarme. They were occupied with questions of intelligence and the recruitment of informers, and also had an internal SS-I service [Special Service for Information] for counterintelligence and the analysis of secret information in Odessa headed by E. Cristescu.[13]

However, the territory between the Dniester River and the Southern Bug River was never completely subordinate to Romanian administration. In distinction from Bessarabia and Bukovina, where the Romanian legal system was active and Romania's official currency was used, the territory of the Transnistria, according to Antonescu's Decree No. 1 from 19 August 1941, solely used the German Occupation Reichsmark. For a short time after the occupation in Odessa, the Soviet ruble was also in cirulation. Thus, Bucharest constantly had to appeal to Berlin for currency, which also didn't bolster the confidence of the members of the Romanian administration in the Transnistria, even though they were well-paid for their work. They received pay in the Romanian leu and in an equal amount of German Reichsmark.[14]

Lines of communication (railroads, sea and river routes, etc.) and both telephone and telegraph communications were under the operational control of the *Wehrmacht*. A special German transportion command was created in Odessa to control key and major stations – the German transportion commandant offices. Only in March 1942 was Bucharest able to place a portion of the Transnistria railroad system under Romanian administrative control. A commandant office of communications of the German Army was also installed in Odessa headed by General von Rotrich, which was supposed to "facilitate the responsible representatives of Romanian authority in the economic exploitation" of the oblast, but for all practical purposes the activity of the Romanian administration was subordinate to the Germans. Emissaries from Bucharest were only allowed to

---

11   V.N. Stanko [chief ed.], *Istoriia Odesy* [*History of Odessa*] (Odessa: Druk, 2002), p. 402.
12   *Molva*, 20 May 1943.
13   *Odessa*, 19 September 1942.
14   DAOO, F. R. 1820, S/393, Op. 1, Spr. 411, Ark. 128.

"present Romanian interests". The post of "agricultural expert" was introduced into every district and county of the Transnistria – German advisors in military uniforms.

Berlin considered the local German population, who were taken under the wing of the SS secret service for assisting individuals of German origins on the territories occupied by Germany – the *Volksdeutsche Mittelstelle* – to be a reliable bulwark of support on the territory between the Dniester and Southern Bug Rivers. This service from the very start of its activity created compact German zones on the territory of the Transnistria, from which members of non-German nationalities were expelled, as well as those in neighboring villages. In order to secure the German settlement zones, paramilitary groups of local ethnic Germans formed, led by SS officers. The members of the Romanian occupation authority had no right to interfere in the administrative affairs of the German settlements; even in cultural and awareness-raising work, only the *Volksdeutsche Mittelstelle* was allowed to conduct it. According to a convention on the status of the German population of the Transnistria, signed on 13 December 1941 by Alexianu and SS *Oberfuhrer* Hoffman, the *Volksdeutsche Mittelstelle* received the right to send representatives from 12 German businesses into the Transnistria with the aim of "purchasing local goods and sending them back to Germany."

In Bucharest, a unified leadership organ was created to oversee the activity of the Romanian occupational administration in all the adjacent lands – the "Civil and Military Office for the Administration of Bessarabia, Bukovina and the Transnistria", headed by the General Secretary of Romania's government. I. Antonescu tried not only to "administer and exploit" the Transnistria. On 26 February 1942 in front of a government assembly he declared: "It is no secret that I'm not inclined to lose that which we've already acquired. The Transnistria must become a Romanian oblast; we will make it Romanian, having expelled all foreigners from there. ... We must create living space for Romanians."[15]

Thus, Romania's leadership plainly had no intention to view the land beyond the Dniester River as a temporary possession. Even so, Bucharest didn't openly announce its claims on the Transnistria, first of all out of concerns that Hungary would then assess this step as compensation for Northern Transylvania. Despite the discernable "caution" on the part of members of Romania's government, from the outset the Romanian administration tried to gain firm footing on Ukrainian soil. On 16 December 1941, I. Antonescu gave instructions to the governor of the Transnistria G. Alexianu: "Act there as if Romanian authority has been established on this territory for two million years."[16]

The main task of the Romanian administration was to create a path toward colonizing the Ukrainian territories. Already in November 1941 during a celebration to mark Romania's decision to join the Axis states, its Vice Admiral M. Antonescu said, "With respect to the Slavs it is necessary to adopt an unshakeable position, and therefore any partition ... or occupation of Slavic territory are legal acts." Hitler supported him:

> You are right – the Slavs present a biological question, not an ideological one ... In the future, there must be two races in Europe: German and Latin. These two races must work ... to decrease the number of Slavs. ... We must resort to colonization and biological means in order to destroy the Slavs.

---

15 Stanko [chief ed.], *Istoriia Odesy*, p. 404.
16 Ibid.

He then added, "My mission, if it is successful, is to destroy the Slavs."[17]

I. Antonescu in a message to the members of Romania's occupational administration on Ukrainian soil demanded "… in the economic sphere, do not allow the Ukrainians to take a single step forward", while those engaged in politics were "to be sent to camps." However, the Ukrainian people of the Transnistria couldn't take a single step in other spheres of public life either, in particular in the development and spreading of the Ukrainian language and culture. True, here the Romanian occupational administration tried to show some flexibility: it promised to allow the publication of a Ukrainian newspaper, and even opened a Ukrainian theater, although it was quickly closed. Only one individual and two schools out of 50 worked in the Ukrainian language for teaching. The Romanian counterintelligence special service was identifying local activists as Ukrainian "separatists."[18]

Immediately, the migration of Romanians to the conquered territory began. In the governor's order from 26 January 1942, there is the statement:

> Romanians, who were born beyond the Dniester River, are returning from Romania to the Transnistria. These Romanians, returning in the middle of winter to their native places, are finding their homes occupied by communists and don't have an accommodation and the necessary food for existence, since it is impossible to find work. We are requesting measures to be taken to present them with the needed produce from the reserve of collective farms. Especially take notice that this is the only class thanks to which it might be possible to awaken a Romanian spirit in the hearts of the local population.[19]

Given the arrival of repatriates from Romania this proved insufficient, so they simply began to drive Ukrainian peasants out of their homes and expel them from villages.[20] Many villages were completely emptied of the local inhabitants and colonized by German settlers.[21]

The occupiers established a regime of unbridled terror and violence in the city of Odessa. Embittered by the city's lengthy defense, the occupiers on the day after entering Odessa perpetrated savage reprisals against its population. They were breaking into apartments, robbing and murdering the residents, not sparing old men, women or children. Gallows were set up on the streets and in public squares. The bodies of the hanged victims weren't taken down for several days in order to terrorize the population.

Sweeps of the city were conducted periodically. In the process, they were arresting primarily Jews and sending them to the police or the commandant's office. Only a few were able to bribe their way out of trouble, and they were temporarily released; the rest were sent to prison, from which few returned. On 17 October, some of the arrested people were forcibly driven to the airfield and compelled to trample the grounds in order to prove the absence of mines.[22] On the first day of the occupation, three citizens were demonstrably hanged in Odessa's Il'dichevsky District, including the 63-year-old K. Lysenko, because the Red Army commander N. Ushakov and female Komsomol member L. Kovaleva were found hiding in his home. On the next day the occupiers arrested everyone on the streets and in the buildings of the city's central sector, where the Romanians had decided to create the so-called "official quarter". Several thousand women, chil-

---

17   I.E. Levit, *Krakh politiki agressii diktatora Antonesku* [*Failure of dictator Antonescu's politics of aggression*] (Kishinev, 1983), p. 162.

18   DAOO, F.R. 2242, Op. 1, Spr. 1098, Ark. 53-54.

19   DAOO, F.R. 558, S/1985, Spr. 26, Ark. 3.

20   DAOO, F.R. 1820, S/393, Op. 1, Spr. 293, Ark. 5.

21   DAOO, F.R. 558, s. 1985, Spr. 27, Ark. 21; Op. 1, Spr. 26, Ark. 126.

22   D.Z. Starodinsky, *Odesskoe getto: Vospominaniia* [*Odessa ghetto: Recollections*] (Odessa, 1991: p. 18.

dren and old men were shepherded along Novoarkadinskaia Street in the direction of the Arcade. Outside one of the former sanitariums, the fascists stripped these people to their underclothing, before leading them into a quarry and shooting them there.

The most terrible deed was perpetrated a day later: the fascists rounded up an enormous number of Jews – men, women, elderly people and children – as well as captured Red Army soldiers and sailors, and gathered them into nine former powder magazines on Liustdorfskaia (today Chernomorskaia) Street. Then they doused the magazines with fuel from hoses and set them on fire. Military historians maintain that the mass burning of people alive was a brainchild of the Romanians, and was used for the first time right in Odessa. The reason to resort to this was the eternal poverty of the Romanians: this way they could spare the rifle cartridges …. The powder magazines smoldered for several days and the wind wafted a black smoke carrying a pungent odor over the city.[23] After the liberation of Odessa, an Extraordinary State Commission discovered the remains of 22,000 people at the place of this malignant deed. The archives preserved the news-paper *Bol'shevistskoe znamia*'s for 6 May 1944, which describes how this happened. In order to better understand the pathology of Romanian fascism, it makes sense to cite the article in full:

> Crowds of people are being led out of the city. They are being taken from their apartments and simply right on the streets. Women were told to fetch their children. Mothers are carry-ing babies. There goes one mother. She has an infant boy in her arms. Two a bit older are spasmodically clutching at her skirt. Children are carrying toys, baskets of provisions, bottles of milk; after all, on the road they'll get thirsty.
>
> Here is Novoarkadinskaia Street. Clouds of dust are billowing up from it. The dust hangs in the air like a thick cloud. The people are tormented by thirst and ignorance of what is happening. Many begin to lag behind, and they are being prodded on with rifle butts. One of the mothers fell. A Romanian soldier kicks her with his boot. She rises, and barely moving her feet, shuffles onward, but her strength is running out, and having taken several steps, the woman falls again. The Romanian cocks his rifle. The breech clicks. A shot. The woman collapses onto her side. Blood streams onto the dust of the road like a scarlet rivulet.
>
> "Mommy, get up, why are you joking around?" asks the little boy, tugging at his mother's dress, and a smile of disbelief freezes on his little face. He falls forever at the feet of his mother, impaled by a bayonet.
>
> People trudge onward. Here's the sanatorium. Here they are made to undress down to their underclothing. Off to one side of the road is a rock quarry. It is 18 meters deep. Here they were shot.
>
> …
>
> Liustdorfskaia Street. A place where there were once artillery stockpiles. Now there is a wasteland here. The Nazi scoundrels tried to wipe away the traces – they levelled this place to the ground. In vain, though! The population in the surrounding neighborhood remembers those cruel days. One old collective farmer Pavel Sklifasovsky says, "The blood freezes in the veins when we recall this horror." What happened here?
>
> On the day of 17 October 1941, four groups of 2,500 to 3,000 people each were driven out of the city. Soviet people – women, children, the elderly – driven like cattle, they were forced into warehouses with rifle butts. The doors were closed and locked shut with deadbolts, and they were sealed up inside. They [the Romanians] then took apart the roof and poured

---

23   S. Ia. Borovoi, "Gibel' evreiskogo naseleniia Odessy vo vremia fashistskoi okkupatsii" ["Death of the Jewish population of Odessa during the fascist occupation"] *Istorichni zoshiti*, No. 4 (1991), pp. 3, 74.

gasoline into the warehouses, before setting them on fire. Eleven thousand women, old people and children were burned. Burned alive.

No mercy for the executioners! There is no place on earth for them![24]

In the act of the Extraordinary Government Commission to ascertain and investigate the atrocities of the German and Romanian aggressors and their accomplices, the statements of eyewitnesses of this inhumane act have been preserved. A female resident of Odessa M.N. Bobkova:

> On 19 October 1941 the Romanians began to drive peaceful residents who'd been arrested in their thousands – men, women and children – into the premises of powder magazines, located on Liustderdorfskaia Street near my home. Once they had crammed nine empty warehouses with people, they then rolled up drums of fuel to the warehouses … I personally watched as the Romanians pumped fuel out of these drums and were using hoses to pour the gasoline into the warehouses, which were holding the residents of the city. When the warehouses were doused with fuel, the Romanian soldiers set them on fire. A terribly cry arose … Women and children, enveloped in flames, were screaming "Save us, don't kill us, don't burn us! The warehouses set ablaze by the Romanians continued to burn for several days. When the blaze died out, the Romanians forcibly drove residents of the city to the place of the conflagration, where they were made to dig large trenches, each with a length of about 100 meters, a width of 5-6 meters, and a depth of approximately 3 meters. Then Romanian soldiers appeared, and they were dragging charred corpses into these trenches and buried them.[25]

Unendurable torments were the fate of the prisoners of war that fell into hands of the Romanians. In freezing weather, they were driven barefooted and half-naked through the snow to a concentration camp, and there killed off. Many even had their lips bound together with rings so that they couldn't talk.[26] For example, 38 Red Army prisoners were executed on the outskirts of the city of Bălți. Junior Sergeant S.M. Kuz'min, who survived by some miracle, remembered:

> It was around 6 or 7 o'clock in the evening. They led us into a barn and ordered each prisoner to pick up an armful of straw, as if to make a bed out of it for the night. Once we had spread out the straw, a German officer ordered everyone to lie down. Not even a half hour had passed, when the same officer issued an order to fall into three ranks, as if for an inspection. The prisoners carried out the order. Suddenly, through the half-open door the bright light of a floodlight was directed at us, and a machine gun began to chatter. Everyone fell. We began to crawl toward any sort of furrow we could find. When the shouts and cries ended, two Germans entered and began to saturate the walls, floor, ceiling and bodies with gasoline, before setting them all ablaze.[27]

On the evening of 22 October at a radio signal from the Crimea, the building on Marazlievskaia Street, which had been wired for demolition with powerful explosives even before the evacuation of the Soviet troops, blew up. The building now contained a Romanian commandant's office, the headquarters of the Romanian 10th Infantry Division and German signalers. As a result of the explosion, approximately 100 German and Romanian officers and soldiers were killed, including

---

24   *Bol'shevistskoe znamia*, 6 May 1944.
25   *Odessa v Velikoi Otechestvennoi voine Sovetskogo Soiuza. Sbornik dokumentov i materialov* [*Odessa in the Great Patriotic War of the Soviet Union. Collection of documents and materials*] Vol. 1 (Odessa, 1947), pp. 46-47.
26   DAOO, F. Memuarnykh dokumentov, Op. 1, Spr. 18, Ark. 1.
27   *Chernomorska kommuna*, 8 January 1946

the military commandant of Odessa – the commander of the 10th Infantry Division General Ion Glogojanu. In response, the occupiers unleashed a wave of repressions on the city. Already within 3 hours after the explosion, the newly appointed commandant of Odessa General Trestorianu in his first report announced: "I have taken measures in order to hang Jews and communists on the public squares of Odessa." The executioners seized the first men that they came across on streets and even buildings, and hung them from trees. Those who resisted were shot on the spot. By the morning of 23 October, the streets of the city presented a terrible scene: hundreds of bodies of Odessans blackening on columns and trees. The most horrible scene opened on Aleksandrovskii Prospect: bodies were dangling here along the entire length of the alley. Gallows were erected on the square in front of the train station, at the Landing, in the New Market and in other places. On 23 October, the commander of the Romanian II Army Corps General Macici arrived in Odessa from Tiraspol, and the villainous killing of totally innocent people rose to even larger scales. In the course of several days, approximately 5,000 residents of Odessa were executed. On 24 October the fascists escorted more than 250 men of various ages under guard to Alekseevskii City Garden, on the corner of Stepovaia and Mel'nichnaia Streets, where they shot them with machine guns.[28]

The official organ of the municipality – *Odesskaia gazeta* – in its first issue dated 25 October 1941 made it known to the people that after the "terrorist act, perpetrated against the military command, 200 Bol'sheviks were shot for each dead officer or civilian bureaucrat, whether German or Romanian, and up to 100 Bol'sheviks for each soldier." The announcement also revealed that hostages had been taken, which in the event of a repeat of such acts would be shot together with their families.[29]

In such a predatory, beastly face the occupation of the "New Order" appeared in Odessa from the very first days. Yet the main representative of this "New Order" in Odessa G. Alexianu in his declaration promulgated in *Odesskaia gazeta* insincerely proclaimed, "We are here for the defense of faith, for the emancipation of souls … so that belief in a better world is reborn again in the hearts of everyone, which affirms noble motives, life and human ideals."[30]

The introduction of Bucharest's colonization plans regarding the Transnistria began with the resolution of the "Jewish problem" in the Nazi spirit. The first wave of the destruction of Odessa's Jewish population rolled out almost as soon as the Romanians entered Odessa. The second wave began after the commandant's office was blown sky-high on 22 October 1941. It was at the end of October that the first batches of Jews were shipped from Odessa to the Transnistria's "Majdanek" – a concentration camp set up by the Nazis at a State Farm that raised feeder pigs in Bogdanovka (Domanevskii District), and was located back then in the northeastern corner of Odessa Oblast.

In November 1941, the extermination of the Transnistria's Jewish population moved to a planned scale. On 8 November the occupation's mouthpiece *Odesskaia gazeta* printed an order from the Romanian military command, according to which all draft-age males of "Jewish origin" had 48 hours to appear at the city prison under the threat of being shot on the spot. On 17 November the occupiers took the next step: this same newspaper printed another order: "All individuals of Jewish origin, living in Odessa, are compelled by 1200 19 November 1941 to report all the valuable items in their possession – stones and metals (platinum, gold, silver) in any form."[31]

A new wave of shootings rolled out in connection with the "evacuation" of Jews from Bessarabia and Bukovina to the Transnistria. Back on 8 July 1941, when the Romanian and German forces

---

28   *Molva*, 11, 13 April 1943.
29   *Odesskaia gazeta*, 25 October 1941.
30   Ibid., 8 November 1941.
31   Ibid., 17 November 1941.

had arrived at the line of the Dniester River between Chernovtsy and Bălți, I. Antonescu at a meeting of the Romanian government peremptorily stated:

> I stand for the compulsory expulsion of the entire Jewish element from Bessarabia and Bukovina ... I'm also for the compulsory emigration of the Ukrainian element, which at the given moment don't even belong here. I'm indifferent if we enter history as barbarians ... Never before in history has there been a more suitable moment for us. If the need arises – shoot them from machine guns.

On 16 December 1941, at another session of the Romanian government, Antonescu demanded from Transnistria's governor G. Alexianu to "purge" the Jews from Odessa, without waiting for Berlin to make a decision on this matter. He ordered: "Bury them in the catacombs, drown them in the Black Sea. I don't want to know anything about it. Let hundreds die, let thousands die, as long as they all perish."

So they began killing and killing the Jews. They didn't even take the time to remove their corpses from the streets of Odessa. A preserved report from one of the Romanian bureaucrats of the Department of Propaganda stated:

> In the area of the 2nd Toll Gate, at the Old Market, between Aleksandrovskii Prospect and Uspenskaia Street, beyond Slobodka and on the road to Slobodka there are piles of the frozen corpses of Jews; some of the bodies are bloody ... These Jews had been previously shot or killed and left on the road. A small number of corpses are at Sortirovochnaia, in railcars, on the railroad line and in other places.[32]

Another, similar report revealed, "On the 24th of this month at Privoz ... two Jews were shot by German soldiers. When checking their documents, it turned out that they had Russian passports, which were taken from them, and they were shot on the spot at the market and their bodies tossed into a waste bin."[33]

On 20 December 1941, an execution detachment arrived in Bogdanovka, which had become the main point for the transfer of Jews from all the territory occupied by Romanian troops and where moreover by this time was holding more than 55,000 Jews. On 21 December, mass shootings began. Altogether in these days at the end of December, in Bogdanovka and other ghetto camps that were located in the Domanevskii District (Marinovka, Marenburg, Novoselovka, Vladimirovka, Moldanovka and others), the executioners killed no fewer than 74,000 Jews. The fascists forced the prisoners to construct an earthen embankment that would hold back the currents of blood that were streaming down the slopes of the ravine into the Bug River. In this same camp of Bogdanovka, more than 2,000 people, including many children, were burned alive.

In addition, the Romanian administration prepared the mass expulsion of Jews from Odessa with the aim of their subsequent elimination. On 10 January 1942, an order went out to the army and Odessa's garrison, according to which "... all Jews without exception, who are located on the territory of Odessa and its suburbs" had to appear within two days at Slobodka-Romanovka, where a Jewish ghetto had been created. This same day became the beginning of the "evacuation" of the Jewish population of Odessa and its suburbs to settlements in the north of Ochakovskii and the south of Berezovskii Counties, which had been chosen for this by the administration.[34] Thus,

---

32 DAOO, F. R. 1826, S/339, Op. 3, Spr. 4, Ark. 6.
33 DAOO, F. R. 1926, S/399, Op. 3, Spr. 8, Ark. 65.
34 *Odesskaia gazeta*, 12, 14 January 1942.

the ghetto at Slobodka played the role of a staging point, and in light of the frigid temperatures that occurred that winter and the conditions of the evacuation, there is the belief that this from the outset was part of a deliberate plan for the physical extermination of the people. The city stood transfixed with horror. Over just one month alone, between 12 January and 18 February 1942, more than 30,000 people were forcibly driven out of Odessa to the Berezovskii County concentration camp. They were doomed to death on the way. Those who nevertheless managed to reach Domanevka went through a sorting process and the weakest people were sent on to "Gorkii" (on the outskirts of Domanevka) or to the "Akmechatka quarters" (a State Farm that raised feeder pigs 12 kilometers outside the village of Akmechatka), where a slow death from hunger and the lack of medical attention awaited them.

According to official data, the total number of Jews that were tormented and killed in the camps of the Domanevskii District alone is measured at 116,000. All of this refutes the existing, widespread opinion regarding the relative humanity of the Romanian occupational authority in comparison with the German occupation. If a portion of the Jewish population of Odessa and the region survived, then first of all it is thanks to the humanity and compassion of Odessans and the rural population of the places of deportation, which sometimes concealed entire Jewish families at the risk of their own lives.[35] In February 1944, I. Antonescu summed up the results of his "activity" in the following way: "In not a single country, other than Germany, have such measures been taken to eliminate any influence or activity of the Jews."[36]

Altogether, concentration camps that held approximately 1,600,000 Soviet people were organized in various populated places of Odessa Oblast. Over the time of the occupation, hundreds of thousands of citizens of the city and oblast of Odessa were shot, hung, burned alive, buried alive, tortured in torture chambers or driven into slavery.[37]

Having taken out their fury on the defenseless population, the occupiers then had to introduce terror into "legal" frameworks. An order published by them banned "any type of meeting, procession or grouping of a political nature and any other associations."[38] With this order, any movement or lingering on the streets of local citizens that numbered more than 3 individuals was forbidden, and a total curfew went into effect at 10 o'clock each night. The punishment for the violation of any of these orders was one and the same: execution. It was also announced that for each incident of an attack against German or Romanian soldiers, 500 citizens would be shot.[39]

On 17 October, a demagogic proclamation to the people, which had yellowed with time and had obviously been prepared by the enemy command back in the days of the unsuccessful August assaults against the city, was put on display in the city. It called the residents to obedience:

> To the citizens of the city of Odessa! ... I advise you not to commit hostile acts with respect to the army or the officials who will be governing the city. Turn in those who have terrorist, espionage or sabotage tasks, as well as those who are concealing a weapon ... Consider it your duty to inform us in the event that someone isn't adhering to a decree ... [he] will be punished by being shot on the spot.
> General de Corps de Armata Adjutant I. Iacobici
> Chief of Staff General N. Tataranu[40]

---

35   Stanko [chief ed.], *Istoriia Odesi*, pp. 405-406.
36   Levit, *Krakh politiki agressii diktatora Antonesku*, p. 162.
37   G.A. Karev, *Odessa – gorod-geroi* [*Odessa – hero city*] (Moscow: Voenizdat, 1978), p. 132.
38   *Odessa v Velikoi Otechestvennoi voine Sovetskogo Soiuza*, Vol. 1, p. 9.
39   Ibid., p. 10; *Odesskaia gazeta*, 20 November 1941.
40   *Odessa v Velikoi Otechestvennoi voine Sovetskogo Soiuza*, Vol. 2, p. 6.

Fighting on the approaches to Odessa.

Pilots of the 69th Fighter Aviation Regiment getting ready for a mission.

The "For the defense of Odessa" medal, established by a Decree of the USSR Presidium of the Supreme Soviet on 22 December 1942.

Citizens at work on a barricade on one of Odessa's streets, 1 August 1941.

Sailors from the destroyer *Shaumian* during a lull in the fighting on the outskirts of Odessa, August 1941.

Sailors attack an enemy position on the outskirts of Odessa.

Sailors in the defense of Odessa.

The defense of Odessa 1941: The city of Odessa on fire.

The defense of Odessa 1941: Barricades in front of the Opera House.

The famous Potemkin Stairs, the formal entrance into Odessa from the direction of the sea, in 1941.

Odessan residents inspect a captured gun.

The construction of an armored train in Odessa, 1941.

Odessa on fire, 1941.

A Romanian He-112B-2 of German manufacture shot down over Odessa.

A Soviet artillery crew mans a gun in a cornfield near Odessa.

A Soviet I-16 fighter revs its engine as it readies for take off.

It was forbidden to leave one's place of residence without a special pass; to sell or trade prod-ucts of one's own labor without official license; go out onto the street after the onset of darkness; approach any closer than 100 meters to a railroad bed; keep a weapon; discuss military or political topics, etc. The population was punished with particular cruelty for any contact with partisans or members of the underground. Each such order ended with the phrase: "The guilty will be punished by death."

Even long before the fascist invasion of the Soviet Union, Hitler's government had worked out a detailed plan that foresaw the seizure of material and cultural valuables of the Soviet people, the plundering of the civilian population, the establishment of a regime of penal labor, famine and bloody reprisals in the conquered areas. In the document "The 12 commandments for the behavior of Germans in the East and their handling of the Russians", compiled as an instruction guide for the occupational officials and bureaucrats assigned to the East, said among other things: "... the Russian sees a higher being in the German; take care to preserve this authority of the German" and "... you must take the harshest and most pitiless measures, which the government expects of you."[41]

These predatory plans found their reflection in the innumerable orders issued by the occupiers. For example, the "Directives on the leadership of the economy in the newly occupied eastern oblasts" (the "Green folder"), which was compiled in Berlin in June 1941 and signed by H. Göring, foresaw the "requisitioning, confiscation and export to Germany of raw materials, fuel (oil), agri-cultural products, manufactured goods and any type of assets." In order to implement this larce-nous plan, a special apparatus was created in the form of an "economic command", "economic staff", "special inspectors", "detachments to collect the means of production", "detachments to collect raw materials", an "Institute of Military Agronomists", "agricultural officers", etc.

Following this fascist program, I. Antonescu in his turn issued a series of orders, which prompted the army to mass looting and killing. Order No. 24220 from the chief of staff of the Romanian 14th Infantry Division Colonel Nicolaescu stated, in part: "Bread, cattle, goats and sheep, and chickens – all this must be taken from the population for the army. Careful searches must be conducted in each home and everything without exception must be seized. For the slightest resist-ance – shoot the perpetrators on the spot and burn down the homes."[42]

An entire army of marauders flooded into the occupied territories for easy loot. They brought out of Odessa everything that was possible to carry away. Thugs from specially commissioned "Organization-1" teams broke into clinics, hospitals, sanatoria, museums and other facilities, as well as into residences, and plundered medications, equipment, instruments, precious works of art, and everyday items, declaring everything to be "military trophies". On 3 December 1941, the "Odessa service for the seizure and collection of trophies" was created. At sessions of the Romanian government, Antonescu cited ever-greater plan numbers for the evacuation of material valuables from Odessa Oblast: "... worth 50-60, possibly even 100 billion leus." Practically everything that could be taken from Odessa was brought back to Romania in the form of "trophies": By July 1942, around 4,000 rail cars containing looted property, including the furniture and accessories of kindergartens and nurseries, schools and libraries, opera and other theaters, etc. returned to Romania.[43] However, the main emphasis in the matter of plundering the Transnistria was placed on food exports. Everywhere, the occupiers conducted the forcible confiscation of bread and food products. In order to plunder the people, a special 400,000-strong army of "authorized requisition agents" was created, which received Governor Alexianu's strict instructions: "Everything down

---

41   TsS IDK, F. 70221, Op. 148, Ed. kr. 12, Ark. 3-9; *Voenno-istoricheskii zhurnal*, No. 8 (1991), pp. 10-13.
42   Shternshtein, *Morskie vorota – Odessa*, p. 148.
43   DAOO, F. R. 1234, Op. 7, Spr. 193, Ark. 54, 115-117.

to the last seed must be surrendered to Romanian storage facilities. Do not stand on ceremony with the Soviet population; do not allow any indecisiveness or any hesitations." Alexianu assured Antonescu that in the case of the slightest insubordination or sabotage, he would "act with particular cruelty."[44]

One of the orders from the commander of Odessa's occupational force dated 3 November 1941 to General N. Gineraru and Military Prosecutor Lieutenant Colonel K. Grecharnaca said, "Individuals, living in the city, who know about any stockpiles or hidden reserves of abandoned property, food goods, materials, machines or instruments that are still unknown to us are obliged to report about them to the corresponding district police within 12 hours of the publication of the given order; individuals who live in villages must report to the rural councils within this same time period. Those guilty in concealing stockpiles and reserves are to be given the death penalty."[45]

The archives have preserved a multitude of reports of G. Alexianu directly to I. Antonescu about the export to Romania of tens of thousands of heads of cattle and thousands of sheep. One of the messages from 21 February 1942 informed that at that time, "The total number of rail cars carrying exports to Romania amounts to 11,399 ...."[46] Agricultural machines, tractors, trolley cars, trolley buses, rails, railway sleepers, engines, stakes, tires and print shops were looted and sent back to Romania, all and sundry.[47] One can judge the quantity of the plundered goods brought out from a report of the Romanian General Staff to the governorship of the Transnistria about the quantity of exported food items and property for just the one and a half months between 1 November and 14 December 1943 (see Table 8.1).[48]

With the aim of accelerating the export of plundered valuables, Antonescu's government decided to repair Odessa's port partially so as to connect it with Romanian ports. A letter of order from the Vice-Secretary of State for Naval Matters P. Păis to the governor of the Transnistria stated:

> According to a decision of Sir Marshal Ion Antonescu ... we have the honor to request kindly that you take charge of the bestowed 10,000,000 leu in order to get work going to put the undamaged facilities of Odessa's port back into operation, in view of the need to stockpile and ship seized property and items, which must be delivered by right of ownership of the government, according to the instructions of the Council of Ministers' Decree No. 1403/1941.[49]

In order to organize the work, a group of officials arrived in Odessa from Constanţa. This was especially noted in the article "Odessa's port resumes its work" published by *Odesskaia gazeta* on 30 November 1941. The newspaper announced: "Work will be organized in Odessa according to the system used by Romania's ports." Together with the port director Popescu, his engineers Grecu and Burlacu and host of other functionaries of lower rank together with their secretaries arrived. The port's headquarters was located in one of the intact buildings of the Kherson Court.

Simultaneously, *Capitani* (Naval *Siguranţa*) were created at the port, the job of which was to carry out the functions of the gendarme. The *Capitani* were to track ships as they came and went

---

44   Shternshtein, *Morskie vorota – Odessa*, p. 149.

45   *Odesskaya gazeta*, 5 November 1941.

46   DAOO, F. R. 1820, S/393, Op. 1, Spr. 677, Ark. 75; Spr. 314, Ark. 104.

47   DAOO, F. R. 1820, S/393, Op. 1, Spr. 1909, Ark. 12, 13; F. R. 2509, S/1082, Op. 1, Spr. 3, Ark. 21; F. R. 2514, S/1087, Op. 1, Spr. 136, Ark. 15; F. R. 1824, S/397, Spr. 113, SKK, Ark. 1; F. R. 1926, S/399, Op. 1, Spr. 17, Ark. 1.

48   *Odessa v Velikoi Otechestvennoi voine Sovetskogo Soiuza*, Vol. 1, p. 70.

49   DAOO, F. R. 1968, S/541, Op. 1, Spr. 5, Ark. 19. Machine-typed copy translated from the Romanian (*Diretirenea Portului Odesa din Gudernamantulu Transnistriei*) – (Management board of Odessa's port of the governorship of the Transnistria)

Table 8.1: Plundered farm animals, food products and other agricultural items exported to Romania (in number of rail cars with a 10-metric ton capacity)

Items	1 to 30 November 1943	1 to 14 December 1943	Total
Butter	3	–	3
Sugar	84	70	154
Various food products	296	64	360
Wheat	477	128	605
Rye	33	20	53
Light grains	202	292	494
Corn	15	37	52
Bran flour	4	4	8
Cattle and birds	952	134	1,086
Oil seed	91	45	136
Various machines	527	201	728
Agricultural machines	1,398	442	1,840
Scrap iron	514	209	723
Ferrous metals	7	8	15
Luggage	87	46	133
Leather	12	5	17
Millwork	50	42	92
Ore	139	3	142
Various loads	868	394	1,262
Cattle, hogs and sheep, driven to stations from Bessarabia	521	-	521
Horses, driven to stations from Bessarabia	1,429	301	1,730
Total	7,709	2,445	10,154

at the port and keep order at the berths, as well as to keep an eye on the trustworthiness of the workers. They were also in charge of the distribution of passes. Officers of the *Capitani* were vested with unlimited authority; among their functions was keeping watch over the civilians that were being forced to work at the port. All of the work at the port was done by hand and required physical strength exclusively. The workers carried enormous loads over long distances on their shoulders, including stones, logs and iron. The Germans were raising sunk cutters, vehicles and other valuables from the bottom of the sea and were selling them on the spot at a speculative price to scalpers, who flocked to Odessa from Romania. A White Russian émigré N. Liubomirov directed this side work.[50]

An incessant rivalry was going on between the German and Romanian "conquerors", on the one hand, and among the separate Romanian business firms that were striving to squeeze a little more profit from the rapacious exploitation and pillaging of the port, on the other hand. The repeated interventions by the naval minister, governor and major military officials, who were in turn bribed by one group or another, led nowhere.

At the direction of the German command, an agreement was hammered out between the German and Romanian authorities about sharing the port's facilities and equipment, while

---

50 *Odesskaia gazeta*, 27 May 1942.

functions to exploit the port were strictly demarcated. The Romanians managed civil affairs and were in charge of the processing of agricultural and similar loads of a non-military nature. The German command at the port, on the other hand, handled only military loads. A circular from the Vice Chief of the General Staff General Arbore addressed to Governor Alexianu dated 20 May 1942 is of interest; it required of the command of units and elements to render the broadest assistance to the collecting of marine trophies in the Black Sea, and "to report their available evidence about the materials seized by the Germans and collected in ports, loaded onto ships, etc., since we are due 40% of all the material which has already been taken or will be taken in the form of loot."[51]

The situation of the population in the Transnistria was desparate. In fact it was doomed to extinction, which the fascist newspaper *Porunka vremii* was even recognizing: "Since the past year and to the present day, prices have gone up by 300 to 500%. ... Children are being fed weeds. In the cities over recent times, there have been no potatoes at all."[52] When village *starosta* gave the order to requisition feathers and down, they reported, "Since the people have no chickens or other birds, there is no possibility to gather down and feathers."[53] Almost the entire inventory of agricultural items was confiscated from the population, taken "as a military contribution to the soldiers who are fighting at the front"; this went so far as to include stockings, socks and gloves, as well as felt boots.[54]

However, Odessa's population managed to avoid hunger due to the confluence of several fortuitous circumstances. The fact is little-known and officially hushed up: Before the war's outbreak, a host of goods and loads had accumulated in Odessa's port, which because of the panic and confusion hadn't been evacuated to the rear. The fact that the city's authorities had the wisdom prior to the surrender of Odessa not to burn or blow up the stockpiles (so that the fascists wouldn't get them), but to distribute the goods to the rest of the population, reflects well upon them. The wares didn't reach everyone and it wasn't allocated evenly, but nevertheless practically throughout the entire extent of the occupation, many Odessans had no deficit in light textiles or tea, which they could exchange for other products. There is even more information on this subject, characteristic for both Odessa and other cities of the oblast. After the retreat of Soviet forces (which as a rule went rather quickly) and prior to the appearance of the enemy's forward detachments, there was a period of a vacuum of authority (sometimes for several hours, sometimes even for entire days). During this period, facilities, factories and shops were opened and nothing was being guarded. Enterprising individuals and simply the brave hauled away everything that they could carry off. This also allowed many to survive somehow that terrible time, including by trading wares and domestic things for food.

Not only were the initial months of occupation very hard on life, but also the winter of 1941-1942. However, already from the spring of 1942 to the summer of 1943, the material and food supply of the city dwellers improved somewhat; the population had adapted. Workers in the cities for an 8-hour workday were receiving 4 to 8 Occupation Reichsmarks daily. This allowed a family to get by, since in the shops of the municipality, the rations were sufficient and at a relatively low price. For example, 1 kilogram of bread per ration card cost 0.9 Reichsmarks, while resellers were selling it for 2.75 Reichsmarks; 1 kilogram of sugar by norm cost 3 Reichsmarks, while 1 kilogram of unrationed sugar could be purchased for 20 Reichsmarks; 1 kilogram of rationed butter cost 6 Reichsmarks, and could then be turned around and sold for 30 Reichsmarks. Each worker in Odessa received the following rations at fixed prices per month: 0.5 kilogram of fat (butter or

51   DAOO, F.R. 1968, S/541, Op. 1, Spr. 3, Ark. 7; machine-typed copy translated from the Romanian.
52   Shternshtein, *Morskie voroty Ukrainy*, p. 148.
53   DAOO, F. R. 2056, S/629, Op. 1, Spr. 109, Ark. 13.
54   DAOO, F. R. 2539, S/1113, Op. 1, Spr. 3, Ark. 67; F. R. 2509, S/1082, Op. 1, Spr. 3, Ark. 28; F. R. 2056, S/629, Op. 1, Spr. 6, Ark. 155; Spr. 104, Ark. 111; F. R. 1820, S/393, Op. 1, Spr. 1918, Ark. 37.

rendered pig fat); 1 liter of sunflower oil; 1 kilogram of sugar; 5-6 kilograms of kasha, macaroni and white flour; 2 kilograms of meat; a half-liter of vodka; and 300 cigarettes. In free trade it was possible to buy goods at higher prices without any restrictions. If only they'd been brand-name goods …. Even more, anyone desiring for corresponding remuneration could obtain a license to open their own shop or other small enterprise and legally run a business. Already by the summer of 1942, Odessa was full of all types of goods. Romanian merchants were also drawn to the city, where they opened dry good shops, variety stores and groceries.

The occupational authorities made no effort to decide the social problems of the residents of Odessa.[55] The level of medical service was plainly insufficient – the quantity of infectious diseases rose constantly in the city. In the spring of 1943, there was an outbreak of venereal diseases. Treatment was on a paid basis; consultation with a doctor cost 12 Reichsmarks, an X-ray cost 20 Reichsmarks, and an operation – anywhere beyond 20 Reichsmarks.[56]

On 18 March 1942, the governor of the Transnistria G. Alexianu issued an order regarding compulsory labor conscription, with lengthy prison times and exile to camps for violations of this order. The occupiers implemented this order with all their known cruelty.

K.F. Sokolova talked about how her 65-year-old father, who'd been badly wounded on 15 October 1941 during an air raid on Odessa and had since been confined to bed, was sent four summons from the labor bureau, which all began with the common threat: "avoidance of work is punishable". She added, "On 17 March 1943, during the funeral ceremony for my father, policemen headed by an inspector of the labor bureau burst into the house with an order to send him off to the camps for failing to show up for work."[57]

The situation of the workers at Odessa's rebuilt factories was exceptionally hard; they were treated like slaves. Every German or Romanian, from the factory director to the pettiest pen pusher, could abuse and beat up an employee. The application of physical force was a matter of course. One port longshoreman A.I. Shevchenko recalls:

> We worked all day long, surrounded on every side by Romanian guards, before they led us under guard to dinner, which consisted of lukewarm, disgusting slop. Only late at night were we dismissed to go home with the warning to show up for work the next day almost at daybreak. For the slightest insubordination they promised a thousand kicks and blows, and it must be said that they carried out this promise. It was agonizing to load our wood, furniture, grain and other goods for shipment to Romania. The situation was intolerable, and many times we ran away from the port, but the labor bureau would track us down, forcibly return us to the port, and pitilessly beat us in the *Capitani*'s office.[58]

Because of the down time of the industrial plants, far from everyone found work. The number of unemployed in Odessa during the period of occupation reached 80% of the total population, but far from everyone was able to enroll at the labor bureau. Later, the local power structures began to try to resolve this problem by sending the unemployed to compulsory work in Germany, but also by setting up small-scale production and a handicraft trade. However, this didn't lead to perceptible changes: in the spring of 1943 there were only 12,000 workers or owners of private workshops.[59] Only the food and pharmaceutical sectors were of natural interest to the occupiers. Here was where they exerted their efforts.

---

55   *Molva*, 11, 13 April 1943.
56   Ibid., 15 April 1943.
57   Shternshtein, *Morskie vorota Ukrainy*, p. 152.
58   Ibid.
59   *Molva*, 8 April 1943.

With the aim of effectively using the labor force, in August 1942 a Labor Cohort was created. The governor's order for this stated: "All males who have reached 20 years of age and who live on the territory of the Transnistria are obliged to join the organization's cadres." The young men were to be used at "field works and as community guards, and guards of firms, neighborhoods and facilities." Those who declined to join were sent to prison. The amount of work had no effect on the daily ration of 200 grams of bread for each person.[60]

The occupational authorities didn't even blanch at engaging children of 7 to 12 years of age in slave labor. At an order from the praetor of the Odessa District and the chief of the Land Department on 30 July 1943, the rural *starosta* "were obligated to send all children from 7 to 12 years of age to the Khadzhibey (Koroleva Mariia) State Farm for doing agricultural work."[61]

The press of the Transnistria filled their pages with announcements of "launch of a new line", "rehabilitation of one more workshop", the production of "new" goods and so forth. However, almost all of the output of such enterprises went to Romania, or was used in place to supply troops or meet the needs of the occupational administration. For example, of the 2,612 rail cars of ground sugar produced by factories of the Transnistria in 1942, just 322 rail cars were left for the social welfare system that existed in the Odessa municipality; the rest went to Romania or were turned over to Romanian bureaucrats and merchants. Of the 774 metric tons of the produced soap, the Romanian Army received 430 metric tons, and the rest was distributed among Romanian office employees and so forth. The cigarettes, wine and salt that were produced in industrial enterprises were considered a state monopoly and sold only in special government stores, as were postage stamps.[62]

The level of pension support was very low and included people of pension age selectively – depending on their utility to the new regime. That portion of the intelligentsia that served the new regime received pensions. For example, at the petition of the rector of Odessa University, the city chief G. Pynța fixed up 65 professors in the spring of 1943 with academic pensions through the university, discounted rents for an apartment, and a 50% discount in the costs of electricity and heat. In addition, the Bureau of Culture of Transnistria's governorship in the first semester of 1942/1943 academic year relieved 862 students from payment for their education – the offspring of office employees of provincial and municipal officers and university staff. At that time, 1,800 students were studying in all the academic departments of the Odessa University, or which only 302 were Romanians and Moldavians.[63]

In the lengthy chain of crimes committed by the fascists, the forcible round-up of citizens of Odessa for slave labor in Germany occupied a special place. Special trains carrying the captives stretched through the city. Recalled a port watchman V.S. Balan, "I remember how young men and women from the Crimea and other places were delivered to the port on barges for shipment into hard labor in exile. Haggard, shabby and hungry, they were shoved into rail cars and hastily sent off."[64] The archives have preserved testimonies about the deportation of 56,100 residents of the Odessa area into slavery.[65]

One of the main directions of the activity of the new regime was the struggle against Communist ideology and for Romanian influence on the people's social conscience. In Odessa, gramophone records by Soviet composers and Jewish composers were banned, as were books published under

60 *Odessa v Velikoi Otechestvennoi voine Sovetskogo Soiuza*, Vol 2, p. 174.
61 DAOO, F.R. 2056, S/629, Op. 1, Spr. 91, Ark. 108.
62 A. Dallin, *Odessa, 1941-1944: A case study of Soviet territory under foreign rule* (Santa Monica, CA: RAND Corporation, 1957), p. 164; Stanko [chief ed.], *Istoriia Odesi*, pp. 407-408.
63 *Odesskaia gazeta*, 13 March 1942; *Molva*, 9, 10 April 1943.
64 Shternshtein, *Morskie vorota Ukrainy*, p. 153.
65 DAOO, F. R. 2527, S/110, Spr. 8, 17, 23, 26.

Soviet rule and the singing of Russian and Ukrainian songs. Streets, cities and settlements received new names. The fascists were pitting Ukrainians against Poles, Poles against Ukrainians, and those and others against Russians.[66]

The governor of the Transnistria attempted to fill various organizational forms of socio-economic and cultural life with a pro-Romanian content. He started with education and culture – the primary links of influence on a society. Already on 7 October 1941, there was the announcement of the opening of a single higher education institute on the entire territory between the Prut and Southern Bug Rivers – the Odessa University, the rector of which was Professor of Medicine P.A. Chasovnikov. Within the university, an "Institute of Anti-Communist Propaganda" was created. In the city, periodic publications came out with increasing frequency; the information they contained boiled down to communiques from the fronts in a major key, and bringing Romanian laws to Ukrainian lands. The publications were full of the poison of fascist ideology and anti-Semitism. From 20 June 1942, a newspaper in the German language began to come out: *Der Deutsche in Transnistrien* [*Germans in the Transnistria*]. On 6 September 1942, the first issue of the daily newspaper *Pobeda* [*Victory*] in the Romanian language came out. From 1 December 1942 the daily newspaper in the Russian language *Molva* [*Talk*] began circulation, which became in April 1943 the official organ of the governor's administration. Almost from the first days of the occupation, the *Odesskaia gazeta* – the official organ of the mayor's office – entered daily circulation.[67]

An entertainment industry took root intensively: movie theaters with a corresponding repertoire, and a broad network of theaters, including privately-owned ones. A talented acting troupe, who performed a repertoire of masterpieces of world and domestic classics, worked in the Odessa Opera House. The sole Romanian spectacle, Paul Constantinescu's ballet *Nuntâ în Carpați* [*Wedding in the Carpathians*], quickly disappeared from the stage, because it wasn't popular with the viewing public. The opera house opened on 7 December 1941, premiering the opera *Evgenii Onegin*. The operas *La Traviatta, Rigoletto, Madame Butterfly, Aida, Tosca, Faust* and *Carmen* enjoyed the greatest public popularity. The repertoire of ballets included *Swan Lake, Sleeping Beauty, Le Corsaire* [*The Pirate*] and *La petite Fadette*. The famous tenor E. Marinescu and other Romanian singers from Bucharest and Timișoara performed on the stage of the Odessa Opera House; a leading tenor of that time T. Scipano sang lyrical sentimental and other songs. The German conductor G. Lessner conducted performances of *La Boheme*, while the well-known Italian conductor B. Molinari conducted *Aida* and *Rigoletto*.[68] Concerts were often performed with the participation of the orchestra and soloists of the theater.

The Odessa Opera House was the genuine cultural center of the city in the years of occupation. On 21 February 1943, soon after the German Sixth Army capitulated at Stalingrad, the walls of the opera house became filled with the patriotic aria from Glinka's *Ivan Susanin* (about the sorry fate of aggressors), and Tchaikovsky's *Slavonic March* and *1812 Overture*, which prompted the indignation of Germans who were attending the concert. The customary tradition in Odessa of admiration for the operatic arts continued to attract a significant number of visitors, and primarily young people. For many of them, a visit to the Opera House became a basic cultural need and pastime.

Christian churches re-opened in the city, which conducted active religious proselytization. On 30 November 1941, the *Odesskaia gazeta* included an article entitled "Tserkvi" ["Churches"], which announced that "by the end of 1941, Odessa will be enriched with 10-12 new churches."[69] The

66   DAOO, F. R. 1826, S/399, Op. 1, Spr. 84, Ark. 63, 68; *Molva*, 8 September 1943.
67   Stanko [chief ed.], *Istoriia Odesi*, pp. 406-407.
68   DAOO, F. R. 2249, Op. 3, Spr. 18, Ark. 5; A.Ia. Golovko, *Starye Odesskie interv'iu* [*Old Odessan interviews*] (Odessa: Astroprint, 2000), pp. 7-9.
69   *Odesskaia gazeta*, 30 November 1941.

Orthodox Church cathedral at the Monastery of St. Il'ia from the beginning of the occupation became the center of the Orthodox Church life of Odessa. Over the years of occupation in Odessa, there existed 22 faith-based communities centered on the Orthodox churches and cathedrals. By the beginning of 1944, in Odessa alone there were up to 30 churches and two monasteries: for men, the Panteleimonovskii Monastery, and for women – the Sviato-Mikhailovskii Monastery. The occupation authority didn't interfere in this process, giving a release to the religious feelings of the population. On the other hand, by strengthening the foundations of ideological influence, it tried to take possession not only material valuables, but also place the very soul of the people under control. The Romanian authorities and their Orthodox mission regarded Ukrainian and Russian priests with hostility. The metropolitan mission of V. Puju ordered services to be held only in the Church Slavonic language, and sermons – in Romanian or Russian. It was banned to conduct services in the Ukrainian language, and the assignment of churches for six priests of the Ukrainian Apostolic Orthodox Church was denied. Subsequently they had to leave Odessa. In a spiritual seminary based in Odessa, both Russians and Ukrainians studied, but instruction was given only in the Russian or Romanian languages.[70] It was as if adherents of other religions, especially Jews, didn't even exist in Odessa.[71]

The youth of the Transnistria were raised in a religious spirit. The governorship's propaganda was aimed at inculcating an ethnographic Moldavian element, in order to instill a Romanian spirit and create a situation acceptable for the Romanian administration, so this same element exerted maximal efforts in arable farming and industry, as well espoused the Christian faith.[72]

Parallel in the city with the authorization of C. Vidrascu, a network of brothels appeared in the city, which were officially called "Houses of Assignation to Service German and Romanian Military Personnel".[73] From the very first days of their existence, however, they didn't serve only servicemen.

70   *Ideia i chin*, No. 4 (1943).
71   *Odesskaia gazeta*, 20 November 1941.
72   *Transnistria, 1941-1943* (1943), pp. 67, 70.
73   DAOO, F. R. 2522, S/1116, Op. 1, Spr. 42, Ark. 3.

9

Odessa resists the occupation

Odessa was still offering resistance, and in the rear of the Romanian and German forces a movement of popular resistance was already developing in the Odessa region. Toward the end of August 1941, the leadership of Odessa Oblast together with the Military Council of the Coastal Army redeployed 130 men to occupied districts of the oblast, who provided the core for forming seven partisan detachments. The partisan detachment led by A.F. Soldatenko operated boldly. On the territory of the Beliaevskii and Frunzovskii Districts, he crushed the headquarters of a Romanian battalion, killed 150 Romanian soldiers and officers, and knocked out two anti-aircraft guns.[1]

A Sovinform communique from 31 August 1941 announced that in the course of the previous week, partisans of the Odessa region had conducted around 20 major attacks against enemy supply columns, moving along roads close to Shiriaevo, Perestal', and the villages of Antonovka and Demidovo in the Berezovskii District. The partisans destroyed 47 German trucks carrying large-caliber shells, 27 barrels of gasoline and 42 horse-drawn wagons carrying food. In the fighting against the combat elements guarding the motorized columns and wagon trains, more than 120 enemy soldiers were killed.[2]

Another Sovinformburo communique from 28 September 1941 announced: "Partisan detachments of Odessa Oblast are operating boldly in the rear of the German and Romanian forces. A detachment of partisans with fire from a captured machine gun destroyed a launch carrying 9 enemy soldiers. … The partisans are creating intolerable conditions for the foe. Under interrogation, one of the prisoners declared, 'Partisans – this is a second Soviet army, which we don't see, but which doesn't allow us to live.'"[3]

The enemy's Supreme Command, frightened by the scale of popular resistance to the "New Order", demanded from the division commanders: "In view of the enemy's widespread use of actions in our rear, it is necessary to take measures to secure headquarters both during marches and at stops. Staff officers, moving alone, must be escorted by 1-2 soldiers with machine pistols and grenades; any columns, whether on foot, horse-drawn or motorized, must take thorough measures for an immediate defense."[4]

On 2 October 1941, the Sovinformburo reported:

One of the partisan detachments in the course of September conducted 18 attacks against enemy columns heading toward the Odessa front. In the combats with the fascists, the

---

1   *Kniga Pamiati Ukrainy: Odesskaia oblast* [*Book of Memory of Ukraine: Odessa Oblast*] Vol. 1 (Odessa: Maiak, 1994), p. 28.
2   Ibid.
3   *73 geroicheskikh dnia. Khronika oborony Odessy v 1941 godu, izd. 3* [*73 heroic days. Chronicle of the defense of Odessa in 1941, 3rd edition*] (Odessa: Maiak, 1988), p. 235.
4   S. Vol'skii, *Velichnii podvig* [*Great achievement*] (Kiev, 1967), p. 170.

partisans killed more than 20 soldiers and officers, and seized a lot of weapons and ammunition. A different detachment, operating northwest of Odessa, destroyed 7 large bridges and mined roads in 16 locations. Six vehicles carrying infantry triggered mines, and up to 100 enemy soldiers were killed. West of Odessa another partisan detachment destroyed 17 railway tank cars filled with fuel and two motorized columns transporting shells for the enemy's artillery.[5]

The resistance movement against the occupiers was being organized in the Odessa region even before the territory was captured by the occupiers. Various groups operated independently from each other, but primarily Party organs formed partisan detachments and underground organizations, while central and local security organs formed reconnaissance- sabotage groups. A clandestine oblast committee of the Communist Party, created in Odessa and headed by A.P. Petrovsky and S.S. Sukharev, was coordinating the activity of the underground district committees of the Party. One hundred and eighteen Communists were selected for underground work in Odessa and its surroundings, who were organized into 29 primary cells of three members each, as well as into six underground Party district committees according to territory: Leninskii, Vodnotransportnyi [Shipping], Il'ichevskii, Primorskii [Coastal], Tsentral'nyi [Central] and Prigorodnyi [Suburban]. Each of the six was headed by two secretaries and had liaison groups, clandestine apartments, money, weapons, ammunition and agitation literature.[6] Seven detachments operated on the basis of five of the district committees.[7] Nine more partisan detachments were additionally formed in the oblast.

In the Nerubaiskii catacombs and in Odessa separately from the Party structures, two reconnaissance-sabotage detachments of the NKVD prepared for actions. One was led by Captain of Security V.A. Molodtsov (code name – Pavel Badaev), who arrived in July from Moscow. The second, rather larger detachment of 32 men was created by the headquarters of the NKVD in Odessa Oblast. Militia organs also left behind small sabotage groups and separate individuals on occupied territory.

Members of T. Semchishin's Southern March Group also operated on the territory of the oblast. Their activity, primarily, was directed at the restoration of the Ukrainian government on Ukrainian territory. March groups of the *Bukovinskii Kuren'*, organized in July 1941 by Ukrainian patriots led by P. Voinovsky on the territory of Bukovina, were also oriented at work in Odessa Oblast.[8]

Separate popular resistance groups were created and operated independently. For example, on 25 October 1941 the Sovinformburo reported about the actions of a partisan detachment of the Rybolovetskii Collective Farm in the enemy rear in Odessa Oblast. The partisans made their way along a river to some Romanian stockpiles and set them on fire, and then attacked a Romanian element that was in laager. In panic the enemy soldiers and officers started to run away, but they were caught by mounted men and cut down. Altogether during the nighttime clash the Romanians lost 60 men killed and 50 wounded. Two mortars, three wagons of ammunition, four machine guns and 90 rifles wound up in the partisans' hands.[9]

---

5   *73 geroicheskikh dnia*, p. 244.
6   TsDAGO Ukraini, F. 1, Op. 9a, Spr. 65, Ark. 174.
7   DAOO, F.R. 11, Spr. 2113, Ark. 13-15 [Otchet o podpol'noi i partizanskoi deiatelnost'v Odesskoi oblasti – Account of the underground and partisan activity in Odessa Oblast]
8   P. Voinovsky, *Moe naivishche shchastia: Spomin* [*My greatest happiness: Memoirs*] (Kiev, 1999), pp. 245-247; Stanko [chief ed.], *Istoriia Odesi*, pp. 397-398.
9   *Soobshcheniia Sovetskogo Informbiuro* [*Communiques of the Soviet Information Bureau*] Vol. 1 (Moscow, 1944), p. 322.

The famous Odessa catacombs became the main base for Odessa's resistance movement. Odessa was built upon steep coastal banks, the foundation of which is composed of a 12-16 meter layer of Pontian limestone, covered by brownish-red clay and loess-like loam. It was in the layer of limestone of varying degrees of density that the Odessa catacombs developed. Catacombs are a network of underground passages and labyrinths. At the present time, their total length reaches approximately 2,500 kilometers, which exceeds the Paris underground labyrinths and Rome's famous underground (according to various estimates, their total lengths range from 300 to 500 kilometers). The majority of the Odessa catacombs are underground quarries, to which reinforcing walls of building stones – shell or shell rock, used for constructing the city – have been added. In addition, cavities of natural or man-made origin are part of the system of catacombs – karst and dilatancy caverns, construction trenches and pits, cellars and vaults, underground shelters, drainage tunnels, catchment basins and similar underground cavities. The first underground quarries began to appear in the first half of the 19th Century, during the feverish building of Odessa as a source of inexpensive building material – shell rock, or more accurately, Pontian limestone. The excavation of rock was done with the help of saws, and was so intensive that already in the latter half of the 19th Century; the extensive network of underground cavities began to cause problems for the city. At the beginning of the 20th Century, in connection with the increasingly frequent settling and collapse of buildings, a ban was introduced on the excavation of rock within the city's limits. However, the excavation of limestone continues in mines, located in Dofinovka, Buldynka and the Fominaia balka, and thus the extent of Odessa's catacombs continues to grow even to the present day.

The Odessa catacombs are multi-tiered; their galleries lie at various depths from the surface of the ground, forming a unique underground city, consisting of passages, grottoes, dead ends, niches, chambers and so on. Tunnels from building cellars lead into many catacombs (in Odessa, such passages are mostly called "mines"). Usually the mines extend beyond the perimeter of the buildings, and passing under streets and public squares, often link up with the overall labyrinth of the catacombs.[10]

Since long ago, Odessa's residents have used the opportunity of reliable shelter in the catacombs against natural woes and the enemy. In the early 20th Century the catacombs were used by Odessans as a base for forming resistance detachments and storing weapons for the struggle against the Czarist regime and the repulse of the Austro-German, Anglo-French and other invasions. When Odessa fell into the hands of the fascist aggressors, the catacombs again became a combat camp, where resistance detachments took shelter.

The Party's underground Prigorodnyi District Committee consisting of 13 people led by S.F. Lazarev established itself in the Odessa catacombs.[11] A host of items were brought into the underground camp, including 10 rifles, 5,000 cartridges, 200 grenades, 50 kilograms of explosives, entrenching tools, kerosene lamps, kerosene stoves, enough food and fuel to last a year, clothes, a radio receiver, a typewriter, and paper for printing leaflets.[12] One of the partisan detachments led by A.F. Soldatenko was also based in the catacombs beneath Odessa's Il'ichevskii District. In the catacombs beneath the village of Krivaia Balka were two partisan detachments under the command of E.I. Voroshilov and V.F. Dushechkin. In the catacombs below Frunze Street was the operating base of V.A. Kaloshin's and V.A. Kuznetsov's large reconnaissance-sabotage detachment.[13]

---

10   *Odesskie katakomby, Izd. 3-e* [*Odessan catacombs, 3rd ed.*] (Odessa: Maiak, 1974).

11   DAOO, Memuarnyi fond, Vospominaniia S.F. Lazarev [Recollections of S.F. Lazarev], p. 1.

12   DAOO, F. 11, Op. 45, Spr. 3, Ark. 41.

13   G.A. Karev, *Odessa – gorod-geroi* [*Odessa – Hero City*] (Moscow: Voenizdat, 1978), pp. 133-134.

Partisans in the catacombs prepared for battle with the occupiers and took loyalty oaths. Upon joining a partisan detachment, they voluntarily took on commitments and swore before their comrades:

> In the ranks of partisan detachments, to conduct struggle against the fascist occupiers and their henchmen with a weapon in my hands to the last drop of blood. I will carry out all orders promptly, clearly and without questioning; I will not share secrets involving the group, detachment or Committee with my own family or kin, and also not with other individuals and offices of the fascist yoke and their henchmen. In case of betrayal of the oath I've given aloud in the presence of comrades, let the strict hand of the field partisan tribunal punish me at the place of my betrayal, whereupon I am giving my signature.[14]

Romanian authorities realized the threat that the catacombs presented. Thus they gave them unflagging attention; already on 5 November 1941 the command of the occupational forces demanded:

> Article 1. All residents of the city of Odessa and neighboring surroundings are obliged to declare in written form to police departments (their military law sections) about any exits from the catacombs known to them, as well as the location of mines in homes, yards, sheds, cellars and other places known to them; the declaration must be made within a seven-day period from the date of publication of the present order. Primarily the janitors of the corresponding homes and their residents, who failed to make the declaration within the indicated period, will answer for the failure to report about the catacombs and mined locations.

> Article 2. Residents of buildings, where catacomb entrances or exits, or mined locations are discovered after the indicated time expires will be punished by death. All of those who live near the catacombs or mined places, and aware of their presence, fail to report them will face the same sentence – just like those who know individuals who are using the catacombs, but fail to report on these people within the indicated time period. Young violators of the order will be punished just like adults.
>
> General P. Tib. Petrescu, Military Prosecutor G. Soltan[15]

The occupiers sought to brick up all the catacomb entrances and exits known to them, but the Odessans were resisting the sealing of the catacombs in any and every way. The commandant's headquarters on 20 November 1941 announced:

> On the morning of 13 November, two Romanian soldiers were killed by Russian Communist-terrorists while they were working to seal a catacomb. Notice is hereby given that such terrorist acts will be mercilessly punished by the Romanian authorities. Every citizen of Odessa who knows about the location of Communist-terrorists lurking in buildings, cellars, catacombs or any other shelters are obliged to report about this immediately to the district police office. In the event of an attack on Romanian or German soldiers, 500 Communists will be shot for each episode of a terrorist act. First of all, neighbors will be shot.[16]

---

14   DAOO, F. R. 213v, S/711, Op. 1, Spr. 39, Ark. 87.
15   *Odesskaia gazeta*, 5 November 1941.
16   Ibid., 20 November 1941.

The occupiers took active measures to try to suppress the least hint of organized actions and to destroy underground organizations and partisan detachments promptly. The Romanian security force, the Gestapo, the police and the gendarmes entangled the city with a dense network of spies, provocateurs, informants and both open and secret agents. Each had their own torture chambers for interrogating and torturing suspected partisans. The torture chambers particularly occupying the premises of a former movie theater in the Slobodka District in order to punish partisans and members of the underground were notorious. Here the torturers came up with refined ways to apply the cruelest agonies and torments. The occupational administration also established a harsh dictatorial regime:

> The support and concealment of suspects is strictly prohibited. Those who admit a military prisoner, Jew, partisan or former Communist activist who is on the loose into their apartment and give him aid without authorization will be shot. Those who are aware of suspects loose among the population, but who doesn't immediately report this through the head of the city, district or village to the corresponding organs of German authority will also be punished.[17]

Thus, underground partisan organizations never got the chance even to get to work before the blows of the fascist secret police began to fall upon them. At the end of October 1941, the 1st Secretary of the underground Party Oblast Committee A.P. Petrovsky was arrested. At the same time the *Siguranța* smashed the Party's underground Leninskii and Primorskii District Committees. In early 1942, the majority of the members of the underground Party organizations of the Il'icheskii District was arrested, followed a short time later by those of the Central District Committee.[18] Many members of the underground also fell into the hands of the Romanian secret police coincidentally during the mass round-ups of Jews. Far from every patriot adhered to the rules of a conspiracy. Safe houses were sometimes set up right next door to the pre-war residence of an underground member, where he or she was well known (as happened, for example, with the revelation of the 1st Secretary of the Party's underground Oblast Committee A.P. Petrovsky). Quite often, important documents about the membership of underground district committees and groups, and information about passwords, safe houses and so forth fell into the hands of the foe. All this led to further setbacks.[19]

Thus, the first wave of the underground-partisan movement, which was organized back during the period of Odessa's defense, was rather quickly neutralized by the occupiers. Among the reasons for this, one can cite the weak preparation of the partisan detachments; the hastiness in choosing recruits; the lack of a mindset toward a prolonged struggle in the enemy rear; and the disparate nature of the actions of partisan detachments and groups. One must also consider the geographic factor: the expansive, open steppes of Ukraine's south weren't amenable to the creation of a mass partisan movement. It never became the main form of popular struggle against the occupiers, like it did in the northern, western and eastern areas of Ukraine. Subsequently, the main form of the resistance movement on territories occupied by Romania became the underground's propaganda work and subversive activities within the limits of a specific town, village or settlement, and also the sabotage of occupational administration projects.

Broad work among the population of the city and surrounding villages was deployed. The main means for conducting it was the printing and distribution of leaflets. This material gave refutations to the lies of fascist propaganda about the defeat of the Red Army, provided information about

---

17 *Nove zhittia*, 27 September 1942
18 DAOO, F. P. 11, Op. 45, Spr. 1, Ark. 13.
19 V. Fabiansky, "Dvoinaia igra" ["Double game"], *Iug*, 14 April 2001.

the real situation at the front, and explained the essence of the fascist regime. One of the leaflets declared:

> Workers, peasants and employees! Bloody Hitler and his toady Antonescu continue to trample our holy land with filthy, fascist boots … What have the fascists brought to Ukraine's occupied area? Hangings, shootings, racks, whips, beatings, and jails they've organized in every county.[20]

Leaflets came out almost daily. In just the first three months of the enemy occupation alone, the members of the underground printed and circulated more than 7,000 leaflets and appeals among the population of the city.[21] On the eve of the 1942 New Year a leaflet circulated in the city, in which the partisans congratulated the residents with the arrival of the New Year: "I'm informing you that we are alive and well, which we also wish for you. We also wish to work in 1942 on free socialist soil. The fascists have spoiled our mood a little, but never mind, they won't be running things much longer. Their days of existence are numbered."[22]

One leaflet that circulated among the railroad workers appealed, "Frustrate the orders of the German vampires; disrupt haulages; destroy steam engines and wagons; derail trains on slopes. Add not residual fuel oil to grease boxes, but sand; set fire to trains and fuel tanks; create bottlenecks at stations; by every means possible disrupt the transportation system of the hated occupiers."[23]

Odessa's workers actively responded to such appeals. Soon, alongside the word "partisans", the no less frightening word "sabotage" began to appear in the occupier's documents. Odessa's longshoremen, the workers of the Dzerzhinskii, Red Guards, January Uprising and October Revolution factories and of other enterprises were actively undermining the efforts of the occupational powers to restore the port, factories and plants and get them operating again. The collective farmers of the nearby villages sharply reduced the planting of winter crops, slaughtered cattle and were hiding food products, resisting the payment of taxes in kind. Sabotage became one of the most important forms of struggle by the population of Odessa and its suburbs against the German and Romanian aggressors.

The port had particular significance. Here, resistance went along two channels. Together with the "Stalin" detachment (Commander S.I. Drozdov, Commissar D.I. Ovcharenko), which had been created by Party organs, other underground partisan groups that had arisen spontaneously were operating. A group of 11 longshoremen and sailors, organized in December 1941 by a port engineer named A.I. Pashchenko, was the first to initiate activities. A group of underground saboteurs, which consisted primarily of workers of the railroad depot at Odessa's port, began to operate in the wake of Paschchenko's group. Other small underground sabotage groups and solitary patriots began to follow suit. The command of the "Stalin" partisan detachment devised special instructions regarding acts of sabotage, diversions and damage with the aim of frustrating the loading and unloading operations at the docks. Underground groups also conducted propaganda and diversionary acts in order to undermine work at the port; organized assistance to persons in custody and wounded Red Army prisoners; carried out special missions at the behest of the Red Army command; and saved the port's property from plundering, and the port's facilities and equipment from destruction.

20   *Odessa v Velikoi Otechestvennoi voine Sovetskogo Soiuza. Sbornik dokumentov i materialov [Odessa in the Great Patriotic War of the Soviet Union. Collection of documents and materials]* Vol. 2 (Odessa, 1947), pp. 135-136.
21   S.F. Lazarev, "V tylu vraga" ["In the enemy rear"] *Chernomors'ka kommuna*, 20 June 1944.
22   DAOO, F. R. 1820, s/3939, Op. 1, Spr. 1101, Ark. 40.
23   Lazarev, "V tylu vraga", *Chernomors'ka kommuna*, 20 June 1944.

However, the main efforts of the port's patriots were directed toward the frustration of restoration and repair work at the moorings, in the harbor's services and with water supply, and the organization of subversive activities with respect to loading and unloading operations. For example, when repairing the wooden docks that had been built in front of the stone walls of the coastline, which had been destroyed by air raids and artillery barrages during the period of Odessa's defense, systematic sabotage was organized. The workers here together with the foreman Iakunenko were deliberately idling, delaying the completion of all the tasks. As a result, not a single dock was repaired according to schedule. Only at the year's end did the Romanian administration notice that all the while, Iakunenko's team, which consisted of 60 men, hadn't repaired even 60 meters of the dockage. Iakunenko and his group of workers were fired and turned over to trial for sabotage.

N.A. Alekseev's plumbers were sabotaging the restoration of wells and the repair of the city's water lines. Well No. 2 was blocked up with rocks and cobblestone, after which all attempts by the Romanians to get it working again proved unsuccessful. As a result, water supply to the port worked fitfully with lengthy outages. Frequently because of the untimely delivery of water, ships and trains were being delayed.

Senior Mechanic Florchuk of the tugboat *Floros* spent two years "repairing" the ship's main engine. When it became no longer possible to drag out the work any longer, he arranged an act of sabotage – he failed to attach a necessary capacitor to the engine, as a result of which the engine housing was blown off. For this, Florchuk was arrested and subjected to tortures.

During the loading of barley aboard the steamship *Tsar Ferdinand*, V. Naidenov's labor brigade made a so-called "umbrella", meaning it left a hollow cavity in the middle of a hold which had been otherwise been filled to the brim, so it was missing 300 metric tons of grain. This under-loading not only inflicted economic damage, it also threated the ship's stability at sea. Other labor brigades were also doing such acts of sabotage. In particular hollows and blockages in the holding areas were often made when loading mill cake and other loads.

Acts of sabotage also took place in the ship repair factory, the towing fleet, the port's railroad and other sectors of the port. On 10 April 1942, railroad workers, members of an underground group, left a fuel tank intended for combat ships at the 7th Berth, then twisted off the cap of the drain and allowed the entire tank to empty into the sea.

Switchman Vokhach sent a train of tank cars carrying costly imported fuel oil onto a switched track at the 7th Switch. As a result, the train crashed, and the delivery of the fuel oil to combat units was delayed for 23 hours. Soon, he detained a train of 53 railcars that had been prepared by the Germans for urgent delivery for 13 hours. The train's delay was prompted by intentional damage to the steam engine at a road crossing at the 6th Switch. The most common means of disabling separate railroad cars and entire trains was by clogging the axle-bearings with sand. Inspection teams, having discovered the sand, had to detain the railcars for several days in order to clean out the sand.

Another form of sabotage work was the creation of confusion and chaos in the servicing and running of railroad trains on the port's territory. Railcars originally marked to be sent to a hopper were diverted to the Prakticheskaia [Practice] Harbor, while railcars that were urgently needed at the 23rd Berth wound up at the Devolanovskie warehouses. Trains carrying residual fuel oil intended for dispatch to the electrical power station for heating wound up instead at an oil and gas terminal, where they stood for several days. Over that interim, costly brand-name Turkish fuel oil which had been delivered by mistake to the Port of Odessa's railroad station had to be used up in the burners in view of the late delivery of the residual fuel oil.

Because of the lack of electrical energy in the daytime hours, the corn mill worked only at nights. However, the corn mill didn't work smoothly throughout the entire shift on a single night: a spring bar popped off or a bearing melted, or else a pulley came untracked, rods buckled or a belt snapped. The occupiers were told that the stoppages were due the abundance of dust, the low quality of lubricants or other contrived reasons. As a result, the corn mill over 10 hours of operation processed no more than 10 metric tons of corn in place of the normal 70 metric tons. A. Grigorenko, a man who worked in the port's machinery sector, oversaw the "technical supervision" at the corn mill.

Railcar mechanics slapped an "Unsound" sticker on railcars loaded with plundered equipment and ready for departure to Romania. The "unsound" railcars were unhitched for reloading, which usually took 15-20 days. Over this time, the valuable loads were ferreted away and replaced with useless scrap. Railcars carrying grain were abandoned once beyond the port and the contents found their way to the local population. At the 14th Switch near the Red Warehouses, by means of the uncoupling of a switch, a steam engine pulling five railcars jumped the rails. Several days later the automatic switches at the 2nd Switch near the Krymskii crossroads became stuck. This led to accidents, during which 10 railcars carrying ore were demolished and 150 meters of railroad tracks destroyed. For the incurred losses, the Germans presented the Romanian command of the Port of Odessa's railroad station with a bill for 4,000,000 leu.

Lacking the strength to counter the widespread sabotage, the administration was searching for solutions of the problem through the use of troops, of which the occupiers already didn't have enough at the front. On 26 November 1942, the Romanian Department of the Navy, noting the "lack of a Romanian spirit" and the poor work being done to repair ships and the port, proposed the militarization of the maritime dockyards to the governor of the Transnistria. The message stated, "… taking into consideration that the dockyards are working for the [Romanian] Royal Fleet and German Admiralty, the preservation of secrecy, order and intensive work for military objectives are necessary, for which it is needed to prevent sabotage, which leads to the loss of ships that are very valuable for conducting naval warfare …."[24]

The military commandant of the dockyards and Port of Odessa workshops on 1 October 1943 informed the director of the Port of Odessa about the "plodding, inborn qualities of the Russian workers" and about the fact that their poor work "is explained by the fact that they fear Bol'shevik agents, who are conducting active work among the workers after the end of a workshift." He proposed "to strengthen the supervision by Romanian soldiers, in order to prevent acts of sabotage and to obtain significantly greater efficacy."[25] On 8 October 1943, the Port of Odessa's director reported to the governor, "The boiler stoker, who is complaining that Engineer V. Grecu, the chief of our Maintenance Department, struck him, failed to follow orders and by this delayed the loading of grain aboard barges for several hours."

No matter how much the Romanian secret police raged, the labor productivity at the port remained extremely low. Indeed, if the loading of oil cake onto barges normally required approximately 5 days, then this job would take 15-18 days to complete and be done in an execrable fashion. Failure to show up for work and sabotage of the administration's orders were a common occurrence.[26]

On 2 December 1942, the occupational newspaper *Molva* announced that at the port, "the entire multi-kilometer railroad system had been converted to European gauge tracks."[27] The conversion of the tracks was done with the aim of accelerating the extraction of Ukraine's riches to Germany and Romania. Patriots decided to hinder this. During the conversion of the railroad line, a group of patriots improperly decreased the space between the rails along the line leading to scales. As a result, more than 10 railcars carrying ore crashed. After this accident, it required 5

---

24   Cited by Shternshtein, *Morskie vorota Ukrainy*, pp. 162-163.
25   Ibid., p. 163.
26   Ibid., p. 153.
27   *Molva*, 2 December 1942.

days to mend the tracks. In order to detain the departure of a train carrying ammunition, long-shoremen Nesterov and Pustovitov cut 52 brake hoses.

In order to forestall acts of sabotage, the occupational authorities issued an order to the effect that "anyone caught walking along the railroad line without special authorization" would be shot. In fact, several people were shot, but this didn't intimidate the patriots. On the next train, loaded with grain, 49 brake hoses were again cut and additional accidents followed one after the other.

Suddenly it was discovered that the gutter spouts in the grain warehouses had been jammed and all the grain had become soaked with rain water. The warehouse guard Salata had done this. Engineer Skumbrii who was working as an unskilled laborer contaminated a large quantity of grain with granary pests. Train after train, sent to Romania, arrived at their point of designation empty – the doors in all the railcars were half-open. Near the clock tower, another train of 17 rail-cars loaded with grain jumped the rails and crashed. Someone had undone the switches. Everyone, from a warehouse guard to an engineer, was an implacable foe of the occupiers.

Back in the beginning of 1942, the port's management, convinced of the longshoremen's hostile attitude toward all the measures taken by the occupational authorities and suspecting that each of them was a partisan or partisan sympathizer, adopted a number of measures to put an end to the acts of sabotage. In a report note dated 30 April 1942 to the governor of the Transnistria, the port's director wrote "… we also cannot be responsible for securing equipment and materials located on an expansive territory, if we don't have Romanian military security forces under our direction, in sufficient number and especially assigned for this. Regarding the local guards from the ranks of the civilian population, there cannot be even any talk." The longshoremen were discharged from handling military cargoes; they weren't trusted. Their role was taken over by prisoners of war working under the unrelenting eye observation of German settlers. With the aim of increasing surveillance, detachments of soldiers, who monitored the intensity and quality of work done, were attached to each brigade of freight handlers.

Many longshoremen as punishment for acts of sabotage or defiance were sent to special camps. The port's management sent to the labor board attached to the commandant's office "lists of individuals marked for exile to camps for various reasons, including but not limited to: discipli-nary violations, thefts, voluntary absence from work and others." The threat to be sent to camps didn't break the longshoremen's resistance. A circular dated 18 December 1943 sent to the port's management by the governor of the Transnistria, which authorized the use of weapons against the workers, also didn't frighten them.

Sabotage and subversive activity also took place at other of Odessa's operating enterprises. The occupiers tried to suppress this activity with bloody terror. A military field court ceaselessly issued death sentences, and in order to cow the people the sentences were often carried out in public. However, these measures, as a rule, led to results opposite the ones intended.

At the end of 1941, an engineer of the superphosphate acidulation plant O.E. Boitsun created a small underground group. Its tasks were to protect specialists from being shipped to Germany; conduct propaganda work and acts of sabotage at the factory; and by every way possible lower the quality of the produced product. For these purposes the group acquired three radio receivers, and received and circulated Sovinformburo communiques and other materials. In order to prevent the possibility of copper and valuable equipment being taken away and sent to Romania, members of the group re-worked copper into copper sulfate; purposelessly expended the acid available at the factory; and buried 25 metric tons of copper, 10 metric tons of cast iron pipes, 4 transformers, 1 drill machine and several electric motors.[28]

---

28   DAOO, F. 11, Op. 45, Od. khr. 150, Ark. 32-38.

The damage to telephone communications in the city became a tribulation for the occupational authorities. One of the directives from the headquarters of the Odessa police force to the 2nd Police District, signed by commissars S. Plugaru and N. Vulcu announced that unknown individuals had conducted acts of sabotage, stealing and cutting telephone cables; to wit:

1. On 29 January 1944, approximately 200 meters of cable from the telephone line along Lesnaia Street had been cut and hauled away;
2. On 2 February 1944 at the corner of Pushkin Street and Bazaar Street, two lines had been cut in four places and 100 meters of cable had been snipped away;
3. On 4 February 40 meters of cable had been snipped away and stolen in Romanovka Park;
4. On 5 February 1944 at Birzhevaia Square, between Lanzheronovskaia Street and Theater Streets, the I Romanian Corps' line had been cut away in two places, and 200 meters of the wire had been stolen together with accessories;
5. On 12-13 February 1944, five lengths of cable were cut away.[29]

By early 1943, already more than 40 underground organizations and groups were operating in Odessa. The partisans attacked fascist patrols, units and garrison headquarters and blew up ammunition stockpiles. Underground members arranged acts of sabotage at enterprises, the port, and against railroad transportation; seized weapons and ammunition; hid Soviet soldiers and officers who were fleeing fascist imprisonment; conducted reconnaissance work; and used radio receivers to receive Sovinformburo communiques and other materials transmitted from Moscow, which they subsequently circulated among the population.

People of various nationalities, professions and ages were unified in the underground groups for the struggle against the occupiers. Former judges of the People's Court M.A. Lytkin and M.P. Nikitin;, pensioner V.A. Cheptsov; tanker I.S. Solov'ev who had escaped fascist captivity; artist I.I. Poplavsky; university professor V.I. Litovchenko; a participant in the underground movement during the Russian Civil War B.V. Gumpert; young Komsomol member A. Osadchyi; married schoolteachers V.I. and A.A. Trofimovsky; shipyard electrician V. Zotov; Chief Petty Officer P. Kuprin who had escaped fascist captivity; Dr. M.G. Chernyshev; German political emigrant G.K. Noraiks; and T.F. Latenko, a female worker at the Dzerzhinsky factory all led underground groups ....[30]

In the autumn of 1941, at an order from the USSR NKVD, a 28-man reconnaissance commando detachment headed by V.A. Molodtsov (code name Pavel Baldaev) was created. Subsequently the detachment grew to 65 soldiers. The Odessa NKVD Headquarters assigned experienced officers to Molodtsov's group. Russian Civil War veterans; Chekists [members of the first Soviet secret police agency, the *ChK* (Extraordinary Committee)]; local catacomb mineworkers, who had good knowledge of the multi-kilometer, multi-layered underground labyrinth; workers from factories, workshops and the port; collective farmers and office employees; and Communists, Komsomol members and non-Party members all joined the detachment. The detachment was based in the catacombs at a depth of 25-30 meters below the suburban villages along the Kuial'nitskii estuary – Usatovo, Nerubaiskoe and Kuial'nik. The underground camp had the shape of the letter "T" – two lateral mine tunnels that connected with the Nerubaiskoe – Usatovo main tunnel that led to the mine mouth. The underground camp had accommodations for the headquarters and places of rest for the soldiers, as well as kitchens and storage rooms for weapons and food. The underground members of the detachment laid telephone lines between the detachment's headquarters and the

29   DAOO, F. R. 2509, s/1082, Op. 1, Spr. 314, Ark. 107.
30   Z. Pershina, *Imeni Ianvarskogo vosstaniia* [*The January Uprising Factory*] (Odessa, 1963), pp. 159-163.

sentry posts at the exits from the catacomb. The camp received delivery of 100 rifles, 7 machine guns, 40,000 cartridges, 300 grenades, approximately a ton of TNT, various entrenching tools, warm clothing, and a half-year supply of fuel, flour, kasha, sugar, potatoes and other food products.[31] Bakeries, baths, drinking water wells, a chamber for the headquarters, overnight facilities, a dining hall and a Red Corner [a propaganda reading room] all equipped the catacombs.

Despite all this, the living conditions in the underground camp were hard. Air circulation was poor; the chill, moist air penetrated the people, and things and food products became quickly covered with mold. The members of the underground had to use fuel sparingly, and thus they had to live in semi-darkness, or at times completely abandon the use of kerosene lamps and primitive torches.

V.A. Molodtsov's detachment was split into underground and above ground groups. Approximately two-thirds of the soldiers stayed in the catacombs, and from there conducted combat forays on the surface. The remaining soldiers operated in the city and its surroundings, gathering reconnaissance information and preparing operations by the detachment's main forces. The detachment's responsibilities included the collection of reconnaissance intelligence and their transmission by radio to Moscow; conducting acts of subversion and sabotage; unmasking the fascist regime; and spreading Sovinformburo communiques among the population of Odessa.

The city or "surface" detachment had their own stockpiles of weapons and also had reserves of ammunition, explosives and food. It included three reconnaissance-commando groups of 6-10 men each. One of them was created at the Odessa brewing factory and was headed by P. Prodyshko, while the second was organized among fishermen in the vicinity of Bol'shaia Fontanka and headed by G. Shilin. The third, headed by the 16-year-old Komsomol member Ia. Gordienko, consisted of young city residents. On 12 September Badaev reported to the center in Moscow about Ia. Gordienko, his brother Aleksei and classmates S. Chikov and Sh. Khoroshenko: "I've picked splendid young men for reconnoitering and communications." Time showed that he wasn't mistaken about any one of them.

In addition, in the city and several important areas of the Trans-Dniester area, Badaev's partisans had a small scouting network consisting of around 15 individuals, with which Badaev maintained communications via Ia. Gordienko, T. Mezhigurskaia, T. Shestakova and G. Martsyshek. These were reliable fellow conspirators. Already in 1941, some of them managed to penetrate the occupier's military, their facilities and the police.

Fima, a friend of Iasha Gordienko, gained the trust of the police commissar and received permits and verification letters filled out in the name of "secret police informer Nikolai Bakov". These documents repeatedly bailed Badaev's liaison agents out of trouble; more than once, the "secret informer" supplied the members of the underground and partisans with needed verification letters, visas for residence and passes, and caused the police to follow false leads. When the threat of a defection arose, at Badaev's order Fima holed up in the catacombs, where he in fact later died, remaining for the partisans the unknown "Fima the Electrician". In investigative documents of the Romanian counterintelligence, there is a mention of a Badaev scout Elena, who according to one of the documents, "penetrated the sphere of Romanian officers and gathered important intelligence."

Badaev's partisans initiated combat operations against the occupiers already on 16 October 1941. In the evening, having emerged from the catacombs and taken up position in a ravine at the entrance to a mine, the detachment opened fire at a column of enemy troops that was marching through the village of Nerubaiskoe on their way to Odessa. In a brief combat action, the partisans

---

31   G. Martsyshek, *My na svoei zemle* [*We on our own soil*] (Odessa, 1960), pp. 46-47; G.A. Karev, *Odessa – gorod-geroi* [*Odessa – Hero City*] (Moscow: Voenizdat, 1978), p. 136.

killed up to 45 soldiers and officers and returned to their underground lair without losses. On the next day an enemy train derailed and crashed into a ravine. Up until the end of 1941, Badaev's partisans had several armed clashes with punitive expeditioners, mined roads, destroyed lines of communication, and derailed four railroad trains carrying troops and ammunition.[32]

Many sites in the city, upon the Coastal Army's evacuation, were mined; in particular, more than 100 delayed-action bombs were emplaced. As already mention, they prepared the building on Marazlievskaia Street that housed the NKVD headquarters for remote-controlled demolition. A separate radio-technical platoon of the 82nd Engineer Battalion did the wiring for the explosives and set them in place. A technician, designated to trigger the explosives remotely, was standing by. The building was completely secret, and only the perpetrators were aware of its purpose. Here's how the assistant commander of the Odessa Defense District for engineering General A.F. Khrenov later told about the mission:

> In the cellar they dug trenches. They carried out the dirt at night, in the same bags they had used to bring in the TNT. The explosives were laid into the trenches, packed into niches chosen at two corners of the building above the pediment, and into ventilation ducts that ran in the walls. Altogether, they used almost 3 metric tons of TNT. They carefully filled the primer with stearin, in order to protect the detonation capsule against moisture. The end of the detonator was attached to terminal of a special wireless set; the duplicative set, dialed into the same radio frequency, remained with us. In order to ensure the radio-controlled bombs would work, two 100-kilogram bombs were connected to the wireless set (they managed to leave them under columns in the vestibule). The wireless set itself was booby-trapped, in case enemy sappers came up with the idea of prying up floor planks in the cellar.[33]

In order to fool the enemy sappers, several ordinary blasting charges were also deployed in the cellar.

The code for the radio signal was given to V.A. Molodtsov. Separately, an agreement was reached with him about transmitting the code in the event that any large meeting with the participation of high-ranking officers took place in the building on Marazlievskaia Street.

On the morning of 22 October 1941, A.F. Khrenov received a radio message from V.A. Molodtsov (Badaev): "A concert on Marazlievskaia will begin at 1730 on the 22nd." At 1800 on 22 October, at a radio signal from the Crimea, the explosives were detonated. The bomb worked flawlessly, inflicting heavy damage to the aggressors. Eyewitnesses said that the effect of the explosion was like that of a small earthquake. As a result, approximately 100 enemy soldiers and officers were killed, including General I.F. Glogojanu, the commander of the Romanian 10th Infantry Division. This was one of the first radio-controlled remote explosions conducted by Soviet engineers in the years of the Great Patriotic War.[34]

In the middle of November 1941, V.A. Molodtsov's scouts learned that a train carrying soldiers and officers, as well as fascist bureaucrats of the occupational administration, was supposed to arrive in Odessa on their way to the Sevastopol area. On a dark, rainy night K.N Zalensky, I.I. Ivanov and P.A. Pustomel'nikov stealthily crept up to the railroad bed at a section of the track between Dachnaia and Zastava Stations. The section of railroad track was being intensely guarded by mounted patrols. Having waited for a suitable moment, I.I. Ivanov laid a mine under the rails.

---

32   Karev, *Odessa – gorod-geroi*, pp. 136-137.
33   A.F. Khrenov, *Mosty k Pobede* [*Bridges to Victory*] (Moscow: Voenizdat, 1982), p. 144.
34   *73 geroicheskikh dnei: Khronika oborony Odessy v 1941 godu* [*73 heroic days: Chronicle of the defense of Odessa in 1941*] 3rd Ed. (Odessa: Maiak, 1988), pp. 272-273.

Soon the sound of the clattering wheels of an approaching train became audible. Holding their breaths, the members of the underground waited for the mine's explosion. It blew up beneath the fourth railcar. The fifth car turned out to be loaded with shells, and their detonations increased the catastrophe. Enveloped by flames, one railcar after another toppled from the embankment. Among their wreckage were a lot of dead fascist soldiers and officers. The Soviet patriots returned to the catacombs without any losses.[35]

Badaev's partisans collected military and political information about the enemy, scouted out important military sites and guided Soviet bombers toward them. Badaev's radio set transmitted information to the center about the movement of heavy artillery, the position of enemy coastal batteries in the Odessa – Ochakov sector and the location of major gasoline stockpiles in the city of Pervomaisk. Members of the underground movement acquired the fascist plan for the defense of Odessa in the event of a simultaneously landing of Soviet troops from the air and by sea, and then transmitted it to Moscow. The partisans distributed anti-fascist leaflets and Sovinformburo communiques among the people, and were revealing and killing active accomplices and agents of the hostile counterintelligence service.

Partisans Ia.F. Vasin, I.N. Petrenko, I.A. Grinchenko and others laid mines and spikes on the roads against enemy motorized transports, and destroyed a lot of enemy trucks and the military cargo they were carrying. In addition, I.N. Petrenko was an excellent sniper. In the days of Odessa's defense he had killed several dozen Nazis, and while acting as part of Badaev's band, he increased this score by another 30 killed fascists. [36]

The former Nazi general K. von Tippelskirch later wrote: "When leaving Odessa in the autumn of 1941, the Russians created in the city a partisan cell that was filled with the greatest fanaticism. The partisans were based in the catacombs, the intricate network of which extended for a total length of approximately 100 kilometers, having no equal anywhere in Europe ... The partisans launched nighttime attacks against isolated soldiers and poorly guarded military objectives."[37]

The effectiveness of the resistance detachments was very high. In the specific conditions of Odessa it was measured not only by the number of enemy dead and acts of subversion conducted, but also by the number of the adversary's troops that the underground resistance diverted from the frontlines. In the area of suburban villages alone, where in 1941 there were just 76-80 underground partisans, the occupiers assembled around 16,000 of their troops, including select SS units and of the gendarme, with the aim of sealing the catacomb's entrances and exits.[38] In May 1942, the operation to destroy the partisans in the catacombs of Odessa was being conducted by the forces of an entire garrison division.[39]

After the explosion on Marazlievskaia Street, the occupiers walled up, mined and put under guard all the entrances to the catacombs known to them; poisoned water in the wells; and forcibly drove away the inhabitants of the nearby villages with machine-gun fire. Specialized teams, brought in from Germany, released poison gases into the catacombs.

The evidence found in the archival documents that have preserved the details of those events is interesting:

---

35   TsDAGO Ukraini, F. 1, Op. 9, Spr. 85, Ark. 13.

36   Odesskii istoriko-kraevedcheskii muzei. Otdel Velikoi Otechestvennoi voiny: ekspozitsiia "23 Geroi popol'ia" [Odessa Regional History Museum. Department of the Great Patriotic War: the "23 Heroes of the Underground" exhibition]

37   K. Tippelskirch, *Istoriia vtoroi mirovoi voiny* [*History of the Second World War*]. Translated from German (Moscow, 1956), p. 359.

38   Martsyshek, *My na svoei zemle*, p. 7.

39   Stanko [chief ed.], *Istoriia Odesy*, p. 410.

In the area of the villages of Usatovo and Nerubaisk, the Romanian authorities have assembled a large number of troops. It was as if they were preparing for a major operation. In the daytime artillery and punitive detachments arrived. All of these troops were to operate against the partisans. The officers were giving orders and inspecting weapons, but not a one of them knew or could tell the soldiers where the partisans were or where to direct all this firepower. This uncertainty and fear in front of an invisible adversary were exasperating the Romanians. They rolled up guns and fired shells at pointblank range at the main entrance to the catacombs.

After the barrage, one detachment with torches decided to enter the catacombs. They entered the main entrance. An officer with a flashlight kept checking maps. Further on, the tunnel branched. An officer directed to head to the left. Several minutes later, the hollow explosion of a mine rang out. The soldiers moving in front crumpled, dropping their burning torches. From out of the darkness, a machine gun began to chatter. The unglued Romanians in animal-like fear scurried back to the main entrance. Few of them on this day managed to emerge from the catacombs.

Enraged by the failure, the Romanians perpetrated a brutal reprisal against the residents of Usatovo. They hung old men and women from telegraph poles. They piled the bodies of 30 executed peasants at the main entrance to the catacombs. They poisoned all the nearby wells.

The partisans drilled new wells, created new tunnels and emerged on the surface in new locations unknown to the foe. Once again at nights, vehicles on the roads to the city crashed, wires were cut, and occupational troops slain by unseen marksmen were falling. A week later, yet another military train was derailed in the vicinity of Dal'nik Station.[40]

The partisans managed to divert the poison gases into empty estuarial tunnel shafts; however, they were deprived of regular contact with the city's underground members and the population. Only Badaev himself and separate liaison agents managed to get around the blockade of the catacombs. Badaev repeatedly emerged from underground in order to organize the scouting and subversive activities of the city detachment. On 8 February 1942 he again made his way into the city, but on the night of 9-10 February a traitor informed the Romanians of his presence and he was arrested in a safe house apartment together with Tamara Mezhigorskaia, Iasha and Aleksei Gordienko, and Sasha Chikov. Two days later in the same apartment, the liaison detachment Tamara Shestakova and Shurik Khoroshen'ko fell into an ambush organized by the gendarme.

In the course of February and March 1942, the enemy counterintelligence managed to arrest almost all of the members of the city's reconnaissance-commando detachment. However, they continued to struggle against the foe even in imprisonment. During the interrogations, the torturers subjected the Badaev partisans to the most gruesome torture techniques, but they were unable to break them. Shackled in irons and beaten daily to the loss of consciousness, Badaev continued to refuse to answer the investigator's questions and at night transmitted an order via the prison "telegraph" to his comrades in all the cells: "Endure!" T. Mezhigurskaia wrote words full of the contempt of death and about her readiness to carry out her duties to the end to friends throughout the underground: "Dear comrades! Soon they will shoot us. Don't despair, we're ready for it all and go to our deaths with our heads held high. Tell my son everything that you know about me." Not wishing to answer the inquisitors' questions, N. Shevchenko took poison. The partisan scout and guide miner I.A. Kuzhel' also committed suicide, having slit his veins with a piece of window glass.

---

40   *Odessa v Velikoi Otechestvennoi voine Sovetskogo Soiuza*, Vol. 2, p. 210.

Without having received any confessions from the arrested, the Romanian military field court sentenced V.A. Molodtsov (Badaev) and his 13 trustworthy comrades, including T.U. Mezhigurskaia, T.G. Shestakova, Ia.Ia. Gordienko, and N.I. Milan to death. Having received the sentence of the court and its offer to enter a plea for mercy, V.A. Molodtsov hurled at the faces of the executioners: "We're Russians, and on our own soil we don't beg for mercy from our foes!" The judges were chilled by these words. They were giving a man some hope for life, and he was rejecting it. For him, better death and oblivion than humiliation and betrayal! It was even more chilling for these judges to face the unbending inner strength of these people, when all the sentenced rallied to the words of their commander. Even the pregnant T.G. Shestakova rejected the chance to beg for mercy.

At the end of July 1942, the sentence was carried out. T.G. Shestakova was held in a prison isolation cell until she gave birth, and then they shot her.

The young patriot Iasha Gordienko also held out courageously. Today much has been written about him in essays and tales; the heroic fate of the young man lies at the basis of a play and cinematic film. Schools, Pioneer Palaces, streets and naval ships bear his name, and museum exhibits are dedicated to him. Back then, he was an ordinary teenage boy, a student of Odessa's Special Naval School. At 16 years of age, he enjoyed Badaev's special and deserved trust. Of all the city detachment, he alone knew all of the secret entrances to the catacombs, and only he was allowed at any time at his own initiative to enter the underground camp. In addition to the secret timetable of the train's movement that was blown up on the night of 17-18 November, which he gleaned from the Transnistria administration, he acquired the information about the enormous fascist gasoline stockpile at Pervomaisk. Badaev passed this information to Moscow, and on the third day after the receipt of this crucial information, the stockpile was destroyed by Soviet bombers. A short time later Iasha informed Badaev about the date of a scheduled march of an enemy division from Odessa to Nikolaev. Using this intelligence, a group of Soviet aircraft attacked the enemy's column on the road to Nikolaev and destroyed 129 vehicles and up to two battalions of infantry.

As the commander's runner Gordienko in the daylight hours went around all the underground places of secret meetings in the city, and at night he delivered the gathered information to Badaev in the catacombs. For this it was necessary to pass through the city during curfew hours, when on the darkened streets, anyone without a special pass from the police was liable to be arrested or shot on the spot. Then he had to head out into a field, where mounted fascist patrols didn't even ask for any passes, but opened fire at any suspicious shadow that caught their eye. Next he had to make his way to a secret trap-door, where he would enter the catacombs and make his way along 3-4 kilometers of intricate tunnels and passageways in absolute darkness to the detachment's headquarters. Having given the commander a report and having received the next assignment for the underground groups in the city, that same night Iasha would return to the city. For such work, courage, agility, reckless audacity and dedication to his entrusted task were necessary.

The Romanians were guessing that in addition to Badaev and his runners, no one else knew about the secret entrances to the catacombs or the safe house apartments in the city. Soon they realized that despite any and all tortures, Badaev, Mezhigurskaia and Shestakova wouldn't divulge this secret to them. The enemies were hoping that the 16-year-old runner wouldn't endure the tortures and would spill everything he knew. However, the Nazis terribly miscalculated. They beat Iasha with barbed wire, hung him from his feet from the ceiling, tore all the fingernails from his fingers, and tortured him with red-hot iron rods and electrical currents. The tortures continued for almost five months. However, Iasha didn't betray a single address or a single secret entrance into the catacombs. When on 30 July 1942 the executioners led him half-blinded by tortures and half-deafened by the beatings to the prison yard to shoot him, he began to sing an old revolutionary song "Stout-heartedly, comrades, in step!" Of the 73 members of the two reconnaissance-commando detachments that operated under Molodtsov's leadership, 41 were captured and executed, two committed suicide after unendurable tortures, two fell in combat, and the rest were subjected to terrible torments in fascist torture chambers.[41]

On 3 July 1942, an announcement was published in the *Odesskaia gazeta*:

> Upon the retreat of Soviet forces from Odessa, a group of Communist partisans were left behind by units of the NKVD with the special mission to conduct terrorist, subversive activities and espionage work. Stockpiles of weapons and explosives were left in their possession. Upon the entry of allied forces, this group of Communist partisans hid in Odessa's catacombs, but they were discovered and turned over to a military field court. The court, having examined the deeds of the group's members, who stood accused of conducting subversive terrorist work, espionage and the concealment of a stockpile of weapons and ammunition, rendered its verdict:
>
> Badaev Pavel Vladimirovich, Gofman Artur, Volkov Semen, Muzychenko Nikolai, Muzychenko Ivan, Sinin Grigorii, Milan Petr, Shevchenko Pavel, Mezhigurskaia Tamara, Shestakova Tamara, Sletov Mikhail and Buniakov Mikhail – will be shot.
>
> Khoroshen'ko Aleksei – a life sentence
>
> Kozubenko, Grigorii – 20 years of hard labor
>
> Iudin Nikitin and Gofman Vitol'd – 10 years of hard labor.[42]

After V.A. Molodtsov's death and that of the entire underground group of his detachment, the fascists strengthened the blockade of the catacombs. The partisans were in a desperately difficult situation, but continued to resist. Twenty-six soldiers were assigned to conduct combat operations on the surface. Between 9 and 22 May 1942, they conducted five daring sallies. In one of them the partisans attacked a punitive detachment in the resort area of the town of Kulianika. In open battle the participants in the punitive expedition were utterly routed. From the place of combat, they hauled away three truckloads of corpses. The "SS-I" service in Bucharest announced, "Partisans have again gone over to active operations."[43]

In order to isolate the underground resistance members from the population that was supporting them, all of the homes near the catacombs were leveled, and a complicated system of passes was set up. Anyone who showed up in the vicinity of the caverns was killed on the spot. The fascists exerted strenuous efforts to seek out and seal all of the entrances and even tiniest crevices that led into the catacombs with concrete. They succeeded in finding two traitors, who appear in the documents of the occupiers under the code names "King" and "Tomcat". The latter were quite familiar with the catacombs and pointed out places to the occupiers where entries that hadn't yet been sealed up with concrete remained. With their assistance, the occupiers mined, obstructed and plugged with concrete approximately 400 entrances and exits of the catacombs.[44] Wells, the shafts of which passed through the catacombs, were poisoned with arsenic or filled with oil. As a result of all these measures, the partisans wound up sealed off under the ground, with no current of fresh air and without an adequate water supply. Moreover, by the end of June 1942, they had almost completely exhausted their food supplies. Each individual was given one tablespoon of millet and two teaspoons of coffee a day.[45]

Considering the situation as it now stood, the decision was taken to abandon the catacombs and restage to the Savranskie Woods in the northern area of Odessa Oblast in order to continue

41   Karev, *Odessa – Gorod-geroi*, pp. 140-141.
42   *Odesskaia gazeta*, 3 July 1942.
43   Stanko [chief ed.], *Istoriia Odesi*, p. 410.
44   TsDAGO Ukraini, F. 1, Op. 9, Spr. 85, Ark. 13.
45   TsDAGO Ukraini, F. 1, Op. 9, Spr. 85, Ark. 9.

the struggle, while some would go to the safe house apartments and conduct underground work in the city. However, in order to accomplish this, it was necessary to find a new exit from the catacombs that was unknown to the occupiers. For more than two days, the partisans went round and round the labyrinth, blindly going from one shaft to another, until they finally found a small crevice, approximately 20 kilometers distant from their underground base. Having cleared it out, the exhausted people made their way to the surface and emerged onto a steppe, approximately 15 kilometers from Usatovo.

However, a short time later the majority of them was captured and after cruel tortures, executed. Other underground members still managed to make their way into Odessa unspotted and settle into safe house apartments. Now the core of the activity of the members of the underground became large-scale propaganda and agitation work. For this they used leaflets, newspapers and other printed materials, including those that Soviet aircraft delivered on occupied territory. The bulletin *Vesti s Sovetskoi Rodiny* [*"News from the Soviet Motherland"*], published by the Red Army's Main Political Directorate, and the newspaper *Za Sovetskuyu Ukrainu* [*For Soviet Ukraine*], put out by the Southwestern Front's Political Administration, received the broadest distribution. It was necessary to supply the people with correct information, and to set it against fascist propaganda. The underground movement got the printing and circulation of leaflets which relayed information from the Sovinformburo, up and running among the population. In addition to the leaflets, the information sheet *Za Sovetskuyu Rodinu* was distributed. It contained information about the situation on the Soviet-German front, about partisan actions in the enemy's rear, and about labor successes on the domestic home front. Odessa underground presses also published orders from the Supreme High Command and telegrams from abroad. An information leaflet came out twice a week in 60-100 copies. The underground groups with their own means reprinted it, increasing the print run, and by various means distributed among the people of Odessa. The underground district committee of the water supply system, which resumed its activity, organized the publication of a newspaper in the Russian language, *Golos naroda* [*Voice of the people*] (between April and October 1942, 13 issues of this newspaper came out).

Striving to break the resistance of Odessa's citizens, the occupational authorities, alongside systematic killings, conducted equally systematically malevolent fascist propaganda. In their yellowed pages, over the radio and in public addresses they sought to persuade the people that the Red Army had been defeated, trying to convince them that resistance was useless.

However, the people didn't believe the foe, and disregarding the risk, recognized the truth about the situation at the front. Around that time a Sovinformburo communique became known to the majority of the population. Patriots, not fearing persecution and severe punishments, were secretly listening to the radio and passing news from the front to each other. The occupiers, understanding that the sharpest weapon against their entire propaganda campaign was hearing the truth over the radio, conducted a rigorous struggle against underground radios.

An entire series of threatening orders demanded the immediate surrender of all radio receivers and parts for them, under the threat of the harshest punishments. The population was ordered under the threat of arrest and a drumhead trial to turn in anyone who had a radio receiver, and also to report those who spread "rumors". In the occupation newspapers it was explained that informers would be taken under the special custody of the police. In the *Odesskaia gazeta* on 24 December 1941, an order from the commander of the occupational army was published: "... it is forbidden to discuss, but also to comment upon or express conjecture about combat operations, about the situation and disposition of forces or any other questions connected with the Romanian Army and its ally." Fearing talk among the people, the Romanian command in the following issue of the *Odesskaia gazeta* published an order, which made known that "... the movement or stops on the streets of private citizens numbering more than 3 people is forbidden."[46] In the wake of the publication of these orders, house-to-house searches began. In the event of the discovery of a radio receiver or any component of one, their owner was subjected to arrest, tortures and a court martial trial, which usually carried out a harsh penal sentence.

However, leaflets were continuing to appear in the port in hundreds of copies. Each morning the adversary was stopping in fury in front of new leaflets, pasted up on freight cars, fences and the exterior walls of the port's buildings. One day they were appealing to longshoremen, the next day – to railroad workers, and a day later – to sailors. These leaflets enjoyed great success, were read secretly, handed over to the next person, and were frequently copied. These were genuine heralds of truth and hope. They encouraged the readers and called them to the struggle.

The further the front receded to the east, the more the significance grew of radio transmissions from the rest of the country in the underground's activity. For the population of Ukraine's occupied territories, including the Transnistria, transmissions went on around the clock in the Ukrainian language from the T.G. Shevchenko radio station in Saratov and *Sovetskaia Ukraina* from Moscow.[47]

In December 1941, a patriotic group arose on the territory of the industrial Il'ichevskii District of Odessa; its organizer was installation engineer S.I. Drozdov. In the apartment of A.M. Nikolaenko, the underground members set up a radio set that received Sovinformburo communiques and other important announcements, which were then printed on two typewriters and distributed among the workers. In the summer of 1942, S.I. Drozdov's group linked up with the underground group of A.I. Shaliagin and P.N. Prokopenko. The total number of members of the unified underground organization amounted to 50 people.[48] It worked actively to make contact with patriots who were striving for active struggle and to conduct agitation work among the population. Operating on a railroad, they knocked out steam engines, caused crashes, and detained the movement of trains in the Odessa – Kolosovka sector for 24 hours and longer. At a jute factory and tanning factory, they broke machinery and equipment that had been designated for shipment to Romania. They also set fire to stockpiles of fuel and ammunition.

Underground cells in the Red Guards factory, the Dzerzhinsky factory, at a meat processing plant and in the suburban village of Krivaia Balka (under the leadership of K.A. Timofeev) joined into a single organization consisting of 30 individuals. The organization was based in the catacombs in the vicinity of Krivaia Balka. While undermining attepts by the occupiers to repair enterprises and getting them operating again, the members of this underground organization also conducted a number of bold acts of subversion. Members A.G. Atanasov, A.A. Prudnikov, V.A. Poliansky at the Red Guards factory cannibalized an 80-metric-ton crane. It took the Romanians several months to get it working again. At this same factory, 10 electric motors and 6 lathe and radial drill presses were rendered worthless.[49]

For the acquisition of weapons and demonstrations against the occupational regime, the organization created a special group of 10 individuals. This group operated in the area of Krivaia Balka. It launched attacks against small detachments and individual enemy soldiers and officers, and killed

46   Shternshtein, *Morskie vorota Ukrainy*, pp. 157-158.
47   *Ukrainska RSR u Velikii Vitchiznianii viini Radianskogo Soiuzu 1941-1945: u 3 t.* [*Ukraine Socialist Republic in the Great Patriotic War of the Soviet Union 1941-1945: in 3 volumes*] Vol. 1 (Kiev: Politvidav Ukrainy, 1967), pp. 309-310; *Odesskaia oblast' v Velikoi Otechestvennoi voine 1941-1945: Dokumenty i materialy* [*Odessa Oblast in the Great Patriotic War 1941-1945: Documents and materials*] (Odessa: Maiak, 1970), p. 290.
48   DAOO, F.P. 11, Op. 45, Spr. 79, Ark. 15.
49   TsDAGO Ukraini, F.P. 7, Op. 10, Spr. 90, Ark. 85.

police members and other traitors of the Motherland. Already in the first months of struggle, the group captured 8 rifles, 1500 cartridges, 20 grenades and killed 37 fascists and their henchmen.[50]

Together with their fathers and older brothers, the youth of Odessa also actively struggled against the aggressors. Adolescent boys and girls served the cause as part of all underground organizations, and in separate cases created their own independent Komsomol youth patriotic groups. In the autumn of 1941, adolescent boys and girls who knew each other from joint study in the 59th Odessa School began to organize around Leonid and Liudmila Bachinsky. Soon another 7 individuals joined the organization, including a Soviet officer named V. Skul'sky who had escaped imprisonment. The number of members of this organization grew to 24. Crisp military discipline was introduced. All of the underground members were split into four cells of 5-7 each. The youthful underground members initiated fervent activity. They got their hands on a radio receiver. Receiving Sovinformburo communiques over the radio, they wrote them out by hand and distributed them among the people.

G. Antonius, V. Novitsky and U. Borovsky were cutting telephone lines in various districts of the city and knocked out the power grid. At the behest of the organization, they fixed some longshoremen up with work at a military aviation warehouse. During the transportation of loads, they would imperceptibly cut parachute straps with little pieces of razor blades; when handling aviation radio receivers for shipment they would bump the boxes into hard objects with the aim of breaking fragile components of the receivers, while the boxes remained undamaged. The members of the underground found a way to cut up the rubber tires for the wheels of aircraft and vehicles. From the front, messages often arrived about the death of pilots due to damage to the parachute straps, and about the crashes of vehicles and airplanes.

Another group of adolescent boys – A. Belinsky, P. Gumennyi and A. Piven' – while working at Odessa's Central Station, sprinkled sand into the axle bearings of railroad cars, cut pneumatic lines, and did damage to the station facilities.[51] Wishing to help naval commandoes, L. Bachinsky, P. Skul'sky, E. Maksiukov, P. Kurenkov and others scouted the Black Sea coastline from the Arcade to the port. They noted down the collected intelligence about the location of military objectives on a special map, which would be turned over to the sailors. In order to support further any future naval landing, the youth went about the procurement of weapons, including by means of pilfering them from military stockpiles.

In the spring and summer of 1942, in connection with the sharp deterioration of the situation on the southern front with the start of the enemy's offensive toward Stalingrad and the Northern Caucuses, the lines of communication in the south Ukraine acquired special significance. Assisting the front, the members of the underground resistance movement increased their subversive activities on the railroads of the Transnistria. Acts of sabotage were carried out at the Zatish'e, Berezovka, Odessa Trade and Port of Odessa railroad stations. At the same time, many acts of sabotage took place in enterprises of naval shipping and heavy industry in Odessa itself: at Ship Repair Factories No. 1 and No. 2 (by underground members of B.K. Ovcharenko's and G.S. Trusov's group), and later by N.A. Geft's group in Odessa's port.

From the middle of 1942, a Ukrainian national-liberation underground movement also began to form in Odessa. One of the leaders of the OUN (Organization of Ukrainian Nationalists) in Odessa was V. Lisovsky, and one of its centers was the "Foundation" bookstore in the so-called "round house" on Grecheskaia [Greek] Square. The bookstore belonged to S. Karavansky – a member of the OUN's regional organization that was operating in Odessa. He conducted active

50   TsDAGO Ukraini, F.P. 7, Op. 10, Spr. 90, Ark. 88.
51   R. Chaichuk, "Net bezymennykh geroev" ["There are no nameless heroes"] *Komsomol'skoe plamia*, 28 February 1962.

agitation work, both against fascism and against Communist propaganda. S. Karavansky's book-store became legal cover for the organization, a suitable place for distributing underground liter-ature. Members of the OUN were taking advantage of contradictions between the Romanian and German occupational authorities and conducted work among Romanian soldiers. A former member of the Ukrainian underground movement Odessan A. Legky recalled, "... the Romanians hated the Germans and *vice versa* ... In such a situation the regional organization of Ukrainian nationalists, particularly in the final year of occupation, by every means cultivated an anti-Hitler mood among the Romanians."[52] The "SS-I" service identified the presence of "separatists" among the professors of the university, within the walls of the Ukraine Secondary School No. 1 (today – the premises of the Richelieu Lysée). The deacon of the Historical Philology faculty of Odessa University V.F. Lazursky stood out among them. The OUN members were also active in publish-ing.[53] At the same time in Odessa as the organ of the OUN's oblast connection *Chornomors'ka visnik* [*Black Sea Bulletin*] was coming out, three issues of *Chornomors'ka zbirnika* [*Black Sea Digest*] came out, which was published by the Ukrainian Black Sea Institute, founded by Iu. Lipoi in Warsaw.[54]

Meanwhile the punitive and repressive organs of the occupiers weren't sleeping. All the while they were increasing their activity to uncover and destroy underground cells. A broad network of agents, working for the *Siguranţa*, was created. The patriots were often operating at their own risk; many of them were ignoring the rules of a conspiracy, were unfamiar with the methods and approaches of the work of enemy counter-intelligence, and didn't always know how to recognize and expose enemy agents sent to infiltrate the underground movement. All this unavoidably led to new failures and the death of many dedicated people. The losses were severe.

The occupiers were mobilizing the full apparatus of the Gestapo, the Romanian gendarmes, military counter-intelligence, and the entire network of agents in order to destroy the underground resistance movement. In the spring and beginning of summer 1943, the fascist counter-intelligence once again got on the track of the underground Party Oblast Committee and Vodotransportnyi District Committee. Many leaders of underground groups and organizers of the underground movement wound up in the occupiers' torture chambers, including the First Secretary of the Party Oblast Committee S.S. Sukharev and First Secretary of the Party Vodotransportnyi District Committee M.G. Reshetnikov. The chief of the Romanian secret police reported to Bucharest at this time about the arrest of 124 leaders and members of underground organizations and 171 individuals that were acting independently.[55]

The fall-out of the "Oblast Committee" case, as the occupiers called it, continued for more than six months. The arrested underground members were tormented by the most refined and sadistic torture methods, right up to the use of electric currents, the so-called "airplane" technique, and the crushing of hands, but no one gave up comrades who remained at large. On the matter of the "Oblast Committee" case, in November 1943 the occupiers' military field court sentenced 87 underground members to various periods of hard labor. S.S. Sukharev was killed, ostensibly during an escape attempt.[56] The head of the "SS-I" service E. Cristescu in a report note about the organization and activity of the Odessa underground Oblast Committee observed, "... even

52   A. Bachinsky, "Borot'ba OUN-UPA proti fashist'kikh zagarbnikov na Pivdni Ukrain" ["Struggle of the OUN – UPA against the fascist invaders in southern Ukraine"] *Chornomors'ki novini* [*Black Sea News*] 6 January 1994.

53   P. Mirchun, *Ukrains'ka povstan'ska armia (1942-1952): Dokumenti i materiali* [*Ukrainian Insurgent Army (1942-1952): Documents and materials*] (L'vov, 1991), p. 202.

54   Stanko [chief ed.], *Istoriia Odesi*, p. 411.

55   TsDAGO Ukraini, Inv. 492, Ark. 154.

56   TsDAGO Ukraini, F. 1, Op. 9, Spr. 85, Ark. 7.

though the Oblast Committee (underground) wasn't completely organized, it presented a large threat to the security of the occupation armies and Romanian administration."[57]

At the end of the winter of 1942-1943, the underground Komsomol organization *Partizanskaia iskra* [*Partisan spark*] was destroyed. Possessing a list of names of members of this organization, taking advantage of the loss of contact within the underground organization, the panic that had arisen among the population, and the services of recruited agents, the gendarme began to conduct mass arrests of members of the organization, their family members, and accomplices. Over three days more than 90 people were arrested. Almost the entire membership of the organization was captured. The tortures were horrifying. During the torture of I.A. Pavlenko, his leg bones above the shin were broken; during an interrogation, the fingers on N. Burevich's left hand were held in a door jam and then crushed by the slamming door, and he was beaten to the point of unconsciousness; Kuriatinsky was mashed by a bed of boards; Mogurenko was frightfully beaten until his face was black; and others were burned by lit cigarettes applied to the back or face. After cruel tortures, patriots that were bound in barbed wire were shepherded through the freezing temperatures in their underwear to the village of Krymka, where they were shot on the outskirts. Seven of the members were sent instead to the prison in Tiraspol, where later on 6 April 1943 they were also shot by policemen headed by the chief of police S. Dotsenko at the Petrovka railroad station.[58]

Despite the mass executions, arrests and tortures, the struggle continued – new groups arose to take the place of the destroyed organizations. The Odessa Prigorodnyi District Committee, led by S.F. Lazarev, returned to its underground base in the catacombs beneath Usatovo. He created two partisan detachments: the Usatavo and Kuial'nitskii partisans. By the end of 1943, these partisan detachments numbered 119 men and women. Taking advantage of the fact that the fascists had somewhat weakened their blockade of the catacombs, on 14 April 1943 the underground members that remained at large again returned to their underground base. In the catacombs, the members had to do a lot of physical work. They dug wells, searched for new paths and reinforced the old ones, did combat training, including marksmanship drills.

By January 1944 the Kuial'nitskii detachment had grown to 100 members, and it actively joined the struggle against the occupiers. On one sally, the detachment scattered a group of occupiers that were driving collective farm cattle to Germany. On another one, the partisans attacked an enemy detachment, killing 65 fascists and wounding approximately 60. They took refuge in the catacombs from their pursuers. Striving to force the partisans to surrender, the enemy at first blew up entrances to the catacombs and fired at them from pointblank range from heavy weapons, and then brought up dozens of metric tons of cement and sealed all the exits. The partisans were caught in a stone pocket. It became difficult to breathe because there wasn't enough air. They had run out of food, and their supply of kerosene, their sole source of light, was also running low. To find a way out meant to survive. For six days, the haggard partisans searched for an exit. Weakened by hunger, the partisans were moving at a crawl. There were no shovels or pickaxes, and there was no strength either. Scooping with their hands and scraping with their fingernails until they bled, the partisans cleared a previously blocked-up saving exit that they found.[59]

The resistance to the occupational regime was also growing in the rest of the oblast. The praetor of the Bershadskii District Bunia Florin reported to his superior: "In the middle of the month of October 1943, partisan detachments began to organize, which began killing civil servants working for the Romanian administration, disarming the gendarmes, and inciting the population

57 *Odessa oblast'v Velikoi Otechestvennoi voine 1941-1945*, pp, 224, 293.
58 DAOO, F. 94, Spr. 2, Ark. 13-15.
59 Bachinsky, "Borot'ba OUN-UPA proti fashist'kikh zagarbnikov"; "Pivden' Ukraini pid chas drugoi svitovoi viini (1939-1945): Materiali respublikans'kogo simpoziumu" [South Ukraine during the Second World War (1939-1945): Materials of a national symposium] 1st ed. (Odessa, 1993), p. 71.

to conduct subversive and terrorist acts … We request your assistance by sending additional well-armed military units in order to mop up the villages and woods of partisan detachments."[60] Altogether by the start of 1944, 46 partisan detachments numbering up to 3,000 men and women were operating in Odessa and the rest of the oblast.[61]

The underground "Sverdlov" organization, created on 12 April 1943 by Colonel F.P. Shcherbakov, who had fallen into encirclement and made his way to Odessa, represented a significant force. Its members working at the January Uprising, "Kinap" and Shipyard No. 1 disabled or stashed away machine tools and mechanisms, slowed the repair of enemy torpedo boats, and received and distributed Sovinformburo communiques. In the autumn of 1943, the decision was made to restage to the catacombs, for which purpose a 17-meter shaft was dug into the catacombs from the yard of underground member A.S. Krishmar, through which food, weapons and ammunition were lowered into an underground storage chamber. On 20 March 1944, 54 members of the underground went into the catacombs, where they were joined by approximately 300 citizens of Odessa.

On 2 April 1944, during the entry of the next batch of residents into the catacombs, the entrance was discovered by the Germans. They blew up the shaft, destroyed the home, and cruelly dealt with Krishmar's family by shooting his son, daughter and twin sister.[62]

In May 1943, underground groups at the Red Guards and Dzerzhinsky factories, at a carbonated water plant, in the village of Krivaia Balka, and A. Termzin's group that was operating in Slobodka united into an underground organization of Odessa's Leninskii District. It was headed by a former secretary of the Communist Party's Novoarkhangelsk District Committee of Kirovograd Oblast K.A. Timofeev, who had been left behind in the enemy rear in order to organize an underground movement in his district, but had been forced to make his way to Odessa in order to shake off a manhunt for him. Combat groups of this organization attacked truck columns that were taking away Soviet people into fascist slavery, and organized escapes of prisoners of war from a prisoner camp.

The underground patriotic organization of the Il'ichevskii District, headed by D.I. Ovcharenko, initiated active work.[63] By October 1943, it had grown to 232 members. The organization had two dozen safe house apartments and a base in the catacombs below Golovkovskaia Street. The members had 6 radio receivers, 3 typewriters and their own typograph machine. This allowed the organization to receive Sovinformburo communiques and lead articles of the *Pravda* newspaper regularly; print leaflets, proclamations, slogans and epigrams against the fascist leaders; and publish combat leaflets *Za schast'e Rodiny* [*For happiness of the Motherland*] with their typesetting machine. Its underground members actively conducted agitation work among the occupation troops, and deployed subversive activities on a broad scale. They wiped out small enemy elements, killed fascists and their stooges, seized their weapons, and disabled factory equipment. For example, I.S. Kirsanov's group set fire to an ammunition stockpile and 210 drums of fuel in Blizhnye Mel'nitsy (on the outskirts of Odessa). Another group, led by G.K. Martyniuk, arranged the collision of four steam engines that had been slated for military trains at the Odessa Trade Station, while another steam engine was sent into an impasse at full speed. All five steam engines were wrecked. In connection with this, the fascists arrested 70 people – the depot's entire shift. Many of them spent almost a month in prison under harsh interrogation, but no one betrayed the organizers of the sabotage attack.

60   DAOO, F. R. 1983, s/566, Op. 1, Spr. 78, Ark. 103, 105-106.
61   TsDAGO Ukraini, F. 1, Op. 9, Spr. 85, Ark. 15.
62   DAOO, F. 11, Op. 45, Od. khr. 150, Ark. 44-55.
63   TsDAGO Ukraini, F. 1, Op. 9, Spr. 85, Ark. 16.

At the jute factory, female patriots headed by O.T. Zarembovskaia destroyed 7,000 sacks and threw the equipment of 12 textile machines that were slated to be sent to Romania into a pond.[64] Members of V.A. Molotov's group at the superphosphate factory hid the main components of equipment that produced a workshop's sulfuric acid, electric motors and ball bearings, and thereby kept it all from being sent to Germany.[65]

Given the fact that by this time the Red Army was pursuing a general offensive, the underground groups at the Red Guards, Dzerzhinsky and October Revolution factories and the meat-packing plant, under the leadership of A.G. Atanasov, V.M. Mishenin and A.G. Anosov, changed the nature of their subversive work. If previously they sought to disable machines and equipment for a long time or permanently, then now they began removing and hiding separate parts and components. The occupiers where thereby deprived of the opportunity to use the industrial equipment, but upon the arrival of the Red Army the machinery could be quickly put back into operation. In the Leninskii District's village of Krivaia Balka, at the direction of M.I. Bardenov the collective farmers took apart tractors, hid the parts, and ferreted away 5 metric tons of seed grain, livestock and food.

Saving Soviet people from killings and round-ups for fascist forced labor occupied an important place in the work of the underground members. For example, F.M. Drobot's group, which joined the Leninskii District organization, did important work to prepare the catacombs in Krivaia Balka to receive a large number of refugees. It sought out nine entrances into the catacombs that were unknown to the occupiers and cleared the Romanian-planted mines from three entrances. Four wells for drinking water for the underground were drilled out and repaired. In December 1943, underground member P.E. Pirogov organized an attack against the Nazis, who were taking away adolescent boys and girls to Germany in three trucks. The guard was killed, and the adolescents were liberated. In the area of Peresyp', members of the underground scattered a security escort that was guarding 200 residents of Odessa tabbed for transport to Germany, and they were all freed.

In the latter half of 1943, in connection with the approach of the Ukrainian *fronts* of the Red Army to the borders of the Odessa Oblast, the question arose about strengthening the cooperation of the Odessan underground movement with the attacking Soviet forces. For this purpose, experienced army scouts and military specialists arrived in the oblast.

On 15 August 1943, a group led by Senior Lieutenant I.A. Kukharenko parachuted into the northern area of the oblast. Having established contact with the underground members and partisans in the Savranskie Woods, the group in November 1943 created the "Burevestnik" ["Petrel"] partisan detachment commanded by Senior Lieutenant Kukharenko.

In September 1943, a group created by the Soviet scout N.A. Geft, who was German by nationality, arrived at one of Odessa's largest enterprises, Shipyard No. 1, to engage in subversive work. I.A. Riaboshapchenko, V.L. Tikhonin, M.S. Bereshchuk, I.Ia. Myndru and others joined this group. Geft was so conspiratorial that the members of the sabotage group themselves didn't even guess that the tall, lanky chief engineer of the shipyard, who wore a German uniform, was in fact their leader. Some of them planned to kill Geft as a traiter and fascist sidekick.

In the period between September 1943 and 10 April 1944, this group executed a number of subversive actions, saved some of the shipyard's equipment, tools and other property from being shipped to Germany, and prevented the demolition of two workshops. At the end of March 1943,

64 *Odessa v Velikoi Otechestvennoi voine*, Vol. 2, pp. 196-197.
65 DAOO, F. 11, Op. 45, Spr. 18, Ark. 9.

the occupiers created a concentration camp, which held all the men who worked at the shipyard. With the help of Geft, a large group of workers managed to escape.[66]

The underground members of this group conducted a number of acts of sabotage, as a result of which fascist boats and combat ships that had been repaired at the shipyard were blown up and sent to the bottom of the sea. In one incident, a bomb, camouflaged as an ordinary lump of coal, was tossed into a coal bunker aboard a repaired fascist ship. After a series of previous incidents, the fascists had increased their vigilance, and it wasn't so simple for the young worker V. Tikhonin to enter the ship's boiler room. Nevertheless, he managed to elude the fascists' vigilant watch, found the bomb, and tossed it a little further into the stoker when the ship was already at sea. Soon at the shipyard it became known that the ship sank after the explosion of the boilers.

It didn't even enter the heads of the underground members that the bomb that had been tossed into the coal bunker had been crafted by Professor E.K. Lopatto, who was well-known in Odessa. He was a Doctor of Technical Science and the deacon of the chemical-technological faculty of Odessa's Industrial (Polytechnical) Institute. When Soviet troops had abandoned Odessa, at the direction of Soviet intelligence the professor remained in the city. Not a Communist Party member and the son of a general of the Tsarist Imperial Army, he managed to gain the trust of the occupational authorities and opened a private laboratory, in which he secretly built bombs. The resistance movement at the shipyard used these bombs to blow up an enemy ship and a self-propelled barge, and damaged a transport ship, a tugboat, a river steamer and other boats.

When the threat of the dismantling and shipment of the superphosphate plant to Germany by the occupiers was in the air, Lopatto, who had at one time worked at the plant as the chief engineer, managed to prove to the occupational authorities that to dismantle the factory was the equivalent of destroying it, that it was supposedly impossible to rebuild such an enterprise in a new location, and so it was better to shift the factory to the production of copper sulfate. He managed not only to save the plant, but also reprocessed more than 150 metric tons of copper, of which the German military industry was experiencing an acute deficit, into copper sulfate.

E.K. Lopatto managed to to secure a job as a draftsman in the governorship's industrial administration for his son. There he produced a schematic map of the Transnistria, which depicted the location of all of its industrial sites. The occupiers thought highly of the map. However, Soviet intelligence thought even more of it, once Lopatto had delivered a copy of the schematic map to it.

At the assignment of one of the leaders of the underground V.E. Burzi, Lopatto compiled a list of Odessa's operating enterprises, which showed not only the type and volume of their production, but also the identities and code names of the traitors that worked in these enterprises. With the help of E.K. Lopatto, Soviet organs later neutralized a lot of enemy agents.[67]

After the liberation of Odessa, N.A. Geft, who'd been sent into the enemy rear on the territory of Poland, fell into encirclement in one of the battles, and not wishing to surrender, shot himself. Posthumously he was awarded with the Order of the Patriotic War 1st Degree, the Order of the Red Star, and the medal "Partisan of the Patriotic War 1941-1945".[68]

On the night of 21-22 September 1943, two female Komsomol members, E.N. Butenko and radio operator N.M. Zaitseva were dropped by parachute into Odessa by the Department of Partisans with the headquarters of the Red Army. They landed in the vicinity of the village of Sverdlovo, buried their parachutes, radio and battery, and headed in the direction of the city. Having spotted the airplane, the fascists decided that the Soviets had conducted an operation to

---

66 Istoriia gorodov i sel Ukrainskoi SSR: Odesskaia oblast [History of the cities and villages of the Ukrainian Soviet Socialist Republic: Odessa Oblast] (Kiev: Institut istoriia AN USSR, 1978), p. 135.

67 Karev, Odessa – Gorod geroi, p. 144.

68 DAOO, F.P. 11, Op. 45, Spr. 75, Ark. 3-5.

land paratroops, and promptly established supplementary pickets. Anti-aircraft guns and machine guns were firing all through the night. Mounted police patrols were roaming the entire area. Police round-ups began in the area of the landing.

Recalled Butenko:

> The pilot had missed our targeted drop point by 15 kilometers, and thus it was hard to orient ourselves. We spent most of the night sitting in a ditch. When morning broke we began to sneak down toward a village, where we spotted a woman at a well. Obviously, having noticed that we were strangers, without asking any questions she gave us an understanding look and advised us not to pass through the village, because they were detaining everyone there, and she pointed out a safe route through a balka. So both from the very first step and in all our subsequent work, we felt the support of the people.[69]

Nevertheless, the young women were unable to avoid to bumping into a fascist patrol. Toward the end of the day, Butenko and Zaitsev were caught and sent to the Romanian secret police. A court sentenced them to two years of confinement in a concentration camp in Tiraspol. The retribution might have been more severe, but the wits and composure of the young women saved the situation. They were sentenced for "illegally crossing the Bug River". At the court they behaved confidently and adroitly fooled the judicial officers. At the end of November the two young women escaped the concentration camp. Having arrived in Odessa, they took a room at No. 8 Perekopskaia Pobeda [Perekop Victory] Street, set up a radio in it, and made contact with their higher command. With the very first radio message, their superiors ordered them immediately to set up around-the-clock observation over the port, and report regularly on the loading and unloading of ships, and whenever a ship headed out to sea.

On the next day Butenko took a job in the port as a laborer. Relying on the help of Soviet citizens, the women monitored the movement of all ships that passed through Odessa's port. They learned at what time, with what cargo and along which route the ships were heading, their displacement tonnage, and their onboard weapons and command staff. The scouts learned to orient themselves quickly and accurately. Soon, surveillance over the movement of troops and ships became easier in connection with Butenko's switch to work as a telegraph operator at the Port of Odessa's railroad station. A job in the midst of the enemy requires a person with special tempering, who knows how to anticipate thousands of all-possible coincidences and unexpected circumstances that are capable of upsetting all previously prepared contingency plans. Such a person is characterized by intelligence, bravery, boundless resourcefulness and incessant vigilance. Such was the female scout E. Butenko. Before the war she had worked as a kindergarten teacher. It would seem that there is a large gulf between such a peaceful profession and the dangerous work as a scout. However, the war disclosed her other capabilities.

The radio operator N.M. Zaitseva transmitted the gleaned intelligence to the command. A former collective farm worker from Nikolaev Oblast, she voluntarily joined the Red Army, completed the training courses for a radio operator, and now had been sent to occupied Odessa. From a small room of an unprepossessing cottage in the Moldovanka [a subdistrict of Odessa located close to the city center], the modest young Soviet woman N. Zaitseva conducted a hidden war against the Germans. Clinging to her headset, she would quickly write out the next orders from the command, and then spend a long time transmitting information about the port's operation, about the stockpiles of cargo, about the departure of passenger and cargo ships, about the warships berthed in the harbor, and so forth. The adversaries, alarmed by the accurate information

---

69 Shternshtein, *Morskie vorota Ukrainy*, p. 166.

about everything happening in the port and the methodical attacks by Soviet aircraft, attempted to take a bearing on the radio set. After all, Zaitseva transmitted a total of 460 radio messages, and each of them brought death to the foe. Often, enemy convoys were sunk in the Black Sea by Soviet bombers and ships – and N. Zaitseva had reported their departure.

N. Zaitseva later recalled:

> Often precarious, almost hopeless situations came about during our work in the enemy rear. You always had to be on your toes. I remember such an incident: On a windy, February evening I with difficulty managed to find the right airwave, and I set about transmitting very valuable and urgent information. Five minutes after I had started the transmissions, a female neighbor knocked on my door – she wanted to borrow a cooking pot. I couldn't detach myself from the transmitter. Every minute was counting. A ship loaded with ammunition and equipment, sent by the enemy to the Crimea, might slip away. We were making known the enemy's intention, but to answer the doorknock meant cutting my transmission short, so I decided not to respond. It was difficult to imagine that this quite insignificant event might lead to such far-reaching consequences.
>
> For some reason, my neighbor decided that I had suffered carbon monoxide poisoning. She raised a ruckus in the yard outside. The doorman called the police, and preparations began to break my door down. I somehow managed in the interim to end the transmission, hide the radio equipment and antenna, wrap a wet rag around my head, and present myself to the crowd in this manner. Having thanked everyone for the "concern" they showed, I spent the entire evening applying hot compresses to my head under the touching care of my neighbor.[70]

The intelligence team experienced particularly large difficulties in securing power for the radio. For one-and-a-half months, the radio worked on batteries, purchased from German soldiers supposedly for the manufacture of pocket flashlights. In February 1944, a courier E. Adamchuk was dropped by parachute into Odessa, carrying batteries and spare parts for the radio. The transportation of this valuable cargo to the city was complicated by the circumstance that the fascists, with the aim of plundering, were stopping and searching all passing vehicles and wagons. Disdaining the danger, two peasants of the village of Gniliakovo Nikolai and Aleksandr Ostapchuk, transported this cargo on their sleds. In order to avoid encounters with Romanians, they took roundabout ways.

The days on the eve of the city's liberation were especially stressful for the members of Butenko's group. It was necessary to report on the rapid troop movements, in order to hinder the shipment of the cargo loads that had accumulated in the port. In addition, the two young women had to carry out a number of special assignments.

In 1943 a number of new underground groups and organizations arose in Odessa. B.V. Gumpert (Gromov), one of the leaders of Odessa's Party underground in the years of the Russian Civil War, illegally returned to Odessa in the autumn of 1943. Through I.P. Kalabin, he made contact with 20 men and organized an underground group. Member V.N. Peten with the help of his female relative G.I. Madritsa, who worked for the fascist newspaper *Odesskaia gazeta*, obtained a character font and roller, while her father, a factory worker mechanic, built a primitive printing press. The underground group printed and distributed the text of a declaration by the Allied powers about the fascists' responsibility for the atrocities they had conducted, a number of Sovinformburo announcements, and 17 leaflets. B.V. Gumpert's group managed to conceal valuable instruments

---

70   Ibid., p. 168.

of the Stomatological Institute from being exported, and immediately after the liberation of Odessa these instruments were used to treat Soviet soldiers.[71]

In commemoration of the anniversary of the Russian Revolution and in order to raise the spirits of the residents of Odessa, on the night of 6-7 November 1943, a group of patriots led by M. Vinnitskii unfurled a Soviet flag on the tallest building in the city – on the spire of the Uspensky Cathedral – and painted slogans on the walls of large buildings on Uspenskaia Street and Preobrazhenskaia Street: "Hail the October Revolution!" "Death to fascism!" Only by 1000 in the morning did the occupiers muster the courage to take down the flag – an inscription "Mined" that had been made by the members of the underground had made them apprehensive. An underground group founded by M.G. Chernyshev operated energetically. It consisted of just 10 members, but it organized the escape of more than 100 Soviet prisoners of war from fascist prisons and camps, concealed them, and supplied them with needed documents, food and articles of clothing.

The port, through which the majority of enemy shipments passed, remained one of the main targets of the underground resistance movement's activities. The most effective form of sabotage in the port was introduction of disorganization and confusion in the joint operation of ships and the railroad. Cargoes designated for urgent loading aboard a ship were unloaded from the railcars by the port's longshoremen and placed in remote warehouses, and thus the ship was forced to wait for departure. By sabotaging the ships heading to Romania in every way possible, the dock workers and railroad employees of the Port of Odessa preserved more than 10 metric tons of grain in warehouses until the arrival of Soviet forces. On four ships undergoing repair, members of the underground remetaled bearings with babbit metal that contained a larger admixture of lead than was proper, as a result of which once at sea the ship's engines malfunctioned. On two tugboats, two incorrectly fitted clutch couplings were installed, and soon they had to go to repeat repair. Repair work dragged out under various excuses. The steamships *Antrekht* and *Amur* were in fact never put back into service before the end of the occupation.

However, time was inexorably counting down the final months of the occupier's reign of terror on Ukrainian soil. After the defeat of the Germans at the Battle of Kursk, an unrestrained counteroffensive by Soviet forces across Ukrainian territory began, which gave an additional impulse to the development of the resistance movement in southern Ukraine. A characteristic detail of this period was the creation of centers of leadership of the partisan struggle in counties of the Transnistria, which united the northern areas of Odessa and Nikolaev Oblasts, as well as the southern districts of Vinnitsa Oblast. In the southern, steppe districts of the Transnistria, despite the extremely unfavorable open terrain, the underground organizations also went over to methods of armed, partisan struggle.

Alongside the many successes, however, the Odessan underground movement also had certain shortcomings. The main one of them was the absence of a unified leadership on the scale of the entire city. The underground organizations and groups worked disjointedly, with no coordination of their activity, which reduced their effectiveness, but the approaching front lines demanded an intensification of the blows in the enemy rear as well.

On 16 January 1944, a team of 10 men and women led by D. Avdeev (Chernomorsky), who already had experience in organizing an underground, partisan struggle against the fascist aggressors in Rostov and Donetsk, was dropped by parachute in the area of Zatish'e Station of Odessa Oblast.[72] The team included Commissar Ia.M. Levchenko and the Donetsk miners D.S. Gavshin (Dneprov), E.P. Barkalov, V.G. Rybin, N.G. Shliakhov, L.I. Safonenko and V.I. Deshko. The

71   DAOO, F. 11, Op. 45, Spr. 28, Ark. 25.
72   Shternshtein, *Morskie vorota Ukrainy*, p. 171.

team's radio operator was a young woman from the city of Kalininsk of Saratov Oblast A. Lubian, while the commander's courier was a female partisan from Rostov V. Syrenko (D.A. Mamedova). The team had undergone thorough preliminary training at the headquarters of the partisan movement of the 4th Ukrainian Front and had the task to coordinate and activate the partisan movement in that part of the Ukraine.

Having assessed the situation on the ground, Avdeev sent V. Deshko to the Berezovskii District and Luku Safonenko to the Razdel'nianskii and Grosulovskii (today the Velikomikhailovskii) Districts with the assignment to make contact with Soviet partisans and to direct them to strengthen the struggle against the occupiers and toward cooperation with attacking units of the Red Army. Having been injured when making his parachute landing, the group's commissar Levchenko and radio operator Lubian stayed for a time with collective farm workers in Osipovki, while the team's main cell headed to Odessa.

The Odessan underground members at this time were conducting intensified work to accumulate weapons. The Romanian punitive organs had increased the terror, but despite the new wave of atrocities, the patriots in the autumn of 1943 began increasingly to go over to open partisan actions. The Romanian administration identified the participation of "Ukrainians" in attacks against patrols of the gendarme, railroad stations, etc.[73]

V.D. Avdeev's team arrived in Odessa on 27 January 1944. Despite the fact that the team didn't have any safehouses or passwords, thanks to their great experience it managed in the course of one month to establish contact with all of the underground organizations and groups. The Il'ichevskii underground organization, led by S.I. Drozdov and D.I. Ovcharenko, became the main base for staging the partisan movement in Odessa. Somewhat later Avdeev made contact as well with the Leninskii District's underground organization, led by K.A. Timofeev.

On 3 February 1944, V.D. Avdeev held a conference of all the leaders of Odessa's underground organization and groups. At Avdeev's proposal, the city was divided into six areas, and it was decided to create a partisan detachment in each of them subordinate to the unified leadership of Avdeev's team of parachutists. This partisan formation, based in the catacombs, was supposed to join battle with the enemy units and seize the city upon the approach of Soviet forces. Almost every member of the underground capable of bearing arms joined this formation, and it grew to a total of more than 470 fighters.[74] V.D. Avdeev headed the entire leadership of the underground and partisan struggle in the city. He worked out a plan for a general armed uprising by the people of Odessa.

Special propaganda among the enemy's troops was determined as an important direction of activity. Members of the underground organizations appealed to the Romanian soldiers and sailors as representatives of the Romanian people who were being oppressed by their fascist rulers. Indeed, this work yielded results – after obtaining leaflets that exposed the real meaning of Antonescu's adventuristic policies, the sailors aboard the Romanian cutter *Maria* that was standing in port went on strike. The cutter's departure from the port was delayed for several days. Frightened by the disturbances on their ships, the occupational authorities took urgent measures. The chief of staff of the Romanian 3rd Infantry Division Lieutenant Colonel Zaganescu on 27 July 1943 ordered the commandant of Odessa's port "to put an end, as much as this was possible, to communications between ship crews and local port workers."[75]

---

73   V. Egorov, N. Zotov, and N. Rogozhin, *Geroi ne umiraiut* [*Heroes don't die*] (Odessa: Maiak, 1964), pp. 12-13.

74   *Bol'shevistskoe znamia*, 14 October 1945.

75   TsDAGO Ukraini, F. 1, Op. 9, Spr. 85, Ark. 19-20, 33, 38.

Great attention was paid to work among the military servicemen of the 1st Slovak Division, which was stationed in Odessa. The fascist Tiso government sent Slovak soldiers to war against the Soviet Union contrary to their desire. At the front, as soon as an opportunity presented itself, they went over to the Soviet side in droves. Thus the remnants of this division had been removed from the front and were being used by the German command for garrison duties in rear areas. The members of Odessa's underground established contact with the most active of the Slovak troops and began to conduct work in the division's companies through them. In October 1943, underground members of the jute factory recruited a Slovak soldier P. Gaiduchko, who'd been assigned to guard a military stockpile, into their ranks; Gaiduchko took the partisan oath. P. Gaiduchko actively worked to undermine the loyalty of other Slovaks, calling upon them to go over to the side of the partisans.[76]

Slovak anti-fascists Sergeant M. Konchity, 2nd Lieutenant K. Pogach, Privates I. Kish, Ia. Pavlik and others made contact with underground members of the Il'ichevskii District. Somewhat later, underground members of the Leninskii District established contact with Ia. Kroshlak and other Slovak anti-fascists. Avdeev met personally with P. Gaiduchko, M. Konchity, K. Pogach, I. Kish and other Slovak anti-fascists. He supplied them with the text of the Agreement on Friendship, Mutual Assistance and Post-war Collaboration between the USSR and Czechoslovakia, which had been signed on 12 December 1943, gave them information about the situation at the fronts, and told them about the combat activities of L. Svoboda's Czechoslovak Corps, which was fighting together with the Red Army against Germany. The Slovak underground members conducted anti-fascist agitation in their units, rendered assistance to the partisans with food and vehicles, and handed a radio set to them. Their collaboration with the Odessan underground was so obvious that the German commandant of the city issued an order to send the Slovak division to Tiraspol.

In order to avoid transfer, after negotiations with the partisan leadership, 88 Slovak anti-fascists left their units and entered the catacombs in the Krivaia Balka area, and another 68 entered the central catacombs. To the catacombs they brought 2 mortars, 2 machine guns, 150 rifles, 40 pistols, 300 grenades, 630 kilograms of explosives, and a lot of bullets.[77] The Germans hastily transported the rest of the Slovaks, who hadn't had time to go over to the partisans, out of Odessa.

The creation of the partisan formation was successfully progressing: the partisan headquarters of the six areas were forming combat groups and acquiring weapons and ammunition. Avdeev assigned his assistants – D.S. Gavshin and E.P. Barkalov – to take charge of the operational leadership over the partisan headquarters of the areas and the underground organizations. He systematically met with detachment commanders, urging them to hasten the preparation of the catacombs and to move all the partisans and members of the underground into them. He himself was getting ready to enter the catacombs. However, Avdeev didn't manage to complete the work he had started. On the morning of 2 March 1944, he was arrested. During the arrest, the commander of the parachute team attempted to fight his way free, but failed. He was surrounded, but he had one last bullet in his pistol. Not wishing to wind up in the hands of the foe alive, Avdeev placed the muzzle of the pistol at his temple and pulled the trigger. The bullet knocked out an eye, but the wound didn't prove to be fatal. Three days later, when Avdeev regained consciousness, he put an end to his life by slamming his wounded temple against the iron backboard of his bed. Death came instantly.

The death of their commander and the mass arrests that followed it hindered the members of the underground from fully implementing Avdeev's plan to create a partisan formation, but his

---

76   DAOO, F. R. 1820, s/393, Op. 1, Spr. 312, Ark. 259.

77   *Odessa: Ocherk istorii goroda-geroia* [*Odessa: Sketch of the history of the hero city*] (Odessa, 1957), pp. 260-262; *Odesskaia gazeta*, 5 November 1941.

peers nevertheless managed to prepare the Odessan underground resistance for armed struggle against the occupiers once the liberation of the city began. The chief of staff of the organizing parachute team D.S. Gavshin took charge of the partisan detachment of the Leninskii District and moved it into the catacombs, while team member E.P. Barkalov led the partisan detachment of the Il'ichevskii District into them as well. Then Barkalov headed off to the catacombs below the rural settlement of Leninsk and created another partisan detachment there; it was comprised of collective farm workers of Leninsk, workers of the "Vanguard" State Farm and the January Uprising factory, as well as 12 Slovak soldiers led by I. Kish. Two more partisan detachments, created by the underground Party's Prigorodnyi District Committee established bases in the Usatovo and Kuial'nitskii catacombs.

In the latter half of March 1944, the underground members of the Il'ichevskii District and of a number of other districts of Odessa at the proposal of parachute team members D.S. Gavshin and E.P. Barkalov descended into the catacombs, having an entrance in the yard of Building No. 39 on Kartamyshevskaia Street and joined a partisan detachment being created by the headquarters of the 3rd Microdistrict and by a leader of underground subversive groups A.I. Loshchenko. In addition to the members of the underground, a significant number of civilians of Odessa, who had arrived at the underground members' call to join them in the catacombs in order to take refuge against Nazi repressions, but who had no prior experience in the underground or partisan struggle against the occupiers, joined Loschenko's partisan detachment.

Out of the 1,660 individuals enlisted in the partisans, the command created 10 combat companies, a material supply and support platoon, and a commandant's company subordinate to the commandant of the catacombs G.F. Martyniuk. The detachment had a medical station and an armory. Former soldiers, commanders and political workers of the Red Army, who had wound up in occupied Odessa, as well as the most active underground members, were appointed as commanders and political leaders of the detachment's companies.

The formation of the detachment took place in the inadequately lit catacombs, with a large aggregation of people who were little known to each other, and who needed to be furnished with food, water and protection from the Nazis. The command didn't have an adequate number of weapons and could arm no more than three or four companies of the detachment. It focused its main efforts on guarding and supplying the civilian population that had descended into the catacombs. The partisans were leading civilians into the catacombs, helping them with food, and conducting explanatory work with them.

The Slovak detachment of anti-fascists led by Sergeant M. Konchity and 2nd Lieutenant K. Pogach, rendered great assistance in the defense of the catacombs and giving material support to the people. A special element had been created among them, headed by M. Konchity. It took active part in the struggle against the Nazis, who twice attempted to break into the catacombs. Ideological work in the detachment was led by D.I. Ovcharenko, who came out of prison on 31 March 1944 and immediately headed down into the catacombs. He gave instructions to the political leaders of the companies and the platoon agitators, and kept them supplied with Sovinformburo communiques and leaflets. At the end of March 1944, the partisan detachment began to publish the newspaper *Za schast'e Rodiny*. The newspaper was distributed not only in the catacombs, but also among the city's population.[78]

With the frontlines approaching Odessa, things became particularly lively at the port. Trains were arriving there carrying troops and equipment, and sanitary trains with wounded. Romanian civil servants and merchants together with their families and plundered property were striving to reach the port ahead of the advancing Red Army. The headquarters of the "Stalin" partisan

---

78   *Odesskie katakomby* [*Odessan catacombs*] 3rd ed. (Odessa: Maiak, 1974), pp. 97-98.

detachment, which had made contact with the headquarters of the 3rd Ukrainian Front that was operating on the Odessa axis, gave an order to the underground group of longshoremen and sailors to gather needed intelligence regarding the enemy's fortified coastal points, the size and composition of the security force, the mining of the coastline in the area of the port, and the movement of enemy ships. The group carried out this assignment within the time period set for it by the command.[79]

For two and a half years, the occupiers had been hauling away the riches of Odessa. When they sensed that the final days were approaching, they grabbed everything, right down to scrap iron that they'd stripped from damaged Soviet ships. On 20 April 1944, the port director wrote to the director of the Romanian incorporated community Reşiţa: "We have the honor to request you to deign to order the accelerated collection of scrap iron on the territory of Odessa's port. For example, today only one brigade of yours is working, which at the 10th Mooring is cutting scraps of old iron from the boat *Adzhariia* ..."[80]

The longshoremen and railroad workers O. Boichuk, A. Panasiuk, I. Mospan and A. Pinchuk and many others did whatever they could to disrupt the loading operations. They created disorganization in the stockpiling of the cargo, and a complete lack of coordination arose between the railroad transport and the ships. A locomotive, started up without an engineer, plowed into a train; loaded trains smashed into moving empty rail cars; trains were switched onto occupied tracks. Each day smashed rail cars were sidetracked into a storage area, and everything was done to keep secret the identity of those responsible for the crashes. Cargo boxes of medications or bullets were disappearing, and someone was systematically puncturing the tires on trucks. On the port's railroad, the occupational authorities weren't the masters; here, patriots were setting up their own routines and schedules. They were preventing the shipment by the enemy of an enormous quantity of fuel drums and railcars full of grain, food products, property and equipment especially assembled for dispatch to Romania. At the oil and gas terminal, the occupiers had prepared the shipment of 473 fuel tank cars. They were only able to ship out 50 of the tank cars; their further delivery was halted by the arranged accident involving a locomotive at a switch in the rails. Then the authorities decided to bring up barges and load them up with the gasoline. However, even this plan was thwarted. The gasoline in the fuel reservoir was set ablaze, and 423 cistern railcars of fuel never reached the enemy.[81]

O.E. Boitsun's group was acquiring weapons and ammunition in preparation for the armed uprising. By the spring of 1944, the group's members had 7 pistols, 3 rifles, 1 submachine gun and a large quantity of ammunition. The catacomb was set up for protection against pursuit, and food items, fuel and a lot of other necessary items were stockpiled.[82]

In February 1944 two more teams were parachuted into Kodymskii District, one of which was headed by D.B. Murzin, the other by N.K. Romanov. Out of the number of partisans of the village of Budei and the local population of the village of Pirozhnaia, two partisan detachments were formed, which in the course of subsequent combat operations killed more than 300 Nazis.[83]

In February-March 1944, partisans of the group founded in October 1942 in the Odessan coastal village of Usatovo headed by S.N. Serbulom and N.D. Golubenko sheltered up to 600

---

79 DAOO, F. 1, Op. 45, Spr. 53, Ark. 2.
80 DAOO, F. R. 1958, s/541, Op. 1, Spr. 280, Ark. 15.
81 Shternshtein, *Morskie vorota Ukrainy*, pp. 169-170.
82 DAOO, F. 11, Op. 45, Od. khr. 150, Ark. 32-38.
83 S.A. Vol'sky, "V Odesskikh katakombakh" ["In the Odessa catacombs"] in *Geroi popol'ia. O podpol'noi bor'be sovetskikh patriotov v tylu nemetsko-fashistkikh voisk v gody Velikoi Otechestvennoi voiny* [*Heroes of the underground. On the underground struggle of Soviet patriots in the rear of the German-fascist forces in the years of the Great Patriotic War*] 2nd Ed. (Moscow: Politizdat, 1996).

Soviet citizens who had been threatened with forced labor in Germany, and drove up to 500 head of cattle into the underground. From the end of March 1944 this partisan group conducted 11 combat sallies, as a result of which the enemy suffered 62 killed and 28 wounded, and lost 63 rifles, 2 submachine guns, one machine gun, 20 grenades and other gear to the partisans.[84]

The people of Odessa were waiting impatiently for the arrival of the Red Army. An informational report from the 2nd Police District in the city of Odessa to the department of the *Siguranța* on the morale of the population stated:

> 3. The Ukrainian population comprises the majority of the district's population. Exceptionally receptive to any sort of rumors that touch upon the situation at the front, passing this information along from one to another. This they do commonly in places of a large gathering of people, like at market places and so on.
>
> It should be noted that as soon as hostile radio stations transmit any sort of special announcement, it immediately becomes known throughout the city.
>
> It should also be emphasized that the majority of the population is waiting for the return of Soviet power. This state of morale is being supported by interested agents, who are spreading the rumors.
>
> ...
>
> 10. The press: Newspapers are read by the vast portion of the public with great interest, since everyone is interested by the course of combat operations. Newspaper vendors believe that the majority of the population is waiting for return of the Bol'sheviks, and are striving to the utmost to yell out the names of populated places that have been abandoned [by the Germans]. This they do in particularly crowded locations with evident enjoyment and satisfaction. We consider it necessary to ban such incidents in public places.[85]

Meanwhile Soviet forces, overcoming stubborn enemy resistance, were closing on Odessa. The German command was striving at any cost to maintain possession of the city, in order to block the path to central Romania. Major forces of the German Sixth Army and Romanian Third Army were falling back on Odessa. In early March 1944, retreating Germans entered Odessa and removed the Romanian administration – the city totally went over to German military control.

This led to a further sharpening of relations between the Axis allies. The Nazi command was openly ignoring Romanian "sovereignty" in the Transnistria. I. Antonescu issued an order to abolish the functions of the civilian governor with the Army's High Command on the occupied territory between the Dniester and Bug Rivers." Thus, for the first time since 19 August 1941, the name "Transnistria" disappeared from his orders. All power passed to the hands of the military in the form of Romanian Major General G. Potopeanu.[86]

The representatives of the occupational powers, sensing the end, sharply accelerated the shipment of valuable items from Odessa. According to the 1943 plan alone, the equipment of 63 enteprises was to be shipped out of the Transnistria to Romania. The losses of the city from plundering and deliberate destruction by the occupiers would have been significantly greater, if not for the growing resistance of the patriots.

As the Red Army neared Odessa, the occupiers, intensively shipping material valuables from Odessa, simultaneously became concerned about destroying the traces of their crimes. At the end of February 1944, even a "Commission to investigate the civilian governor of the Transnistria"

---

84   DAOO, F. 11, Op. 45, Od. khr. 150, Ark. 94-96.
85   DAOO, F. 11, Op. 45, Od. khr. 150, Ark. 145-147.
86   *Odesskaia gazeta,* 3 February 1944.

was created in Bucharest. At sessions of this commission, the Vice Premier of the Romanian government M. Antonescu, who even not long before was asserting that he was doing everything so that the Transnistria belonged to Romania, was now claiming that the occupation of the Transnistria "from the beginning had been only of a temporary nature". At the same time, trying to cover up traces, he remarked, "We are interested in dispersing … valuables, possibly to make them inconspicuously available to the Romanian economy, and not to keep them in a compact stockpiles."[87] However, only a few days were left to the occupiers to remain in Odessa: Soviet forces were rapidly approaching. On 17 March 1944, the final issue of *Odesskaia gazeta* came out. On the following day, 18 March 1944, the Germans forced their Romanian allies to sign a "Protocol about the transfer of the military administration of the territory between the Dniester and the Bug to General Auleb as the authorized representative of the Supreme High Command of the German Army." Considering the key strategic significance of Odessa and its port at this stage of the war, the Germans were trying to hold the city; however, in case of a retreat, they began to place mines around the city.

Realizing that they couldn't hold out long in Odessa, the Nazis began to prepare for Operation Flame, which foresaw the complete destruction of the city. The fascists began to mine the best residences, school buildings, hospitals, theaters, industrial sites, the city train station and the port. In the event of their defeat in the battle for Odessa, the Nazis decided to blow up the city and its people and to level it to the ground. Like rabid dogs, the fascists were roving throughout the city, searching for partisans and members of the underground, and resumed mass shootings. In these circumstances, the main task of the underground movement and the partisan detachments was to save the city, kill Nazis, and render assistance to the Soviet troops in the liberation of Odessa.

Soon special detachments of German arsonists and demolitionists were turning enterprises, establishments and residences into piles of ruins. According to a previously prepared plan, the German-fascist aggressors demolished a significant portion of Odessa's factories and plants, and blew up or burned down 2,290 of the most important, architecturally and historically valuable buildings, including the House of the Red Army, the main passenger train terminal, the Sabanskie Barracks, the building of the main post office, the communal bank, the city's hospital and many others.

They meticulously prepared the Port of Odessa for destruction. Back in the last days of February 1944, two companies of sappers had arrived in the port, and they began intensive preparatory work for its demolition. They dug out a trench with a depth of 30 to 40 centimeters along the line of berths, starting from the oil and gas terminal out to the first berth, and from that point they dug pits with a depth of 1.25 meters every 10 meters. Two lines of wire were stretched out in the trench, the ends of which led to the pits. Three boxes of TNT weighing 75 kilograms were placed in each pit. These wires stretched along all the berths in an uninterrupted line. The trenches were painstakingly filled in with sand, and then covered by stones.

In all of the port's warehouses, every 10-15 meters two or three 50-kilogram aerial bombs were stacked on a parallel track. Next to them, barrels containing 150 kilograms of explosive material were set in place. In multi-story buildings, the same amount of explosive material was stacked with the same symmetrical precision on each floor. All of these aerial bombs and barrels were linked by one continuous line of wire.

By 29 March, all of the Port of Odessa's berths and service terminals had been fully wired for demolition. Explosives had been wired in at the oil and gas terminal. Everything was ready to blow

---

87 I.E. Levit, *Krakh politiki agressii diktatora Antonesku* [*Failure of dictator Antonescu's politics of aggression*] (Kishinev, 1983), pp. 242-243.

up the port. Sentries were posted to guard the aerial bombs in the warehouses, at the pits, and along the entire extent of the wires running along the trenches.

To protect the supervisors located at the central demolition post, a protected electric cable linked it with every sector of the port. A section of the Quarantine mole adjacent to the central demolition post, along with the breakwater, sea wall and lighthouse were mined with delayed-action high explosives, in order to allow the demolitionists to reach a safe point out at sea before the explosives went up.

Methodically and steadily, the fascists had prepared an unspeakable crime – the total destruction of the largest port on the Black Sea. For 10 days in a row, the fascists were blowing up cold storage facilities, and spent one and a half weeks systematically demolishing the shipyard. The members of the underground movement were strenuously seeking ways to prevent the total destruction of the port. Port workers O.M. Kitsuk and P.I. Kushansky observed where the fascists had laid out the control wire, and on the night of 6-7 April 1944, skillfully avoiding the sentries, cut the the wired line of explosive devices in many places.

Having sailed out to sea, the German demolitionists sent the signal to the main control panel. The entire port was supposed to go up in explosions, along with all of the factories, buildings, annexes, and the entire above-water and below-water portion of the waterfront. However, an explosion of the expected strength didn't follow. Through the efforts of the patriots, a number of the berths, buildings and warehouses were spared from demolition.

In April 1944, retreating under the pressure of the Red Army, the occupiers also intended to blow up the superphosphate plant. For this purpose they emplaced boxes of explosives in the workshops and on the grounds of the enterprise. Members of a group led by O.E. Boitsun entered the factory via a tunnel that had been dug, disarmed the explosives, and thereby saved the plant from destruction. On 10 April 1944, armed members of the group, exiting the catacombs, took direct part in the liberation of the city together with units of the Soviet Army. In the fighting against the German aggressors, which developed in the area of the superphosphate plant, the group's leader O.E. Boitsun was severely wounded.[88]

In the period between 2 and 10 April 1944, E.P. Barkalov's partisan detachment staged a series of successful combat operations. For example, on 2 April the partisans attacked a German demolition team numbering 11 men. In a short combat action, a German officer and three soldiers were killed, and the rest taken prisoner. On 3 April Barkalov's group of partisans conducted an attack on a large German column of 77 horse-drawn wagons. Having killed or partially captured the armed escort, the partisans liberated Soviet civilans that were being forcibly taken to the west, and captured weapons, ammunition and food.[89]

On the night of 9-10 April 1944, a number of partisan groups of the Il'ichevsky District detachment, led by S.I. Drozdov, A.M. Shaliagin and N.R. Markushevsky took part in the liberation of Odessa and mopping it up of German stragglers, snipers and hold-outs. They were joined in this combat work by the group of Slovak anti-fascists under the command of M. Konchity, which had joined the partisan cause.[90]

The Germans so feared the assistance of the city's residents to the forces of the Red Army that the final declaration by the German commandant of Odessa on 9 April 1944 stated:

> In recent days, the attacks by civilian individuals against military personnel of the German Army and allied army have increased. Therefore, all citizens are forbidden to leave their

88   DAOO, F. 11, Op. 45, Od. khr. 150, Ark. 32-38.
89   DAOO, F. 11, Op. 45, Od. khr. 150, Ark. 113-114.
90   DAOO, F. 11, Op. 45, Od. khr. 150, Ark. 47-52.

apartments. Windows must be closed. Doors also, but not locked. Those who contrary to this appear on the street or show up in a window or open entrances will be shot without warning.

This order goes into effect today at 1500 hours.

Odessa, 9 IV 1944

Military commandant of Odessa[91]

In the liberation of the city from the fascist occupiers, members of the Odessan underground resistance movement and partisans rendered great assistance to the Soviet troops by inflicting painful blows from the rear. Partisan elements commanded by E.P. Barkalov, A.I. Loshchenko, I.S. Kirsanov, D.S. Gavshin and G.P. Kisov in the ensuing street fighting blocked the enemy's path of retreat through Odessa toward Tiraspol. They were knocking out enemy vehicles and creating traffic snarls on the streets, and bringing fire to bear on retreating enemy troops, throwing their columns into panic.[92]

The most important combat operation by the partisans of the Prigorodnyi area was the combat with German demolitionists in the vicinity of the Khadzhibeiskii Dam. Striving to block the path of Soviet troops to Odessa the fascists were wiring the dam with explosives in order to blow it up at the proper moment and flood the Peresyp' estuary. The partisans led by L.F. Gorbel' killed approximately 50 Germans in the battle and prevented the explosion of the dam and the subsequent flooding of the estuary.

Over the time of the fascist occupation, approximately 1,300 partisans and more than 2,000 underground resistance members operated on the territory of Odessa Oblast and helped thousands of residents. The ranks of the "people's avengers" included 930 women, and many of them were leaders of underground organizations and groups.[93]

In Odessa there was not a single enterprise under enemy occupation that didn't have acts of sabotage, subversion, demolition or the agitational activity of underground members in one form or another. More than 3,000 aggressors found their deaths in Odessa at the avenging hands of Odessa's underground resistance members. In the course of liberating the city alone, they killed, wounded or captured 1,214 enemy soldiers and officers. In the course of the entire period of occupation, the resistance movement in the city diverted up to two enemy divisions from the front. They hid approximately 18,000 Odessans in the catacombs at one time or another and saved them from execution or forced servitude in Germany. Altogether along the path of subversion and resistance, the partisans and underground members of Odessa Oblast killed more than 5,000 enemy soldiers and officers and 189 traitors to the Motherland; organized 27 crashes of military trains that were carrying troops and equipment and blew up 16 railroad or road bridges; destroyed 82 kilometers of telephone lines; knocked out or destroyed 2 tanks, 248 vehicles and 13 artillery pieces; captured 1,059 rifles, 62 machine guns and a lot of other military equipment and ammunition; and saved up to 20,000 Soviet civilians from being driven into fascist slavery.[94]

The feats of Odessa's resistance members received high recognition. Many of them received Orders and medals of the Soviet Union. In the memory of generations of its citizens, Odessa will eternally remain an unvanquished city.

91   DAOO, *Kollektsiia unikal'nykh dokumentov perioda okkupatsii* [Collection of unique documents of the occupation period], Op. 1, Spr. 1, Ark. 1.

92   *Bol'shevistskoe znamia*, 14 October 1945.

93   *Kniga pamiati Ukrainy: Odesskaia oblast'* [Book of Remembrance of Ukraine: Odessa Oblast] Vol. 1 (Odessa: Maiak, 1994), p. 31.

94   Karev, *Odessa – Gorod-geroi*, pp. 95, 149; Vol'sky, "V Odesskikh katakombov" in *Geroi podpol'ia*.

10

The 3rd Ukrainian Front's Odessa offensive and the liberation of Odessa

The spring of 1944 turned out to be prolonged, cold and slushy. However, it was a memorable, joyful spring. Now nothing could stop the Soviet armies' offensive. After the defeat of the Germans at Stalingrad, and then at Kursk, the fascists could only retreat, abandoning one city after another. They were still baring their teeth, launching counterattacks and clinging to river obstacles, but the enormous and inexorable power of the Red Army kept pushing them ever further to the west.

After a heavy defeat in the Bereznegovatoe – Snigirevsk offensive operation the fascists managed to fall back behind the Southern Bug River, and on this line they stopped the 2nd Ukrainian Front's offensive. They were holding the city of Nikolaev on the left bank of the Southern Bug River. However, a successful offensive by the 2nd Ukrainian Front in the course of the Uman' – Botoșani operation and the arrival of our forces in the area of Iași and Kishinev, resulted in the deep envelopment of the enemy's coastal grouping from the northwest and forced the Germans to shift part of their forces from the Southern Bug to the Kishinev axis.[1] The 2nd Ukrainian Front's Uman' – Botoșani operation led to the defeat of the German Eighth Army and the rupture of Army Group South's front. At the same time, a maneuver to the south against the front of Army Group "A" at the end of March 1944 substantially altered the situation on the coastal direction, thereby greatly facilitating an advance by the 3rd Ukrainian Front.

On 11 March 1944, in the course of the offensive from the Ingulets River to the Southern Bug River, the *Stavka* of the Supreme High Command with Directive No. 220050 in the midst of the Bereznegovatoe – Snigirevsk operation directed the 3rd Ukrainian Front to increase its pace in the pursuit of the enemy, capture bridges on the Southern Bug in the Konstantinovka – Voznesensk – Novaia Odessa sector and seize a bridgehead on its opposite bank. Subsequently it was to liberate Tiraspol and Odessa and continue the offensive with the aim of reaching the line of the Prut and Danube Rivers – on the national border of the Soviet Union.[2]

The 3rd Ukrainian Front experienced great difficulties in carrying out this order. The offensive's pace was slowed by the spring muddy season, and it was experiencing a shortage of troops and combat equipment, especially tanks. Thus it was unable to prevent the enemy's retreat to the right bank of the Southern Bug River and from the march break through the German defenses here. The Front's main forces reached the Southern Bug only by 22 March.

---

1   *Istoriia Vtoroi Mirovoi voiny 1939-1945, v 12-ti t.* [*History of the Second World War 1939-1945 in 12 volumes*] Vol. 8 (Moscow: Voenizdat, 1977), p. 93.
2   AGSh MO RF, Op. 1795, D. 166, ll. 179-182; D. 8/12.

The German defenses on the Southern Bug River had been previously prepared by engineers, but prior to the start of the operation only its main belt with a depth of 3 kilometers was ready; its forward edge was protected by formidable barbed-wire entanglements. The density of the 3rd Ukrainian Front's troops in the sector of the offensive was adequately high – one division per 10-12 kilometers of frontage. The terrain presented a treeless, coastal plain, which was cut by a large number of rivers, estuaries and balkas. The spring thaw and the flooding of many of the rivers presented a serious obstacle to the attacking Soviet troops. Meteorological conditions restricted air operations.[3] In order to fulfill the task for it set by the *Stavka* back on 11 March, the 3rd Ukrainian Front command worked out a new, Odessa offensive operation.

The German command was giving a lot of significance to the continued possession of Odessa. Its loss would create a threat to the naval lines of communication between the ports of Romania and the Crimea. The abandonment of Odessa and the Crimea would put the position of the fascist armies in southeastern Europe under threat, first of all in Romania, and would have a harmful influence on relations with Turkey. Thus the *Wehrmacht* was hastily bringing up forces from the west; and major populated places were declared "fortresses", which were to be held to the last soldier, contrary to the unjustified desires of the commanders of armies and army groups.

The forces of the 3rd Ukrainian Front were being opposed by the German Sixth Army (which had been resurrected in place of the Paulus' Sixth Army that had been destroyed at Stalingrad) and the Romanan Third Army, which in total had 34 divisions. On the northern and northwestern approaches to Odessa, the enemy created strong defensive fortifications. A frontal attack here would lead to prolonged, costly fighting. The situation required an outflanking maneuver, which would force the adversaries to abandon these positions. However, such a maneuver was complicated by the unprecedented mud on the roads, the lack of transport means and the need to replenish the Front's armies with men.

In order to close the enormous gap that had been torn in the front by the defeat of the Eighth Army, to stop the advance of Soviet forces toward Romania and to prevent the threat of encirclement of the coastal grouping, starting in the last days of March 1944 the German-fascist command had to implement significant force regroupings in the month of April. Antonescu's final reserve, the Romanian Fourth Army (eight divisions and one brigade) was moved up to the Iași area, and seven more Romanian divisions and two brigades were shifted to reinforce the German Eighth Army on the Kishinev axis. Three divisions, including two Romanian ones, arrived in the Eighth Army from Army Group "A". Altogether 8 corps headquarters, 18 divisions and three brigades from Romania and Army Group "A" were shifted to the line opposite the 2nd Ukrainian Front between 21 March and the end of April 1944.[4]

From the end of March, enemy resistance on the Iași and Kishinev directions stiffened. At the same time, the forces of the 2nd Ukrainian Front became extended; in the conditions of the complete lack of roads due to the muddy season, the artillery and rear services were lagging behind. Thus in the middle of April, having halted the offensive, the 2nd Ukrainian Front's troops began to dig in along the Rădăuți, Pașcani, Dubăsari line.

Stavka Representative and Marshal of the Soviet Union A.M. Vasilevsky and the Commander-in-Chief of the 3rd Ukrainian Front General of the Army R.Ia. Malinovsky submitted their plan for the Odessa offensive operation to the *Stavka* on 19 March 1944. In the operation's plan there was the statement, "The 3rd Ukrainian Front on 20 March … arrives at the Bug River in the sector

3   M. Tur, "Razgrom nemetsko-fashistkikh voisk pod Odessoi I v Krymu" ["Defeat of the German-fascist forces at Odessa and in the Crimea"] *Voennyi vestnik*, No. 4 (1954), pp. 39-40.
4   TsAMO RF, F. 243, Op. 2912, ll. 2-7; F. 48a, Op, 1795, D. 416, ll. 179-185.

from Konstantinovka to the south, and without any operational pause for preparations, switches to execute the Odessa operation."[5]

The plan for the operation was as follows: Forces of the 46th and 8th Guards Armies (commanded respectively by General V.V. Glagolev and General V.I. Chuikov) would launch the main attack from the Voznesensk – Novaia Odessa sector. Meanwhile, General I.A. Pliev's Mobile Group, consisting of the 4th Guards Cavalry Corps and 4th Guards Mechanized Corps, and the 23rd Tank Corps would attack in the general direction of Razdel'naia and envelop Odessa from the northwest. The right-flank 57th and 37th Armies (commanded respectively by General N.A. Gagen and General M.N. Sharokhin) received the order to attack in the general direction of Tiraspol.

It was planned to launch an auxiliary attack with the forces of the left-flank 6th and 5th Shock Armies (commanded respectively by General I.T. Shlemin and V.D. Tsvetaev) and the 28th Army (commanded by General A.A. Grechkin) in the direction of Nikolaev, Nechaiannoe and Odessa along the Black Sea coastline.[6]

Pliev's Mobile Group, with the 200 tanks it had available, was designated to develop a success in the Veselinovo (25 kilometers south of Voznesensk), Razdel'naia direction, while the 23rd Tank Corps was to stand ready to exploit a success in the direction of Voznesensk, Tsebrikovo and Tiraspol.

Two days – 21 and 22 March – were given to prepare the forced crossing of the Southern Bug River. The actual crossing was set to take place on the night of 22-23 March, and the crossing forces were to reach a line 5-8 kilometers west of the river. It was planned for the 3rd Ukrainian Front's forces to reach the Zatish'e, Razdel'naia line and seize Odessa by 1 April. The Mobile Group and the 23rd Tank Corps were supposed to take Tiraspol and Bendery by this date.[7]

Marshal of the Soviet Union A.M. Vasilevsky recalled:

> On the night of 19-20 March, the Supreme Commander-in-Chief informed me over the telephone that the considerations we had presented had been approved by the *Stavka*"[8] and that tanks and prime movers would arrive little by little. However, he added that there was now no possibility to provide replenishments with personnel. Meanwhile, the constant rains were again totally disintegrating the dirt roads that were already bad without them. Again, it became possible to deliver everything needed by the troops only with the aid of tractors and jeeps. In connection with this, the Front was forced to postpone the offensive until 26 March.[9]

Somewhat ahead of that date, Senior Lieutenant M. Zagesov's reconnaissance company forced a crossing of the Southern Bug River in the Novaia Odessa area. It stealthily crossed the river and gained a foothold on the opposite bank near the village of Tkachevka. In its wake, other forward units of the 3rd Ukrainian Front began to cross the river.

---

5   AGSh MO RF, Op. 1975, D. 166, ll. 179-182; D. 8/12.

6   TsAMO RF, F. 132a, Op. 2642, D. 36, l. 71.

7   *Operatsii Sovetskikh Vooruzhennykh Sil v Velikoi Otechestvennoi voine 1941-1945* [*Operations of the Soviet Armed Forces in the Great Patriotic War 1941-1945*] Vol. 1 (Moscow: Voenizdat, 1958), p. 161.

8   *Stavka* of the Supreme High Command Directive No. 2022204 from 19 March 1944; AGSh MO RF, Op. 1795, D. 8/12.

9   A.M. Vasilevsky, "Prikaz Stavki: Odessu osvobodit'! ["Stavka order: Liberate Odessa!"] *Oni srazhalis' za Odessu: Sbornik vospominanii uchastnikov oborony i osvobozhdeniia Odessy* [*They fought for Odessa: Collection of recollections of veterans of the defense and liberation of Odessa*] (Odessa, 1998), p. 123.

Stubborn fighting for possession of Tkachevka lasted for more than a week. On the night of 21-22 March a strong wind began blowing in from the sea, seawater surged into the estuary, and flooded conditions on the Southern Bug River began. The pontoon bridges were washed away by the raging river current. The Guardsmen fought to the last bullet. The artillery could not give the infantry serious fire support because of delays in bringing up shells. The water in the river was rising so swiftly that it was threatening to swamp the bridgeheads on the right bank. The Front Commander-in-Chief was forced to issue an order to the troops, who had seized the bridgeheads with fighting, to return to the left bank. The intended crossing of the river by other units was postponed.

By the start of the main operation, the 3rd Ukrainian Front had under its command the 6th, 28th, 57th, 37th, 46th, 8th Guards, 5th Shock Armies; the 23rd Tank, 4th Guards Cavalry and 4th Guards Mechanized Corps; and the 17th Air Army (commanded by General V.A. Sudets). After the liberation of Nikolaev, the air army was withdrawn into the *Stavka* reserve. The 23rd Tank Corps had 88 tanks and 26 self-propelled guns. The 4th Guards Mechanized and 4th Guards Cavalry Corps had a combined 232 tanks and 35 self-propelled guns.

In addition to the 3rd Ukrainian Front's forces, a portion of the Black Sea Fleet was involved in the execution of the Odessa operation. The Fleet was given the tasks to inflict strikes upon the enemy ships in ports and while at sea with high-altitude bombers and torpedo bombers; to deploy no less than seven submarines on the enemy's lines of communications in the Black Sea; and to take part in the liberation of coastal cities and ports.[10] Torpedo boats were restaged to Skadovsk for operations against the enemy's lines of communication in the northwestern area of the Black Sea. On 6-7 March, the first group of nine torpedo boats moved to Skadovsk. Soon they were followed by a second group of six torpedo boats.[11]

A large amount of work was done to make the air force ready. All of the regiments were to a significant extent replenished with aircraft and brought up to strength in personnel. The 43rd Fighter Aviation Regiment was re-formed from scratch, while the 119th Naval Reconnaissance Regiment was converted into the 13th Guards Long-range Bomber Regiment, re-equipped with the latest bomber. The air crews of this regiment were well-trained for operations against the enemy's naval shipping and combat ships on the open sea. By March 1944, the 1st Mine-and-Torpedo Aviation Regiment, the 36th Mine-and-Torpedo Aviation Regiment, the 23rd Storm Aviation Regiment and the 43rd Fighter Aviation Regiment had fully restaged to the Skadovsk airbase, as well as two squadrons of the 30th Reconnaissance Aviation Regiment.[12]

Altogether by the start of the operation, the 3rd Ukrainian Front had 57 rifle divisions, plus one tank, one cavalry and one mechanized corps, which yielded an operational density of one rifle division for each 3-4 kilometers of frontage. In the course of the preceding fighting, the Front's troops had sustained losses which couldn't be replaced in time for the start of the operation, and the strength of each rifle division didn't exceed 3,000 to 4,000 men.[13]

The German Sixth Army and Romanian Third Army, numbering 21 divisions (of which 4 were Romanian and one was Slovak) and 8 brigades of assault guns were opposing the forces of the 3rd Ukrainian Front on a 170-kilometer sector of the front extending from Konstantinovka in the north to the Dnieper – Bug estuary in the south. In connection with the heavy losses in the preceding fighting, approximately half of these divisions had been reduced to divisional combat groups; the numeric strength of the divisions reached 7,500 men each, while the divisional combat groups had 4,000 to 4,500 men each. Two *Luftwaffe Fliegerkorps* and two Romanian air fleets,

---

10   TsVMA RF, F. 167, D. 6059, ll. 171-173.
11   G.I. Vaneev, *Chernomortsy v Velikoi Otechestvennoi voine* [*Black Sea sailors in the Great Patriotic War*] (Moscow: Voenizdat, 1978), p. 322.
12   TsVMA RF, F. 10, D. 39234, l. 82.
13   *Operatsii Sovetskikh Vooruzhennykh Sil v Velikoi Otechestvennoi voine*, p. 162.

numbering a grand total of 620 aircraft, were supporting the troops of the German Sixth and Romanian Third Armies.

Thus, in comparison the Soviet grouping numbered approximately 528,000 men, including approximately 195,000 in the rifle divisions; 6,400 guns and mortars; and 415 tanks and self-propelled guns. The enemy grouping had a total number of around 200,000 men, including approximately 120,000 in the infantry divisions; around 2,000 guns and mortars, and around 160 tanks and self-propelled guns. The re-fitted Soviet 17th Air Army had 540 aircraft. The overall correlation of force by the start of the Odessa operation was in our favor according to every indicator save aircraft: 2.6 to 1 in men, including 1.6 to 1 in the rifle (infantry) divisions; 3.2 to 1 in guns and mortars; and 2.6 to 1 in tanks and self-propelled guns.[14]

When planning the combat use of the artillery in the Odessa operation, three considerations were taken into account: firstly, several formations of the Front's armies were starting the offensive out of bridgeheads that they had seized on the left bank of the Southern Bug River in the course of the preceding offensive fighting; secondly, because of the spring thaw, a portion of the artillery had lagged behind and could not be brought up to their firing positions for the offensive in time, and thus had no way to take part in the artillery preparation; thirdly, the enemy had hastily organized the defense on the left bank of the Southern Bug River with the same formations that had been falling back repeatedly under the blows from the Soviet forces. In connection with these considerations, the planners decided that the artillery preparation for the offensive would continue for 30 to 45 minutes and include the broad use of the guns deployed to fire over open sights.

It was planned to accompany the attack, as well to support the battle in the depth of the enemy's defenses, by means successive concentrations of fire on enemy strongpoints and counterattacking groups that were slowing progress made by the infantry and tanks. The density of artillery and mortars on the designated breakthrough sectors did not exceed 65-70 guns and morters per kilometer of front.

Air support for the operation rested on the 17th Air Army under the command of Colonel General of Aviation V.A. Sudets. The air army was supposed to facilitate a breakthrough by the ground forces into the entire depth of the enemy's defenses with bomber and ground attack aircraft strikes against enemy strongpoints and key road hubs in the enemy's rear, and then harry the retreating enemy colums during a subsequent pursuit.

The staging of the operation took place in very difficult conditions, chiefly because in essence it was conducted in the midst of an on-going offensive. The rains, which had converted the dirt roads into quagmires, were also a serious hindrance. Only tractors and jeeps could bring up the necessary supplies. Nevertheless, by the last days of March, the Front's forces had been replenished with men and supplied with combat equipment, ammunition, fuel and rations. They now had more tanks and artillery pieces than they had by the start of the Bereznegovatoe – Snigirevsk operation, while the number of troops and amount of equipment on the enemy's side had dwindled due to combat losses and the transfer of major forces to the Kishinev direction. The correlation of force in men and combat equipment in the sector of the looming offensive had shifted further in favor of the Soviet forces.[15] In addition, it had become more risky for the enemy to hold a line along the Southern Bug River in view of the deep envelopment of his coastal grouping by the forces of the 2nd Ukrainian Front and the threat of the loss of paths of retreat beyond the Dniester River.

The spring thaw and lack of roads, as well as the slow pace in rebuilding the railroads, were strongly constraining the ability to keep the troops supplied with materiel and equipment. In such conditions, primary attention was given to making the maximal use of local resources of

14   Ibid., p. 163.
15   V.S. Golubovich, *Marshal Malinovsky* (Kiev, 1988).

food and fodder. Yet if this kept the troops adequately supplied with food and fodder, their supply with ammunition and fuel was extremely insufficient. For example, the 37th Army, which was attacking on the main axis, had only 0.6 of a standard combat load and just 0.5 of a refill of fuel and lubricants. The situation was similar among the troops of other armies.

Alongside the regrouping of forces, the creation of stockpiles of materiel, the organization of command and control and the work to secure cooperation among the units and formations of the 3rd Ukrainian Front, a lot of political education work was done among the troops. The primary task of the propaganda and mass agitation work was to create a high attacking zeal in the Soviet troops, and to bolster their decisiveness and ability to overcome the enemy's defense. Political workers also worked with incoming replacements arriving from liberated areas of Ukraine in order to explain the international and internal situation of our country, as well as the tasks and objectives of the Soviet Army in the war. As a result of all this work, a highly aggressive mindset reigned among the Soviet troops and they were eager to start the offensive.

Because of the spring thaw, all motorized transport bogged down in the sea of mud. This not only slowed the movement of artillery and ammunition, it also was delaying the arrival of the standard bridging equipment. Only an insignificant amount of the bridging materiel had been brought up to the river by 25 March. Because of these factors, the start date for the offensive was again postponed from 23 March to 26 March.

Simultaneously with the bringing up of artillery, ammunition, bridging equipment and rear services, the troops of the 3rd Ukrainian Front's right flank were continuing to push toward the river, where the 37th and 57th Armies from the march were able to force the river and seize a number of small bridgeheads in the sector between Konstantinovka and Voznesensk. On 24 March, the 37th Army in fact liberated Voznesensk. In the center, troops of the 46th Army and 8th Guards Army were continuing to battle to expand their previously gained bridgeheads in the area south of Voznesensk and west of Novaia Odessa.

In this period before the formal launching of the operation, the troops of the 57th, 37th, 46th and 8th Guards Armies used only whatever means they could find at hand to cross the river. Thus, the accumulation of strength within the captured bridgeheads went very slowly, and the troops were not able to bring artillery into the bridgeheads until the arrival of bridging equipment. On the 3rd Ukrainian Front's left wing, the 5th Shock, 6th and 28th Armies were engaged in intense fighting to take Nikolaev.

On 26 March, the forces of the 3rd Ukrainian Front formally kicked off the offensive and went on the attack across the Front's entire sector. The armies of the Front's right flank and center set about crossing the Southern Bug River with their main forces. The 57th, 37th, 46th and 8th Guards Armies were using primarily the means at hand and the insignificant amount of light bridging equipment that had arrived. The main bridging equipment had still not come up. As Marshal A.M. Vasilevsky reported to the *Stavka*, in order to bring it up, "… all of the means of the Front and the armies were mobilized, right down to oxen."[16]

Attempts by the troops of the 57th, 37th, 46th and 8th Guards Armies to continue to bring men and equipment across the river during the daylight hours of 26 March led to the loss of the pontoon bridges because of intense enemy artillery fire (in places, direct fire), and were halted. With the onset of darkness, the troops of the right flank and center resumed the crossing of the river and the fighting to expand the bridgeheads they had seized.

In order to aid the offensive by the armies of the 3rd Ukrainian Front's right flank, the *Stavka* of the Supreme High Command decided to take advantage of the success of the 2nd Ukrainian Front's 5th Army, which by that time had forced a crossing of the Southern Bug River north of

---

16   AGSh MO RF, Op. 1795, D. 168, ll. 63-65.

Pervomaisk. It ordered the main forces of the 2nd Ukrainian Front's 7th Guards Army to cross the Southern Bug River in the 5th Army's sector, before pivoting with an attack to the south with the aim of "rolling up" the enemy's defenses on the right bank of the river and facilitating the river crossing of 3rd Ukrainian Front's right flank.

The 3rd Ukrainian Front's 57th and 37th took advantage of the neighboring *front's* success and the 7th Guards Army's subsequent maneuver. They expanded their bridgeheads in the area of Konstantinovka and Voznesensk and brought their main forces across the Southern Bug River.[17] In contrast, the 46th Army and 8th Guards Army to the south failed to overcome the enemy resistance and made no headway.

In this situation, the Commander-in-Chief of the 3rd Ukrainian Front, taking into account the clear success achieved in the sector of the 57th and 37th Armies, as well as the breakthrough made by the forces of the 2nd Ukrainian Front's left flank and their subsequent exploitation to the south in the direction of Tiraspol, decided to shift his Front's main forces to his right flank. Pliev's Mobile Group and the 23rd Tank Corps were to regroup to this point by the morning of 29 March 1944. Pliev's Mobile Group shifted from the sector of the 8th Guards Army to the vicinity of Aleksandrovka in the sector of the 37th Army, while the 23rd Tank Corps redeployed out of the sector of the 46th Army to the 57th Army's sector.

On the morning of 28 March, the forces of the 3rd Ukrainian Front's right flank and center resumed the offensive. On this day, enemy resistance collapsed in the entire sector of the 37th and 57th Armies. Supported from the air, the troops of these armies tore a 45-kilometer breach into the enemy's line and advanced up to 25 kilometers.

The 46th and 8th Guards Armies in the course of 28 March continued to fight to expand their bridgeheads and bring more men and equipment across the river. The troops of these armies, having run into stiff enemy opposition and lacking a sufficient amount of bridging equipment and necessary artillery support, were able to make only an insignificant advance.

Meanwhile, as the troops of the 3rd Ukrainian Front's right flank and center were encountering varying success in breaking through the enemy's front along the line of the Southern Bug River, the troops of the Front's left wing had been continuing to battle to take possession of Nikolaev. Having broken the enemy's dogged resistance, on 28 March the forces of the 5th Shock and 28th Armies, in cooperation with troops of the 6th Army, finally took the city – a major port and enemy strongpoint at the mouth of the Southern Bug River.

In the fighting for possession of Nikolaev, a Soviet raiding party accomplished an immortal feat. In order to help the attacking troops take the city, a small group of troops from the 384th Separate Naval Infantry Battalion and from units of the 28th Army, headed by Senior Lieutenant K.F. Ol'shansky, boarded 7 fishing boats and traveled approximately 15 kilometers up the Southern Bug River from its mouth on the Black Sea. They stealthily landed in the city's port and took possession of several buildings and elevators, which they adapted for an all-round defense. Now the commando group faced its main task – to create confusion in the enemy rear in order to prompt the enemy to pull units from the front in order to deal with it. The Germans discovered the raiding party only by around 0800. At 1000, the enemy launched the first of many attacks. Ultimately, the enemy committed up to two battalions of infantry, four 75-mm guns, several tanks, and machine guns against the small group of Soviet commandoes. However, the Soviet troops were fighting to their deaths and drove back all the enemy's attacks. At a difficult point in the unequal battle, the Nazis gave the Soviet commandoes an opportunity to surrender, but they rejected this offer.[18]

---

17   TsAMO RF, F. 48a, Op. 1795, D. 416, Ark. 295.

18   P. Bolgari, N. Zotkin, D. Kornienko, M. Liubimov and A. Liakhovich, *Chernomorskoi flot: Istoricheskii ocherk* [*Black Sea Fleet: Historical study*] (Moscow: Voenizdat, 1967), p. 261.

Many of the heroic defenders were killed or wounded, but those still able continued to fight. Senior Red Navy Sailor V.V. Khodarev was wounded. His left hand was torn away by a shell fragment, but at just that moment an enemy tank was approaching. The bleeding hero picked up a bundle of grenades with his right hand, rushed toward the tank, and blew it up.

For 48 hours the brave warriors repulsed furious attacks from superior enemy forces, tying them up in combat. The raiders killed up to 700 enemy soldiers and officers, but they in return, having driven back 18 enemy attacks, had suffered heavy losses. Of the 67 men, only 12 remained alive, but they continued to fight valiantly until the arrival of attacking Soviet units. When the severely wounded commander was disabled, Yeoman 2nd Class K.V. Bochkovich assumed command. At a difficult moment during the fighting, the sailors sent a radio message to their command, which stated, "We, fighting men and officers, sailors of Comrade Ol'shansky's detachment vow to the Motherland that the mission given to us will be carried out to the last drop of blood, with no regrets for death." The last five attacks with the participation of tanks, artillery and flamethrowers were the most bitter. Failing to achieve success, the Nazis in the final assault employed poison gas against the Soviet holdouts. However, in spite of everything, the commandoes carried out their order.[19]

The Motherland considered all the men of Ol'shansky's raiding party, including Ol'shansky himself, worthy of the title Hero of the Soviet Union. The name of the heroes has been given to a square in the city center, upon which the residents of Nikolaev have erected a stately monument to the commandoes. One of the streets of the city carries the name of K.F. Ol'shansky.[20] A large amphibious assault ship of the Ukrainian Navy is called the *K.F. Ol'shansky*.

Local fishermen who took the raiding party up the Southern Bug River in their boats, provided valuable assistance to the operation. One of the fishermen A.I. Andreev decided to stay with the raiders after dropping them off. Together with them he reconnoitered, using his familiarity with the city to guide the men, and together with them he fought to repel the foe's attacks. For the courage and valor he displayed, he was posthumously awarded the title "Hero of the Soviet Union."

In the course of 29 and 30 March, the troops of the 3rd Ukrainian Front, overcoming the resistance of hostile troops, forced a crossing of the Southern Bug River along its entire extent between Konstantinovka and Nikolaev. The successful advance by the 2nd Ukrainian Front, which by 28 March had reached the Rybnitsa, Konstantinovka line with its left wing, and the cracking of the German defensive line along the Southern Bug River by the 3rd Ukrainian Front, forced the enemy troops to begin a general retreat to the Dniester River. The troops of the 3rd Ukrainian Front began to pursue the retreating enemy. In the course of the pursuit, Pliev's Mobile Group and the 23rd Tank Corps were committed into the breach in the Domanovka area on the morning of 31 March, and they exploited in the general direction of Razdel'naia. Throughout the night of 30-31 March, units of Lieutenant General T.I. Tanaschishin's 4th Mechanized Corps and the 10th Cavalry Division from the march attacked enemy positions and blocked all paths of retreat to the enemy troops. In the area of Berezovka, heavy fighting developed. With the sunrise, enemy aircraft appeared overhead. A group of 20-30 Focke-Wolf fighter bombers struck our combat formations. The enemy was conducting a constant artillery barrage and mortar fire from beyond Tylihul.

Regiments of the 9th and 30th Cavalry Divisions began to move into jumping-off positions for a breakthrough of the enemy's defenses south of Berezovka. Lieutenant General Tanaschishin reported that the enemy was counterattacking the corps' right flank units and fighting to regain

---

19 Iu. Prokhvatilov, *Ognennye mili matrosovskogo batal'ona* [*Fiery miles of a battalion of sailors*] (Mariupol', 1998), pp. 156-186.
20 O.M. Garkusha, E.G. Gorbunov, Iu.I. Guzeniuk (eds.), *Mikolaivshchina litopis istorichnikh podii* (*Mykolaiiv: Chronicls of historical events*) (Kherson, 2002), p. 410.

possession of captured ground. I.A. Pliev through binoculars saw that the enemy was advancing with large forces of infantry and tanks. This gladdened him, because it was easier to crush an attacking enemy in open battle than it was when the enemy was dug into fortifications, especially because he was aware that he had two more divisions ready to go into battle. He now knew that the fate of Berezovka had been decided. He ordered, "Wait until the Germans get drawn into battle with the 10th Guards [Division], then commit the second echelon against their flank. We'll launch a general attack by the mechanized and cavalry corps."[21]

The Germans realized too late that their counterattack was a blunder. The 9th Guards Cavalry Division with a decisive attack seized the railroad station and burst into Berezovka from the south. The 30th Cavalry Division forced a crossing of the Tylihul River and outflanked Berezovka from the southwest, blocking the path of retreat of its garrison. The 4th Guards Mechanized Corps also broke into Berezovka. The fighting in the Berezovka area continued almost until noon. The defending units here were shattered.

The troops of the Mobile Group then moved on toward Razdel'naia Station. Lieutenant General Tanaschishin, the commander of the 4th Guards Mechanized Corps, was at an observation post on the northwestern outskirts of Berezovka, where he was giving a report on the course of the fighting for Berezovka. He received an order to pursue the enemy. At this moment, a group of Focke-Wolfs appeared overhead, which struck the corps' combat positions and the railroad station. One bomb fell on the observation post on the northwestern outskirts of Berezovka, and General Tanaschishin was killed. His death deeply affected all of his subordinates. His chief of staff Major General V.I. Zhdanov assumed command of the 4th Mechanized Corps. General T.I. Tanaschishin's body was carried to Voznesensk, where it was buried with honors. The mobile troops, overcoming the resistance of enemy rear guard detachments, advanced up to 70 kilometers on this day and reached the Tylihul River in the areas of Striukovo and Berezovka. By the end of 31 March, the rifle formations also arrived at the Tylihul River in the Ivanovka – Berezovka – Tashino sector.

The forces on the 3rd Ukrainian Front's left flank were also making good headway. Troops of the 5th Shock Army on the morning of 30 March resumed the offensive out of its bridgehead in the area of Varvarovka, and on this same day units of the 1st Guards Fortified District, the forward detachment of the 295th Rifle Division and units of the Black Sea Fleet reached Ochakov and Fort Krasnyi Maiak [Red Lighthouse] as a result of a combined attack.[22]

In order to assist the Soviet troops with taking the fortified strongpoint of Ochakov, on the morning of 30 March 40 sailors of a fortified sector of the coastal defense (under the command of Lieutenant Colonel Iu.I. Neimark) disembarked from a yawl and rowboats onto the island of Pervomaiskii. The Black Sea sailors seized the island, and in the process captured six guns and two stockpiles of ammunition. At 1130 the sailors climbed back into their boats, left the island and headed toward Ochakov. A group of sailors led by Senior Lieutenant A. Loktorin successfully landed and became tied up in fighting in the port. Soon a second group of sailors led by Lieutenant Colonel Neimark came up and successfully landed. The landing parties seized the port and captured three seine-net fishing boats and a cutter that were moored there. They also managed to prevent the fascists from blowing up the port's facilities. Thus Ochakov was liberated with a combined attack from the land and sea.

Next, despite the fact that the enemy during the retreat had managed to blow up all the bridges across the Tylihul River and mine the fords, the troops of the 3rd Ukrainian Front successfully forced a crossing of this river and continued to exploit in the direction of Razdel'naia and Strasburg. When a success became evident in the sector of the 57th and 37th Armies, the Front command

---

21   I. Pliev, "Vpered na Odessu" ["Forward to Odessa"] *Voenno-istoricheskii zhurnal*, No. 4 (1984), p. 67.

22   TsAMO RF, F. 132a, Op. 2642, D. 36, ll. 359-360.

again decided to concentrate its main forces here. Pliev's Mobile Group and A.O. Akhmanov's 23rd Tank Corps were committed into the breach and quickly headed in the direction of Tiraspol and Razdel'naia.

Pliev's Mobile Group consisted of the 4th Guards Cavalry Corps, the 4th Guards Mechanized Corps, the 5th Separate Motorized Rifle Brigade and attached assets. As of 1 April 1944, the 4th Guards Cavalry Corps had 18,640 men, 13,070 horses, 89 medium tanks, 34 light tanks, 11 self-propelled guns, 92 76-mm guns, 33 45-mm guns, 36 anti-aircraft guns, 66 120-mm mortars and 99 82-mm mortars. The 4th Guards Mechanized Corps had 6,882 men, 1 heavy tank, 87 medium tanks, 6 light tanks, 5 self-propelled guns, 23 76-mm guns, 41 45-mm and 54-mm guns, 10 anti-aircraft guns, 14 120-mm mortars and 31 107-mm mortars.[23]

The units of the mobile group and tank corps were continuing to make a stubborn advance, and having conducted an outflanking maneuver, reached Razdel'naia in five days. For five days and nights, the men had no sleep: day and night, difficult water crossings and battles continued in the mud of the spring thaw, under enemy airstrikes and in foul weather. Sometimes the Cossacks dismounted and led their exhausted horses. The tanks, self-propelled guns and vehicles were pushing through swamps which seemed impossible to cross even on foot. They were towed, pushed, and crews and drivers were laying logs, boards, brushwood – everything they could find to gain traction, right down to quilted jackets and overcoats – under the tracks and wheels.

The commander of the German Sixth Army committed the fresh 157th Cavalry Division against Pliev's Mobile Group. On that night it was so dark and such a snowstorm was blowing that a column of this division consisting of several elements of mounted men and approximately 60 vehicles with infantry and artillery unwittingly wound up in the midst of the combat formations of our mobile group and was completely destroyed.[24]

The Cossacks and tank crews were deathly tired, but Razdel'naia – a major railroad hub on the enemy Odessa grouping's main path of retreat to Romania – lay in front of them. I.A. Pliev remembered:

> A decision was necessary: attack Razdel'naia right away or allow the tired, utterly worn out men to rest until morning. It was now five days from the hour when our mobile group crossed the front line, and our raid was on-going. Over this time we had forced a crossing of the Ingulets River, brushed aside enemy units that were trying to block our path into the enemy's operational rear, and with decisive night attacks had taken two of the enemy's most important strongpoints – Berezovka and Stalino. Yet over all these five days, not a single Cossack, not a single tanker had obtained some shuteye.
>
> Now Razdel'naia was in front of us; the third by count, and just about the most important station for the Nazis. The only railroad leading beyond the Dniester to Romania runs through Razdel'naia. To take Razdel'naia – meant to close the path of evacuation of equipment, troops and plundered goods from the Odessa fortified area like a stopper. To take Razdel'naia meant to drive the Nazis into a pocket, to doom their troops to destruction – and after all, the enemy's Sixth Army, which had been ordered to hold Odessa, had been created by Hitler himself in order to take revenge for the destruction of Paulus's army at Stalingrad, which carried the same numerical designation. Not in vain had Hitler baptized this new Sixth Army "the army of avengers".

---

23   Pliev, "Vpered na Odessu", p. 67.

24   A.M. Vasilevsky, "Prikaz Stavki: Odessu osvobodit'! ["*Stavka* order: Liberate Odessa!"], in *Oni srazhalis za Odessu:Sbornik vospominanii* [*They fought for Odessa: Collection of recollections*] (Odessa, 1998), p. 124.

It didn't even enter the mind of the Hitler command that anyone might venture an attack through such oceans of mud on a night that was as dark as coal, but I knew that if we attacked now, at night, we'd take the station with hardly any losses. To wait until morning meant to allow the enemy to ready a defense ... and by morning, the enemy likely would have brought up reserves. Finally, with the sunrise the enemy's air force would make an appearance....[25]

So the Cossack cavalry divisions, the tanks and the self-propelled guns plunged on toward Razdel'naia. By midday on 4 April, it had been fully liberated from the fascists. Thus, the final railroad that connected the enemy's formations that were retreating along the coastline together with the rest of the German Sixth Army had been cut. The Soviet troops captured 37 locomotives, 990 loaded railcars and a lot of combat equipment.[26]

However, General Pliev's Cossacks and tankers had no time for rest. The Front Commander-in-Chief General Malinovsky decided to pivot the Mobile Group to the southeast in order to cut the enemy's path of retreat beyond the Dniester. Leaving the 5th Separate Motorized Rifle Brigade in Razdel'naia in order to hold it until the approach of the 37th Army, General Pliev's Mobile Group smashed the enemy troops holding Kuchurgan Station, seized this important enemy strongpoint on the Tiraspol – Odessa highway, and then sharply pivoted to the south.

The enemy's coastal grouping had essentially been split into two parts: to the northwest of Razdel'naia Station were units of the LII and XXX Army Corps and to the southwest of it were units of the XXIX, XXXXIV and LXXII Army Corps. The Sovinformburo on 5 April 1944 announced:

Forces of the 3rd Ukrainian Front continued a successful offensive. Soviet infantry and a cavalry-mechanized formation arrived at the approaches to the town of Razdel'naia. The Germans were stubbornly defending this important communications hub and strongpoint of their defense on the approaches to Odessa. With impetuous blows our soldiers broke the enemy resistance and captured the major railroad hub and town of Razdel'naia. Thus, the Odessa – Tiraspol railroad, as well as the enemy Odessa grouping's main path of retreat to Romania, have been cut by our forces.

Other Soviet units, advancing to the south, took the Odessa Oblast's district centers of Ianovka and Anotono-Kondintsevo and more than a hundred other villages and towns. Retreating under the blows of our forces, the enemy is suffering heavy losses in personnel and equipment. In the course of the day, 25 tanks; 48 guns, of which 11 have a caliber of 150-mm and 7 have a caliber of 210-mm; 460 vehicles, 4 bridging parks and 7 stockpiles of ammunition, food and military property have been captured from the Germans.[27]

With the aim of securing the retreat of their forces, the German command on the morning of 6 April undertook a counterattack out of an area northwest of Budennovka in the direction of Razdel'nia with a portion of the XXXXIV and XXIX Army Corps. The assignment was to link up with units of the LII and XXX Army Corps, reach the crossing sites on the Dniester River at Tiraspol, and withdraw their troops to the right bank of the Dniester River. In the course of savage fighting, the Soviet troops inflicted heavy losses to the enemy, but the bulk of his forces were able

---

25   Pliev, "Stremitel'nyi reid po osvobozhdeniiu Odessy" ["Impetuous raid for the liberation of Odessa"] in *Oni srazhalis' za Odessu: Sbornik vospominanii*, pp. 137-138.

26   *Ukrainska RSR u Velikii Vitchiznianii viini Radianskogo Soiuzu 1941-1945: u 3 t. [Ukraine Socialist Republic in the Great Patriotic War of the Soviet Union 1941-1945: in 3 volumes]* Vol. 3 (Kiev: Vidavnitsvo politichnoi literatury, 1969), p. 37.

27   *Soobshchenie Sovetskogo Informbiuro [Announcements of the Soviet Informational Bureau]* Vol. 6 (Moscow, 1944), pp. 167-168.

to break out of the pocket in the vicinity of Razdel'naia in the 37th Army's sector, and reach the area of Tiraspol.

The commander-in-chief of Army Group "A" was striving at whatever the cost to fix and destroy the Soviet mobile formations and prevent the destruction of the Sixth Army, thereby giving it the opportunity to fall back behind the Dniester River. He was deploying strong blocking detachments in the path of Pliev's Mobile Group and hurling large formations of ground attack aircraft and bombers against it. However, the units of I.A. Pliev, exploiting the nighttime darkness and snowstorm, maneuvering and regrouping, were continuing to rampage through the enemy rear area and were swiftly advancing toward Odessa. By the morning of 6 April, the tankers with fighting broke into Mangeim, while the Cossacks rode into Kagarlyk – into those same populated places where back in the summer of 1941 the heroic defense of Odessa began. Out in front of them were still the bridges across the Dniester River at Karolino-Bugaz and Maiakov, over which the Nazis were hoping to escape encirclement.

Out in front was also Beliaevka, which supplied Odessa with water. In order to liberate it quickly and prevent the fascists from blowing up the water pump station, I.A. Pliev formed a special detachment of reconnaissance troops comprised of his boldest Cossacks and attached a tank company to it. The scouts, using the twilight hours and strong north wind that was carrying rain and snow, made their way stealthily to the 3-meter intake which led into the water, above which a strand of barbed wire had been stretched. The scouts waded around the intake up to their chests in the icy water, and using materials at hand silently negotiated the barbed wire fence. Senior Sergeant S. Larin and Private I. Voichenko took out two sentries without a sound. A third sentry spotted the scouts and opened fire. This raised the alarm, shots rang out, and a hand-to-hand clash erupted between the Cossacks and Nazis. At this moment the tanks, having crashed through the fence, burst onto the grounds of the water pump station. The enemy security detachment was destroyed. The reconnaissance troops and tanks took up an all-round defense. Soon the entire German garrison in Beliaevka rushed toward the station. A fierce battle ensued. However, from the north and east, units of a division of Pliev's Mobile Group were already entering the streets of Beliaevka. When the fighting subsided, sappers cleared the mines from the water pump station and removed several metric tons of explosives.

Meanwhile the adversary, using strong blocking detachments to screen the eastern direction along a line of estuaries, and the northern direction along the Palievo – Vygoda Station line, on the night of 6-7 April directed forces toward Beliaevka. As Lieutenant General I.A. Pliev later remarked, because of carelessness when setting up security, a terrible misfortune almost took place. Knowing that the division was bringing itself back to order, toward morning he decided to get some rest in a home on the northeastern outskirts of Beliaevka. Having spread his felt cloak on the floor, Pliev immediately fell asleep. However, something instantly woke him up. Pliev grabbed a submachine gun and strained to listen. He could hear conversation in the German language coming from an adjacent room. It was already growing light and through an open door he could see two German soldiers. Immediately he fired a burst from his submachine gun at them. Hearing the gunfire, a security platoon of Cossacks rushed into the building and killed the Germans. As became clear, major forces of Germans and Romanians were breaking out of Odessa toward Beliaevka and Maiaki. All of the Mobile Group's available artillery, tanks and self-propelled guns were moved out into direct firing positions, which were covered by minefields and companies of submachine gunners. In the subsequent battle, almost all of the enemy's tanks were knocked out. The Cossacks launched a counterattack. The enemy forces, breaking out toward Beliaevka, were boxed into a swamp and wiped out. Many of them chose captivity over death.[28]

---

28   Pliev, "Vpered na Odessu", pp. 65-73.

Having seized Beliaevka and bridges across the Dniester River on 8 April, units of Pliev's Mobile Group arrived at the gates of Odessa from the west. Just as quickly, the last bridges across the Dniester were captured. The Nazis found themselves trapped between the Black Sea and the broad Dniester estuary. Many German soldiers and officers, seeing the hopelessness of their predicament, ceased resistance and laid down their weapons; there were cases where entire units surrendered in an organized manner.[29]

On 9 April by an order from the 3rd Ukrainian Front's headquarters, Pliev's Mobile Group was given the mission to take Ovidiopol' with part of its forces and to block the path of the enemy's retreat toward the bridges across the Dniester. The Mobile Group's main forces were to reach the Black Sea coastline south of Odessa.

The path of our units, advancing toward Odessa from the direction of Ovidiopol', wasn't easy. The enemy in strong groups began a retreat toward a bridge across the Dniester estuary. The highway became an arena of a fierce clash between Soviet artillerymen and enemy tanks. In the area of Tatarka alone, the Guardsmen of the regiment commanded by Lieutenant Colonel M.S. Sheidin repulsed six enemy counterattacks. In the regiment's anti-tank battery, every shell counted, and thus the artillery crews opened fire only at close ranges. Guncrew commander Sergeant P. Pitaev demonstrated exceptional cool. Eighteen tanks were advancing toward his position. The sergeant allowed them to close and opened fire at pointblank range. With his first shell he knocked out the lead machine. Three more shots thundered – and three more tanks stopped and began smoking. On the boot-heels of the retreating enemy units, Sheidin's regiment burst into Tatarka, where it captured more than 1,000 Nazi soldiers and officers.[30] By the end of 10 April 1944, the main forces of Pliev's Mobile Group had reached the Black Sea coastline.

Meanwhile further to the south on the opening day of the Odessa offensive, forward detachments of the rifle divisions of the 5th Shock Army made rapid progress toward Odessa in a 35-kilometer sector, bypassing enemy strongpoints and destroying enemy detachments on intermediary lines of defense. The forward detachments of the 108th Guards Rifle Division were operating particularly decisively. One forward detachment under the command of Major N.Ia. Chernov by 1500 took the villages of Lombertovo and Nechaiannoe, in the process seizing 50 vehicles, 8 prime movers, 22 guns and mortars, and 8 various stockpiles of items.[31] A second forward detachment of the 311th Rifle Regiment led by Lieutenant Colonel V.P. Fedorov, from the march burst into Tashino and drove the Nazis out of the village.[32]

By the end of day 30 March, the main forces of the 108th Guards Rifle Division after bitter fighting took the villages of Neizats and reached the eastern bank of the Tylihul estuary. Out in front of the 416th Rifle Division, a reconnaissance detachment led by a rifle battalion commander Major V.M. Mel'nik was scouting ahead. In the course of the fighting for Nechaiannoe and further south, units of the 416th Rifle Division together with the 108th Guards Rifle Division successfully routed the enemy. Over the day of combat, more than 900 German soldiers and officers were killed and 230 were captured. In addition, the Soviet troops seized 630 rifles, 118 machine guns, two prime movers and six stockpiles. That evening the 416th Rifle Division took Krasnaia Ukrainka and reached the eastern bank of the estuary that had a 3.5-kilometer dam and three blown bridges.

The 248th Rifle Division was attacking along the Nikolaev – Odessa highway, overcoming enemy resistance centered on strongpoints. By the end of the day it seized the village of Koblevo at the southern end of the Tylihul estuary. On 31 March the 3rd Ukrainian Front's forces in

---

29   *Istoriia Vtoroi Mirovoi voiny 1939-1945*, Vol. 8 (Moscow; Voenizdat, 1977), p. 95.
30   V.I. Chuikov, "Shturm – vpered na Odessa!" ["Assault – forward to Odessa!] in *Oni srazhalis' za Odessu: Sbornik vospominanii*, p. 133.
31   TsAMO RF, F. 1299, Op. 156931, D. 51, l. 41.
32   TsAMO RF, F. 256, Op. 156931, D. 51, l. 41.

cooperation with a landing force from the Black Sea Fleet forced a crossing of the Dnepr – Bug estuary. On 1 April the 5th Shock Army's forces continued the offensive and by the end of the day approached the eastern bank of the Tylihul estuary. A broad water obstacle 15-20 kilometers wide stretched in front of the army's forces across its entire sector of attack.

Intelligence data and prisoner testimonies established that on the approaches to Odessa, just like they did in front of Nikolaev, the Nazi command had prepared four lines of defense:

1. along the western bank of the Tylihul estuary;
2. along the western bank of the Adzhalykskii estuary;
3. along the western bank of the Bol'shoi Adzhalykskii estuary;
4. encircling the city

On all the lines the Germans were deeply entrenched and they had mined the approaches to the Tylihul estuary and the 3.5-kilometer-long dam; all three bridges across the estuary were blown up. They were counting upon the estuary to present a major obstacle to the advance of Soviet forces. On the night of 31 March – 1 April, the 10th Rifle Corps' 86th and 109th Guards Rifle Divisions, in a snowstorm, from the march set about forcing the estuary by wading across a neck of land between the estuary and the Black Sea that had become inundated by the spring floods.

The conditions for forcing a crossing of the Tylihul estuary were simply awful: rain, snow and ice with nothing visible up ahead, and worst of all – the sudden arrival of a cold snap. Everything became soaked and uniforms froze stiff; the horses had icicles and were also chilled to the bone.

From the forward positions of the 86th Guards Rifle Division came reports that the enemy had begun to withdraw from the first line of defense to the second. The army commander ordered for the forward units of the 86th and 109th Guards Rifle Divisions to set about crossing the estuary immediately.[33] The depth of the flooded ground was above the waist. Occasionally up to the shoulders in the icy water, the Guardsmen waded across the 2-kilometer isthmus, overcoming waves that were knocking them off their feet, and seized a bridgehead on the western bank of the Tylihul estuary.

For the next four days, the Germans with uninterrupted counterattacks tried to hurl the Guardsmen back across the estuary. Some of the defensive sectors changed hands repeatedly. The enemy launched a particularly heavy counterattack against the 109th Guards Rifle Division, and it was forced to fall back to the banks of the estuary. The commander of the forward observation post for the 5th Shock Army's long-range artillery group Captain I.I. Makarenko contacted the heavy guns to bring down fire on the counterattacking enemy. After a short interval of time the heavy artillery struck the attacking Nazis; the barrage concluded with a thunderous salvo of fire from a battalion of "Katiusha" rocket launchers. The Guardsmen, having rallied and put the combat formations of the division back into order, rose on the attack, crashed head-on into the enemy that had broken through, and regained possession of their sector of defense.

Simultaneously with the fighting to hold the bridgehead, work was going on to clear the mines from the dam and rebuild the destroyed bridges. The army's 827th Engineer Battalion and the 10th Guards Rifle Corps' 900th Sapper Battalion did the work to repair the bridges under continuous artillery and mortar fire and attacks by enemy fighter-bombers. On 4 April alone, 20 of the combat engineers were killed and several severely wounded. Even so, the sappers and engineers pressed on with the work bravely until all of the bridges had been rebuilt.

Even as this heavy fighting was going on to hold the bridgehead, the commander of the 5th Shock Army decided launch a main attack out of the area of the isthmus between the estuary and

---

33   V. Antonov, "Na Odessu" ["Toward Odessa"] in *Oni srazhalis' za Odessu. Vospominanii uchastnikov*, p. 131.

the Black Sea and to form the army into two echelons. The first echelon – the 10th Guards Rifle Corps – was to breach the enemy's defenses in the Koshary, Hill 45.3 sector and by the end of the day 5 April 1944 reach the Sverdlovo – Novaia Dofinovka line. The second echelon – the 37th Rifle Corps would be introduced into the breach from behind the 10th Guards Rifle Corps' right flank and attack in the northwestern direction toward the "1st of May" State Farm.

Representatives from the 17th Air Army and the Black Sea Fleet arrived at the 5th Shock Army headquarters in order to organize support for the attack. Feverish preparations began. Special attention was given to bringing up ammunition, which was becoming extremely scarce in the frontline units because of the impassable roads. By 4 April, two battalions each of the 11th Guards and 1162nd Cannon-Artillery Regiments were already in their firing positions near the village of Koblevo. Some of the batteries had been deployed to place direct fire. Captain A.S. Skripnikov's 7th Battery performed particularly successfully. The fire of Captain P.I. Ivanov's 4th Battery from defilade positions was also effective; on 4 and 5 April it knocked out two enemy batteries.[34]

On the evening of 4 April, the 10th Guards Rifle Corps (the 86th Guards Rifle, 109th Guards Rifle and 320th Rifle Divisions) with a concerted attack broke through the defenses and crushed the opposing enemy in a night battle. By morning, the corps' forces were continuing to exploit in the direction of Sverdlovo.

At a request from army commander Lieutenant General V.D. Tsvetaev, already at dawn a ground attack squadron of the 5th Guards Storm Aviation Division under the command of Colonel L.V. Kolomeitsev appeared above the army's combat formations. The air strike against the enemy troops was successful, despite the bad weather, and the joy of the men in the rifle units was boundless. All day, every 2-3 hours, our air force struck the enemy, which to a significant extent facilitated an increase in the offensive's pace. The 37th Rifle Corps entered the breakthrough with its main forces and headed in the direction of Koblevo, Koshary and Tishkovka.

The 108th Rifle Division crossed the northern section of the estuary using rafts and boats and pressed on in the direction of Kubanka. In the difficult muddy conditions, the 295th Rifle Division and the 320th Rifle Division forged ahead, smashed the enemy holding the village of Sychavka, took possession of it, and continued to advance in the direction of Vizirka.

At the northern end of the Tylihul estuary, the 108th Guards Rifle and 416th Rifle Division set about making a crossing. The commander of the 108th Guards Rifle Division Colonel S.I. Dunaev readied a first echelon consisting of the 305th Rifle Regiment's 3rd Rifle Battalion. Choosing a moment when the winds had subsided a little, the first echelon set out to make the crossing using rafts and boats. The enemy wasn't anticipating an attempt to cross the estuary in such weather and left only a small screening group in position. With a surpise attack, the Nazis were driven back from the estuary and hurled westward. Behind the first echelon, other units of the division were crossing the estuary.

At dawn on 5 April, the re-assembled 108th Guards Rifle Division struck the northern flank of the Romanian 15th Infantry Division, and the Romanian troops began to flee in panic toward Spiridonovka. The Guardsmen went into a swift advance toward Kalinovka and Novyi Liustdorf, and by the end of the day had taken the villages of Zaria and Trud. A portion of the artillery, motorized and horse-drawn transport was sent around the northern tip of the estuary, where units of the 6th Army were breaking through the enemy's defenses.

Thus, having forced a crossing of the Tylihul estuary and having broken the enemy resistance, the Guardsmen began to advance in two directions. The 5th Shock Army's right flank bypassed Odessa to the north and began to envelop it from the west, advancing toward Ovidiopol', while the left flank pressed on toward the city from the north. Marshal of the Soviet Union V.I. Chuikov,

---

34   TSAMO RF, F. 33, Op. 590155, D. 2567, l. 377.

a twice-Hero of the Soviet Union, recalled "My command and observation posts were mobile. We attacked relentlessly through boggy mud, advancing through Serbka, Blagoevo, Vygoda and Dal'nik."[35]

In the preceding fighting, the 5th Shock Army had achieved its greatest success with nighttime combat operations. So on the night of 5-6 April, the rifle divisions went on the attack, routed the enemy and drove toward the enemy's third line of defense. The Guardsmen of the 108th and 49th Guards Rifle Divisions performed boldy and decisively in the night fighting, and by 0600 on 6 April they took the hills north of Sverdlovo. In the 10th Guards Rifle Corps, the 295th and 320th Rifle Divisions, from the march, slogging through the mud, attacked the enemy in Sverdlovo. The combat for this major populated point was heavy, but the enemy was ultimately defeated and the town was liberated from its fascist occupiers.

The success scored by the Soviet troops in the nighttime combat continued to develop after sunrise as well. The 37th Rifle Corps' right-flanking 108th and 49th Guards Rifle Divisions broke through the enemy's defenses along the Voznesensk – Odessa railroad line, and at 1200 on 6 April, after a short artillery preparation, attacked the enemy on the hills south of Kubanka and broke through to the Kuial'nitskii estuary, while the 308th Rifle Regiment captured Kubanka.[36]

The 248th and 416th Rifle Divisions approached the railroad tracks and northern section of the Il'ichevka State Farm. In the 10th Guards Rifle Corps, the 295th and 320th Rifle Divisions neared the central farmstead of the Il'ichevka State Farm and south of it. There, the enemy greeted our troops with intense and well-organized fire. Preparations began to break through the enemy's defenses. The second echelon 416th Rifle Division out of the Krasnaia Ukrainka area had successfully completed crossing the dam and rebuilt bridges, deployed into a combat formation, and joined battle simultaneously with the other divisions of the 37th Rifle Corps.

Having broken enemy resistance, the army's forces in the course of the day advanced up to 20 kilometers, and reached the line: Ropat'evo, Meshchanka, eastern bank of the Adzhalykskii estuary and approached the enemy's second line of defense. In the course of developing the offensive, the army's commander had concentrated his main force grouping on the army's right flank.

By the end of the day 6 April, the forces of the 8th Guards Army, overcoming every natural obstacle it encountered in its path, the morass of the spring mud, and fierce enemy resistance, approached the Khadzhibeiskii estuary. This presented a serious water obstacle. In its narrowest stretches, the estuary was up to 800 meters wide, and its depth in places approached 2 meters. The fascists had every right to believe that it was here that they would be able to consolidate on the right bank, win time, and organize a defense of Odessa. However, that same night reinforced reconnaissance detachments were crossing the estuary, and at dawn, the 8th Guards Army's main forces followed suit. After heavy fighting that lasted day and night, the forward units took Vygoda.

By 8 April, the forces of the 3rd Ukrainian Front's right flank was looming from the north over the enemy's Odessa grouping, while its left-flank 5th Shock Army had broken through the enemy's third line of defense and cut the Voznesensk – Odessa railroad. Upon reaching the railroad line, the army commander Lieutenant General V.D. Tsvetaev altered the axis of the army's advance from the west to the south. By the morning of 8 April, the 5th Shock Army was already attacking southward between two estuaries, the Kuial'nitskii estuary and the Bol'shoi Adzhalykskii estuary, and by 1000 it had taken Gil'dendorf and Fontanka on the Black Sea coastline northeast of Odessa.

After an artillery preparation, waves of infantry from the rifle regiments rose out of the mud and wet snow and charged the enemy's defenses. In the 248th Rifle Division, Major Shchelkunov's

35   Cited by Karev, *Odessa – Gorod-geroi*, p. 157.
36   TsAMO RF, F. 1229, Op. 12, D. 36, ll. 159-160.

2nd Rifle Battalion led the attack and was the first unit to break into the Il'ichevka State Farm. However, in the subsequent battle the heroic battalion commander was killed. The 295th Rifle Division attacked the central farmstead of the State Farm, and with the assistance of the 320th Rifle Division, Il'ichevka was completely liberated from the Nazis.

The enemy reinforced his forces in this sector with the German 304th Infantry Division with the attached 173rd Field Training Battalion and the the 50th Infantry Division's III/150th Artillery Regiment, in place of the Romanian 15th Infantry Division. From the early morning hours of 7 April, bitter fighting began. The Nazis launched a counterattack and at times the fighting reached the point of hand-to-hand combat. Throughout the day, possession of the Il'ichevka State Farm and railroad changed hands several times. In the middle of the day, the dense cloud cover began to clear, and pilots of the 5th Guards Storm Aviation Division raked the enemy troops with cannon and machine-gun fire. Inspired by the air strikes, the Soviet troops by the end of the day drove the enemy out of the State Farm and spent the following night firmly digging in on the occupied line.

The enemy, striving to check our offensive, on the morning of 8 April again launched counterattacks, which was preceded by air strikes. The *Luftwaffe* in groups of 9-16 Ju-87 and Ju-88 aircraft bombed and strafed the combat positions of the 416th, 248th and 108th Guards Rifle Divisions. At 1100, German attackers out of the area of Aleksandrovka counterattacked the 86th Guards Rifle Division four times. However, the Guardsmen stood firm and repelled all the counterattacks. At 1400 up to a battalion of infantry attacked the 248th Rifle Division out of the Korsuntsy area southwest of Il'ichevka, but had no success.

Having repulsed all of the German counterattacks, troops of the 5th Shock Army resumed the offensive and approached a previously-prepared defensive line with a strongpoint in the village of Gil'dendorf. The enemy met the attackers with organized fire. This line had been built back in 1941 by Soviet sailors when fighting to repel the German offensive. Now the German aggressors were putting up stubborn resistance on this line.

Back on the night of 7-8 April, the commander of the 108th Guards Rifle Division Colonel S.I. Dunaev had sent a small landing force consisting of the 9th Rifle Company of the 308th Rifle Regiment aboard boats along the coastline into the enemy rear. The intense rifle and machine-gun fire from the landing party prompted panic in the defenders and weakened the German grip on the defensive line. Rifle regiments of the 108th Guards Rifle and 416th Rifle Divisions took advantage of the enemy's confusion, and with a sudden and concerted attack broke through the enemy's defenses and took Gil'dendorf.

The 17th Air Army was supporting the combat operations of the 5th Shock Army not only with strikes by ground attack aircraft, but also keeping it supplied with ammunition. On the morning Il'ichevka transport aircraft airdropped boxes of ammunition in the Il'ichevka area, many even without parachutes. In the spring muddy season, the delivery of ammunition by air was a genuine salvation for the troops.

The troops of the 5th Shock Army resumed the offensive between the Kuial'nitskii and Bol'shoi Adzhalyksii estuaries. The 416th Rifle Division from the march attacked German positions in the village of Anatol'evka, and after stubborn fighting, the village was liberated.[37] The commander of the 108th Guards Rifle Division formed a landing force aboard boats with the aim of forcing a crossing of the Kuial'nitskii estuary and launching a sudden attack along its western bank toward Sortirovochnaia Station, which was located on a strip of land between the estuary and the sea.

On the night of 8-9 April, the landing party left on its raid. On that same night the 108th Guards Rifle Division, jointly with the 416th Rifle Division, took the hamlet of Shevchenko and nearby saltworks in heavy fighting. The 248th Rifle Division was continuing to attack along the

---

37   V. Antonov, "Na Odessu", p. 138.

railroad to the south in the direction of Sortirovochnaia Station. The 10th Guards Rifle Corps' 86th Guards Rifle and 320th Rifle Divisions, having taken Aleksandrovka, with a decisive attack broke through to the Black Sea and by 2300 drove the German occupiers out of Kryzhanovka, isolating Odessa from the east. Thereby, the 3rd Ukrainian Front's forces, operating according to a unified plan, routed major enemy forces, and having overcome numerous water obstacles in unbelievably difficult weather conditions reached a jumping-off line for the assault on Odessa by the morning of 9 April 1944.

In the course of the day, with the infantry's arrival on the northern outskirts of the city, the commander of the 5th Shock Army Lieutenant General V.D. Tsvetaev, the commander of the 17th Air Army Colonel General V.A. Sudets and the leader of an operational group of Black Sea steamships Captain I.M. Pis'mennyi worked out an agreement to begin a simultaneous assault on Odessa from the ground, air and sea.

In front of the troops of the 5th Shock Army lay the final, city defensive line on a 2-kilometer isthmus between the Kual'nitskii estuary and Black Sea. The defense of Odessa was placed on the shoulders of the specially-assigned LXXII Army Corps under the command of German General von Forster. The city's defensive line had strong wire obstacles, which on individual directions consisted of three separate belts of wire. Bunkers had been constructed in the area of Luzanovka, and concrete pillboxes on the street intersections and public squares of Odessa. The city had been thoroughly prepared not only for an all-round defense, but also for fighting within the city.

The Soviet forces meticulously prepared to storm Odessa. The formations and units were assigned axes of attack and clusters of blocks and buildings that they were supposed to take. Command and observation posts were moved up closer to the city; intelligence was obtained about the enemy's defenses and strength; and artillery was brought up in order to support the attacking infantry and to counter the approach of enemy ships to the city from the direction of the sea. In front of the soldiers lay the war-torn outskirts of the city, and city buildings and the roofs of apartment buildings were visible. They knew that all of the city's best buildings, port facilities and factories had been mined and wired for demolition. The fascists intended to convert the city into ashes and ruins. It was necessary to attack as quickly as possible. Before the final assault, a decision was made for the artillery not to bombard the city, but to place only direct fire on identified enemy locations and equipment; pilots were not to bomb sectors of the city.

The commander of the 5th Shock Army in connection with the enemy's deeply-echeloned defense ordered the commanders of the rifle corps to arrange their divisions into two echelons. The commander of the 37th Rifle Corps opted to withdraw the 49th Guards Rifle Division into the rear echelon, while in the 10th Guards Rifle Corps the 109th Guards Rifle Division went into the second echelon.

At dawn on 9 April 1944, the assault began on Odessa's urban defensive fringe. After a brief, powerful barrage by the 5th Shock Army's artillery on the isthmus lying between the Kuial'nitskii estuary and the Black Sea, the troops of the 5th Shock Army rose on the attack. The 248th Rifle Division's attack initially made good headway. Its 905th Rifle Regiment (commanded by Colonel D. Filatov), reinforced with the 384th Separate Naval Infantry Battalion, was the first to break through toward Sortirovochnaia Station. The immediate surrounding terrain made for heavy going. The Nazis had blown up the dam in the Luzanovka area, and the resulting flood had covered the station's adjacent ground. The advance was only possible along a railroad embankment that was being swept by enemy fire. The Germans opened heavy fire at the attackers from the direction of the Zhevakhov and the Shkodova hills, as well as from the city.

The commander of the 248th Rifle Division Colonel N.Z. Galai requested air support. The ground attack aircraft suppressed the enemy's artillery on the Zhevakhov and Shkodova hills. At 1400 the attack was resumed. The regiment commander Colonel D. Filatov personally led the attack against Sortirovochnaia Station with Captain Z.M. Salikhov's rifle battalion. The rest of the

248th Rifle Division's rifle regiments joined this attack. Some by wading, others by swimming, the attackers advanced, broke into the station and took possession of it.

On the right flank, the decisive actions of the 108th Guards Rifle Division's reconnaissance battalion, which made a crossing of the estuary, facilitated the 416th Rifle Division's advance toward Sortirovochnaia Station. To the left of the 248th Rifle Division, the divisions of the 10th Guards Rifle Corps were attacking. The 295th Rifle Division swiftly broke into the first enemy trench line, and having overwhelmed the Nazis in hand-to-hand combats, continued to advance. When the dam that had been blown up by the Germans appeared in their path, the soldiers and officers with no hesitation entered the cold water and waded across the icy water obstacle. At 1700 Lieutenant Colonel S.G. Artemov's 1042nd Rifle Regiment became engaged in combat for Kuial'nik Station, while Lieutenant Colonel V.N. Liubko's 1038th Rifle Regiment, jointly with the 248th Rifle Division on its right, completed the storming of Sortirovochnaia Station before pressing on toward the suburb of Peresyp'.

The 86th Rifle Division (commanded by Colonel V.P. Sokolovsky) broke through the positions on the approaches to Peresyp' and fought its way into the eastern portion of the suburb. Subsequently, together with a portion of the 295th Rifle Division, with decisive actions it crushed the enemy occupying Peresyp' and approached the eastern outskirts of Odessa.

The 320th Rifle Division was attacking along the coastline of the Black Sea on the 5th Shock Army's extreme left flank. Its 478th Rifle Regiment attacked with particular elan, and with its energetic actions helped the 86th Guards Rifle Division in the assault against Peresyp'.

By 1900 the army's formations had breached the final German defensive line on the 2-kilometer-wide isthmus between the Kuial'nistkii estuary and the Black Sea and were closing on the outskirts of Odessa. At 2000 the assault against the city began without any artillery preparation. On the evening of 9 April, a division of night bombers under the command of Colonel G.I. Belitsky and the 244th Bomber Aviation Division commanded by Lieutenant Colonel P.V. Nedosekin began to strike enemy ships in the city's port.[38] A directive from the 3rd Ukrainian Front headquarters went out to all the units: the artillery was not to open fire on the city, nor were city districts to be bombed from the air!

Partisans and the underground resistance movement in Odessa rendered significant assistance to the Red Army's forces in the liberation of the city. Exiting the catacombs, they entered into open clashes with the adversary and eliminated enemy detachments that were trying to demolish the city. They brought intelligence to the command of the 3rd Ukrainian Front about the enemy forces, the locations of his batteries, places where the enemy was trying to regroup, and so forth.

The newspaper *Izvestiia* published an article on this day about the Red Army's approach to Odessa:

> Across the flat Odessan steppe, among abandoned cornfields and burned vineyards, past salty estuaries and balkas, full of spring floodwater, the Red Army is swiftly advancing toward the beautiful, battered Odessa.
>
> Down below, beneath the boulevard, lies the enormous port. Sailors around the world know about it. Its first-class facilities have become rusty. Solitary swallows and seagulls circle around the white tower of the darkened lighthouse. The port has died in Romanian possession. Even the *Völkishcher Beobachter* [the official newspaper of the National Socialist German Workers' Party] wrote on 19 July 1943: "Only an insignificant amount is unloaded in Odessa's port in comparison with the previous quantity of commodities."

---

38   TsAMO RF, F. 370, Op. 6518, D. 294, ll. 16-17.

The city is also empty. The cinders and dust of destruction rises above it. In place of the collapsed buildings are piles of "Odessa stone", the yellowish porous limestone. The famous black locust trees that once lined all of Odessa's streets have been chopped down.

That's how Odessa, which the Romanians announced as the capital of the Transnistria, looks now ....[39]

The commander of one of the Soviet divisions later recalled:

The Germans didn't believe in the possibility of such an unprecedented dash by the Soviet troops. They were duped by the speed, by the attacks from the march, when our troops never asked for rest, but demanded combat and attacks, even though this soldier had only recently stormed Nikolaev and taken Ochakov from the Germans. However, I understood my soldiers. That morning I saw what was giving them the strength for the final assault; together with them I caught sight of the walls of Odessa.[40]

On the evening of 9 April, units of General V.D. Tsvetaev's 5th Shock Army entered the northern part of Odessa. That night, troops of the 8th Guards and 6th Armies and of Pliev's Mobile Group also closed in on the city.[41]

Colonel D. Filatov's 905th Rifle Regiment was the first to break into the city; fighting began for each block and each building. Fire was coming in from every direction. Nevertheless, the soldiers were advancing up the Seliansky slope. The gray sky began to grow light. A new day was dawning. The 416th Rifle Division was assaulting the western side of the city. Street fighting continued with growing intensity. Captain Nuraliev's rifle battalion was making the greatest progress in the division; in incessant attacks, it was fighting its way into the southwestern quarters of the city.

In the 295th Rifle Division, the commander of the 1038th Rifle Regiment's 2nd Rifle Battalion Major I.U. Gashenko was born in Odessa and grew up in the city. He had the good fortune to liberate his native city, and took first the machine-building factory, and then the tannery with an impetuous attack. In order to accelerate the pace of the offensive, the commander of the 1040th Rifle Regiment instructed his deputy Major F.N. Zaveriukha to take command of a group of submachine gunners. During an attack against one enemy strongpoint in a large building, the soldiers under Major Zaveriukha crept up to a point immediately adjacent to the building, showered the Germans with grenades, and then burst into the building. In the course of hand-to-hand combat, 10 Nazis were killed and the rest taken prisoner. However, Major F.N. Zaveriukha fell courageously in this action, and he was buried on the grounds of the Odessa Infantry School on the day of the city's liberation.

The 248th Rifle Division, commanded by N.Z. Galai, set about assaulting the city in the direction of Moskovskaia Street, advanced as far as the bridge on the Seliansky slope, then pushed on further along Korolenko Street to the Opera House and the naval port. It was the first to reach the city center. Troops of the 905th Rifle Regiment captured the Sabaneev Bridge and a group of submachine gunners hustled toward the Opera House. The combat in this area was brief. The Opera House had been wired for demolition, but partisans had been able to cut the wires, while the division's combat engineers checked every nook and cranny of the building, disarming and removing every powerful delayed-action bomb they came across.

---

39   *Izvetsiia*, 9 April 1944.
40   Cited by Shternshtein, *Morskie vorota Gorod-geroi*, p. 197.
41   R.K. Rokossovsky, *V boiakh za osvobozhdenie Ukrainy* [*In the fighting for the liberation of Odessa*] (Kiev: Ukraina, 2000), p. 60.

Meanwhile, Major General D.M. Syzranov's 416th Rifle Division, Major General I.I. Shvygin's 320th Rifle Division and Colonel V.P. Sokolovsky's 86th Guards Rifle Division were fighing their way into the northeastern and northern sectors of the city. Major General Shvygin's 320th "Enakievo" Rifle Division was engaged in fighting in the city's industrial area, attacking toward Peresyp'. That evening I.I. Shvygin ordered a group of reconnaissance troops to be formed, comprised of the most audacious soldiers, who were to break though to Odessa, sow panic in the enemy rear and thereby hinder demolition work in the city and port, as well as the evacuation of enemy troops. At 2200 the group of scouts, headed by General Shvygin himself, under the cover of darkness stepped off on the attack and managed to fight their way to the port. Major General Shvygin reported about this over the radio to the commander of the 5th Shock Army V.D. Tsvetaev. Reinforcements hastened to the port area, and soon it was mopped up of the enemy. All night, fighting went on on the streets of Moldovanka, in the suburb of Krivaia Balka and on the western outskirts of Odessa. The enemy offered especially tough resistance along the coastal streets and in the port.

Captain I.M. Pis'mennyi together with an operational group from the Black Sea Shipping Company was situated in the area of Zhevakhov Hill. They were reporting to the commander and army headquarters that the 2nd Brigade of Torpedo Boats, Black Sea Fleet pilots and submarines were operating on the enemy's lines of communications, preventing the evacuation of troops and plundered property by sea.

Aircraft of the Black Sea Fleet operating from the Skadovsk airfield were taking part in strikes against enemy transports in Odessa's port and on the open sea. Three groups of naval aircraft in the course of the day sank an enemy transport that displaced 3,000 metric tons of water, and damaged a patrol boat, two barges and a transport carrying 1,500 metric tons of cargo.

On the morning of 10 April, troops of the 5th Shock Army began wrapping up the fighting in the city. The 108th Guards Rifle Division drove the enemy out of the northwestern sector of the city. In the street fighting, Odessan privates T.D. Eshotkin, I.M. Tolstokorov, I.I. Evsiukov, A. Kozyev and L.L. Shamin stood out, as did Sergeant I.A. Dudin. During the fighting for the city, the division killed 500 fascist soldiers and officers and captured 150 more, and seized 200 vehicles, 16 guns, 23 prime movers, 7 military trains and 15 various stockpiles.[42]

The 416th Rifle Division was engaged in combat in the southwestern sector of the city. The enemy was resisting with heavy and continuous fire from attics and cellars. However, the experience acquired in the street fighting for Melitopol and Nikolaev came in handy for the troops, and from building to building, cover from cover, eliminating the enemy, they kept making progress. A rifle company under the command of Senior Sergeant Zuev forged ahead and was the first to reach the southwestern outskirts of the city. Upon reaching the western and southwestern outskirts of Odessa, the 108th Guards Rifle Division and 416th Rifle Division at 1000 linked up with forward units of the 6th and 8th Guards Armies and Pliev's Mobile Group. The 905th Rifle Regiment of the 248th Rifle Division was fighting its way toward Artema Street, and ran into heavy rifle and machine-gun fire coming from a corner building. Sergeant I. Sokolov's squad, moving around the building to the rear, attacked and wiped out the enemy nest. The advance resumed, but from out of the ruins of a building on Krasnaia Gvardiia Street, the enemy opened up intense machine-gun fire. Anti-tank rifleman A. Mamedov with several accurate shots from his anti-tank rifle silenced the machine-gun crew, while Senior Sergeant I. Petrov's squad broke into the ruins and captured a large group of enemy soldiers and officers.

The 295th Rifle Divison was also mopping up the final resistance in the city center. A large amount of military loot was captured by units of this division in the city: 825 vehicles; 20

---

42   TsAMO RF, F. 1229, Op. 1, D. 9, l. 145.

locomotives; 500 railcars, the majority of which were loaded with inventory; and 18 fueltank cars filled with gasoline. It also captured 142 enemy soldiers and officers.[43]

The 86th Guards Rifle Division was mopping up the city's eastern sector. The 320th Rifle Division had fully taken the sea port and the areas adjacent to it. In the course of the night of 9-10 April and on the next morning, troops of the 5th Shock Army were mopping up the final pockets of resistance within the city in the areas of Bankovskaia, Tovarnaia Station, south of the train station, south of the October Revolution Square, the city park and on Chumki Hill, and by 1000 they had taken complete possession of the city.

The famous Stalingrad sniper V. Zaitsev performed valiantly in the fighting for Odessa. By this time he was commanding an anti-aircraft company of the 79th Guards Rifle Division. The anti-aircraft machine-gun crews of Zaitsev's company, while covering the vanguard elements from enemy aerial attacks, often engaged enemy ground troops – infantry and anti-tank riflemen. On the approaches to the southwestern outskirts of the city, in the vicinity of the jute factory, Zaitsev personally led his company, operating as an ordinary rifle element, on the attack, and in conjunction with Lieutenant Vladimir Burda's rifle company, captured a military airbase. The attack was so swift that a squadron of German fighters that was operating from this airbase didn't have time to take off. The entire squadron of 18 Messerschmitt fighters became a trophy for the anti-aircraft gunners.[44]

The 384th Separate Battalion of Naval Infantry, the Novorossiisk 2nd Brigade of Torpedo Boats, Black Sea Fleet pilots and submarines all took direct part in the battle for Odessa. The submarines and torpedo boats operated against enemy sea lines of communication, preventing the enemy from evacuating troops and plundered items by sea to Romanian ports. In the skies above Odessa, the pilots of the 5th Guards Torpedo Bomber and 40th Divebomber Aviation Regiments particularly stood out: Major M.I. Burkin, Captain A.G. Alfimov, Lieutenant V.I. Minakov, Captain I.I. Kutsenko and others. Fighter pilots of the 11th Guards, 6th and 36th Fighter Aviation Regiments also fought heroically.

Once the fighting subsided, thousands of jubilant residents of the city emerged onto the streets and public squares. They were embracing the liberating soldiers and volunteering to serve as guides and drivers. Women and old men, having armed themselves with whatever they came across, were ferreting out Nazis still hiding in attics and cellars, and turning them over to Soviet troops. The residents were bringing tables out into the middle of the street and offering to all the troops whatever food they had available.

Soviet sappers were also moving along streets from building to building, leaving behind laconic signs: "Checked. No mines". Meanwhile at the order of Colonel Galai, the regiment commanders of the 248th Rifle Division each selected a battalion that had most distinguished itself in the street fighting. At midday, the battalions fell into a full-dress assembly in front of the Opera House and froze at the command, "Ten-hut!" The division commander together with the regiment commanders and flagbearers emerged on the balcony of the Opera House and hoisted a scarlet banner in ceremonial silence.

Owing to the energetic, well-coordinated actions of the troops of the 3rd Ukrainian Front and the fighters of the underground resistance movement, the city was saved from complete destruction. The enemy had been beaten and hurled back beyond the Dniester River. A large amount of loot was captured in the city: thousands of vehicles, guns and mortars; more than 100 tanks; and a lot of other military inventory. Altogether in the fighting for the city, the adversary lost more than 5,000 killed and wounded, and 1,100 soldiers and officers taken prisoner. The remnants of the

---

43   TsAMO RF. F. 295, Op. 139082, D. 1.
44   Chuikov, *V boiiakh za Ukrainu*, [In the fighting for Ukraine] (Kiev: Politizdat, 1972), p. 271.

shattered German IV and XVII Army Corps and the Romanian III Army Corps were in retreat toward Ovidiopol'.

On this same day, in honor of the liberation of Odessa, Moscow gave a 324-gun salute of 24 volleys. The exploits of more than 13,000 soldiers and officers – the liberators of Odessa – were noted with high government honors.

In the fighting for Odessa, the 248th, 416th and 6th Guards Rifle Divisions; the 4th Guards Cavalry Corps; the 9th Composite Aviation Corps; the 62nd Engineer-Sapper Brigade; the 87th Guards Mortar Regiment; the 91st Separate Signals Regiment and many others particularly distinguished themselves. The units and formations that stood out were honored with Orders and the Guards title, and 27 of them received the honorific designation "Odessa".[45]

It should be particularly noted that the operations of the 3rd Ukrainian Front was marked by a high degree of coordination, including as well with the fighters of Odessa's underground resistance movement. The commander of the 8th Guards Army General V.I. Chuikov had every justification to write later: "The entire Odessa operation, undoubtedly, has entered history as one of the most glittering with respect to the excellent, smooth coordination that had been instilled in the armies of the 3rd Ukrainian Front. Several armies were operating in one and the same rhythm, at one and the same tempo, each carrying out its assignment in its own sector."[46]

The troops of the Red Army and sailors of the Black Sea Fleet, together with popular militiamen and the workers of the city back in 1941 had defended Odessa for two and a half months against a vastly superior enemy force. Soviet troops, in contrast, liberated the city in 24 hours. The enemy's Odessa grouping had ceased to exist. An order from the Supreme Commander-in-Chief stated, "Today, 10 April, as a result of a skillful outflanking maneuver by infantry and mobile formations, in combination with a frontal assault, troops of the 3rd Ukrainian Front seized an important economic and political center of the country, an oblast' capital of Ukraine, and a first-class port on the Black Sea – Odessa – a powerful strongpoint in the German defenses, covering the path to central areas of Romania."[47]

The operation to liberate Odessa became, obviously, one of the the least-bloody in the history of the Great Patriotic War. The losses sustained during the storming of the city were so light, that it is paradoxical but a fact that they've been concealed up to the present day, so as not to cast a shadow over other operations. Thus, the liberation of Odessa can be called one of the most brilliant operations of the Second World War, because it cost so little blood. Over the course of two weeks the enemy's Odessa grouping was enveloped from the north by an impetuous dash. In essence, Odessa became caught in a pocket. When you compare the liberation of Odessa with the liberation of other cities, the impression forms that Rodion Malinovsky, a native Odessan, surpassed everyone else in his desire to spare the city and residents of Odessa. When implementing his plan, the Marshal of the Soviet Union Malinovsky didn't commit a single strategic error! His subordinates also matched him in this desire to protect the city. With little cost in human blood or damage to the city, the fascists were simply forced out of it. This stands in contrast to the general manner of force operations conducted by the Soviet command, which simply took no consideration of the losses suffered by fellow countrymen. In the liberation of Odessa, there was no heroic self-sacrificial hurling of a body onto the muzzle of a nearby enemy firing point in order to block the fire coming from it, no suicidal dash beneath an enemy tank with a bundle of grenades. The city was liberated intelligently, swiftly and decisively.

45   Chuikov, "Shturm – vpered na Odessu", p. 136.
46   Ibid., p. 142.
47   Cited in Shternshtein, *Morskie vorota Ukrainy*, p. 198.

11

Odessa rises from the ruins

The most damaging and irreplaceable were Odessa's demographic losses: whereas the 1939 Census showed more than 601,600 people were living in Odessa, then at the time of the city's liberation in April 1944, this number had fallen to around 250,000.[1] If at the beginning of January 1941 Odessa's industrial plants employed 79,600 employees (including 50,600 workers), then after the war in the best case the number of workers was in the hundreds.

The damage done by the occupiers to the city's cultural and historical treasures, created by the talent and labor of multiple generations of Odessans, was enormous, irreplaceable and not fully calculated even to the present day. An investigation done by the Extraordinary Government Commission immediately after the city's liberation discovered that rare museum valuables had been plundered from Odessa's art museums by the occupational authorities: more than 200 paintings done by masters of the paintbrush (Repin, Ivanov, Kuindzhi, Savrasov, Makovsky, Nesterov and others), dozens of porcelain objects, sculptures, bronze items, ivory articles, ancient weapons, artistic furniture sets, tapestries, rugs and so forth. The plundered Odessan archives, libraries, museums and other exhibits have still not been able to restore their collections to the point that existed prior to the war.

Retreating under the blows of the Soviet Army, the Nazi vandals had strived to destroy Odessa completely: they burned, blew up and converted factories and plants into ashes and ruins, as well as some of Odessa's most famous buildings, including the A.S. Pushkin Museum, the Sabansky Barracks and other monuments of material culture from the early 19th Century. At the cost of unparalleled efforts and at the risk of their own lives, Soviet troops and partisans managed to save the majority of the city, but the fascists still inflicted enormous damage to it. Of the 990 plants and factories in Odessa Oblast, 733 were partially or completely destroyed. The port and railroad station lay in ruins. Almost all of the businesses of the food industry and consumer services had been destroyed: not a single bread factory remained intact, and not a single bank was working. The occupiers plundered and ravaged 17 hospitals and polyclinics, 55 nurseries, and 29 health spas, and burned down or blew up 2,290 major buildings that were of great architectural or historical value.[2] The damage done to the residential areas of Odessa and Odessa Oblast was also enormous: 954,000 square meters of floor space and 2,900 residential and administrative buildings in the city had been wrecked, and 13,000 residences on the territory of the oblast had been destroyed. The total damage done to Odessa Oblast equaled 27.5 billion rubles.[3]

1   DAOO, F.R. 1234, Op. 7, Spr. 405, l. 27.
2   *Niurnberg protsess: Sbornik materialov; v 2 t.* [*Nuremburg trials: Collection of materials, in 2 volumes*], Vol. 1 (Moscow, 1955), p. 767.
3   DAOO, F.R. 1234, Op. 1, Spr. 20, Ark. 15.

The chairman of the City Executive Committee during the occupation and restoration of Odessa B.P. Davidenko recalled:

> On many of the streets, the skeletons of buildings were smoking; other buildings lay in piles of rubble or had gaping holes in the walls. The fascists had inflicted more than 1,250 million rubles worth of damage to municipal facilities and services. Late one night I took a detour road through the city and arrived at the city executive committee, which at the time was temporary located on Lev Tol'stoy Street. The first resolution that was taken, and that was posted on 11 April around the city, was dedicated to resuming work at industrial enterprises and in the city's departments and offices.[4]

The port was in particularly bad shape. In an Act regarding the losses and damage inflicted by the Nazi German aggressors and their allies, which was compiled by a specially-created commission, there is the note: "The entire port has been damaged with the exception of five quays and 90% of the storage space." There follows a list of destroyed facilities, machinery, floating rigs and residential buildings. The damage done to the port was put at 218 million rubles. The Military, Platonovsky and Oil and Gas docks were almost completely destroyed, as were the New, Coal and Watermelon wharves together with the warehouses, machinery, service buildings and other facilities located at them. All of the port's floating rigs were completely destroyed and only 10% of the port's machinery remained functional. Of the port's residential and service buildings, 58% lay in ruins.[5]

Foreign specialists visited Odessa in 1944. Seeing the damage done to the port, they were shaking their heads: "This is long-time damage. This is very long-time damage."[6] However, despite all the pessimistic prognoses – the port was put back into service again in the shortest time-span. Preparation to rebuild the Port of Odessa began in essence back when the war was in full swing, long before the city's liberation, when the intense struggle between the German demolition teams and the Soviet patriots, who were striving to save the port's dockage and infrastructure from complete destruction. Already on the afternoon of 10 April, at a time when the discharges of artillery pieces were still audible, work to rebuild the port got underway.

The springtime sun was illuminating the long rows of ruins of charred buildings. Stockpiles of inventory and grain were still smoldering. The port's territory and offshore area had been mined, and the port was cluttered with shells and bombs that had been wired by the fascist to trigger the detonation of explosives, burned out fueltank cars and railcars, and piles of rubble and plundered property. Motor boats, barges, dredgers and other watercraft had been sunk on the berth, blocking the approach of ships. The harbor breakwater had been damaged, and waves were crashing through gaps in the seawall and inundating the wharves. The legendary Vorontsov lighthouse was no longer indicating to ships the safe route in storms and bad weather. They were only able to make their way cautiously into the port through the wreckage following lanes cleared by sappers. It was dangerous to diverge from the course, because all the surrounding water still held mines.

Early on the morning of 11 April 1944, machine operators, field engineers, freight handlers, workshop laborers and sailers were already showing up outside the Black Sea Shipping Company. Throughout the period of occupation, they had evaded labor duties and were working to undermine all of the measures enacted by the occupational regime. Yet from the very first day after

---

4   Cited in Karev, *Odessa: Gorod-geroi* [*Odessa: Hero city*] (Moscow: Voenizdat, 1978), p. 163.
5   Shternshtein, *Morskie vorota Ukrainy* [*Maritime gates of Ukraine*] (Odessa: Odesskoe oblastnoe izdatel'stvo, 1958), pp. 198-199.
6   Cited by Karev, *Odessa: Gorod-geroi*, p. 167.

the liberation, more than a thousand people actively set to work to restore the vandalized and damaged port complex. For the first step it was necessary to clear the territory and offshore area of mines, shells, bombs and all sorts of "cunning surprises" left behind by the foe with the aim of converting the port into a stealthy death zone. The front was demanding replenishments and ammunition, and the port had to get back to work as soon as possible. Together with the sappers, dockworkers set to work to disarm and remove high-explosives, clear booby-traps, and raise the sunk ships, wagons, vehicles and artillery pieces from the bottom of the harbor. Step by step, at the risk of life, they were regaining each meter of the port's territory. A.G. Rump recalled, "Shells were still exploding on all three floors of the Northern Warehouse, and passing vehicles were still encountering mines, but the recruited labor brigades were saving grain in the burning warehouses, clearing rubble and filling in craters. This work didn't go by without casualties."[7]

In the course of 42 days, 24,689 artillery shells, 987 aerial bombs, 570 hand grenades, 80 demolition charges (with a total weight of 5,460 kilograms), as well as booby traps, wired artillery shells and howitzer shells, anti-personnel mines and other dangerous devices were disarmed and removed from the grounds and offshore area of the port.[8] The rapid clearing of explosives, wreckage, captured guns from the territory and the painstaking sweeping of the port's waters made it possible to initiate repair work quickly.

By the middle of May 1944 the port's labor collective now consisted of 2,200 workers, employees and engineers. By this time, a large amount of the repair work had been completed: five dry-cargo and oil-loading terminals for large-capacity ships were operational; the repair and construction site had been repaired; a number of the annexes had re-opened; eight gantry cranes were back in operation; the piles of rubble of demolished buildings had been cleared; an artesian well with a flowrate of 40 cubic meters an hour had been repaired; and motorboats were back in working order.

On the first day of liberation the executive committee of the Odessa City Council of Workers' Deputies announced the resumption of work of the city's industrial enterprises. Odessans in a multitude of meetings and gatherings swore to make their contribution to the ultimate destruction of the foe and to repair and rebuild their native city as quickly as possible. They were declaring, "Odessa will be reborn from the ashes and ruins; Odessa will be even more beautiful than it once was!" At a meeting attended by the Commander-in-Chief of the 3rd Ukrainian Front R.Ia. Malinovsky, a fellow townsman and liberator of his native city, citizens took on the full responsibility for its restoration: "We consider it a duty of our civic honor to repair everything in Odessa that was destroyed by the German and Romanian occupiers and to revive our full-blooded social life. We firmly believe that our beloved Odessa will again quickly enter the leading ranks of the blossoming cities of Soviet Ukraine."[9] The Ukrainian authors M. Ryl'sky and Iu. Ianovsky in the April days of 1944 wrote: "By his very nature, an Odessan is an optimist. The humor of a resident of the south is coupled with activity and enterprise, a cheerful song with a zeal for work. He immediately gets to work. Odessa will rise out of the ashes and ruins."[10] With rough and dangerous work, the arduous period of the city's rebirth began.

One of the first and most important tasks was the cleansing of Odessa's streets from the fascist filth that remained in the city in the form of names given to the streets under occupation and

7   Shternshtein, *Morskie vorota Ukrainy*, p. 200.

8   Ibid.

9   V.I. Chuikov, "Shtum – vrpered na Odessu!" [Assault – forward to Odessa!"] in *Oni srazhalis' za Odessu: Sbornik vospominanii* [*They fought for Odessa: Collection of recollections*] (Odessa, 1998), p. 135; *Odessa v Velikoi Otechestvennoi voine Sovetskogo Soiuza: Sbornik dokumentov i materialov* [*Odessa in the Great Patriotic War of the Soviet Union: Collection of documents and materials*] Vol. 3 (Odessa, 1951), p. 28.

10   B. Davidenko, "Gorod vozrozhdaetsia" ["The city returns to life"] *Geroicheskaia Odessa: Sbornik statei i materialov* [*Heroic Odessa: Collection of articles and materials*] (Odessa, 1945), p. 118.

their associated road signs – free Odessans couldn't live on A. Hitler Street or Antonescu Street. Thus on 12 April the executive committee of the Odessa City Council issued Decree No. 5 "On the restoration of the previous names of the streets of Odessa and the removal of signs and notices with German or Romanian lettering". The decree gave three days for all responsible individuals to remove from buildings all the "signs, placards, notices, announcements, sign posts, etc., written in the German or Romanian languages, and in the same period of time to post new ones with their former names and to freshen up the numbering on the buildings."

In the city there was not a single block or sidewalk paving stone without damage. Soon the streets were cleared of the rubble of buildings; the gaping holes in the walls of the buildings were patched with stone; and glass once again sparkled in the windows. Over 25 days, the public water supply system and power station that had been blown up by the enemy were rebuilt – the city again began to receive water and electrical energy. One after another, industrial enterprises were put back into service and began supplying the front with their output. With time, the large craters caused by bombs were filled in, and the hollows marking the locations of former barricades were leveled out.

In May 1944, railroad service resumed on the Odessa – Kiev and Odessa – Moscow railways. On 27 June 1944, the first passenger trains departed Odessa for Kiev and Moscow. Similarly, on 24 June the State Committee of Defense enacted a special decree "About initial measures to rebuild the ports and shipyards of the People's Commissariat of the Fleet in the cities of Odessa, Nikolaev and Kherson", which established a concrete program for making these ports operational again.

The frontlines still ran not far from Odessa. Fitfully clinging to defensive lines, the German forces were offering stubborn resistance to the units of the advancing Soviet Army. The city and port were subjected to enemy airstrikes. In the course of 5 August 1944, 298 fragmentation bombs were dropped on the grounds and offshore area of the port. The city's headquarters of the Local Air Defense system, just as back in the days of the city's heroic defense, contined to work efficiently and strenuously. Bomb shelters were re-opened, slit trenches were dug, and command centers were re-equipped. First-aid teams and ambulances were constantly on duty.

The ruins were yielding under the concurrent on-slaught of Odessa's workers. Neither enemy air strikes nor the absence of electrical power, water supply and necessary materials slowed the rapid pace of the rebuilding work. Tens of thousands of workers, primarily women, arrived at the port and at plants and factories to repair the damaged buildings. Voluntary Saturday workdays and clean-ups were systematically organized. People arriving from evacuation and returning, demo-bilized troops after the victorious conclusion of the war were quickly included in the process of repairing and rebuilding Odessa.

The rapid restoration of operation to the enterprises contributed to a piecemeal return of evacu-ated factory equipment and machinery, as well as supplies from the central regions of the country. For example, if in the first weeks after liberation workers of the January Uprising factory and the shipyard repaired only military equipment and vehicles, then already in May 1944 they began to produce their basic types of production. The labor collectives at the October Revolution, Red Profintern, Starostin and other factories of Odessa were stubbornly working to get production up and running again.

In the city, regular peacetime life began to return. On 21 April, classes at Odessa State University resumed. Altogether in April 1944, seven of Odessa's higher education institutions re-opened, and by the end of the year, fifteen. A majority of the scientific research institutions also resumed opera-tion. Collectives from the higher education and academic institutions rendered real help to the recovery of the city, its communal economy, industry and agriculture.[11] Already in April 1944,

---

11   *Chornomor'ska kommuna*, 6 May 1944.

the oblast newspapers *Chernomorska kommuna* and *Bol'shevistskoe znamia* resumed circulation, as did 28 district newspapers. The articles they published were calling for the mobilization of all the resources and exertions to restore the city and oblast economy that had been destroyed by the war in the shortest time possible.

On 28 May 1944, the Odessa State Academic Theater of Opera and Ballet opened. By the end of the year, seven theaters and eight movie theaters were open again in Odessa. Theatrical troupes were traveling to the front to put on shows, as well as giving on-site performances for the oblast's workers.[12]

In September 1944, the city schools re-opened. By the end of 1945, the school children of Odessa and Odessa Oblast were studying in more than 1,300 schools (including 75 primary, 7-year and middle schools in Odessa).[13] The insufficient qualification of the majority of the teachers; the large gaps in the knowledge of the students because of the absence of appropriate education during the years of occupation; the significant number of so-called "over-age children", who were no longer school age; and almost the complete lack of material, study guides, notebooks and textbooks were all hindering the teaching process. The occupiers destroyed almost all of the school libraries, and in the first school year they were partially restored in only 383 schools.[14]

On its 150th anniversary, marked by new labor accomplishments in September 1944, Odessa again felt the concern and attention of other cities of Ukraine. Kiev residents in their greeting wrote, "… the fascists inflicted heavy wounds on Odessa. However, already a powerful symphony of creative reconstructive work is pealing on the shore of the Black Sea and the picturesque streets and squares of the belle Odessa – Ukraine's southern outpost. The labor of the Odessans is closely aligned with the labor of the citizens of Kiev, Stalingrad and Leningrad."

The captains of many ships were preparing to journey to Odessa from the first day of its liberation, considering it an honor to be the first of the Black Sea merchant sailors to arrive at the Port of Odessa. In order to bring the desired moment closer, the sailors in many of the country's ports donated their weekly earnings to the fund to get the Port of Odessa re-opened, and on 7 October 1944 Odessa's port became operational again, when the first Soviet ships – the *Kalinin* and the *Dmitrov* docked at its quayside. Less than six months was necessary to get the almost fully destroyed port complex working again; foreign specialists had considered the damage irreparable.

Navigation pilot S.S. Dymchenko demonstrated great skill when guiding the first ships into and out of the port. The port's immediate offshore area was still strewn with enemy mines, and the guiding of ships required a great deal of job knowledge and caution. The dockworkers began to load ammunition supplies, weapons, food and other cargo in order to assist the Soviet troops that were driving the enemy to the west. On 25 October 1944 the Soviet tanker *Sovneft'*, loaded with 10,000 metric tons of fuel, arrived at Odessa's port. Given its draft of 8.85 meters, its navigation along the channel that still hadn't been completely cleared of mines wasn't without risk. Having carefully studied the situation and having convinced himself that there was a narrow passage between the sunken ships that were obstructing the entrance to the oil terminal, V.I. Koval' steered the ship through the opening. Thousands of metric tons of fuel began to leave the Port of Odessa, bound for the Danube River. The tanker fleet was inadequate, so the the petroleum tankcars that had been abandoned by the enemy were coupled, filled with fuel, and towed to the Danube.

The most rapid restoration of Odessa's port had an important military-strategic significance and for the significant deliveries to the USSR through Lend-Lease. Throughout the war, there were three primary routes for the shipment of Lend-Lease supplies, and in particular armored

---

12 *Chornomor'ska kommuna*, 30 May 1944.
13 DAOO, F.R. 2000, Op. 3, Spr. 31, Ark. 99.
14 DAOO, F.R. 2000, Op. 3, Spr. 30, Ark. 101.

vehicles: a northern route to the ports of Arkhangel'sk and Murmansk; a southern route to the ports of Odessa and Baku; and a Far East route to the city of Vladivostok. A significant share of the American M4A2 Sherman tanks and of the 149 British Valentine tanks that arrived via Lend-Lease in 1944 at the southern ports went by the shortest route: through Odessa to the front. The route through liberated Odessa, where due to the winding down of the Baku operations in February 1945 a new department to handle the arrival of armored fighting vehicles was opened, became the last major direction for Allied deliveries. The delivery of fuel and other types of products via Lend-Lease actively passed through the port.

Soviet citizens, freed from fascist slavery, returned to their native land aboard ships that arrived in Odessa, as did national assets that had been plundered by the fascist aggressors. The property and equipment of the Kinap and Red Signal factories, medical instruments, and the inventory of the opera and ballet theater were returned to Odessa aboard the ships *Terek* [a river that rises in the Caucusus and winds its way north and east to the Caspian Sea], *Syzran'* [an oblast in Samara Oblast] and *Odesskii Gorsovet* [*Odessa City Council*].

The city's enterprises, higher education institutions and schools were gradually getting back to business. The city's transport, communications and water and drainage systems were put back into working order. Through the efforts of the population, 35,000 quadratic meters of living space were rehabilitated. It was on these days that the observation of the central *Pravda* newspaper appeared on its pages: "The occupiers tried to stop the city's development and to set it back dozens of years. However, the love of the Odessans for their own city, their energy, enterprising spirit and tenacity at work gives every justification to hope that the city will quickly be rebuilt. It will become even more marvelous than it was before."[15]

Many cities of the country assisted in getting the devastated Odessa back on its feet. Locomotives from Kolomensky [a municipal district of Moscow Oblast], vehicles from Moscow's Automotive Works, machine tools from Gor'kii, and electric power carts from Sverdlovsk were arriving. Ships came in from Leningrad and Vladivostok, in order to change their port of origin to Odessa. Ship repairers from Leningrad and Baku, machine-tool builders from Moscow and Gor'kii, metallurgists from Dnepropetrovsk and Kuznetsk, miners from the Donbass and lumberjacks from the Carpathian Mountains, and hundreds and thousands of the country's production, scientific and cultural collectives were coming to the aid of Odessa. They were arriving not only to help rebuild and restore, but also to create new production, social and other facilities.

Odessa's longshoremen already in the first month of operation (October 1944) handled 18 ships. By the end of 1944, the trans-shipping turnover of cargo at the Port of Odessa amounted to 89,100 metric tons of the 61 ships that were processed. On 20 February 1945 the first ocean-going ships carrying hundreds of thousands of tons of cargo designated to revitalize the economies of Ukraine, Belorussia and Moldavia arrived at Odessa's port. In these days one of the ship convoys delivered powerful overhead gantry cranes for Odessa's port as well. The caterpillar-tracked cranes ready at hand on the decks were started up by crane operators, disembarked under their own power, and went into operation.

The port was working intensively. In the harbor there were long lines of ships loaded with cargo needed for the front or the national economy. In the course of the last three months of 1944 and the first quarter of 1945, 300 large-tonnage and oil tankers were already processed. By the end of 1945, the number of port workers exceeded the pre-war number by 20%. Already in the war years, in 1944-1945 the USSR national budget allocated more than 63,000,000 rubles to the rebuilding of Odessa's port.[16] However, the main resource for the re-opening of Odessa's port, which had been conceivably set back in its development by a dozen years, was the vitality of its residents.

---

15   Cited by Shternshtein, *Morskie vorota Ukrainy*, p. 209.
16   Ibid., p. 213.

In January 1945, already 215 plants and factories that had been fully or partially rebuilt were now operating in Odessa. Approximately 159,000 square meters of living space had been rehabilitated (74,500 of which through the efforts of the people themselves). In 1945, 308 industrial enterprises became operational. However, this was only the start of the rebuilding work, since when resurrecting their city the Odessans directed their main efforts to assist the front, in order to bring about the long-awaited moment of final victory more quickly. Two squadrons of combat aircraft were created through the donations of Odessa's residents to the Victory Fund in 1944-1945.[17]

In the Five-Year Plan for the resurrection and development of the USSR's national economy for the years 1946-1950, Odessa was included on the list of seven high-priority cities of Ukraine that required the immediate reconstruction of housing and communal services.[18] For the rebuilding of industry in the years 1946-1950 the city received 1.2 billion rubles on a centralized basis.[19] The amount of capital investments in the city's economy over the same time period amounted to 770,000,000 rubles.[20] Particular attention was paid to developing the the light and food industries, which met the needs of the city's population in clothing, nutrition and social services.

For the further restoration and reconstruction of Odessa's port, 120,000,000 rubles were allocated, which allowed two deep-water berths to be built and put into operation; to restore and reconstruct the quayside area of the Coal and New moles; to erect new gantry cranes; and to construct tens of thousands of square meters of storage space. In this same year, the legendary *Slava* fleet of whalers set out for the first time from Odessa's port, bound for the shores of the Antarctic.[21] The Black Sea Shipping Company was replenished with such large ships as the *General Cherniakhovsky, Admiral Ushakov, A. Pushkin* and *Chernigov*. A number of additional ships were acquired through reparations. Among them were large passenger ships, which received the names *Rossiia, Pobeda [Victory], Ukraina*, and later, the *Nakhimov*.

The profile of output that the city's enterprises produced before the war was maintained after the war: the Red Guards factory produced drill rigs and suction pumps; the January Uprising factory – railroad cranes; the October Revolution factory – plows and agricultural machines; the Starostin factory – freight car scales and other scales of special construction; the superphosphate plant – superphosphate and sulfuric acid; the A. Marti factory – the building and repair of ships; the roofing factory – Ruberoid roofing and bituminous cement. By the end of 1946, 197 State industrial enterprises and 144 industrial cartels were now operational. Together with the reconstruction of destroyed enterprises, new plants and factories entered service immediately after the war: an automobile assembly plant, the Kirov heavy machine-building factory, a printing equipment factory and others.

Already in 1948, industrial production in the city reached its pre-war level. In 1949, a weaving and sewing factory, a cement factory, a toy factory and a bed factory became operational.[22] In this same year Odessa's industry fully withdrew from government subsidies, became self-financing, and generated profits of tens of millions rubles.

17 *Geroicheskaia Odessa: Sbornik statei i materialov [Heroic Odessa: Collection of articles and materials]* (Odessa, 1945), pp. 118-119.

18 *Druzhba, sotrudnichestvo i bratskaia vzaimopomoshch': Dokumenty i materialy (1917-1982) [Friendship, collaboration and brotherly mutual assistance: Documents and materials (1917-1982)]* (Odessa: Maiak, 1985), p. 107.

19 *Istoriia gorodov i sel Ukrainskoi SSR:Odesskaia oblast' [History of the cities and villages of the Ukraine SSR]* (Kiev: Institut istoriia AN USSR, 1978), p. 140.

20 DAOO, F.R. 1234, Op. 7, Spr. 405, Ark. 436.

21 *Bol'shevistskoe znamia*, 7 February 1948.

22 DAOO, F.R. 1234, Op. 7, Spr. 403, Ark. 18-19.

In 1950, Odessa's industrial cooperative produced more than 70 new types of consumer goods. In 1949, the city's enterprises had implemented approximately 3,000 economizing proposals, which saved the government 25 million rubles. The production capacity of the October Revolution, January Uprising, superphosphate, cable and other factories and plants had grown significantly. Approximately 12,000 new pieces of equipment had been put into service in the city's factories.

By the end of 1950, Odessa's industrial output exceeded its pre-war level. The transshipment of cargo at the Port of Odessa exceeded the pre-war level by 1.5 times. Operations were conducted to tow dozens of light rivercraft to the Volga – Don Canal. From Odessa's port, motorboats were sailing from Odessa to the Caspian Sea and Baku via the Sea of Azov, the Tsymliansk Reservoir, the Volga – Don Canal and the Volga River.

The port's central sector below the coastal boulevard was set aside for passenger voyages. On the location of the cold storage facility that was blown up by the fascists, a passenger ship terminal was set up with boat landings deep enough to allow ocean-going passenger ships to enter the port. By the end of the 1950s, the Port of Odessa became the main base for the anchorages and repair of the Black Sea's merchant fleet. By this time it had acquired powerful technical means, a large motor-vehicle pool, and an extensive network of railroad lines that serviced the port. A significant share of the USSR's foreign trade freight traffic began to pass through the Port of Odessa. Large passenger ships began to conduct regular tourist cruises. Everyday, up to 20 railroad trains were arriving with freight for shipment by sea and departing again into the country's interior after being unloaded.[23] The port became the largest in the nation. It was processing millions of metric tons of industrial and agricultural cargo.

Substantial changes occurred in the social sphere as well. Immediately after the liberation of Odessa, in April 1944 six departments of social welfare and consumer devices were established for family members of Red Army servicemen. In 1947, the social welfare organs were supporting 47,600 war and labor invalids. They were receiving pensions, lump sums of cash payments, ration coupons, while their children were receiving meal tickets and free trips to children's health camps. With the aim of attracting invalids back to work, they were given prosthetic care, treatment and job retraining. On 1 October 1947, 90.6% of the registered invalids were employed.[24]

In the course of two years following the city's liberation, many destroyed medical facilities were rebuilt, furnished with instruments and equipment, and staffed with qualified doctors and nurses. The quality of healthcare assistance to the people rose considerably. The construction of Polyclinic No. 13 and the premises of the factory health clinics of the machine-building factory, the January Uprising factory, the October Revolution factory and the jute factory were completed. In 1947 the city had two clinical hospitals with 1,400 beds, 24 outpatient clinics, 4 tuberculosis dispensaries, and 66 medical clinics at enterprises.[25] The restoration of the healthcare service for patients caused a significant decrease in morbidity from typhus, dysentery and malaria.

In September 1950 the first new steam power plant came on line, followed by a second one in the first half of 1951.[26] After a high-voltage electrical transmission line was installed between Odessa and Beliaevka and Pump Station 3 was built on the Dniester River, a significant increase in the supply of water to the city was achieved, up to 90,000 cubic meters a day. In 1950, the city's water supply reached its pre-war level.[27]

---

23   *Bol'shevistskoe znamia*, 3 August 1958.
24   DAOO, F.R. 1234, Op. 7, Spr. 534, Ark. 32.
25   DAOO, F.R. 1234, Op. 7, Spr. 188, Ark. 9.
26   Ibid.
27   DAOO, F.R. 1234, Op. 7, Spr. 403, Ark. 18-19, Ark. 6-7; Spr. 534, Ark. 2, 8; Spr. 659, Ark. 11; Spr. 828, Ark. 52; Spr. 998, Ark. 4.

The trolley car system was fully restored. In 1948-1950, streetcar Routes No. 8 (Kuial'nik), No. 13 (Ul'ianovsky State Farm), No. 20 (Khadzhibeiskii Resort), No. 23 (Sverdlova Street – City Center), No. 28 (Komsomol'skaia Street – Shevchenko Central Park of Culture and Rest), No. 30 (Odessa Station – Tovarnaia – Frunze Street) were rebuilt and put back into service. The re-opening of the multi-kilometer streetcar line to the Chernomorka resort village had important significance.

The construction of a trolleybus line in Odessa had started in 1941, but the Romanian occupiers purloined the trolleybuses and equipment. In 1945, the trolleybuses and equipment were returned and the first trolleybus route began to operate between Tol'stoy Square and the passenger train station. A second route connected the passenger train station with the Arcade. At the beginning of 1951, 6 bus routes were operating in the city; 18 buses daily on average ran the routes, and on days off in the summertime, this increased to 24. Citizens and visitors to the city also had available a taxicar service that consisted of 48 taxis of the Pobeda ["Victory"] brand. After the war, a cable car line that was closely connected with the history of Odessa's development was rebuilt and upgraded.[28]

In the picturesque resort suburbs of Odessa – Luzanovka, Arkadiia and Bol'shoi Fontan – passenger wharves were built, between which comfortable motorboats and port hydroplanes began to shuttle vacationers. Odessa was developing into a major resort center with a large number of spas, rest homes and treatment facilities. The medicinal qualities of mud from the Kual'nitskii estuary had been long famed locally, and became well-known far beyond Ukraine's borders. Prior to the end of the 1950s, four medicinal spas, designed to serve 300 people a year, were rebuilt and the construction of new ones was underway.[29]

From 1950, Odessa undertook a difficult, but necessary program for a resort city – the creation of new woodlots in the naturally treeless Black Sea coastal zone. Special attention was given to the planting of trees and shrubs along the streets and roads. In order to do the work, labor teams from enterprises, collective farms, State farms and various institutions and organizations were recruited. A green, forested protective belt was created around the city from Kryzhanovka to Burlatskaia Balka, which extended for 35 kilometers and was 200 meters wide. In order to create comfortable conditions for rest and with the aim of erosion protection, decorative trees, shrubs and flowers were planted along the city's coastline, from Lanzheron to Liustdorf. A network of greenhouses and hotbeds with corresponding equipment and boiler system was created. The overall area of green plantings increased from 348 hectares to 1,600 hectares.

Measures were taken to improve the city's appearance and create well-landscaped residences. The outdoor lighting of streets and squares was resumed and improved; drinking fountains were installed; public restrooms were built; and traffic lights were established on the city's main thoroughfares.[30]

The well-being of the citizens was also growing. After the ration card system was abolished in 1947, commerce thrived; the turnover of commodities in the city in 1950 exeeded the pre-war level.

In the following years Odessa quickly developed. Enterprises had mastered the production of new, more technologically complex goods, which were answering the growing demands of the people. New multi-story apartment complexes sprang up on empty lots in Bol'shoi Fontan, Slobodka, Luzanovka and other areas. The structure of the city's macro-economic complex was changing. If in the pre-war years and in the years immediately following the war machine-building

28   V.N. Stanko [chief ed.], *Istoriia Odesi* [*History of Odessa*] (Odessa: Druk, 2002), pp. 435-436.
29   DAOO, F.R. 1234, Op. 7, Spr. 403, Ark. 8-9.
30   DAOO, F.R. 1234, Op. 7, Spr. 403, Ark. 44.

was dominant, then by the end of the 1950s the role of maritime shipping and the port was growing, where 20% of the city's workers were employed. The reconstruction of Odessa's port had been completed, and satellite ports built in Il'ichevsk on the Sukhoi estuary and in Iuzhnyi on the Grigor'evskii estuary. In Il'ichevsk, a ferry service was opened to Varna. A portion of the flow of cargo was shifted from Odessa to the Port of Il'ichevsk, while Odessa's port became primarily a passenger terminal. In 1978 the Odessan portside plant in the town of Iuzhnyi went into operation to produce nitrogen fertilizer with a capacity of 200,000 metric tons of urea, 900,000 metric tons of ammonia and a number of other chemical products. This factory exports 2 million metric tons of ammonia, which flows into the Tol'tti – Gorlovka – Iuzhnyi pipeline. The factory's output goes to export to Italy, Spain, Morocco, China and other countries.

The population of Odessa grew quickly until the 1980s (in 1973 already 1,000,000 residents were registered in the city), but in the 1990s the tendency of a reduction in the pace of population growth became increasingly noticeable. The mass emigration of Odessans to continuous residence abroad began. The problem of an aging population began, and socio-economic problems and difficulties in maintaining the social welfare net for people of retirement age increased. With the transfer to a market economy and the closing of many factories, an excess of labor appeared. The limited demand for labor led to a rise in unemployment and difficulties in job placement for the graduates of academic institutions.

Even the leading branch of Odessa Oblast's economy – shipping – underwent substantial changes. The collapse of the Soviet Union presented many property and legal problems over the partition of the shipping fleets. This was painfully reflected on the business of the Black Sea Shipping Company. During the "legal vacuum" it lost the majority of its best ships. Only now are certain signs appearing about the economic revival of the ports of Odessa Oblast. The Port of Odessa and its oil terminal have been reconstructed and modernized. The port's grain terminal has revived to process the enormous flow of export grain to Europe. A grain transfer complex designed to store 20,000 metric tons of grain at any one time has opened at the port. A contemporary Omega Terminal has opened for processing chemical loads, including transit ones.

Today Odessa is one of the major and largest business, economic, cultural and international tourist centers in the south of Ukraine. Odessa, as before, stands out as Ukraine's main maritime gateway and largest port complex. Odessa has been recognized as a center of education and science, scientific-technical analysis and innovation.

Odessa's port and railroad hub now transport grain, sugar, coal, petrochemicals, cement, metals, jute, lumber and the output of the machine-building industry. The port serves as the base for a fishing fleet and Ukraine's navy. The main branches of Odessa's industry are oil processing, machine-building, metalworking, woodworking, agriculture, chemicals, light and food. Oil and petrochemicals predominate in the city's commercial export structure; they comprise 40% of all exports. Metals and metalware, food products, chemical products, machinery and equipment trail behind. Russia, Ireland, Turkey, Italy, Spain and Germany are Odessa's largest trading partners. The city is also a major scientific, education and cultural center in Ukraine.

The city has become a major resort center, with a gentle climate; in the resort season, the city's population swells with arriving tourists and vacationers who flock to the area resorts, spas, therapeutic baths and miles of sandy beaches, protected by coastal barriers. A *Trassa Zdrorov'ia* [Corridor of Health], which is closed to automobile traffic, runs along the coast and links the city center with the beaches.

No matter from which direction guests travel to Odessa, they are first of all greeted by obelisks of the memorial park Belt of Glory, which follows the main line of defenses that existed back in the autumn of 1941 on the city's outskirts. Among the immense green fields and fragrant verdure of oak woods stand 20-meter monuments that rise into the sky, and catching the rays of the morning sun, they seem like enormous torches that burn on the locations of past battles. Inscriptions are carved into the granite with the names of regiments and divisions that stood to their deaths. On the obelisk in the village of Gniliakovo, beneath the chiseled profile of a soldier and sailor going on the attack, the words of Ukraine's national poet Pavel Tychin have been carved into the granite: "I am the people, of such force of truth that has never been conquered before." There, where back in 1941 the 411th Coastal Artillery Battery stood on the defense, a memorial park to the heroic city has been opened: Silent guns, which once hammered the foe from the first to last hour of the defense, stand in neat row; armored trains and tanks, which were produced in Odessa's factories back in those menacing days, stand on plinths; ships, that once defended Odessa from the sea, now stand frozen on concrete slabs; and a streetcar which once delivered ammunition to the front stands, snarling with mounted anti-aircraft guns. The Military History Museum and the Museum of Partisan Glory are always crowded. Blossoms planted along the Alley of Glory in the T.G. Shevchenko Central Park never fade. It has become a gracious tradition to conduct the laying of wreathes on the graves of the heroes here on memorial days and holidays, and young couples come here after their wedding ceremony in the Wedding Palace. Official delegations and simple people lay flowers on the gravestones of the heroes of the defense, the underground resistance movement and of the liberation of Odessa. The Alley ends at the sea at the obelisk to the Unknown Sailor, where an eternal flame burns.

Odessa today is a contemporary European city, with a multinational population of over a million people, which was rated by the journal "Focus" in 2011 as the top city in Ukraine for quality of life. Many well-known people call Odessa their home, even if they've only lived in it for a short time. The writer Oles' Gonchar had every justification to write, when addressing the residents of Odessa: "You live in a city of legendary glory, known to everyone around the world; in a city of sun, of nautical romance, of high heroism; in a city of resilient, cheerful and talented people."

Index

INDEX OF PEOPLE

INDEX OF PLACES

INDEX OF SOVIET MILITARY FORMATIONS & UNITS